Revolutionary Armies

CW00750009

The New International History Series

Edited by Gordon Martel

Professor of History at the University of Northern British Columbia, and Senior Research Fellow at De Montfort University.

Explaining Auschwitz and Hiroshima
History Writing and the Second World War, 1945–1990
R.J.B. Bosworth

Ideology and International Relations in the Modern World
Alan Cassels

Global Communications, International Affairs and the Media since 1945
Philip M. Taylor

Forthcoming:

War and Cold War in the Middle East
Edward Ingram

North East Asia
An International History
John Stephan

Russia and the World in the Twentieth Century
Teddy Uldricks

Revolutionary Armies in the Modern Era

A revisionist approach

S. P. MacKenzie

Routledge
Taylor & Francis Group

LONDON AND NEW YORK

First published 1997
by Routledge
2 Park Square, Milton Park, Abingdon, Oxon, OX14 4RN

Simultaneously published in the USA and Canada
by Routledge
711 Third Avenue, New York, NY 10017

Routledge is an imprint of the Taylor & Francis Group, an informa business

First issued in paperback 2014

Transferred to Digital Printing 2005

© 1997 S. P. MacKenzie

Typeset in Times by Routledge

All rights reserved. No part of this book may be reprinted or
reproduced or utilized in any form or by any electronic,
mechanical, or other means, now known or hereafter
invented, including photocopying and recording, or in any
information storage or retrieval system, without permission in
writing from the publishers.

British Library Cataloguing in Publication Data
A catalogue record for this book is available from the British Library

Library of Congress Cataloguing in Publication Data
Mackenzie, S. P.
Revolutionary armies in the modern era : a revisionist approach / S.P.
Mackenzie
(The New international history)

Includes bibliographical references and index.
1. Military history, Modern. 2. Armies–History. 3.
Revolutions–History. I. Title II. Series: New international history
series.
D214.M33 1998

355.02'18'09–dc 97–16910

CIP

ISBN 978-0-415-09690-4 (hbk)
ISBN 978-0-415-86777-1 (pbk)

Cover illustration: *Death of General Montgomery at Quebec.*
Reproduced by kind permission of Anne S. K. Brown
Military Collection, Brown University Library.

Contents

Series Editor's Preface   vii
Acknowledgements   ix

Introduction   1

1 **The New Model Army in the English Civil War, 1645–6**   5

2 **The Continental Army in the War of American Independence, 1775–82**   19

3 **The armies of the French Republic and the War of the First Coalition, 1792–7**   33

4 **The armies of Bolívar and the war for the liberation of Gran Colombia, 1811–24**   51

5 **The Voortrekkers, Blood River, and the Zulu War of 1838–40**   68

6 **The armies of the Heavenly Kingdom and the Taiping Rebellion in China, 1850–68**   78

7 **Sepoys in the Indian Mutiny, 1857–9**   96

8 **The International Brigades in the Spanish Civil War, 1936–9**   116

9 **The Waffen-SS in the Second World War, 1939–45**   134

10 **The Viet Cong in the Second Indochina War, 1960–75**   158

Conclusion   175

Notes   178
Index   236

Series Editor's Preface

What we now refer to as 'international' history was the primary concern of those whose work is now recognized as the first attempt by Europeans to conduct a truly 'historical' investigation of the past, and it has remained a central preoccupation of historians ever since. Herodotus, who attempted to explain the Persian Wars, approached the subject quite differently from his successor, Thucydides. Herodotus believed that the answers to the questions that arose from the confrontation between the Persians and the Greeks would be found in the differences between the two cultures; accordingly, he examined the traditions, customs and beliefs of the two civilizations. Critics have long pointed out that he was haphazard in his selection and cavalier in his use of evidence. The same has never been said of Thucydides, who, in attempting to explain the Peloponnesian Wars, went about his task more methodically, and who was meticulous in his use of evidence. Over the next two thousand years, men like Machiavelli, Ranke and Toynbee have added to the tradition, but the underlying dichotomy between the 'anthropological' and the 'archival' approach has remained. Diplomatic historians have been condemned as mere archive-grubbers; diplomatic history as consisting of what one file-clerk said to another. The 'world-historians', the synthesizers, have been attacked for creating structures and patterns that never existed, for offering explanations that can never be tested against the available evidence.

The aim of 'The New International History' is to combine the two traditions, to bring Herodotus and Thucydides together. While drawing upon the enormous wealth of archival research conducted by those historians who continue to work in the political tradition of formal relations between states, the authors in this series will also draw upon other avenues of investigation that have become increasingly fruitful since the Second World War. Ideology and culture, immigration and communications, myths and stereotypes, trade and finance have come to be regarded by contemporary scholars as elements essential to a good understanding of international history, and yet, while these approaches are to be found in detailed monographs and scholarly journals, many of their discoveries have not been presented in a readable and accessible form to students and the public. 'The New International History', by providing books organized along thematic, regional or historiographical lines, hopes to repair this omission.

In spite of the apparently obvious connection between military organizations and the conduct of international affairs, the two themes have too often been treated as discrete entities. Historians of diplomacy have sometimes permitted the military to enter the story they tell when the answer to the question of how a war began appears to be found in the ambitions, aggressiveness or xenophobia of certain high-ranking officers. Historians of the military have rarely transcended the national boundaries of their subject, preferring to focus their attention on national traditions, bureaucratic realities and political rivalries that appear to have little to do with the management of international relations. Paul MacKenzie has broken new ground here in attempting to place the military's place in the modern world within a broader international setting. By examining the changing patterns in relations between the military and society in different revolutionary contexts, he has provided students of international history with an illuminating, comparative perspective on the subject. Like its predecessors in this series, this book is challenging in its perspective and ambitious in its breadth; it is to be hoped that others will follow this bold example of 'the new international history'.

Gordon Martel

Acknowledgements

In researching the subjects covered in this book I have been greatly helped by the staffs of Robarts Library and the Thomas Fisher Rare Book Library at the University of Toronto; the British Library; the Bodleian Library, Oxford; and above all the diligent members of the inter-library loans department of Thomas Cooper Library, University of South Carolina. Without their assistance in retrieving and making available rare and obscure titles, this book would have been infinitely poorer in content.

A study of this kind, essentially a work of synthesis and interpretation, necessarily is built upon the foundations laid by those scholars who have specialized over the last twenty years in the subject areas discussed in each chapter. Though my conclusions may be at variance with those of, say, Ian Gentles on the New Model Army, Charles Royster on the Continental Army, or John Lynn on the armies of the French Revolution, I am keenly aware of the serious archival research that they have undertaken and how important their publications are in terms of presenting both opinion and – vital for a project of this sort – hitherto neglected evidence. In short, this book could not have been written without the preceding work of dozens of other specialist historians.

I am also indebted to Wesley White, Owen Connolly, and David Hall, all of whom suggested one or two sources that I might otherwise have missed and read draft chapters. The editorial staff at Routledge have also been helpful in preparing the manuscript. Finally, I owe thanks to the series editor, Gordon Martel, who went beyond the call of duty in providing detailed comments on an earlier version of the manuscript. The accuracy of the facts and strength of the arguments contained herein remain, of course, my responsibility alone.

Introduction

My original plan for this book was simple. I was going to write a straightforward narrative on revolutionary armies, using material published in recent years to update earlier comparative studies by Katherine Chorley, John Ellis, and Jonathan Adelman.[1] Once I began to immerse myself in the secondary and primary literature on particular armies, however, I began to see problems with what might be termed the standard approach to studying the forces and wars associated with particular socio-political movements.[2]

The first problem had to do with the comparative analysis employed in these earlier works, important and useful though each book is in different ways. 'So-called thematic history', as David Lowenthal has perceptively written, 'traces illuminating parallels but plays down the fact that people at *each* of these times lived lives, acted from motives, and fashioned milieux that were distinctively different.'[3] The hazards of reductionism are of course present in the works of even the most highly regarded of comparative or macro historians,[4] and as a process historical synthesis perhaps inevitably involves a certain blurring of distinction. Yet it seemed to me that the range and sophistication of the newer secondary literature allowed for a more nuanced and possibly less structuralist study of revolutionary armies.

The second and related problem, which encompassed many specific as well as comparative studies, had to do with the almost a priori assumption that revolutions have generated new ways of war and above all a new and more effective type of soldier. Universal and fervent belief in a revolutionary cause, to put it in very simple terms, is assumed to translate into military innovation and greater effectiveness on the battlefield: or, to simplify even more, right equals might.

Studies of historical consciousness and collective memory from Halbwachs to Foucault have tended to confirm the possibly obvious but often ignored fact that how we perceive and interpret the past is conditioned by the needs of the present.[5] The contemporary uses of history determine what is studied, how it is studied, and above all the conclusions that are drawn. What became striking as my research progressed was the extent to which certain needs influenced how revolutionary armies were studied both individually and collectively. Again to simplify somewhat, what began to emerge was a foundation myth – a tendency to accentuate the positive, the selfless, the heroic, in the revolutionary context, in order to legitimize a particular set of societal beliefs.[6]

Revolutionary regimes have traditionally sought to place themselves in opposition to the immediate past as well as seeking more distant historical precedents, a contemporary viewpoint which in many cases helped shape later historical analyses. Use of the term 'revolution' itself is the most basic indicator of this tendency towards accepting that something new, innovative, and – as often as not – positive had occurred. Just as revolutionary regimes are taken to have produced new and progressive societal forms, so too the armies associated with the new order are assumed to possess the moral essence of the revolution and thereby become successful. Citizen-soldiers, embodying revolutionary socio-political principles, evolve innovative tactics and through their commitment to the cause carry all before them. The foundation of a new socio-political order, in short, lies behind the foundation of a new and progressive military order.

Like all myths based around actual events, this image of revolutionary armies fulfils a very human need. At root it is a morality tale in which the forces of light *ipso facto* overcome the forces of darkness.[7] But while by no means wholly fictional, the common image of revolutionary armies is not fully grounded in fact.

History is not a moral science. Depressing as it may be, since the beginning of recorded time success in war has been a matter of better arms, skill, luck, and big battalions rather more often than superior virtue. From the Assyrians to the Khmer Rouge the human saga has been replete with examples of repellent regimes succeeding in fighting their way to success. Moreover, even in societies which are considered to be on the side of the angels there are always those who are unwilling to risk their lives for the sake of principle or the general will.

The morale of troops – their normative will to serve and fight – is of course an important factor in war, but high *esprit de corps* and belief in the cause are poor substitutes for superior firepower and training. 'An army's efficiency gains life and spirit from enthusiasm for the cause for which it fights', Clausewitz conceded, going on to caution: 'but such enthusiasm is not indispensable'.[8]

Yet it is striking the degree to which all those responsible for representing the past – everyone from university-trained historians to scriptwriters, novelists, artists, and illiterate purveyors of oral traditions – have allowed a subjective desire for at least a modicum of success in human affairs to shape their reading of revolutionary armies.[9] Even professional soldiers, supposedly more hard-headed, knowledgeable, and realistic than other observers, have been known to sacrifice rational calculation on the altar of faith in the moral qualities of their men.[10]

Total objectivity is of course an impossible ideal. The past is a foreign country, and all those seeking to recover it inevitably lack complete data and unconsciously impose onto it the personal and societal values, priorities, hopes, and fears of their own age. Like memory, writing history involves 'a process of active restructuring, in which elements may be retained, recorded, or suppressed'.[11]

It might be argued, furthermore, that in making use of recent literature which has explored the lives of those left out of more traditional histories and in highlighting the mythical elements surrounding accounts of revolutionary armies, I am myself merely representing the relativist, antiheroic pessimism of the postmodern age. This may be so. Yet if the past is to be recovered at all, and history is more than a semantic game (à la Derrida), then – as most historians still accept in practice[12] – pursuit of the Rankean ideal of objectivity brings the truth closer. A new look at a traditional approach thus still seems worthwhile. The fact that the Sir John Falstaffs and Chocolate Cream Soldiers of this world do not fit the profile of the heroic and selfless warrior does not mean that they – and their influence – should be ignored.

The aim of this book, therefore, has become rather more ambitious than simply to update the work of others. The hope is now to provide the reader with an account of how the standard views have arisen in academic (and to a lesser extent popular) culture, and to reassess these interpretations in light of the available evidence: to explore, in other words, the gap between the rhetoric and reality.

But why these particular armies? There are many other revolutions and armed forces that might have been picked. These ten, however, possess individual and collective attributes which made them appear particularly worthwhile subjects of study.

Taken together, the cases chosen highlight important differences as well as similarities. They are situated in a variety of times and places around the world from the mid-seventeenth century to the mid-twentieth century, hopefully providing the reader with a truly international and historical perspective. I have also endeavoured to include armies arising out of reactionary as well as progressive revolutionary movements; hence the presence of the Voortrekkers and the Waffen-SS beside forces more commonly considered revolutionary, such as the armies of the French Republic.[13]

Many of the images connected with these revolutionary armies are sociopolitical and nationalist in nature, as one might expect in the modern world. But modern nationalism is not always at the root of the myths surrounding a particular army, as illustrated through the inclusion of cases involving religio-social (Voortrekker) and transnational (International Brigade and – to a lesser extent – Waffen-SS) ideologies.

The degree of dominance in popular and professional discourse enjoyed by particular mythologies also varies. The power of the Voortrekker myth is waning, for example, while the mystique surrounding the Waffen-SS, once discredited, is slowly growing stronger. The episodes studied also encompass the range of attitudes towards the role of heroic individuals in the formation and leadership of revolutionary armies.[14]

The case studies also possess features in common. The foundation mythology surrounding a selected army and the political events with which it has been associated, though it may not always date from the period in question, continues in each case down to the present. Hence a chapter on the People's Liberation Army of China has been omitted because (outside the People's Republic at least) the orthodox account of Maoist success has already been re-evaluated.[15] Likewise the Red Army of the Russian Civil War is excluded, the myths surrounding it – already long subject to critical scrutiny in the West – collapsing along with the Soviet Union itself.[16]

One further linkage should be noted. In most instances the case for the 'revolutionary' nature of these particular armies by contemporary observers or later analysts has been made in part through reference to other such armies familiar to observers, thereby providing at one and the same time both an interesting unity of discourse and a thematic thread.

A volume of this kind, a work of synthesis and interpretation, involves making choices. Where sources are available in English, translated editions have been cited to assist the general reader. I have attempted to base each chapter on as comprehensive a reading of available printed and visual sources as possible, and to make clear in the endnotes whence relevant information comes. Doubtless there will be critics who will disagree with some of the arguments. This is as it should be: within the accepted rules of supporting evidence there is plenty of room for disagreement. And after all words, to paraphrase Tom Stoppard, as well as images, are all we each have to go on.[17]

1 The New Model Army in the English Civil War, 1645–6

Saints in arms?

Pray raise honest godly men . . .

Oliver Cromwell, August 1643[1]

I think these New Modellers knead all their dough with ale, for I never saw so many drunk in my life in so short a time . . .

Sir Samuel Luke, June 1645[2]

That the New Model Army should be regarded as somehow revolutionary is not perhaps surprising. It did, after all, bring to a close the first English Civil War (1642–5) with quite unprecedented success and rapidity.

By the end of 1644, several major battles and hundreds of minor engagements between cavaliers and roundheads in over two years of war had brought the Parliament of England apparently no nearer its goal of forcing King Charles I to accept its authority. When a 'new model' force was created from the remains of three earlier armies in a desperate effort to revitalize Parliament's flagging war effort, its success seemed far from assured and the possibility of a royal victory remained frighteningly real.

Yet within a matter of months of taking the field in April 1645, the New Model Army had decisively beaten the main royalist field forces at Naseby (14 June) and Langport (10 July). Over the following year the remaining cavalier strongholds were reduced by its regiments, one after another, to the point where by June 1646 the King was forced to admit defeat.[3] As Sir Henry Vane put it in a letter to his father: 'The success is hardly imaginable which accompanies Sir Thos. Fairfax's army.'[4] All in all, a quite revolutionary change of fortune.

The New Model Army had thus produced an *annus mirabilis* for the parliamentary cause. But how? What had allowed this army to succeed so brilliantly when earlier armies had failed or allowed defeat to be snatched from the jaws of victory? What was new, revolutionary, about the New Model?

In a manner that would heavily influence later generations of historians, many contemporary observers and participants – reflecting the religious assumptions and preoccupations of the age – tended to explain victory in terms of spiritual and moral superiority. This was particularly true in reference to Oliver Cromwell, the Lieutenant-General of Horse, and his famous regiments of Ironsides.

Cromwell, equating the cause of Parliament with God's will, had from the first believed that the Lord's work could only be accomplished by 'honest godly men'.[5] From the moment he began raising his first troop of cavalry in Huntingdon as a farmer-turned-captain, Cromwell had spared no effort to recruit men of good moral character. In his view 'a few honest men' were better than any number of men of questionable repute; and 'sober Christians' were the most reliable of all.[6]

What was more, as the number of volunteers coming forward between September 1642 and September 1643 led to the expansion of his original band into a force of ten troops – soon to become the shock arm of an entire Eastern Association Army and in turn eventually incorporated into the New Model – Cromwell did not shrink from choosing as officers men whose social position and denomination did not match their high moral qualities. 'I had rather have a plain russet-coated captain that knows what he fight for, and loves what he knows', he stated bluntly in one of his most oft-quoted letters, written in 1643, 'than that which you call a gentleman and nothing else.'[7]

Whether this meant that the Ironsides were led by 'common men, poor and of mean parentage', as one critic alleged, or 'freeholders and freeholders' sons' as an admirer claimed,[8] the reputed behaviour of Cromwell's troopers in and out of battle seemed proof – especially to those Puritan clergy who thought along the same lines – that 'godly honest men' who believed in the cause were better soldiers than those who had little faith and honesty.

According to the Reverend Richard Baxter, the original Ironside troop had seen itself almost as a congregation, a 'gathered church';[9] and even after it expanded tenfold and more, the troops were so sober and well disciplined, in the opinion of a partisan writer for a parliamentary newspaper, that they did not get drunk, steal, or engage in any of the usual soldierly vices harmful to the civilian populace; 'insomuch', it was claimed, 'that the countries leap for joy of them, and come in and join with them'.[10] More to the point, as their performance at engagements from Gainsborough to Marston Moor demonstrated, such men of conscience were 'more engaged to be valiant' and would 'stand firm and charge desperately' in battle.[11]

The success of the New Model Army, organized by Sir Thomas Fairfax with the Ironsides at its core, was therefore ultimately a matter of religious zeal – at least according to the chaplains who accompanied it. William Dell recalled with admiration the 'spirit of prayer' within the army, and other chaplains such as the famous Hugh Peters wrote of the huge audiences their sermons drew. The New Model, indeed, soon gained a reputation as a praying army in which every man carried a Bible and troopers rode into battle singing psalms.[12]

Its commanders set the tone. Joshua Sprigge, for instance, wrote that Fairfax believed that nothing was impossible 'for man to do in God's strength, if they would be up and doing'.[13] As for Cromwell, whom the Earl of Clarendon saw as acting 'in the name of Fairfax' as a sort of *de facto* chief of staff, Naseby and subsequent victories only confirmed that 'God made them [the impure royalists] as stubble to our swords'.[14]

In 1645, therefore, the New Model appeared to mark a radical break with the past in relation to links between motivation and effectiveness in battle. Though bitterly denounced for buttressing Cromwell's personal dictatorship in the latter 1640s and 1650s and held up as an object lesson of the dangers of standing armies from the Restoration onward, the verdict on the original New Model reached by historians in the modern age has tended to mirror the accounts contained in the correspondence and other records of leading figures in the war.

Thomas Carlyle, in editing the first published collection of Cromwell's letters in the mid-nineteenth century, stated that the New Model Army began 'an entirely new epoch'. S. R. Gardiner, the first historian to approach the civil wars with supposedly scientific impartiality, concluded that, while not the whole story behind Parliament's victory, the New Model had indeed been pervaded by a 'revolutionary spirit'. And despite the detailed research conducted by one of Gardiner's pupils, C. H. Firth, at the end of the nineteenth century – which revealed among other things that there was far less saintliness among the troops than commonly assumed[15] – the general histories of England published in the first decades of the twentieth century still tended to lean towards the Puritan ethos in explaining the New Model's success. George Macaulay Trevelyan, for instance, in *England Under the Stuarts*, first published in 1904 with a new edition in 1925, stated that Cromwell's horse regiments in the New Model were fighting 'to win themselves civil and religious freedom', and that 'they had in them a spirit which soon leavened the whole army'.[16] F. C. Montague, writing a similar volume a few years later, used almost exactly the same words: 'the puritan zeal common to most of the officers and some of the men leavened the whole body'.[17]

This emphasis on the positive effect of religion in the New Model Army was taken further by those historians who saw Cromwell's lack of religious sectarianism and emphasis on ability over birth as revolutionary in a socio-political as well as a military sense. 'It was an assemblage of citizens', claimed Lieutenant-Colonel T. S. Baldock in the 1890s, 'each of whom, whilst submitting to the strictest military discipline whilst under arms, believed that he carried with him into his military life all his rights and responsibilities as a citizen.'[18] Sixty-odd years later left-wing British historians, with Christopher Hill as standard bearer, took this line of analysis to its logical conclusion. The new 'democratic army', Hill argued, was 'the common people in uniform' commanded by officers such as Cromwell who recognized 'the fact that free men consciously motivated by a belief in their cause could get the better of mere professionals simply by superior morale and discipline'.[19] Brian Manning, in attempting to write a history of the war from the common people's perspective, was equally convinced that the New Model was an unusually motivated force:

> There was a puritan leaven in the parliament's forces, especially amongst the junior officers, sergeants and corporals, and concentrated in the horse regiments; and no doubt some of the common soldiers were influenced by the ideas they heard preached and discussed, learning for the first time about the religious and political issues at stake in the war.[20]

The troopers of the New Model Army, it appeared, were fighting for religious and political freedom, which made them better soldiers. The royalists, meanwhile, according to Joyce Malcolm, found it more difficult to fill the ranks of their armies because few ordinary people actively supported the King and his reactionary cause.[21]

All this has been grist to the mill of those who seek to draw broad connections between military effectiveness and political revolutions. The New Model Army, so it was claimed, was a revolutionary step into the future. Men volunteered out of conscience, promotion was based strictly on merit, good order was maintained through moral cohesiveness and firm discipline, and high morale was constantly fostered by regimental chaplains acting, in the words of political scientist Jonathan Adelman, as 'the seventeenth-century version of modern commissars'.[22]

The men of the royalist armies, 'neofeudal forces', were in contrast 'illiterate thieves, rogues and vagabonds', led by 'a very thin stratum of wealthier nobles in favour with the court and without any military capabilities'.[23] Modern organization and above all revolutionary politico-religious zeal thus virtually guaranteed the triumph of the New Model Army. The string of unbroken victories from Naseby onward was no accident. Victory went to the side best attuned to the currents of history, the side most able to harness the forces of change and progress.

This is a comforting view for those, left wing or otherwise, who think that holding the moral high ground eventually translates into control of the state. It is worth stressing that, from Carlyle to Hill, those who have written about the New Model Army tend with varying degrees of detachment to view the King's defeat as a victory for what they believe to be right and good in English history. For Whig historians, it represented an important stage in the forward movement of the English constitution; for Marxists a chance for 'The People' to achieve a degree of class-cum-national consciousness.[24]

Not surprisingly, such views have heavily influenced contemporary popular and textbook representations of the English Civil War. In the 1970 Columbia Pictures release *Cromwell*, for example, the King's army is portrayed as being three times as large as the New Model. Yet victory at Naseby goes to Parliament because the New Model, under the influence of Cromwell, is the more dedicated and disciplined army (and a far cry from the feebly led Parliamentary Army which had lost to the cavaliers at Edgehill in 1642).[25] Lacey Baldwin Smith, in a popular American university textbook on late medieval and early modern England first published in 1966 and into its seventh edition by 1996, writes that Parliament 'had forged a weapon of righteousness and discipline' in which promotion was 'based on merit, not blood' and staffed by men of conscience.[26]

Unfortunately, a closer examination of the sources on which this view of the New Model's success is based, and of contrary evidence, suggests that this is an idealized and overly deterministic image. The chances of failure for the New Model Army were quite high, and in many respects the force that won at Naseby was far from revolutionary.

The meaning of the speeches, proposals, and counter-suggestions in Parliament in the winter of 1644–5 which eventually led to the creation of the New Model Army remains a subject of considerable debate. They may well have been a calculated attempt by Cromwell and other hawkish MPs to wrest control of the war effort away from the more dovish parliamentarians who supported the cautious strategies of the existing senior commanders, the earls of Essex and Manchester. On the other hand, though there was much friction between the various parties concerned, key pieces of legislation such as the Self-Denying Ordinance (which barred members of the Commons and Lords from serving in the field) may have been products of a widely held desire for reform and unity.[27] But whether the New Model was the result of a new consensus or an outright victory of the win-the-war party in the Commons, very little about its actual organization and behaviour suggests that it was very different from any other parliamentary (or indeed royalist) force.

The senior commanders whom Parliament chose to lead the new army, Sir Thomas Fairfax (Commander-in-Chief) and Philip Skippon (Sergeant-Major-General of Foot), were, as events were to show, more committed than previous leaders such as Essex to fighting the King to the finish. Neither man, however, was a particularly radical figure. Sir Thomas was a moderate Presbyterian who had risen to command the Horse of the small Northern Army led by his father, Lord Fairfax. His initial career pattern thus matched that of many leaders on both sides in the first two years of war, in which birth and family influence competed with valour and battlefield success as the prime criteria for command appointments. Fairfax, though unquestionably brave under fire and not a bad leader overall, did not always win his engagements. Yet he had been far enough away from London in late 1644 to be untainted by the unseemly squabbles between Cromwell and the war party on the one hand and Manchester, Essex, and the peace party at Westminster on the other. Most importantly, Fairfax was of noble blood yet not disqualified as a sitting Peer by the Self-Denying Ordinance from holding a command. Those who voted against him may well have done so because of the terminal implications for the careers of the generals commanding the three existing parliamentary armies in the south (which would be superseded by the new army) rather than out of suspicion of Fairfax himself.[28]

Skippon's career fitted another pattern common in both parliamentary and royalist armies: the professional soldier who had fought on the Continent and had risen through bravery and skill to command large formations in the Civil War. A man of considerable talent, Skippon had moved from leading the London Trained Bands to command the Foot in Essex's army. A bluff soldier whose Puritan piety appears to have been of a somewhat utilitarian nature – 'Come my boys, my brave boys', he had shouted to his men at Turnham Green in 1642, 'let us pray heartily and fight heartily and God will bless us' – Skippon was the natural choice to lead the New Model infantry. He had risen through proven ability, and as Essex's Major-General of Foot already commanded the largest single body of parliamentary infantry – no small matter when it is remembered that the new force had to be created by breaking up the old armies.

Cromwell, who was eventually exempted from the Self-Denying Ordinance (on a temporary basis) and given command of the New Model cavalry, was somewhat exceptional in not having seen service on the Continent and not being well connected by birth. Even he, however, as true radicals such as the Levellers and Diggers were to discover to their chagrin, was more of a pragmatist and less of a zealot than commonly realized.

Cromwell's emphasis on merit and godliness over birth in the selection of officers, though probably more obvious than in other commanders, was not unique. Manchester, under whom he had served quite happily until the full implications of real victory over the King caused a rift to develop, had also sought godly men, and even in the King's army merit could overcome low social standing.[29] Cromwell's recruiting technique was also, as we shall see, born of necessity rather than dissatisfaction with the social status quo. Moreover, Cromwell was not above the kind of favouritism found in more conventional generals. One of his first acts on joining the New Model Army was to make sure that Henry Ireton, a long-time protégé who would marry one of his daughters before the end of the year, was made Second-in-Command of the Cavalry (Commissary-General) over the heads of more experienced and senior candidates.[30]

Colonels for the new army's regiments were also chosen by a parliamentary committee with reference to past service and socio-political importance, and the remaining officers – a list of whom had to be approved by both Houses – were chosen by Fairfax with an eye to transplanting whole regiments, with experienced officers, from the armies of Essex, Waller, and Manchester into his own. This inevitably meant taking in men of a variety of political and religious persuasions, and there is evidence to suggest Fairfax drew up his list with balance very much in mind.[31] The House of Lords, to be sure, increasingly worried over Puritan influence in politics and military affairs and possibly seeking greater balance than even Fairfax thought necessary, voiced its concern over fifty-seven of the 193 proposed appointments. But this still meant that less than 30 per cent of the officers were perceived as radical; and, under pressure from the Commons, even the

Lords accepted that the danger from the King outweighed the danger from a minority of officers.[32]

If there was a victory for the war party in the choosing of commissions, it was purely defensive in nature. The avoidance of a purge by the Lords of radicals already serving in the old armies, rather than the ousting of the moderates and the creation of a corps of Ironside-type officers, had been achieved.[33] In any event, those who were to lead the troops and regiments of the New Model Army were by no means the homogeneous body of Puritans that some accounts assume.

What, then, of the men whom these officers were to command? The ordinance which Parliament passed for the new army called for a force of eleven regiments of Horse, twelve regiments of Foot, a single regiment of dragoons (mounted infantry), and an appropriate artillery train: in all, about 22,000 men.[34] This was all very well on paper; but the process of actually assembling the New Model demonstrated the extent to which it suffered from the same problems of recruitment and discipline as any 'old model' army of the period.

The three existing armies in the south, particularly the Foot, had become enfeebled over the winter of 1644–5 owing to poor administration, arrears in pay, and widespread desertion. Sufficient cavalry were available, but taken together the existing field forces could produce only about half the 14,000 infantry specified for the new army. Consequently Parliament resorted to a recruiting technique common on both sides since 1643: conscription.

In theory impressment was a reasonable way of making best use of available manpower in the war effort. In practice it was a means for local authorities to empty cells and clear the streets of vagabonds, thieves, and other social undesirables. Conscripts, as Colonel John Vann put it despairingly, were 'scum ... men taken out of prison, Tinkers, Peddlers and Vagrants that have no dwelling and such as whom no account can be given'.[35] Only those worth less than £5 in goods or £3 in land could be drafted, and students, clergy, and members of various professions were exempt regardless of their financial status.[36] Those who remained were not particularly suited for duty in the ranks: 'old decayed serving men and tapsters and such kind of fellows', as Cromwell recognized, lacked the requisite physical strength and psychological motivation.[37]

Soldiers newly pressed into service were liable to run away at the first opportunity. Conscripting men was a notoriously inefficient process. Recruits received a shilling of 'pressed money', but were so prone to desert that guards had to be provided to escort them from their homes to assembly points and to the army. A foot soldier's pay in the 1640s was little better than that of a day labourer – seven pence – and in all armies pay and other necessities were more often than not in arrears. What motive was there to serve? Men 'did daily run away', and well under half of the pressed men actually arrived at their regiments.[38] 'Conscripting infantry in 1645–6', a leading historian of the New Model Army has written, 'was like ladling water into a leaky bucket.'[39]

The result, as Robert Baillie, the Scottish Commissioner in London put it with only moderate exaggeration, was that 'this New-modelled army consists for the most part of raw, inexperienced pressed soldiers'.[40] The armies of Essex and Manchester, as well as the royalist forces, had experienced the same sort of problem;[41] but this only illustrates how traditional, as opposed to revolutionary, the New Model Army really was. Soldiers who knew what they were fighting for were, among the infantry, few and far between indeed.

The absence of anything approaching real commitment to the cause among the Foot is highlighted by the enthusiasm with which defeated royalist infantry were enrolled into the ranks of the New Model Army. After Naseby over a hundred prisoners were taken on, followed by several hundred more former King's men after further victories. By 1647 there were 4,000 former royalists in the ranks – about 20 per cent of the entire army.[42] The older armies, it is worth noting, did exactly the same thing. (A thousand of the parliamentary garrison of Bristol, for instance, joined the King after the port surrendered in July 1643.)[43] When the climactic battle of Naseby took place, it is quite possible that among the Foot on both sides were men who had served the opposing cause.

What then of the supposed 'leaven', the men of the cavalry, paid far better than the infantry (two shillings per day), coming from a higher social stratum, and mostly genuine volunteers? Here again the reality does not quite match the orthodox image of sober zealousness, even among the Ironsides. It was certainly true that Cromwell – and later Manchester as Commander of the Army of the Eastern Association – actively sought to enrol godly men who could be relied upon and promoted by merit.[44] But as the cavalry troops expanded in number so too did the possibility of less-than-perfect recruits making their way into the ranks and the godly straying from righteousness. Hence the reputation the Ironsides also gained for harsh disciplinary measures.

Cromwell, it is too often forgotten, regarded gentlemen as the best natural material for cavalrymen. The cavaliers, he later remembered exclaiming early in the war, tended to win because they were 'gentlemen's sons, younger sons, persons of quality', and when arguing for 'a plain russet-coated captain' over 'that which you call a gentleman and nothing else' he added a caveat which is usually omitted in secondary accounts: 'I honour a gentleman that is so indeed.'[45] It was for practical rather than ideological reasons that Cromwell turned to the more sober of the lower classes to fill his ranks – 'better plain men than none'[46] in view of the fact that the 'quality' had mostly sided with the King – and from the first natural godliness was heavily reinforced by strict punitive measures. One of the commonest problems in all armies, for instance, was met with an order that 'if [any trooper] be drunk he be set in the stocks or worse'.[47]

If such measures were necessary amongst the most committed of units, it is hardly surprising that even harsher deterrents were necessary in the more heterogeneous New Model, where only about a quarter of the horse regiments could be counted as Cromwellian in character.[48] Within weeks of taking the field, New Model horse troopers gained a reputation as plunderers, and drunkenness was common. 'These new modellers', Sir Samuel Luke (the parliamentary garrison commander at Newport Pagnell) wrote in disgust, 'knead all their dough with ale. I have never seen so many drunk in my life in so short a time.'[49] Unauthorized absences, moreover, though heaviest in the infantry, were not unknown among the cavalry: by February 1646 even Cromwell's own brigade was 600 troopers short owing to illness and desertion.[50] Fairfax responded in a manner designed to *encourager les autres*, imposing the death penalty on those found guilty of plundering, deserting, or refusing orders – the last a sporadic occurrence which had affected even Cromwell's troopers.[51]

Surely, though, the zealous piety of the New Model Army set it apart from its opponents? Here again the negative evidence at least balances the positive. For those who see the New Model as an ideologically driven force, the accounts of chaplains are a key form of evidence. Too often, however, their testimony is viewed with an insufficiently critical eye.

To begin with, the actual number of radical clergy serving with the new army needs to be taken into account. The famous Hugh Peters, for example, who, according to one source, 'rode from rank to rank with a Bible in one hand and a pistol in the other exhorting the men to do their duty' before Naseby, may not even have been attached to the army as a chaplain at all. In total only nine radical 'Saints in Arms' can be linked firmly with the New Model Army in 1645 (a total which shrank to four by the spring of 1646). No wonder that one of the constant complaints from Fairfax and other commanders was the *lack* of chaplains.[52] How much influence could such a small number of clergymen really have had? A chaplain preaching a sermon, however powerful of lung and charismatic, cannot even have been heard by more than a few hundred men at once.

No doubt some parliamentary chaplains, encouraged by Fairfax, did effectively foster the belief among some of the troops to whom they preached that God was with them. But the King also took a keen interest in the moral tone of his army, and there were brave and charismatic chaplains among his forces too.[53]

As for lay piety, stories of spontaneous prayer and lay preaching, and of soldiers commonly carrying pocket bibles, need to be taken with a grain of salt. No doubt men in the New Model Army did invoke the name of God in battle; but so too did the royalists. At the battle of Cheriton, for instance, some confusion must have ensued when it was realized that both sides had chosen 'God is With Us' as their battle cry.[54] The more godly of the King's men were also known to sing psalms while marching to war.[55] And can pocket bibles really have been a version of Mao's little red book in an age when around half the adult male population was completely illiterate?[56]

It is true that both Cromwell and Fairfax heavily punished those caught blaspheming, but so did the King; and the mere fact that harsh retribution was even necessary again suggests that there was something of a gap between the image and reality of the New Model.[57] As one critical observer put it, though there were plenty of pious men in the New Model, there were also 'many as ungodly as ever I saw'.[58]

Still, the fact remains that this army won the war for Parliament. If the New Model was not quite the revolutionary force it is often made out to be, then what was it that made it successful?

In terms of experience and talent, there was not much to choose between the two sides. Both armies when the campaigning season opened in 1645 contained a good number of experienced officers and veteran soldiers. Prince Rupert had developed an almost legendary reputation as a royalist cavalry commander, and as Cromwell himself recognized, the cavaliers he led were among the best horsemen in Europe. Lord Astley, in command of the royalist Foot, was a bluff veteran of the Dutch wars who understood his profession as well as Skippon and had fewer new recruits to contend with. And while the King's army was still plagued with problems of rank and precedence in a way that the New Model was not, three years of war had forced the royalists to dispense with social rank as the sole criterion for commissions. The proportion of senior officers who had served on the Continent was even greater than in the parliamentary armies. The lesser gentry rather than the aristocracy tended to command regiments. And former tailors, waiters, millers, and shoemakers could be found among the junior ranks (though in smaller numbers than among Cromwell's troops).[59] Morale on both sides appears to have been quite high on the eve of battle.[60]

Tipping the scales in favour of Parliament, however, was the fact that the New Model was the better organized army – a question of differing degrees of holding administrative and financial chaos at bay rather than one being 'modern' and the other 'feudal'[61] – and had a decided numerical advantage over the King. Despite propaganda claims to the contrary, Fairfax had at least 4,000 more men in the field at Naseby than the King, which meant that if the New Model could hold together for long enough the King's 9,500-odd Horse and Foot would eventually be borne down by weight of numbers.[62]

Numbers alone, however, cannot explain the defeat of the King's army any more than assumptions of ideological superiority. For what is striking about Naseby is the way in which the New Model Army came perilously close at one point to losing the battle, despite having 1,000 more cavalry troopers than the King's force and a quarter more men overall.

Both armies had arrayed themselves in traditional form, with the pikemen and musketeers of the Foot drawn up in phalanx-like blocks in the centre, and with the Horse on the flanks. The few pieces of artillery deployed on each side played a negligible role in subsequent events.[63] After some manœuvring by both sides to deploy on the best ground – eventually placing them on opposing gentle slopes to the north-west of Naseby – the battle began with a general advance by the smaller of the two armies.

Prince Rupert, commanding the royalists in the name of his uncle the King, correctly recognized that his only real chance of victory was to try and break the cohesion of the New Model Army and force a rout before weight of numbers began to tell.[64] To accomplish this meant driving the enemy's cavalry from the field, thereby leaving Skippon's infantry regiments in the centre exposed to attacks on their flanks and rear by the royalist Horse. An all-out attack on the enemy line, with the best portion of the Horse aimed at breaking the enemy's left flank, was therefore quite logical. What was far less logical was Rupert's decision to place himself at the head of the cavalry on the royalist right, an action for which he has been severely criticized by generations of military historians. An overwhelming desire to get away from the intrigues of the King's headquarters and into the thick of the fighting undoubtedly played a role in this decision. Yet in an age when commanders were expected actually to lead, rather than just direct, Rupert's decision may also have been a calculated gamble that his presence among the advancing cavaliers would boost morale and perhaps make a difference at the crucial moment.[65] If so, the mistake was to focus more on the moral effect of his presence in a charge and less on how he was to control his cavaliers if they succeeded in beating the enemy's left-flank Horse under Colonel Sir Henry Ireton.

For a time it looked as if the King might beat the odds. The royalist regiments, advancing 'in a very stately way', according to a senior parliamentary witness, came upon the New Model just as it was assembling for battle.[66] In the centre, Lord Astley's infantry advanced steadily, exchanged a volley of musket fire with Skippon's men at close range, and then came to 'push of pike' (hand-to-hand combat with pikes and musket butts). Despite being outnumbered nearly two to one, the royalist Foot seem to have had the advantage of momentum. The first ranks of New Model infantry were pushed back, units began to lose cohesion, colours were lost, and much to the dismay of the men around him Skippon himself was badly wounded. Uncertainty and fear began to spread in the manner of all crowds, and without help a parliamentary defeat in the centre was a distinct possibility.[67]

An attempt at help, led by Ireton, was made by some of the New Model cavalry on the parliamentary left; but this only had the effect of weakening the parliamentary cavalry lines after they had advanced to meet Prince Rupert. Despite having to advance uphill, and being harassed by fire from a regiment of dismounted dragoons behind a hedge to their right commanded by Colonel John Okey, the cavaliers managed in their second charge to break through the parliamentary Horse.

This was the moment when victory was nearest for the King. With the enemy centre giving way, the left flank partially open, and a number of key figures killed, wounded, or captured – Ireton himself was brought down, wounded, and made prisoner when he tried to assist the New Model infantry – an attack by Rupert's cavalry on Skippon's hard-pressed infantry might have turned fear into panic and produced a wholesale slaughter. 'After this', Okey later admitted, 'we gave ourselves [up] for lost men.'[68]

As it was, however, the momentum of Rupert's charge carried the cavaliers right off the battlefield until they reached and attacked the large parliamentary baggage train a mile distant. In effect this meant that the victory over Ireton's cavalry could not be exploited and half the royalist cavalry were absent from the main scene of action for over an hour and a half.

This had been the great weakness of the cavaliers in earlier battles – the tendency to get carried away, an inability to rally quickly, and charge again in a different place. This may have arisen, as Charles Carlton has suggested, out of a habit of regarding a cavalry charge as akin to a fox hunt – the kind of riding gentlemen were used to – in which cohesion counted for less than the thrill of the chase.[69] Rupert himself seems to have been carried away by his initial success. Charging the parliamentary baggage train, which put up a spirited resistance, was entirely pointless if the main battle still hung in the balance.[70] But it seems unlikely that once the cavaliers began to advance at a full gallop there was much he could do to control events. The emotional excitement and heightened aggressiveness such an all-out charge generated in both horse and rider, coupled with the noise and speed, meant that even the most charismatic leader would be unable to regain control until both horses and men were spent. A charge at a gallop had the advantage of great shock effect, but the disadvantage of being virtually beyond control once launched.[71]

Meanwhile, as Rupert's men careened off the field, the tide of battle was turning in favour of the New Model on the other flank. As on the left, two bodies of horsemen clashed; but this time it was the royalist Northern Horse, outnumbered and facing a brigade of disciplined roundheads led by Cromwell himself, that broke and scattered. And, in marked contrast to Rupert, Cromwell was prepared and able to rally his men – who advanced at a slower but more controllable 'good round trot'[72] – and turn the bulk of his force towards the flanks of the royalist Foot in the centre.

Three hours into the battle, the New Model began to wrest the initiative from the King's army. Fairfax, normally a rather shy man with a stammer, was transformed by battle into a figure of heroic proportions. Having either lost or discarded his helmet early on in the fight, he was easily recognized by his men, exhorting them to stand fast when things looked worst and urging them on to victory when the tide turned. As one of his officers wrote, his presence and courage 'did so animate the Soldiers as is hardly to be expressed'.[73] Deserted by their own Horse, faced by cavalry on either flank (the dragoons having mounted and joined Ireton's troopers in a counter-attack at the other end of the line from Cromwell), and a reinvigorated body of infantry to their front (shattered ranks having been restored and reserves brought forward), the numerically inferior Foot regiments of the royalist centre began to give way. The more experienced troops were able to make a stand and fend off repeated assaults with their pikes; but many of the Foot, seeing the writing on the wall, began to sue for quarter. A last-ditch charge by the King's reserve was stillborn, and by the time Rupert and his men returned to the field there was nothing to do but beat a hasty retreat with Fairfax's men in hot pursuit.[74]

As Cromwell himself admitted, for several hours the outcome of Naseby had been 'very doubtful', a judgement echoed by other contemporary observers.[75] Once the battle had been won, however, the royalist war effort was doomed. Well over 4,000 prisoners had been taken on top of the several hundred killed on the field, most of them infantrymen whom, at this stage in the war, the King could not replace. With the exception of the fight at Langport the following month, where the New Model defeated Lord Goring's demoralized army of 10,000 men – a victory achieved through a mixture of luck, daring, and artillery fire – the last year of the war consisted of storms and sieges of the remaining royalist strongholds.

Naseby was a decisive victory for the parliamentary cause in general and the New Model Army in particular. It was not, however, as Christopher Hill would have it, a victory of the 'new' way over the 'old' way. In terms of overall structure, motivation, and behaviour, there was more which linked the New Model as a whole to other forces of the day *circa* 1645 than set it apart.[76] Even in 1647, when political agitation in the ranks undoubtedly existed, as shown by the famous Putney Debates and subsequent demonstrations, the real meaning and significance of the unrest is open to question.[77]

The phrase 'New Model' ('New Noddle' to the royalists[78]) is itself part of the problem. Officially the force was titled 'The Army of Parliament under the Command of Sir Thomas Fairfax'. Terms like 'New Model' or 'New Modelled' army were used colloquially to distinguish Parliament's 'new' army from older forces such as the Army of the Eastern Association and the Northern Army. It did not necessarily imply a qualitative change. The victory at Naseby, indeed, caught almost everyone by surprise.[79]

Despite a natural tendency for later observers to infer otherwise, a hard look at the evidence reveals nothing particularly revolutionary about this 'New Model' army in its first years beyond the absence of peers and MPs from command positions (in itself not particularly significant beyond the removal of Essex and Manchester); and even in the case of the Self-Denying Ordinance, a tremendously significant exception was made for Cromwell. In terms of organization, manning, and motivation, traditions acquired in the older armies outweighed any innovation. If there *was* anything significantly different about this army it was that it stayed in being long enough for both officers and men to acquire considerable experience working together. This was a practical rather than an ideological development, but one which nevertheless helps explain (along with Cromwell's generalship) the army's continued success against newly raised enemy forces in subsequent wars. 'To play his part in battle', as Brigadier Peter Young put it, 'a trained soldier does not need to be a religious fanatic.'[80]

The New Model, in short, evolved over the years into England's first standing army – with momentous consequences for how it was viewed in the following century. In the wake of the Restoration, the soldiers who had supported Cromwell's personal rule in the 1650s tended to be seen as symbols of political repression rather than of revolutionary commitment and zeal (the latter image only coming back into fashion in more modern times). Yet rather paradoxically it was a desire to avoid the supposedly repressive tendencies of standing armies like the postwar New Model which helped develop within the Thirteen Colonies in America a high regard for the 'plain russet-coated soldier who knows what he fights for and loves what he knows'.

2 The Continental Army in the War of American Independence, 1775–82

Virtue in arms?

Spirit and confidence . . . the best substitute for discipline.

John Adams, October 1775[1]

When men are irritated, and the Passions inflamed, they fly hastily and cheerfully to Arms; but after the first emotions are over . . .

George Washington, September 1776[2]

The War of Independence has always enjoyed enormous resonance within American society. It was, after all, the event which brought the United States into being on the basis of constitutional forms and principles which (it is claimed) are as relevant today as they were over 200 years ago. And in consequence, the patriotic myths surrounding the struggle for independence remain enormously potent.[3]

From the first, those who supported the American Revolution portrayed the war in essentially moralistic terms. The virtuous colonists, united in their cause, had been forced to take up arms in defence of their natural liberties against a despotic monarch and his avaricious ministers who were attempting to subvert those rights. This was how the Continental Congress and colonial legislatures explained the course of events after Lexington and Concord, and – since the past is almost always written up first by the winners – also the terms in which the earliest histories of the War of Independence were written. Virtue had triumphed over vice.[4]

The justness of the American cause, moreover, had been reflected in how each side had approached the military aspects of the conflict. The British had relied on a standing army – in and of itself a symbol of despotic tendencies – the ranks of which were composed of the dregs of society, men motivated only by the desire for pay and plunder and fear of the lash. Lord North had even hired foreign mercenaries, the dreaded Hessians, whose outlook and conduct was even more reprehensible. Such troops were liable to misbehave or desert if given the slightest opportunity, and therefore had to be kept under constant surveillance, forced to fight and manoeuvre *en masse*, in rigid linear formations unsuited to the terrain of the New World. As for the upper-class officers, they were the personification of aristocratic haughtiness: lazy, unwilling to think and adapt, and dismissive of people's rights.[5]

The American war effort, in contrast, was characterized by selflessness, unity, and a uniquely adaptive way of war. Commitment and individual initiative were the keys to American success. Those who took up arms in freedom's cause, from the minutemen who drove back the British column at Lexington and Concord in 1775 to the 'ragged Continentals' who forced the decisive surrender at Yorktown in 1781, were true patriots. They were honest, sober, yeomen volunteers who more than made up for their lack of orthodox military skill by understanding that they were fighting for their own future. As such they were infinitely more committed to the struggle than the unthinking mercenary foe, and could be trusted to operate flexibly, in ways suited to the French and Indian War heritage – in open order, making use of cover, camouflage, and aimed rifle fire.[6]

Those who fought for America were proof of the long-standing Radical Whig assertion (dating from the Cromwell experience) that propertied citizens, defending their homes and liberties in time of crisis, were both safer and even more effective than a standing army.[7] Led by General Washington – a supremely virtuous gentleman-farmer rather than a professional officer – and other natural leaders of men, the American forces were both literally and figuratively citizens in arms, and thus a revolutionary departure from the eighteenth-century tradition of military professionalism.[8]

In the course of the nineteenth century this image of the War of Independence as a triumph of principle lost none of its intensity, as countless histories of fearless patriots and dramatic paintings attest.[9] The following extract from a volume in the popular *World's Best Histories* series, published in 1898, indicates the overheated patriotic prose style commonly employed.

> In every village you could see the farmers shouldering arms and marching to and fro on the green, while an old man played the fife and a boy beat the drum. They did not concern themselves about 'regimentals' or any of the pomp and glory of battle; but they knew how to cast bullets, and how to shoot them into the bull's-eye. In their homespun small clothes, home-knit stockings, home-made shirts and cowhide shoes, they could march to the cannon's mouth as well as the finest scarlet broadcloth and gold epaulets. Their intelligence, their good cause, their sore extremity, made them learn to be soldiers more quickly than seemed possible to English officers who knew the sturdy stupidity of the English peasant of whom the British regiments were composed.[10]

Even Charles K. Bolton, in his otherwise highly regarded and innovative work, *The Private Soldier Under Washington* (1902), asserted that the Continental rank and file were motivated by high idealism, and unlike their foes 'were not a rabble recruited from the low ranks from which a city mob is drawn'.[11]

Ever since Federalist days, to be sure, there were those who had used the War of Independence to try and make a point about the foolhardiness of America relying on amateur forces.[12] In the decades after the Spanish American War, moreover, the works of Emory Upton (a major-general turned historian-polemicist) inspired a generation of US Army officer-scholars to write books designed to debunk the people-in-arms myth and promote the cause of a large peacetime military establishment.[13] But in spite of – or perhaps because of – the vehement and partisan nature of works like *America's Duty as Shown by Our Military History* (1921),[14] these Cassandras had very little impact on what was by now a firmly entrenched set of popular assumptions about the nature of the Revolutionary War.[15]

Meanwhile, as the twentieth century advanced, the military dimensions of the struggle were becoming less and less central to most professional historians' interests. A brief examination of some of the better-known general histories of the United States and of the revolutionary period published in recent decades, however, strongly suggests that when the military aspects *are* touched on the traditional interpretation of virtuous citizen-soldiers triumphing against the odds against corrupt mercenaries is still very much taken for granted.

Allan Nevins and Henry Steele Commanger, for example, in *A Short History of the United States* – in its sixth edition by the mid-1960s – argued along lines that would have been entirely familiar to their nineteenth-century predecessors. They stated that the defeat of General Burgoyne and his invading British army in 1777 'proved that a patriotic yeomanry could be unbeatable'.[16] The Chicago History of American Civilization, under the editorial direction of Daniel J. Boorstin, took a similarly conventional approach to the war. Edmund S. Morgan, in *The Birth of the Republic 1763–89*, first published in 1956 and in revised form as late as 1979, argued that the struggle with Britain had been 'a people's war', fought by patriots whose frontier way of life had 'given them a familiarity with firearms that common people of the Old World lacked'. Their 'greatest asset', however, was 'their desire to be free'.[17]

Howard H. Peckham, meanwhile, in the volume dealing specifically with the military aspects of the Revolution, showed that the essentials of the revolutionary myth remained firmly in place.

> The American in arms was a citizen-soldier. He had volunteered because he had an idea of how his political life should be ordered. He introduced a new concept into war: patriotism . . . . The American's own honor was at stake. He was fighting to determine the destiny of his country and therefore of his children. Once he received some military training he usually could defeat the professional soldier and the mercenary because he had higher motivation, more initiative, and greater hope. These embattled farmers and artisans fought as men possessed – possessed of a fervent and ennobling desire to be free men.[18]

As one of the most recent academic histories of the revolution put it: 'common soldiers unflinchingly endured adversity and the hardships of service'.[19]

Even the US Army came round to this view. The volume *American Military History*, first published by the Office of the Chief of Military History for senior ROTC classes in 1969, makes clear that the need for role models weighed against 'Uptonian' biases in recent decades. Though by no means uncritical of the American effort, the chapter on the Revolutionary War not only ends by stressing the greatness of Washington and other generals but also contrasts the dedication and endurance of the Continental rank and file with British and Hessian soldiers who 'never showed the same spirit'.[20]

Those few historians in academe who have dealt with military affairs since 1945 appear to have succumbed to some extent to the mystique of the Revolution. Don Higginbotham, for example, one of the leading contemporary authorities on the War of Independence, holds that the war was the first instance of a people-in-arms, thus creating 'not only a political revolution but a military revolution as well'.[21]

It therefore comes as no surprise to find James R. Morris, author of the most recent college-level textbook on the American armed forces, confidently asserting that the colonists' greatest asset was 'the cause for which they fought', which meant among other things that '[a]s a fighting force, the Continental Army acquitted itself well despite its lack of professional training'.[22]

Under such circumstances it is only to be expected that popular historians have also by no means given up virtue as the key element in American success. The British, in the opinion of Pulitzer-prize-winning author Barbara Tuchman, 'forgot the extra weapon that is possessed by those who are fighting for a cause. Training is usually the criterion of military effectiveness, but not this time.'[23]

Re-enactments, memorials, and Hollywood films from D. W. Griffith's *America* (1924) to John Millius's *Red Dawn* (1984), have all reinforced the patriot image in public American consciousness.[24] George Washington, for example, remains by far the most recognizable of American heroes.[25]

What Katherine Chorley asserted in *Armies and the Art of Revolution* in 1943 still holds true: 'In most people's minds . . . the American War of Independence will come as the supreme example of revolutionary success against professional troops.'[26]

In fundamental ways, therefore, the contemporary view of the War of Independence mirrors, indeed is derived from, that of the patriots themselves.[27] But how accurate is this view? To what extent were the American forces truly revolutionary, fundamentally different from the enemy in terms of who they were, how they behaved, and why they fought? Despite the longevity of the standard position on this question – virtue and independent commitment triumphing over vice and mass coercion – detailed study of particular aspects of the struggle in recent years suggests that the two sides quickly became, of necessity, remarkably similar.

George Washington, though himself a supreme embodiment of citizen-soldier virtues,[28] quickly recognized a yawning gap between the ideal citizen-soldier army being promoted in the Continental Congress and the real nature of the New England militias surrounding Boston after he was appointed their Commander-in-Chief in the summer of 1775. It was true that in the first action of the war a British column sent to seize arms at Concord in April had been forced into a humiliating retreat by Massachusetts minutemen and militia; that subsequently a force of over 18,000 men from the north-eastern colonies had voluntarily assembled around the British forces in Boston; and that these same men had inflicted severe casualties when the British had stormed Breed's Hill (usually mis-labelled Bunker Hill). But the kind of training which had allowed the minutemen and militia to assemble rapidly, successfully harass a column, and battle a frontal assault from entrenchments, did not make them into an effective army.[29]

The central problem was a lack of discipline and unity among the contingents present. The assemblage of militias besieging Boston, indeed, was in a state of near anarchy. Officers, often with little or no military experience, had either been appointed for political reasons or been elected by their men. Orders were constantly questioned, issues of seniority fiercely debated, and with every man standing on his rights it became impossible even to impose the standard disciplines of camp life. The elementary rules of hygiene were ignored, and there were a steady trickle of wounds caused by men teaching themselves how to shoot: contrary to myth, the north-eastern seaboard was by the late eighteenth century almost as domesticated as western Europe, which meant that volunteers as often as not did not know how to take proper care of either their weapons or themselves in the field.[30] The net result, as one loyalist-leaning observer wrote after inspecting the Boston encampment, was 'as dirty a set of mortals as ever disgraced the name of a soldier'.[31]

Washington and his appointed senior commanders in what was now officially the Continental Army were slowly able to create a little order out of the chaos; but it was an uphill struggle. The terms under which the men had joined up were not propitious. Terms of enlistment varied, but the longest only stretched to the end of the year. Washington's ability to enforce discipline, moreover, was circumscribed by the articles of war adopted by the individual colonies. Only desertion in the face of the enemy and betraying the password were capital crimes, and all other offences – including desertion out of battle – could only involve a fine or a maximum of thirty-nine lashes (biblically correct but a far cry from the maximum thousand lashes set in the British articles of war). If a soldier felt that what he was being asked to do did not match his conception of his duty, or simply became homesick – a major problem – it was easy enough either to ignore orders or to decamp and go home.[32] The Commander-in-Chief, a man of immense self-control, was driven to exasperation by the attitude and behaviour of the New England men, whom he characterized in an uncharacteristic fit of temper as 'an exceedingly dirty and nasty people'.[33]

The units from the various colonies encamped around Boston in 1775 were not, to be sure, behaving very differently from the colonial contingents raised to assist the British during the Seven Years War.[34] But as Washington recognized, in the past Americans had always been backed up by a regular army – this time they faced that very same regular army, and alone. The only option, in his mind, was to try and transform the colonial forces into a regular force. Drawing on his experience with the Virginia Regiment in the 1750s, Washington thought it highly unlikely that short-term volunteers, with little training and many civilian commitments, would be able to confront professional soldiers successfully in the field in what was likely to be a drawn-out war. As he explained to John Hancock in September of 1776, after the first of a number of disastrous engagements around New York:

> Men just dragged from the tender scenes of domestic life, unaccustomed to the din of arms; totally unacquainted with every kind of military skill, which being followed by a want of confidence in themselves, when opposed to troops regularly trained, disciplined, and appointed, superior in knowledge, and superior in arms, makes them timid, and ready to fly from their own shadows.[35]

Washington did not entirely discount the effectiveness of the local militias, and indeed they were to play a vital role in suppressing loyalism, harassing British troops, and supplementing the ranks of the Continental Army when depleted. Militia units, on one or two occasions, were to perform well again in battle, most notably in the north during the Saratoga campaign (1777) and in the south at King's Mountain (1780) and Cowpens (1781).[36] The colonies might have used the parochialism and amateur, semi-civilian nature of the militia to even greater effect by waging a full-scale guerrilla war, as Major-General Charles Lee and one or two other officers advocated early on.[37] But as Washington saw, waging war in this manner would create a struggle so bitter, unrestrained, and drawn out that it would tear the fabric of colonial society apart and render the fruits of victory bitter indeed. Furthermore, if Congress was to gain international recognition and possible aid from the enemy's traditional European rivals, then it would have to prove that – contrary to British propaganda – the war was something other than a mass of rebellious subjects in revolt. For that, and to keep British forces concentrated if not always to defeat them in battle, what Washington called 'a respectable army' was called for.[38]

Already, in 1775–6, Washington had tried to structure the Continental Army along lines very similar to that of the British Army. The administrative system, for example, bore a striking resemblance to that of the enemy, positions such as Adjutant General, Mustermaster General, and even

Brigade Major being consciously based on British precedents.[39] But as the New York campaign demonstrated, the key problem remained terms of service.

Those who had signed on to serve until the end of 1775 had not, as the idealists had expected, re-enlisted in large numbers. (On paper, indeed, the army had only enlisted 9,675 men on 1 January 1776.[40]) As it had become clear that the war would not be over in a matter of weeks or months, and as the discomforts of military life became apparent, the *rage militaire* ebbed away – and with it the strength of the army. Men simply decided that they had done their bit, and that civilian commitments (farms, businesses, etc.) now demanded their attention. The retreat from New York in the late summer of 1776 lowered morale and increased desertion still further, and by September Washington was anticipating the 'dissolution of our army' unless something was done to change how it was recruited and run.[41]

What Washington was asking of Congress was that Whig ideals be set aside in the face of the cold hard fact that the bulk of men were demonstrably motivated more by self-interest than by selfless commitment to a common cause. They needed concrete incentives, both positive and negative, to learn and perform the skills necessary to meet the British Army on equal terms. 'To march over dead bodies', as Major-General Nathanael Greene, one of Washington's principal lieutenants, brutally put it, 'to hear without concern the groans of the wounded, I say few men can stand such scenes unless steeled by habit or fortified by military pride.'[42] The men of the Continental Army, in short, needed to become more like their opponents.

Congress, frightened by the defeats of 1776, gave Washington much of what he wanted in the autumn.[43] If voluntarism was not working, then something other than appeals to patriotism would have to be employed. Generous bounties were now offered to those who signed on for the duration, along with promises of 100 acres of free land after the war. Such offers were most enticing to those with little or no economic stake in society; and though enlistment quotas were set for each state, and a form of conscription introduced in some, the better off could usually purchase the services of substitutes. As detailed studies of enlistment papers have shown, the result was that the ranks of the Continental Army from 1776 to 1777 onward were increasingly filled with young men from the margins of colonial life. Both Congress and Washington might have preferred more upstanding citizens, but most tradesmen and farmers were content to serve in the militia during emergencies and avoid long-term service in the army. Early restrictions on who could not enrol, such as blacks or enemy soldiers, were progressively abandoned as the need for manpower grew more desperate. Soon unemployed labourers, indentured servants, drifters, enemy deserters, and POWs, even slaves, were encouraged to enlist.[44]

At the same time as the enlistment profile was changing, Washington was endeavouring to impose greater discipline and more regular training on his troops – once again in conscious imitation of the British Army. Congress agreed in late 1776 that the articles of war should be considerably expanded to make them more like the British articles, with more crimes listed, a greater number of capital offences (including desertion out of battle), and the maximum number of lashes raised to a hundred.[45]

At the same time as the social profile of the enlisted men was changing, the Commander-in-Chief was attempting to make his officers more distinct from those they commanded. When officers and men treated each other as equals, and 'mixed together as one common herd', then discipline suffered. Officers who did not hold themselves aloof in gentlemanly fashion would not, in Washington's opinion, 'meet with the respect which is essentially necessary to due subordination'.[46] Though only somewhat better off financially than the men, the officers of the Continental Line were encouraged to assume an attitude of gentlemanly aloofness.[47] Washington even by the end of 1777 came to support the rather unrepublican idea of giving them half-pay pensions after the war as a means of avoiding resignations by keeping up their sense of distinction and self-esteem.[48]

Training, as developed during the winter of 1777–8 at Valley Forge and after, was designed to instill the kind of battle discipline found in conventional European armies. With the help of the colourful Baron von Steuben and other European advisors motivated by a mixture of hope for advancement and faith in the cause, the Continental Army adopted a uniform drill code and developed engineering and artillery skills. It drew on a number of European styles, and did depart in some respects from conventional British deployment and tactics (principally in the creation of brigades and the emphasis on aimed musket fire). In all essentials, however, the men of the Continental Army were being trained to fight in the same tactical manner as the enemy – in the open, in thin ranks, standing shoulder to shoulder, firing together on command.[49]

All in all, then, the Continental Army and the British became remarkably similar. The strategic aims of both sides were quite orthodox, centring on the protection or rupture of lines of communication through manœuvre, the capture of key strategic positions, so as to bring the enemy army to battle on the best possible terms.[50] Organized and run along conventional eighteenth-century lines, both armies suffered from severe logistical problems brought on by the distances involved and by the limitations of eighteenth-century state organization and a reluctance on the part of governments to interfere too directly in the economy.[51] Such were the strategic aims of, and constraints on, both Washington and his opponents from Gage to Cornwallis – though Washington, with a weaker army, had to be more careful in deciding when and where to give battle.[52] As for the actual fighting, both armies adopted conventional linear tactics, the actions of the main armies being complemented by light troops and auxiliaries acting as skirmishers and partisans. Contrary to legend, the British were not the proverbial fish out of water in the American wilderness, having developed the techniques of irregular warfare both in Europe and North America in the Seven Years War.[53]

Those who led the fight on both sides, moreover, had a lot in common personally. Many of the more senior British commanders had fought alongside their Revolutionary War opponents in North America during the Seven Years War, and Washington and Gage had been personal friends.[54] Charles Lee and Horatio Gates, respectively appointed Major-General and Brigadier in the Continental Army, had been living in the colonies as half-pay officers of the British Army when the war broke out. Richard Montgomery, another brigadier, had served as a captain in the British Army for many years before retiring to New York.[55] Washington himself had tried several times to gain a regular commission in 1755.[56] The American generals saw themselves as being forced to fight in order to preserve traditional English liberties in the colonies; and while the British saw Washington and his men as rebels, they did not – with the exception of the Hessian officers – view them as beyond the pale in ideological terms. As General William Phillips wrote, 'we cannot forget that when we strike we wound a brother'.[57] Despite the fact that the war was technically a domestic rebellion, therefore, the senior commanders on both sides in the War of Independence generally conducted themselves as if this were a limited, eighteenth-century dynastic struggle in Europe.

Both sides, for example, in a practice quite standard in the dynastic wars of the age, did not hesitate to seek out help from any foreign troops who would serve their cause. The British brought Hessians and other German mercenaries into the colonies under contract. Congress, meanwhile, accepted offers from a wide sample of Europe's itinerant officers – Lafayette being only the most famous example – and, of course, eventually augmented the effectiveness of the Continental Army by allowing a French Royal Army expeditionary force to operate in North America.[58]

Officers taken in battle were generally treated courteously, and often exchanged. When senior commanders believed the enemy was not playing by the rules, they thought nothing of writing a letter of complaint directly to their opponent. Efforts were made in both camps to restrict the effect of major military operations on the civilian population. Though the struggle between loyalist and patriot partisan forces could at times be quite savage – especially in the south – the War of Independence at the level of the main armies was, in many respects, the last war of the *ancien régime* rather than the first war of the era of revolutions.[59]

A common military experience and outlook among senior generals was matched by similar problems in maintaining an effective hierarchy of command. Disunity, rather than harmony, characterized the planning and execution of many operations on both sides.

Relations between British generals and admirals serving in North America, and between the Commander-in-Chief and the North ministry in London, were fraught with misunderstanding, distrust, and jealousy. Time and again, initially successful British operations were sabotaged by poor co-operation between generals and admirals. Serious problems of communication existed between Burgoyne and Gage, Burgoyne and Carleton, Burgoyne and William Howe, Clinton and Richard Howe, and Clinton and Cornwallis – to name only some of the more prominent figures.[60]

That much is common knowledge. Yet the American war effort was no less noteworthy for its disunity. Efforts by Congress to co-ordinate strategy, recruiting, and supply were thwarted at almost every turn by the jealous parochialism of individual colonies. As for the nominal Commander-in-Chief, Washington had to contend with truculent subordinates such as Charles Lee and John Sullivan, men every bit as prickly over their personal honour and position as their British counterparts, and just as willing to complain bitterly, disobey, feud with one another – Horatio Gates versus Philip Schuyler – and engage in political intrigue behind his back. Benedict Arnold, although the only American commander actually to switch sides – his name thereby becoming a synonym for traitorous behaviour in the United States – was far from unique in his sense of injured pride and grievance against his superiors.[61]

As for the forces which these commanders led, the Continental Army, as we have seen, was shaped in conscious imitation of European forces – not least the British Army itself. Officers were gentlemen, or were expected to behave as such; indeed, in aping the manners of their opponents American officers, if anything, behaved more arrogantly towards one another and their men than did officers in many European armies.[62] The rank and file, generally speaking, came from those segments of society with little to lose, and were kept in order by a strict punitive disciplinary code. Though punishments still tended to be more draconian in the British Army, it is worth noting that on several occasions Washington and other American generals thought it necessary on the eve of battle to warn their troops that any man who ran in the face of the enemy would be summarily shot.[63]

Both sides experienced problems with plundering. Especially in the first years of the war, British soldiers were rather indiscriminate in seizing crops and livestock to supplement their rations, and the Hessians gained a possibly undeserved reputation for wanton destruction of civilian property.[64] However, the troops of the Continental Army, chronically short of essentials, were equally inclined to prey on a civilian population which they regarded as indifferent or hostile. Washington was forced to keep his men away from heavily populated areas and in early 1777 issued a reminder that the army's function was 'to give protection and support to the poor, distressed inhabitants; not to multiply and increase their calamities'.[65]

Desertion was also a difficulty not confined to the supposedly more coarse and mercenary British troops. The Continental Army was constantly being drained of its effective manpower by soldiers who decided that they had a right to go home. Indeed, with communities unwilling to turn over to the authorities local boys who had returned, and the prospect of a new life on the frontier beckoning for those with less sympathetic neighbours, desertion was a far greater problem for the Americans than it was for the British. Around one-third of all enlisted men in the Continental Army went absent at one time or another, while the British Army – the men stationed overseas, far from home – suffered losses from desertion of only about 8 per cent over the entire war.[66]

Among those deserters, moreover, were men who joined the opposing army. As well as employing foreigners, both sides actively recruited from amongst enemy prisoners of war in order to fill out their own ranks. In most cases, those who chose to change sides were motivated simply by a desire to escape the often intolerable conditions of captivity. Once in enemy ranks, several hundred such men deserted back to their own lines. No figures exist for the total number of men who changed sides, but it was certainly in the thousands. General Nathanael Greene, looking back on the war near the end, drily remarked that 'we fought the enemy with British soldiers and they fought us with those of America'.[67]

A further indication that the men who fought each other in America were not that dissimilar was the way in which they responded to arrears in pay and shortages of food and clothing. Neither side possessed the administrative and financial structures necessary to meet properly the logistical challenges of protracted war – a chronic problem that would not really be solved until the latter part of the nineteenth century – and in consequence soldiers were rarely paid on time, did not always receive replacements for worn-out clothing and kit, and often lacked provisions. Soldiers could and did endure much hardship, but there came a point on both sides where individual sub-units chose to go on strike – to mutiny – until their grievances were attended to.

In 1777, elements of four different British regiments serving in America refused to obey orders until they were properly clothed and paid, and in 1778 the men of the Seaforth Highlanders mutinied *en masse* over arrears in pay.[68] American militia units were notoriously prone to go on strike in 1777, and mutinies occurred regularly in 1778–9 in various regular garrisons and camps. In the winter of 1780–1, elements of the Pennsylvania and New Jersey Line refused to obey orders, marched out of camp, and threatened Congress and the New Jersey government with force if their demands to be paid and allowed to go home were not met.[69]

The fact that these units refused offers from the British to change sides has sometimes been portrayed as a sign of their underlying patriotism, but British troops in revolt were equally emphatic in declaring their loyalty to the Crown (as opposed to their officers).[70]

In any event, commanders on both sides viewed such mutinies as prejudicial to military discipline, and after allowing some concessions took steps to stop the rot. Washington, indeed, showing less clemency than did King George with the mutinous Seaforths, had two of the New Jersey ringleaders seized and shot at once in front of the rest of the regiment *pour encourager les autres*.[71]

Perhaps, as some have suggested, a hard core of enlistees and dedicated officers like Washington himself truly were committed to the cause, allowing them to endure hardships and setbacks that otherwise would have led the Continental Army to collapse.[72] And, when all is said and done, the British did eventually concede defeat. But even if republican virtue really did exist at some level, it clearly was not the central reason for American success in the War of Independence. What, then, were the keys to American victory?

On one level the war may have been lost for Britain before the first shots were fired at Lexington. Up to a third of the population in the Thirteen Colonies was loyalist, but in the months leading up to Lexington and Concord it was the patriots who gained control of key local and regional institutions such as the militia in 1774–5, thereby severely limiting indigenous support for the British cause. Redcoats could take and hold ports and towns, but the manpower simply did not exist to garrison every town and village. Perhaps under these circumstances it was unlikely that the rebellion could ever have been successfully repressed once the struggle for local control had been won by the rebels.[73]

On the other hand, the war went on for eight years, and there were times when even the most ardent patriots must have wondered if they could ever win. And when the actual course of events is considered, what is striking is the degree to which significant campaigns and battles might easily have turned out differently. Washington and other American commanders, it is worth remembering, were not always right in considering their next moves, any more than Howe, Burgoyne, and the other senior British generals were wrong. A plan by Washington, for example, to assault Boston with his ill-trained army in March of 1776 – a city strongly fortified and garrisoned by the British – would certainly have led to disaster if bad weather had not led to its cancellation.[74] The difference was that the Americans were lucky enough to be saved from the consequences of their own mistakes while the British were usually forced to pay dearly for theirs.

If the British had acted more vigorously in the late summer of 1776, Washington's army would have been cornered and destroyed during its brief and fragmented effort to defend New York later that year – an event which might well have drained the life out of the rebel cause. Instead the Continental Army survived to deliver several sharp counter-attacks and live to fight another day.[75] General Burgoyne, leading his ill-fated army down from Canada in 1777, almost managed to save himself at Saratoga by luring the leading brigades of General Gates into an ambush. Only the betrayal of the plan by a deserter allowed Gates to avoid the trap with only minutes to spare. The subsequent American victory at Saratoga was what finally convinced the French to join the war, turning a colonial rebellion into a worldwide war and greatly reducing the resources Britain could spare for the struggle in America. As contemporaries said, that Burgoyne rather than Gates ended up surrendering was truly an act of providence.[76]

Even after 1777, with the French in the war, there was nothing necessarily inevitable about the decisive British defeat at Yorktown in 1781. Like earlier disasters, this defeat was due in large part to strategic blunders by British commanders (in this case Cornwallis in overreaching himself and neglecting to keep proper contact with the Royal Navy off the south-east seaboard), but also to a great deal of luck on the part of the enemy. In 1781, when Washington at last felt strong enough to return to the attack after five years of mostly defensive campaigns designed to preserve and strengthen the Continental Army, he favoured an assault on New York. If the French commanders had not persuaded him otherwise, Washington's forces would have been in the north, fruitlessly assaulting the strongly entrenched main British army at Manhattan, rather than being in an opportune position to trap Cornwallis against the sea in Virginia.[77]

Overall, then, luck and circumstance were more important to success and failure in the American War of Independence than the moral status of the contending armies. So too, on occasion, was battlefield leadership. Washington was not a brilliant strategist, and lost as many battles as he won. But he could be fearless in placing himself in the position of maximum danger in order to rally wavering troops by personal example, as at Harlem Heights, Princeton, and Monmouth. Washington, though more olympian in manner than either Cromwell or Fairfax had been in the English Civil War, also possessed the crucial ability to inspire otherwise rather ordinary men to unusual feats of bravery and fortitude.[78]

The image of selfless patriots acting as citizen-soldiers against selfish mercenary professionals allowed Americans to view the Revolution in terms of a vast morality play, but the truth of the matter is that after 1775 the contending armies were remarkably alike. Though the citizen-soldier would remain central to republican political thinking during and after the war – so much so that the United States entered the War of 1812 without a regular army[79] – the failure of this theoretical ideal to operate successfully after 1775 forced Congress to depend on a semi-professional force. When all is said and done, the Continental Army emerges as a force not unlike the New Model Army: in theory the embodiment of certain war-winning virtues, but in practice, like their foes, a cross-section of the more desperate sections of the male population, motivated by fear and the hope of profit and emerging victorious through a mixture of luck and leadership.[80]

Yet the ideal of the citizen-soldier, tied in with supposed 'natural' virtues, was by no means dead. It had first emerged, rather paradoxically, in reaction to the kind of professional army the New Model Army had evolved into in the 1650s. Collective amnesia concerning the true circumstances of the War of Independence was to ensure its dominance in American politico-military thinking well into the nineteenth century. Even more significantly, the way in which the American Revolution was reported by sympathetic French observers and propagandized by Benjamin Franklin in Paris – the American people in arms, fighting for their natural liberties, unencumbered by distinctions of class and social rank – was to serve as an inspiring ideal in the wars of the French Revolution.[81] Once again, however, ideals would have to adapt to realities.

3 The armies of the French Republic and the War of the First Coalition, 1792–7

Aux armes, citoyens?

Zeal and above all patriotism . . . often makes up for talent.
Jean-Baptiste Bouchotte, War Minister, 1793[1]

I would like to see these so-called patriots surrounded by drunken and wild soldiers who threaten anyone who dares to talk to them of the laws.
Adjutant-General Jean-Louis Vieusseux, Army of the Rhine, 1792[2]

In the minds of scholars and public alike – and not just in France – the exploits of the armies of the French Revolution are without parallel. Like the political revolution from which they sprang, so it is said, the armies of the First Republic not only saved Revolutionary France from its many enemies but also began a military revolution. How did this occur?

The army of the *ancien régime*, its strength and sense of purpose undermined by conflicting loyalties, was transformed between 1791 and 1794 into the modern world's first citizen army – a truly revolutionary force in every sense. A series of volunteer drafts, culminating in the famous *levée en masse* of August 1793, radically increased the size and widened the social profile of the French Army – a force led increasingly by talented former NCOs and soldiers rather than hidebound aristocrats. No longer separated from their officers by boundaries of class, and serving a revolutionary regime which served the interests of the people at large, these new soldiers were truly committed to the defence of the Republic.

These were men who were the very antithesis of the typically eighteenth-century 'professionals' they fought, soldiers motivated more by fear of punishment than by any normative cause who had to be kept under close supervision and constantly drilled to prevent desertion. As for tactical proficiency, the French volunteers made up for what they lacked in formal drill manoeuvres through sheer revolutionary zeal, their willingness to press home attacks at the point of a bayonet, combined with an ability to think and act independently.

The result, from the first great victory at Valmy in September 1792 and through the later campaigns which sent coalition forces reeling in the Low Countries, along the Rhine, and in Italy, was an army which appeared to mark the end of the dynastic wars of kings and the start of the modern wars of nations, of peoples in arms fighting for their personal and collective cause. 'From this day and place', the young Goethe concluded after watching Valmy from the Prussian side, 'commenced a new epoch in the world's history.'[3]

Like most other accepted beliefs, this view of the armies of the Republic as essentially revolutionary has its origins in the rhetoric of contemporary ideologues. Much as in the American Revolution, such rhetoric revealed more about prevailing philosophical ideals than it did about the actual state of affairs. Ministers, deputies, and publicists of both radical and moderate political persuasions – everyone from Robespierre to Brissot – emphatically subscribed to Enlightenment faith in the citizen-soldier. Leading *philosophes*, including such luminaries as Voltaire, Diderot, Montesquieu, and Rousseau, as well as military thinkers such as Guibert and Servan, had all argued in favour of a citizen army. Details and nuance might vary, but the common assumption was that citizens in arms would be both more committed and more effective than the eighteenth-century regular soldier; that citizens with established liberties and rights to defend would be more reliable and fight more aggressively.[4]

'Every citizen should be a soldier by duty', as Rousseau put it in *The Social Contract*, 'none by trade. If a foreign war comes, the citizens march off calmly to combat; none thinks of flight, they do their duty.' It was this sort of ideological leaning which animated Jacques-Pierre Brissot, leader of the war faction in the Legislative Assembly: 'every advantage is on our side', he cried while successfully urging deputies to declare war on Austria and Prussia in April 1792, 'for now every French citizen is a soldier and a willing soldier at that!'[5]

Willingness and commitment, moreover, made citizen-soldiers much better at attacking than their mercenary foes. Consequently offensive action was always being urged, and the praises of the bayonet charge constantly sung. 'Without cease act offensively', urged Jean-Baptiste Bouchotte, Minister of War, to the commander of the Army of the Moselle, 'it is necessary to haggle with our enemies no longer, but to march intrepidly at them and charge them with the bayonet.'[6] With muskets in short supply and cold steel thought to be crucial in allowing volunteers to express their love of *La Patrie*, pikes – not used for over a century – were manufactured and issued to the troops.[7]

Setbacks in the field did little to dampen such rhetoric. The famous declaration by the Assembly on 11 July 1792, while implicitly acknowledging that all had not gone well by calling for volunteers to buttress existing forces – 'Citizens, the country is in danger!' – assumed that 'those who want the honour of being first to march in defence of all they hold dear' would be animated by the knowledge that 'they are French and free'.[8] When the National Convention and the Committee of Public Safety faced new military crises in 1793, they not only redoubled efforts to bring in more volunteers – culminating in the famous *levée en masse* decree of August –

but also sent representatives to the armies both to keep an eye on the political reliability of the generals and to reinspire the men with republican enthusiasm.[9]

The representatives-on-mission, for the most part, saw what they expected to see in the armies. In the Army of the North and Ardennes, for instance, hard pressed in the spring of 1794, Saint-Just could report to the Committee of Public Safety that 'the spirit of the army is triumphant, joy reigns here'; while another representative wrote that 'our brave soldiers are marching into combat singing and dancing the *Carmagnole*'.[10] As for the continual pressure on French generals to attack, another Jacobin representative-on-mission, Delbrel, had claimed in September 1793 that 'every time that we [in the Army of the North] have attacked we have won, and . . . every time we have been attacked we have almost always been defeated'.[11]

Radical newspapers such as *Père Duchesne*, meanwhile, vast numbers of which were distributed to the armies by the government during the Terror, continued to extol the virtues of the citizen-in-arms. 'Eight days of enthusiasm', Sébastian Lacroix had claimed in July 1793 in reference to the volunteers' lack of military experience, 'can do more for *La Patrie* than eight years of combat.'[12] Revolutionary enthusiasm on the part of *sans-culottes*, armed with cold steel and zeal for their cause, was bound to triumph. Little wonder, therefore, that the Committee of Public Safety should happily confirm its own predispositions by declaring in March 1794 that experience had shown that 'the success of our armies is due principally to the use of the bayonet'.[13]

Combined with the evident successes of the revolutionary armies in the field, this ideological frame of reference produced a highly idealistic image of the revolutionary soldier:

> a committed Republican, a man of principle who opposed tyranny and privilege with the same passion that he reserved for the armies of Austria and Prussia . . . marching out of his village with gaiety in his heart and the cheers of his fellow villagers ringing in his ears . . . the *Père Duchesne* in his knapsack and a Continent at his feet.

All in all the Army of the Republic 'was in every sense a revolutionary army, different from any army that Europe had known'.[14]

Historians in nineteenth-century France, often Jacobin in sympathy, usually accepted, perpetuated, and sometimes even augmented this image of the heroic and committed citizen-soldier. 'By so many heroic actions in the utmost struggles for liberty', as the great Michelet himself put it, 'they magnified human nature.'[15] Historians of the Revolution in the twentieth century, influenced to a greater or lesser degree by Marxism, tended to concentrate less on *la patrie* and more on *égalité*, but the result was essentially the same – the military virtues of the citizen-soldier.[16]

On the significance of Valmy, Albert Mathiez, the first of the great twentieth-century historians of the Revolution, agreed with Goethe. 'Professional armies', he wrote in the early 1920s, 'trained in a passive discipline, were being succeeded by a new army, animated by a sentiment of human dignity and national independence.'[17] Georges Lefebvre went on to state in the 1940s that the French victories were won 'by the sans-culottes, who rushed the enemy to the martial strains of the *Marseillaise* and the *Carmagnole*, swamping the adversary with sheer force of numbers'.[18] For Albert Soboul, who held the Sorbonne chair in the history of the French Revolution in succession to Lefebvre from 1959 to his death in 1982, the soldiers of 1793–4 were 'fighting for their own cause'.

> In the year II the army of the Republic was a truly revolutionary army, intimately tied to the popular classes of society and an instrument of defence for the social and political conquests of these classes. Its inflexible morale, supported by an enthusiasm emanating from the very depths of the people, its exceptional ability to create and reconstitute its officer ranks, to reform itself and recover after defeats, allowed it to face up to the enemy in the most difficult conditions, and then to achieve victory.[19]

The Committee of Public Safety could hardly have put it better. Even in more recent and more detailed analytical studies of the French revolutionary armies by talented historians such as Jean-Paul Bertaud and John Lynn, the traditional image has been qualified but by no means abandoned.[20]

Under the Third, Fourth, and Fifth Republics, meanwhile, this heroic image has literally been carved in stone. Hundreds of monuments, inscriptions, songs, and speeches have been produced over the last 200 years celebrating the defenders of the Revolution. Though rather less martial in tone than the 1879 celebrations, the recent bicentenary festivities still involved a good deal of glorification. The international TV miniseries *La Révolution Française*, directed by Robert Enrico, for instance, included a faithfully heroic rendering of Valmy. And the national anthem itself, the *Marseillaise*, is a perpetual reminder of the revolutionary call to arms.[21]

Not surprisingly in view of prevailing opinion, the armies of the Republic figure prominently in general studies of the (positive) impact of political revolution on military effectiveness. 'The French private', Katherine Chorley concluded in *Armies and the Art of Revolution*, 'realized that for the first time in his long history he was being exhorted to spend his blood in his own cause', the response being 'loyal and unhesitating'.[22] The armies of the Republic, Jonathan Adelman has asserted more recently in *Revolution, Armies, and War*, 'had become a politically conscious national force inspired by a new sense of patriotism'.[23]

At the same time, military historians of varying persuasions from Jomini onwards have portrayed these armies as heralding a military revolution – the end of the dynastic wars and the beginning of the wars of nations. Positively rather than negatively motivated, unlike their opponents, French troops could fight independently, in swarms of skirmishers, and *en masse* in the famous column of attack which skirmishers protected until it was close enough to charge home against the enemy line and begin a rout. 'Two patterns of warfare', as Gunther E. Rothenberg succinctly put it in analysing Valmy, 'the one limited and now becoming obsolete, and the other, potentially unlimited, had collided for the first time.'[24]

Perhaps so, at least in broad terms. A critical examination of the available primary sources, combined with the statistical analyses conducted in recent decades, however, suggest that the abruptness of the transition from one way of war to another and the degree and effectiveness of revolutionary enthusiasm at work in the armies of the First Republic have been greatly overstated.

It is certainly true that the volunteers of 1791–3, and even more so the conscripts of the *levée en masse* of 1793, were an essential supplement to the shrinking numbers of the old Royal Army, allowing the Republic to field armies totalling in excess of 700,000 men by 1794. Whether they were substantially more committed, and therefore more effective, is a more debatable issue.

By the time the Assembly declared war in April 1792, the Royal Army was suffering from a variety of ills which severely limited its effectiveness. Officers, many as nostalgic for the *ancien régime* as Louis XVI, were resigning in record numbers – 6,000 junior and senior officers, or approximately 60 per cent of the authorized total, had resigned or simply fled abroad by the end of the year.[25] The rank and file, meanwhile, freed of harsh punitive discipline by a series of government measures which limited the disciplinary powers of officers and NCOs, and living in an atmosphere of constant political upheaval and turmoil, responded with various acts of insubordination (a full-scale mutiny of several regiments at Nancy in August 1790 being among the more extreme) and by deserting by the thousand. Over 5 per cent of total strength was lost through desertion in 1792.[26]

The Assembly, meanwhile, had been attempting to develop a coherent plan for the future of the army. The problem of officer emigration was at least partially met through the promotion of NCOs, many of whom took a far more professional attitude to soldiering than their aristocratic predecessors.[27] The rank and file, however, remained a problem. Improved conditions of service did little to stem the flow of deserters, while insubordination only grew worse (the Assembly being understandably reluctant to restore the kind of coercive measures associated with the *ancien régime*).[28] Disbanding the army's foreign regiments, however necessary in political terms, only added to the manpower crisis.[29] There was considerable debate on the merits of some form of selective conscription – the army, after all, now served the nation, and military service could be seen as one of the obligations of citizenship. In the end, however, the Assembly maintained the voluntary principle, the manpower problem being addressed through a call in the summer of 1791 for National Guardsmen near the frontiers to form volunteer battalions which would be mobilized to help the Line army in the first campaign.[30]

This, the first of the volunteer levies, met with great enthusiasm. At first a ceiling of 26,000 was set, but by August this had been raised to 101,000 and 169 battalions were formed (though it is worth noting that even at the height of patriotic enthusiasm a fair number of volunteers were in fact deserters from the Line army – 20,000 men under strength – seeking better conditions). Young, mostly *petit bourgeois* in origin, and not yet having to face the rigours of war, the volunteers of 1791 were genuine enthusiasts.[31]

As we shall see, the effectiveness of volunteers in battle left much to be desired; but even in terms of numbers it soon became apparent that the revolutionary enthusiasm of the population was far from limitless. In the wake of the first battlefield disasters after war was declared in April 1792, the Assembly dramatically declared *la patrie en danger* and called for a second volunteer levy of forty-two battalions (33,600 men) from the entire male population, and an increase in the Line army of 50,000 men.[32] In some regions – in Paris, for example, where 15,000 men came forward to join the volunteers – the response was as enthusiastic as in 1791.[33] In many areas, however, the number of recruits was disappointing. The more ardent souls had already joined up, and faced with the prospect of real fighting – something that had not been the case for the men of 1791 – the remainder, especially the peasantry, evidently required incentives.

In order to meet recruiting goals in the departments of the interior, the government had to authorize bounties of 80 to 120 livres to attract recruits, and in some areas quotas could only be met through the use of a highly unpopular ballot system (in other words a form of selective service).[34] The disappointingly small number of volunteers for the regular army, meanwhile, gave rise to great efforts to attract soldiers from the disbanded foreign regiments, particularly the Swiss, back into the ranks in the autumn of 1792.[35]

None of these measures was enough. In February 1793 the new National Convention proclaimed an additional levy of 300,000 18- to 40-year-olds. Departments were allocated quotas, but not told, in light of the fact that true volunteers were unlikely to be forthcoming, how they were to proceed.[36] Bounties were once again offered, but had to be supplemented by balloting and by public nomination (*scrutin révolutionnaire*). Since both the ballot and *scrutin* were open to abuse by local officials, and since the whole process was essentially coercive, there was a good deal of resistance in the form of bribes, threats, draft evasion, and even – in the West – armed rebellion. Not surprisingly, those who ended up leaving for the front tended to be either very young or rather old, and almost always of humble means. By mid-year, this latest 'volunteer' levy had yielded only 150,000 men.[37]

It was the failure of volunteer recruiting, combined with desertion – something we will turn to shortly – which drove the government to proclaim the famous *levée en masse* in the autumn of 1793. Though usually hailed as a masterly effort at total mobilization and as the pinnacle of revolutionary zeal ('young men will go to battle; married men will forge arms and transport provisions; women will make tents and clothing and serve in the hospitals; children will shred old linen') the fact of the matter was that the *levée en masse* meant conscription of a large number – at least 300,000[38] – of the remaining 18- to 25-year-old males.

To be sure, there was much less overt resistance to the *levée en masse* than there had been with the two previous levies, and Jacobin propaganda was not slow to build up an image of those conscripted as 'brave and selfless, cheerful and chivalrous, youngsters offering themselves with carefree generosity to the revolutionary cause'.[39] The burden of military service was being shared more equitably and the nation was clearly in danger, which – coupled with more efficient administration – lessened popular hostility. Still, even now the fact that married men were exempted caused thousands of young men to rush to the altar in some regions, while the Convention found it necessary to impose the death penalty on anyone speaking out against the levy in December 1793.[40]

Contributing to the manpower problem, and strongly suggesting that volunteers were not always as willing to make sacrifices as revolutionary propaganda would have it, was wide-scale desertion. Many of the volunteers of 1791, having signed on for a single campaign, were quite prepared simply to go home at the end of 1792 when the foreign threat had diminished – very much like Washington's troops in 1776. As one volunteer related of a confrontation with an officer who questioned his decision to go home:

> I had no hesitation in replying that I had thrown up everything and that I would always throw up everything for my country, that I was ready to start again on twenty campaigns if she was in danger, but he knew very well that nobody made serious war in winter, and that I wanted to spend the winter at home to continue my studies which I had interrupted for the sake of the nation.[41]

In the summer of 1791, 470,000 men served in French armies. By the beginning of 1793, despite the 1792 levy, the number had shrunk to 350,000.[42] The desertion rate that year was approximately two to four times the annual average for the old Royal Army in the 1780s; even in 1794, with the more willing citizen-soldiers of the *levée en masse* appearing in the field, the desertion rate was at least as high, if not higher, among the volunteer recruits as it had been among the 'mercenaries' who had served the King.[43]

As for the less zealous recruits of 1792–3, and even the supposedly more committed men of the *levée en masse*, life in the ranks was not at all attractive. Homesickness was a serious problem, and serious shortages of clothing, equipment, and food did little to inspire loyalty.[44] On the march, new recruits had to be kept under close supervision to avoid desertion. 'We need a building easily guarded', as one conductor put it in reference to shelter for these groups, 'because at first these country people think only of deserting.'[45] Even with guards, however, men slipping away home, in the words of representatives-on-mission, remained 'a drain that has no end'.[46]

In the departments of the Aisne, Finistère, Gard, Oise, and Tarn, for example, the number of deserters was estimated in the hundreds. In the Haute-Loire, 30 per cent of recruits sent to the army in May 1794 failed to arrive. The district of Saint-Céré, and Châteauneuf in the Main-et-Loire, both lost 25 per cent of their drafts in May 1794 and March 1793 respectively.[47] Once at the front, moreover, desertion continued. Of seventy-one soldiers sent to Saint-Flour from Aurillac in the spring of 1793, for instance, only nineteen had not disappeared by mid-August, while a battalion from Ruffec went from a maximum strength of 2,304 down to 94.[48] Entire units could disappear, as did a company of the 6th Ariege Battalion in December 1793. The prospect of being sent to the Vendée to fight against royalist counter-revolutionary guerrillas only made matters worse: of 15,000 recruits from Charente, 5,000 deserted rather than serve in the Vendée.[49] Among those who stayed in the ranks, there was little condemnation of those who left beyond a minority of hard-core *Jacobins* – the greater concern being to prevent younger brothers from being called up.[50] And as families and even entire villages were more than willing to cover for sons needed on the land, desertion remained an insoluble problem.[51]

Still, thousands of blue-clad volunteers organized in several hundred brigades were helping to augment the strength of the white-coated regular army regiments – and indeed became line troops themselves when the two forces were amalgamated into demi-brigades beginning in the summer of 1793.[52] Numbers, however, were offset to a considerable degree by lack of discipline and training.

The disciplinary problems in the line army have already been mentioned. The volunteers, however, were if anything even less inclined to obey commands they did not like. Officers were as often as not elected on the basis of popularity as much as military experience, and even the most innocuous orders could be – and usually were – contested by the rank-and-file citizen-soldier revelling in the spirit of *égalité*. The 1st *Fédéré* Battalion from the Pas-de-Calais, for instance, had the sense to elect a former regular NCO as their lieutenant-colonel but came near to lynching the unfortunate officer – a 'despot who despises Liberty and Egality' – when he tried to teach his men the fundamentals of drill.[53] 'Now that the time of the *sans-culottes* has arrived', as the radical newspaper *Père Duchesne* triumphantly explained in November 1793, 'those who command and those who obey are equal.'[54]

Not all volunteer units, to be sure, were as highly politicized as the *Fédérés*, originally raised for internal defence and almost as lacking in discipline and training as the later notorious *armées révolutionnaires*.[55] One regular lieutenant even went as far as to write in 1792 of several volunteer battalions that they were 'much better instructed and disciplined than our regiments'.[56] Yet there were also plenty of indications that problems were growing. 'The volunteers of the most recent levy are more trouble than they are worth', A.-L. Biron complained while commanding the Army of the Rhine the same year: 'All the generals to whom I wish to allocate them are afraid of them rather than eager to have them.'[57] Even the most supportive observers concur that indiscipline and lack of proper training could and did seriously undermine military effectiveness.[58]

The first months of the war were not auspicious. The campaign of 1792 opened with an advance by French troops into Austrian-held Belgium in April. One column of 2,300 men, after advancing towards Tournai, began to retreat when contact was made with a small Austrian force. Without any help from the enemy the retreat turned into a rout as a rumour of treason spread. The French commander, General Théobold Dillon, was first wounded and then lynched by his own men.[59] A second column of 15,000 men, under the Duc de Biron, also began to retire before reaching its objective, Mons. At the first contact with enemy cavalry, two French cavalry regiments panicked, crying to their fellows 'Every man for himself! We are betrayed!' The column broke and ran, and Biron was lucky to escape the same fate as Dillon.[60] An advance on Courtrai in June with a force of 20,000 men was swiftly abandoned at the first sign of Austrian resistance – the commanding general, Luckner, evidently fearful that his badly equipped troops would be unable to withstand a serious counter-attack.[61] Little wonder that the Austrians should derisively claim that the revolutionary battle cry ought to be '*ne pas vaincre mais courir*' rather than '*vaincre ou mourir*'.[62]

French armies did, to be sure, manage to win some battles later in the year – notably at Valmy and Jemappes – and even more in 1793; all of which would appear to indicate that after initial encounters both volunteers and line troops (most of the latter having enlisted since 1789) were managing to translate revolutionary enthusiasm into effective tactics. On closer inspection, however, the circumstances of these victories did not herald the superiority of the revolutionary over the professional soldier.

Valmy (20 September 1792), in which there was little direct contact between the opposing sides, was won mostly through the steadiness of the French regular artillery – the arm least affected by the upheavals of the Revolution – and by the fact that the forces of the enemy commander, the Duke of Brunswick, were ravaged by dysentery and lack of supplies owing to heavy rains turning the roads to mud. When they arrived at Valmy, a force of 130,000 Austrians, Prussians, and émigrés had been reduced through wastage (as well as garrisoning captured fortresses) to a weak and ill body of 40,000 men. Once it became evident that the French volunteer infantry would not simply collapse outright and that the French artillery was willing and able to support them, Brunswick prudently withdrew to rest and refit his men (who were, quite apart from anything else, outnumbered five to three by the French). Though a strategic victory for France, insofar as the enemy march on Paris was halted, Valmy was at best a draw at the tactical level.[63]

Jemappes (6 November 1792), the result of yet another attempt to invade Belgium, was a more clear-cut case of the French overcoming their foes in battle. But it is worth remembering that despite outnumbering the Austrians almost four to one, French assaults – columns deploying rather clumsily into line at close range and heavily supported by artillery – were repeatedly beaten off by the disciplined volley fire of the conventionally trained Austrian infantry and by spirited thrusts by Austrian cavalry on the flanks. The offensive zeal of French infantry units notably cooled whenever their artillery support slackened, and on two separate occasions French troops came close to panicking when counter-attacked. Only constant badgering by the French commander, General Charles Dumouriez, and the inspired intervention at a crucial moment of a junior officer and future Orléans king, Louis Philippe, averted disaster and allowed the Austrians to be overwhelmed by weight of numbers.[64]

Similarly, at Hondschoote (8 September 1793), where the French again enjoyed numerical superiority – 14,600 French troops against 9,000 Hanoverians – the initial attacks were far from universally successful. In the centre, indeed, counter-attacks threw the French brigades into such disarray that the commanding general, Houchard, believed the battle was lost – as it might well have been if a final assault with the last French reserves had not been launched. As it was the Hanoverians were driven off, but not destroyed, and a week later the French themselves were forced to retreat after receiving a drubbing at the hands of ever-dangerous Austrian cavalry.[65] 'Soldiers of the mass levy', General Elie wrote after the Army of the North had won the battle of Wattignies (15 October 1793), 'are frightened by the *chasseurs* on their flanks, whom they mistake for the enemy. They fire on their own skirmishers, and then flee.' In the same engagements a separate division broke and ran at the mere sight of Austrian cavalry, and once again the terrible cry '*nous sommes perdu!*' was heard.[66]

These victories, moreover, were counter-balanced to a considerable extent by major defeats. At Neerwinden (18 March 1793), 45,000 French troops attacked 39,000 Austrians, and were soundly defeated by well-drilled musket fire and by Austrian cavalry attacks on the flanks. French casualties were double those of the enemy, and General Dumouriez was forced to retreat from the United Provinces.

Given all of this, the survival of Revolutionary France probably had very little to do with revolutionary enthusiasm among line and volunteer troops, and much to do with the fact that Prussian and Austrian attention was focused on the partition of Poland. The need to keep troops at the ready in the East meant that only 42,000 of the 170,000 troops of the Prussian army, and 70,000 of the 180,000 men of the Austrian army, were deployed against France; and the effectiveness of those armies which were sent against France was diminished still further by Austro-Prussian suspicions and unclear war aims.[67]

Allied generalship during the War of the First Coalition was, to be sure, rather ineffective. Brunswick, the Duke of York, and practically every other allied commander thought and acted in conventional eighteenth-century terms. Advances were slow and cautious, every move made with reference to securing lines of communication and maintaining supplies. Slow sieges, rather than lightning attacks, were seen as the key to winning wars – a frame of mind which could be taken advantage of by French commanders daring enough to run more risks.

And, it is often asserted, even the most faint-hearted French commanders were constantly encouraged to be more aggressive and act decisively by the representatives-on-mission attached to the armies. The Assembly and later the Convention and Committee of Public Safety were, as we have seen, intellectually predisposed to view the attack as the 'natural' way of war; and in the wake of the defection of General Lafayette and (especially) General Dumouriez, lack of aggressiveness could and did lead to denunciation, cashiering, and even execution. Though initially disruptive, the high turnover in senior army commanders thus produced tended to bring to the fore younger, more active, and effective officers – including Napoleon himself.[68]

It can, however, be argued that the armies lost more than they gained from the insistence of the more zealous *commissaires* and representatives-on-mission such as Saint-Just that enthusiasm for offensive action was the true measure of revolutionary consciousness in a commander. Tactical ability and political conformity were not necessarily synonymous.

It was true that through the rapid turnover in general officers – 593 were nominated and suspended in late 1792 and the first half of 1793 alone[69] – the rapid promotion of talented, energetic men was made possible. Louis-Lazare Hoche, for instance, a sergeant in 1792, was a 24-year-old general two years later; another sergeant of that year, Jean-Baptiste Jourdan, rose even faster, being promoted to general in 1793; and, of course, the high dismissal rate allowed the young Lieutenant Bonaparte to demonstrate his skills and become a general in the same year.[70]

Yet it should be borne in mind that of the hundreds of generals dismissed and often executed, there were plenty of competent men. The hard-driving A.-P. Custine, for example, commanding the Army of the North in the spring of 1793, did much to improve the quality of his troops through the setting up of training camps and imposing harsh disciplinary measures – only to be relieved and guillotined in the summer for speaking his mind and opposing the constant pressure emanating from Paris to launch what he regarded as premature offensives.[71] Even after the fall of Robespierre and the creation of the more moderate government of the Directory, perceived ideological incompatibility could threaten the career – even the life – of a rising star of the battlefield. Napoleon Bonaparte was briefly imprisoned and under threat of execution in the summer of 1794 because of his independent attitude and his Jacobin connections.[72]

Conversely, by no means all of those promoted were fitted for the task. Even Danton, though a Jacobin, admitted that while the 'admission into important and difficult posts of new men, whose patriotism was proven', was a good thing, there was a clear drawback: these were also men 'whose talents were not yet aided by experience'.[73]

A case in point was General Houchard, a brave former ranker promoted above his ceiling to command first the Army of the Rhine and then the Army of the North in the summer of 1793. Though achieving victory at Hondschoote, he was unable to co-ordinate a proper pursuit; which in effect meant that the enemy escaped to fight another day. Rather unfairly, the unfortunate Houchard was relieved and executed as a traitor.[74] Men like Houchard, however, were far from exceptional. General Jourdan, complaining about the quality of one of his subordinate commanders, acidly wrote that:

> Fromentin, a citizen devoted to his Patrie and full of courage, ignored the first elements of the art of war and literally believed what is ceaselessly repeated from the podium of the Convention and the Jacobins – that all the talent of a general consists of charging at the head of his troops against the enemy, wherever he may be found.[75]

This was certainly the kind of thought and behaviour the Committee of Public Safety wished to promote. Lazare Carnot, the member who was to do most to bring some semblance of order to the French war effort, did not think twice in appointing representatives-on-mission – each with the power to override generals – completely lacking in military experience. Political reliability – 'we know you' – and faith in the cause would allow such men to do the right thing. On asking for instructions, one such representative was simply told: 'They are in your heart and head; they will come out when needed. Go on, and succeed.'[76]

For those officers who doubted that attacking was always the best course of action, the fate of Custine and others and the presence of representatives-on-mission was a strong deterrent to caution, however well advised. Saint-Just was particularly terrifying (though by no means unique among the representatives). In October 1793, while on mission to the Army of the Rhine, he had argued that at least one general ought to be executed *pour encourager les autres* – and proved to be as good as his word.[77] Saint-Just could demand the impossible, and retaliate against both senior and junior officers when the inevitable consequences of his orders developed.[78]

Little wonder, therefore, that competent officers should be wary of promotion. Lieutenant-Colonel Claude Jacques Lecourbe, denounced and imprisoned once already for lack of aggressiveness in the Army of the North, expressed fear in the summer of 1794 at the prospect being put in charge of a brigade in what would become the Army of the Sambre and Meuse. 'It is with pain that I accept the employment which is destined for me', he wrote to his brother on 18 May; 'the position of general is so risky.'[79] Colonel Jean Louis Reynier went so far as to decline promotion to general in June 1794 on the grounds that at age 23 he was simply too young (a handicap he promptly forgot once the Terror had ended). Other reluctant officers were simply dragooned into command, having been told in no uncertain terms that failure to accept promotion would be viewed as virtual treason.[80]

Members of the Committee of Public Safety, meanwhile, were coming to recognize the gap between the rhetoric and the reality of the revolutionary war effort. The conversion of Carnot, the *de facto* war minister, to a position of pragmatism over ideological orthodoxy was particularly important. Serving as a representative-on-mission to the Army of the North, Carnot had witnessed the way in which after taking enemy-held towns French troops were in the habit of pillaging and getting drunk on local stocks of wine. 'With well-ordered troops we would feel no hesitation', he reported, 'but we must fear, with ours, that once they have made the assault they would scatter into the houses, and get so drunk that in two hours some of them would be slaughtered like cattle on the street corners.'[81]

This experience, combined with more general evidence of indiscipline (pillaging, desertion, and so on), led Carnot to adopt a draconian philosophy far more reminiscent of Frederick the Great than Rousseau. 'If every soldier who steals a pin is not shot on the spot', Carnot concluded, 'you will never accomplish anything.'[82] More radical figures such as Robespierre and even Saint-Just also began to see that discipline by consent would have to be buttressed by coercive measures. Hence, in 1794, a new and stringently harsh disciplinary code was introduced into the French armies, involving the death penalty for crimes such as desertion to the enemy, surrendering without just cause, and abandoning posts.[83] Though problems were still officially blamed on counter-revolutionary elements rather than human nature, by 1794 the authorities had come to tacitly accept that revolutionary enthusiasm and soldiering by consent could interfere with military effectiveness.[84]

Indiscipline by no means disappeared as a result of coercion – in 1795 General Jacques Goguet was killed by his own men after he called them cowards for refusing to charge[85] – but it did make a difference. The annual rate of desertion, for instance, dropped by half between 1793 and 1794.[86] The men of the armies, meanwhile, were becoming more efficient soldiers the longer they campaigned – the *levée en masse* being the last major wave of recruits to don uniform until 1799 – and battlefield performance improved accordingly.[87] One of Napoleon's future marshals, Gouvion Saint-Cyr, recalled that by 1794 the troops he commanded in the Army of the North were 'passably seasoned and disciplined, and sufficiently trained'.[88]

Revolutionary zeal, however, whatever role it played in the early years of the war, had faded away almost completely by 1797. This has been explained by supporters of the revolutionary army thesis as the result of *sans-culotte* alienation from the more conservative government of the Directory in the years following the overthrow of Robespierre and the radical Jacobins in July 1794, as well as from a civilian population indifferent to the sacrifices the soldiers had made.[89] It seems possible, however, that such alienation was of a social rather than a political kind.

By the second half of the 1790s the men in the ranks were, in essence, professional soldiers rather than civilians in uniform. They had chosen to stay rather than desert (when deserting was comparatively risk-free out of battle), and had made army life their own.[90] Old links with the former world of family, town, and village necessarily faded over the years, creating something of a gulf in perception between soldier and civilian. To the civilian, men in uniform came to be feared and avoided as natural despoilers, while in the eyes of soldiers the villagers and townspeople (both abroad and at home) came to be viewed as selfish individuals who had to be made to disgorge the food and other supplies needed by the army.

Indeed, even when Jacobin propaganda within the armies was at its height (involving large-scale distribution of radical papers, patriotic festivals, the activities of representatives-on-mission, *commissaires* and other agents, and much else besides), the complete lack of reaction to the sudden overthrow of Robespierre in 1794 – as well as continuing desertion – suggests that the majority of soldiers may never have been as politically committed as propagandists supposed.[91] Representatives and agents tended to see what they wanted to see.

Bonaparte probably came closer to the true motives of the average man in the ranks when, on assuming command of the Army of Italy in March 1796, he promised that 'I will lead you into the most fertile plains on earth. Rich provinces, opulent towns, all shall be at your disposal; there you will find honour, glory and riches.'[92]

The course of the war itself from 1794 through to the Treaty of Campofiormo in 1797 also suggests that political awareness had never been the single key motivating factor in the ranks. If one assumes that troops did become alienated where once they had been committed, then one would expect their battlefield performance to deteriorate. After all, if love of *liberté* and *égalité* had been a key factor in the victories of 1793–4, then one might legitimately expect to see the troops becoming less effective under the oligarchical Directory. Yet the war went on much as before, with French defeats in one theatre or campaigning season balanced by victories in another theatre or season, without any indication that the fading of the 'Spirit of Year II' (assuming it ever existed on the scale supporters believe) was undermining morale and battlefield effectiveness. If anything, the French position improved in these years; but the key factors were, in almost every case, competent generalship and above all luck rather than the political feelings of the men.[93]

As for the 'revolutionary way of war' supposedly introduced to the world by the committed *sans-culottes* in the ranks, *circa* 1793–4, there is plenty of evidence to suggest that the changes wrought were not as sweeping or novel as is commonly supposed. Certain salient points ought to be borne in mind.

To begin with, the way in which French troops fought varied over time and from one theatre to another, much depending on how much training the men had received. Thus in the Army of the Moselle, the 'old' line formations tended to dominate, while in the Army of the North and the Army of the Ardennes 'new' open-order skirmishing and columns were more common.[94]

Furthermore, the manual on which generals were to base their tactics – the famous *règlement* of 1791 – was the product of a debate over the merits of line, column, and open order which had been going on for decades prior to 1789 and cannot, therefore, be directly connected with the fall of the Old Regime.[95] There were, to be sure, differences between how generals in the field deployed and used their columns and what the *règlement* advised;[96] but given the limited skills of the volunteers this can be seen more as the art of the possible as much as trying to harness revolutionary passion.

In addition, though they were used in a more restricted and orthodox fashion than in the French Army, light troops equivalent to the French *tirailleurs* existed in the armies of the major foes of Revolutionary France. Like the debate over the best use of line infantry (line versus column), discussion of the role of light infantry in open order had been going on for decades, and – as we shall see – the evidence in favour of French practice was by no means overwhelming.[97]

Even the concept of charging home with the bayonet, the idea of a revolution-inspired *furia francese*, was rooted in the Old Regime. Voltaire, commenting on the strengths and weaknesses of the old Royal Army, had argued that while French musketry was often far from good; 'It can be said with as much truth that the French nation attacks with the greatest impetuosity and it is very difficult to resist its shock.'[98] Marshal de Saxe – who proposed that the pike be revived – and several other eighteenth-century military *philosophes* agreed, including the Comte de Guibert, who wrote in the 1770s that the French were by nature 'redoubtable in all attacks with cold steel'.[99]

The supposed impact of revolutionary fervour, in short, was grafted onto an existing set of assumptions concerning the martial nature of the French people – a natural aggressiveness which observers in other states attributed to their own conscripts and took account of in their own regulations. In Russia, the great General A. V. Suvorov always emphasized the moral importance of the bayonet charge by serf conscripts, a not uncommon attitude that dated back to the days of Peter the Great.[100] In Prussia, the infantry regulations of 1796 stated that a close-order attack was the only way to win a battle. 'Regular, trained, and solid [Prussian] infantry', the regulations explained, 'if it advances in closed ranks, with rapid steps, cannot be held up . . . . It should close with the enemy as rapidly and orderly as possible, so as to drive him back and decide the action quickly.'[101]

Finally, if French tactics and collective commitment had been as revolutionary as is usually supposed, one might legitimately ask why the coalition allies did not try to emulate their enemy. None of the major adversaries of France, after all, engaged in any root-and-branch reform of their military practices as a result of the War of the First Coalition.

The British contribution to the land war was, to be sure, too small to allow for proper comparison and potential change, while it can reasonably be argued that the Spanish Army, reflecting the decayed and hidebound nature of the monarchy, was simply incapable of reform. Prussia, which was much more directly involved, eventually began reforms on the basis of what Scharnhorst and others took to be the overwhelming power of nationalism. But this was after 1806, in the wake of total defeat and invasion at the hands of Napoleon, rather than in the 1790s.[102]

Though Prussia had gained little between 1792 and 1795, when a separate peace with France was negotiated, it had at the same time not been decisively defeated. Very much along the lines of the dynastic wars of the previous century, Prussian fortunes had risen and fallen, battles had been won and lost. And at the end of the day, also very much in eighteenth-century fashion, the Treaty of Basle acknowledged that for France to gain territory on the left bank of the Rhine, Prussia would have to be given compensation – hardly a dictated peace.

Social conservatism and slavish adherence to the old Frederickean model did, of course, play a role in preventing Prussia from engaging in military reform. But the conservatives, down to 1806, could justifiably argue that no evidence existed to show that the existing eighteenth-century-pattern army had become truly outmoded.[103]

What was true of Prussia was even more true of the senior coalition partner, Austria, possessing as it did the 'most formidable army which the French had to face in the last years of the eighteenth century'.[104] As T. C. W. Blanning has put it:

> If [the Austrians] had lost Belgium after their defeat at Jemappes on 6 November 1792, they had won it back again after their victory at Neerwinden on 16 March 1793. If they had lost it again after their defeat at Fleuras on 26 June 1794, who was to say that they would not win it back again at some future date?[105]

Napoleon, to be sure, had been such a success in Italy in 1796 that Vienna had been forced to call a halt to the fighting and negotiate a disadvantageous settlement the following year. Yet failure in Italy had to some extent been counter-balanced by the successes of Archduke Charles on the Rhine, and there was no sense in Vienna that full-scale military reform was necessary if France were ever to be challenged in future.

After all, when all was said and done the fact remained that whenever the Austrian troops had met the French on equal numerical terms – battles with Napoleon excepted – discipline and firepower had usually broken revolutionary *élan*. Hence the continued Austrian reliance on the patterns established by Maria Theresa and Joseph II.[106] Austrian commanders, with the vital exception of Archduke Charles, might be rather cautious and unimaginative;[107] but this was only really a danger against a truly outstanding opportunist like Napoleon.[108] And whatever their motivation,

Austrian troops proved time and again their willingness to cross bayonets successfully with the enemy.[109]

This is not to suggest that the War of the First Coalition was simply a carbon copy of earlier conflicts. The mobilization of the French nation during the Terror, of which the *levée en masse* was only a part, was truly unique and (for the most part) effective in producing men and equipment.[110] The armies of the Republic, especially in the wake of the various levies, tended to be far more socially diverse and reflective of civilian society than the men of the coalition armies.[111] Among the French troops, moreover, were men who were truly dedicated to and motivated by the revolutionary cause – as their letters reveal.[112] It was an impressive feat to create large forces virtually from scratch which were able (albeit with a great deal of luck at times) to preserve the Revolution and indeed augment French territory.[113] Yet at the same time it also seems clear that the image of the zealous citizen-soldier driving all before him, with love of liberty in his heart and the fire of revolution in his eye, as typical of French troops, was largely a Jacobin myth. Selfless volunteers of this kind did indeed exist, but a hard look at disciplinary problems, desertion, and performance in battle suggests that they were by no means in the majority and did not, *ipso facto*, make good soldiers. Moreover, as with the propaganda efforts of the government itself, attempts by this committed minority to spread revolutionary enthusiasm among the rank and file faced insurmountable obstacles – obstacles that were overlooked in the panglossian reports of the representatives and agents of the Convention.[114] For what they failed to acknowledge, other than in terms of treason, was that the outlook, hopes, and expectations of the Parisian revolutionary did not by any means necessarily match those of the peasant conscript from the more distant provinces.

The fact of the matter was that France did not possess anything approaching a homogeneous society. Among the peasantry – roughly 80 per cent of the population and therefore the main recruiting base of the *levée en masse* – much of what the Revolution stood for was, both figuratively and literally, quite incomprehensible. In regions where little had changed since the Middle Ages, the Enlightenment principles on which the Revolution was based could and often did appear alien and threatening. Doing away with seigneurial rights might be popular, but anticlericalism, conscription, and state intervention in general definitely were not. The great peasant uprising in the Vendée in 1793, as well as smaller revolts in other regions, were symptomatic of a much wider unease with the more radical features of the Revolution.[115] Within the frontier armies, for instance, many soldiers expressed deep shock at the desecration of churches by their Jacobin comrades and clearly identified more with the life of their village than with the rather more abstract national Revolution.[116]

The countervailing influence of regional and local loyalty was augmented by the problem of language. Illiteracy among the peasantry was widespread, making the influence of the radical press problematic. The existence of dozens of regional languages and dialects made the problem of communication, both specific and cultural, even more difficult. In 1793 the National Convention learned from the Abbé Grégoire that 6 million inhabitants of the Republic spoke no French at all, and another 6 million could not sustain a conversation in what was their second tongue. In effect over one-third of the population of France was not French in any meaningful sense.[117] To the conscript peasant from, say, Lower Brittany or Auvergne, the Parisian *sans-culotte* was just as much a foreigner as the Austrian *Grenzer* or Prussian *Jager*.[118]

The armies of the First Republic, in short, were neither as politically motivated nor as militarily innovative and successful as the Jacobins (then and later) claimed was the case. One might even argue that a better appreciation of the true nature of the War of the First Coalition might have prevented the disastrous effort by the Government of National Defence in 1870–1 to recreate citizen armies along the lines of 1794 that would drive out the Prussians by sheer zeal and numbers.[119] But then of course the true lessons of the past are always notoriously difficult to grasp, and there was at least *some* element of truth to the myth of the revolutionary soldier – something that, as we shall see, could not really be said of the wars of liberation in South America that broke out some years after Napoleon had come to power in France.

4 The armies of Bolívar and the war for the liberation of Gran Colombia, 1811–24

Morir o vencer?

My troops . . . are comparable to and even better than the best of Napoleon.

General Bolívar, December 1814[1]

My command is imaginary and theoretical; my troops have deserted, the officers are left alone, and are so bad that, leaving out a dozen, those who are not in prison should be there.

General Sata y Bussy, February 1815[2]

Over the past century and a half, popular and scholarly interest in the struggle for Latin American independence has focused almost exclusively on the actions of a few revolutionary heroes. And of these, none looms larger in the collective consciousness of the peoples of northern South America, and indeed the world at large, than *El Libertador* himself – Simón Bolívar.

Celebrated in innumerable equestrian statues and heroic paintings in towns and cities all the way from Venezuela to Peru as the liberator of five future states, Bolívar since the 1840s has been a figure of mythical proportions.[3] In Venezuela in particular he remains the cult-like object of something approaching religious worship, the supreme embodiment of heroic striving for perfection in virtually every sphere of public life.[4] 'To evoke the personality of Bolívar', as the president of the Institute of Spanish American Cooperation put it during the birthday bicentenary celebrations in 1983, 'is to give life to the essence of our community ideals.'[5]

Bolívar, it is asserted, was a true giant among men: a political philosopher and writer of great virtue, a statesman of visionary stature, and – last but not least – one of the great captains of history. It was he, after all, who managed, with the help of a small band of devoted lieutenants, to organize and lead armies to victory against the best troops Spain could muster. It was he who had planned the series of campaigns, carried out over great distances and against great odds, which had brought victory. Who else but the Liberator could have conceived and carried out the brilliantly daring crossing of the Andes amidst unbelievable hardship in 1819? In the eyes of Vicente Lecuna, the leading twentieth-century Venezuelan scholar of the War of Independence, Bolívar was comparable to Clausewitz in terms of strategic understanding and easily a match for Caesar or Napoleon in tactical brilliance and leadership.[6]

As for the men whom Bolívar led, they were, in the words of one patriot general, not only brave but also 'quick at learning their duties, supple in limbs, hardy, and cheerfully subordinate under fatigue and privations'.[7] Moreover, though often treated as no more than docile spear carriers in the drama of the Great Man's life, the men of the armies of the Liberator have been implicitly – and sometimes explicitly – linked to his revolutionary greatness. Bolívar's burning thirst for freedom, for an end to Spanish tyranny, is shown to have communicated itself to the officers and men of his forces. His example, so it is said, led patriot soldiers to unparalleled feats of endurance on the many long marches in hostile climates, and to acts of individual and collective heroism in battle. Time and again, battles were won through a willingness to close in and engage the enemy in hand-to-hand combat on horseback or on foot, engagements in which the burning desire to be freed from the colonial yoke, sheer revolutionary aggressiveness on the part of freed slaves, natives, mixed-blood *pardos* and *zambos*, white creoles, and the fierce *llanero* horsemen of the Venezuelan plains, won out over the superior numbers and equipment of Spanish regulars and colonial troops.[8]

Not that Bolívar and the patriots had to fight alone: the justness of their cause was underlined by the hundreds of British and other European veterans who volunteered individually and in special units to fight in South America. Once adjusted to the climate and conditions, these troops would be remembered as having done sterling service by adding a touch of professionalism to the patriot forces, 'Victory or Death' as their motto. These men, moreover, were also idealists, choosing to fight in freedom's cause. One English historian has even suggested that the spirit which motivated them was the same as 'the spirit which took young men off to fight in the Spanish Civil War in the 1930s'.[9]

The origin and persistence of this view of the Liberator and his men, and of the Bolívar cult in general, can be explained through reference to four interrelated factors. The first is the way in which European romanticism influenced the work of the first South American writers dealing with the war. To literary figures such as Felipe Larrázabal and Juan Vicente González, the Liberator was a potent symbol of the human struggle, an almost superhuman figure whose life deserved to be admired and exalted in verse and prose. The second influence was the need for new nation states to legitimize themselves through the creation of suitably uplifting accounts of their immediate past. And, as when nationalist sentiment began to appear elsewhere in the world, a history which fitted patriot expectations in South America quickly came to involve, perforce, a certain degree of myth-making concerning the struggle for independence from foreign domination. Once Bolívar himself was no longer on the scene and sufficient time had elapsed – a decade or so after his exile and death in 1830 – the need for national symbols was exploited by some of the reigning *caudillos* who had once been bitter enemies of the Liberator. This was the third, and perhaps most crucial factor at work in the creation of the cult of Bolívar. The story of the Liberator – and by extension his followers as well – was a useful metaphor for ongoing struggles, of dreams yet to be fulfilled in a region where poverty and social ills remained highly visible in the decades after liberation. Bolívar had died still trying to create a stable and lasting political, social, and economic fabric for northern South America in the wake of the wars; it was a common duty for citizens to carry on the fight.[10] Hence the otherwise rather odd statement by Señor Yañez-Barnuevo that a man who had died a century before 'has much to do still in our America'.[11]

The fourth and final factor which helps explain the awe in which Bolívar has been held, especially among the document-loving professional historians of the late nineteenth and twentieth centuries, is the way in which the image-conscious Liberator portrayed the struggle for independence in his numerous declarations, speeches, and letters. Bolívar was adept at displays of frankness and selflessness which, more often than not, hid more than they revealed about his actions and intentions. Taken at face value – which, for reasons of patriotism even those Latin American historians, such as Lecuna, supposedly working in the Rankean tradition of objective fact gathering and analysis, proceeded to do – the writings of the Liberator could only support the heroic legend. Supported by the memoirs of devoted followers such as O'Leary, the writings of Bolívar – published from the mid-1870s through to the mid-1960s – shed an almost entirely favourable light on their author.[12]

Testimony which conflicted with the image of an unfailingly brilliant and humane statesman and general was dismissed as the petty sniping of lesser mortals, and those few historians who attempted to cast a critical eye on Bolívar and the wars of liberation were strongly criticized for being everything from 'ungenerous in spirit'[13] to grossly materialist in denying the significance of the Liberator 'as the axis of the transformation of the Hispanic American world and the decisive guide in its march toward the future'.[14] As a Spanish biographer put it in the 1950s, even the most cautious questioning of the Liberator's self-image invariably led to defensive counter-attacks by 'a stout battalion of valiant pens'.[15]

Myth, it seems, nearly always takes precedence over the search for historical truth. This is unfortunate, given that even within the voluminous correspondence of the great man himself there are indications that the struggle for independence in the north was not quite the national crusade that is usually assumed. Viewed objectively, most soldiers in the armies of Bolívar were serving for reasons that had very little to do with patriotism, and were led by officers – not least the Liberator himself – whose amateur military talents generated defeat as often as victory.

The basic problem was that, from first to last, only a minority of inhabitants actively supported the revolutionary cause. In the Captaincy-General of Venezuela and the Viceroyalty of New Granada, the native Indians of the interior, as well as the mixed-bloods and poor whites of the cities and plains, had little in common with the dominant creole minority. When the French invasion of Spain in 1808 created a crisis of authority in the colonies, it was only the more ambitious and Enlightenment-influenced creoles who really supported a formal break with the Crown and the setting up of republics in 1810. Lacking legitimacy in the eyes of the Church and much of the population, divided over constitutional questions, and insolvent, the new regimes were unable to protect themselves effectively from anarchy and royalist insurgency in 1811–12.[16]

Patriot armies were formed, but while some officers had seen service in the old colonial militia,[17] the rank and file were unwilling conscript peasants. Effectively unpaid and left without adequate clothing or even food for months at a time, these soldiers had neither training nor any personal allegiance to the republican cause.[18] Conscripts soon began to desert to the enemy in droves, tipping the balance in favour of the initially weak royalist forces. 'A little while ago', General Francisco Miranda commented despairingly on learning that a key arsenal had suddenly fallen to the newly powerful enemy in July 1812, 'we thought that all was secure. Yesterday Monteverde [the royalist leader] had neither weapons nor ammunition. Today he has both in abundance.'[19] The first Venezuelan republic collapsed like a house of cards through incompetence and lack of popular support.[20]

Bolívar, who had played only a supporting role in the rise and fall of the First Republic, had fled east in 1812 and placed himself at the disposal of the government of the United Provinces of New Granada (themselves in a state of virtual civil war), and managed to convince the president that it was both necessary and feasible to launch an attack on the royalists in Venezuela in the winter of 1813. This campaign would mark the true beginning of Bolívar's career as a legendary leader in freedom's cause – not least in terms of the emerging gap between the heroic image of revolutionary struggle promoted by the Liberator and the savage and often rather sordid reality.

Starting with an initial force of only a few hundred men, Bolívar managed to advance and take a series of small enemy positions along the Magdalena river in preparation for moving into Venezuela itself. However, despite the aura of victory generated by successful skirmishes and the arrival of reinforcements, lack of popular support and desertion were as much a problem for Bolívar as they had been for the First Republic.

The Liberator's troops, lower-class New Granadians and a few Venezuelans, either had been pressed into service or were essentially amateur mercenaries without any commitment to the cause. Pay and supplies were at best erratic, and conditions often appalling. Bolívar, according to O'Leary, 'swept them along with his vigour and enthusiasm', his sheer force of personality making up for cold and danger on the difficult ascent from Ocaña to Mompox.[21] By the time Mompox was reached in December 1812, however, desertion had become so endemic that Bolívar had to shoot a few recaptured men to set an example. A more successful expedient was to allow the troops to loot the town of Cúcuta in February 1813, where captured royalist gold was also distributed to make up arrears in pay. In a letter to the president of New Granada some months later, Bolívar defensively claimed that he had never formally encouraged looting – 'I have never uttered such words to my troops' – but with uncharacteristic frankness went on to write: 'I should have done it, to encourage them, for they came most discontented, and they deserted by the hundred.'[22]

Nor was it easy to get the troops (still numbering only in the hundreds) to obey those orders which Bolívar did issue. The advance from New Granada back into Venezuela was made particularly problematic through the opposition of New Granadian officers who disliked the idea of fighting someone else's war. Bolívar had to force their ringleader to move by a direct threat. 'March!' he insisted, 'or, by God, I'll shoot you.'[23]

Once in Venezuela, however, Bolívar was once again confronted with the indifference of the peasantry. The royalist leader Monteverde had through sheer ineptitude and cruelty managed to alienate much of the population since overthrowing the First Republic, but that did not mean that the ordinary inhabitants were keen to see their local economy and way of life destroyed by a full-scale civil war. Most wanted simply to be left alone.

This attitude, however, was something that Bolívar was not prepared to tolerate. If Latin America were to be liberated, the failures of 1812 had shown that true patriot armies (as opposed to small bands of revolutionaries) were needed to stamp out royalist resistance. The people could not be allowed to remain passive or neutral; which in turn meant that the native population – creole, black, and native – had somehow to be divided from the *peninsulares*. Bolívar's answer to this problem was publicly to declare 'War to the Death' in June 1813. Henceforth no Spaniards, civilian or military, would be taken prisoner unless they deserted to the patriot cause. All Spanish property would henceforth be regarded as forfeited. Americans, on the other hand, would always be spared and offered the opportunity to serve their true cause in the patriot army.

The Liberator and his supporters, then and later, claimed that 'War to the Death' was just retaliation for Spanish atrocities,[24] but as Bolívar himself later admitted in private, the real reason was to force people to choose sides. Turning the struggle into a total war along racial lines – leaving no room for civilian neutrality, offering desertion to the patriot cause as the only way for Spanish troops to avoid death – was calculated blackmail. Survival now depended on taking sides, and by making a clear distinction between *peninsulares* and Americans the Liberator hoped to force all but the hard-core creole royalists to have second thoughts.[25] Even a few people changing sides justified the policy in his mind. 'To win four insurgents', Bolívar later explained, 'it was necessary to declare this war to the death.'[26]

Up to a point, calculated terror seemed to work. 'The ranks of the patriot army', O'Leary later claimed, 'were notably increased with the addition of Americans captured from the enemy, deserters from the enemy ranks, and the volunteers who appeared from all quarters to enlist.'[27] The campaign to liberate Venezuela was in many respects a replay of the war in 1812 with the players reversed. This time it was the royalists who found their conscripted forces melting away. By the eve of the key republican victory at Tagaunes on 28 July, the number of patriot troops had quadrupled and republican forces vastly outnumbered the royalists.[28] By August, when Bolívar triumphantly rode into Caracas, the Second Republic was a reality.[29]

It had been a *Campaña Admirable*. Yet, almost as soon as he arrived in Caracas, Bolívar began to embellish the truth. Official proclamations, evidently designed to link his military skill with that of Napoleon and echoed by his supporters, greatly inflated what had been accomplished. Despite lack of formal military training, the Liberator had manœuvred decisively and with skill, inspiring his men to win against superior numbers. In all, five enemy armies, totalling 10,000 men, had been defeated.[30] This was, to say the least, an exaggeration. As one jaundiced observer put it:

> All this bombastic description contains no more truth than the names of the cities and the speed of progress which was impressive; but there were neither battles, but only skirmishes and dispersions or withdrawals; nor armies, but tumultuous gatherings of persons without discipline, who all put together, would not add up to half the numbers boasted of.[31]

Even Gerhard Masur, in his generally sympathetic and admired scholarly biography of the Liberator, had to admit that Bolívar's conduct of the campaign 'resembled not so much the considered moves of chess player as the headlong sallies of a gambler'.[32]

Moreover, though in control of Caracas and the major towns of Venezuela by the latter part of 1813, Bolívar soon discovered that even with 'War to the Death' still in operation, resistance in peripheral regions continued. The pendulum of fate, indeed, seemed by the beginning of 1814 to be rapidly swinging against the Second Republic.

Perhaps the most basic difficulty was that in the countryside the majority of people were unconvinced that the Crown would not ultimately return to impose its will on Spanish America. Despite 'War to the Death', many creoles and (especially) those of mixed descent refused to accept Bolívar. 'Some of America's native sons', O'Leary conceded of this period, 'were the most stubborn enemies of independence.'[33]

Bolívar also lacked anything much in the way of an arms industry. A small number of muskets and other firearms, along with ammunition, could be brought in aboard foreign merchantmen, but with Spain pressuring both Britain and the United States not to intervene in what was presented as a domestic affair, and the Spanish Navy imposing at least the semblance of a blockade by 1814–15, the number of firearms in service never kept up with demand.[34]

Economic conditions made the situation even worse. With trade and revenue falling precipitously amid the anarchy of war, the officers of the

Republic resorted to confiscation of property, forced loans, and press-gang tactics to support their forces in the field. Not surprisingly, this further alienated the lower classes.

The enemy had operated in the same manner under these conditions when Monteverde was in power, but popular discontent naturally tended to focus on what was, at least nominally, the new government. The interior plains of Venezuela, beyond the reach of state authority, became a haven for the destitute and deserters, and the recruiting ground for a primitive yet effective mounted guerrilla army under the leadership of the ferocious bandit leader José Boves.[35] The struggle for Venezuela in 1813–14 soon became something very much akin to a class war: a battle between diverse lower-class elements led by various nominally 'royalist' chieftains attempting to maintain their traditional autonomy against the encroachments of a distrusted creole-led government with its own agenda. Government troops, unwilling conscripts operating almost entirely on foot, were often no match for the ferocious, spear-armed *llaneros*; and though some victories were achieved (Araure in December 1813, for example), the Second Republic was in serious danger. In May 1814, Bolívar was losing so many men through desertion that, though chronically short of men, he ordered one in five of those deserters caught to be shot as a deterrent.[36]

Bolívar, meanwhile, continued to represent events in terms favourable to his own image and sometimes very much at variance with the truth. The patriots held the moral high ground, and under his inspired leadership were fighting, against the odds, for the liberty of the people.

It was the royalists, according to Bolívar, who invariably killed their prisoners – whereas in fact after the republican defeat at Barquisimeto in October 1813, patriot prisoners had been spared by a Spanish regular colonel while those royalist prisoners taken had been slaughtered by order of the Liberator. As the strategic situation worsened, the killing of royalist prisoners – including Americans – grew more frequent, culminating in the cold-blooded massacre of 800 imprisoned at La Guaita. Such atrocities were not uncommon against patriot prisoners, especially those taken by Boves. But, propaganda aside, Bolívar and his associates were far from morally superior in this or any other respect.[37]

Bolívar also sought to disguise the fact that the conscript patriot forces were unlikely to fight to the death in freedom's cause. At Barquisimeto, for instance, a rumour of retreat had caused the republican infantry to panic and flee *en masse* in the face of the enemy.[38] On 7 April 1814, desertion became such a problem that Bolívar, despite a severe shortage of manpower, ordered as a deterrent that all recaptured deserters be shot.[39] Yet in official communiqués patriot forces fought bravely, even heroically. The repulse of Boves during an attack at San Mateo on 25 March 1814, to take the most famous piece of patriot propaganda, was attributed to the actions of one Ricuarte, a patriot officer, who with fifty men under his command valiantly defended an estate house until – on the verge of being overwhelmed – he set a match to the gunpowder store and blew the whole place up. Bolívar later admitted, with some pride, that this was a complete fiction. 'I am the author of that tale', he told Peru de Lacroix,

> I made it up to raise the spirit of my troops, to frighten the enemy and to extol to the highest pitch the soldiers of New Granada. Ricuarte died . . . marching downhill from San Mateo in retreat with his men, and I found him on the path face downwards, dead, with his back burnt by the sun.[40]

This sort of thing continued even after the great defeat at La Puerta (15 June 1814) which effectively ended the Second Republic and forced Bolívar once again to leave Venezuela for New Granada. 'My troops', Bolívar claimed of the Venezuelans who were now fighting on the side of the central government in the New Granadian civil war, ' . . . are comparable to and even better than the best of Napoleon.'[41] These were the same troops whom Bolívar allowed, contrary to surrender terms, to kill prisoners and loot the town of Santa Fe in December 1814 in order to ensure their loyalty. Another patriot officer admitted that while some were 'brave soldiers and virtuous men, many are the acme of corruption, prone to robbery, murder, drunkenness, debauchery and indiscipline'.[42] As always, numbers had to be made up through press-gang methods.

The Liberator and his few thousand men, in fact, had become little different from the dozen or so other squabbling regional warlords – *caudillos* – who had filled the power vacuum created by the collapse of Spanish rule and the initial republican experiments. Though nominally royalist or patriot, these forces were bound together by fealty to a leader who could provide protection and booty rather than by adherence to an ideological cause.[43] Involvement in the civil war in New Granada, as Bolívar came to realize, did little to further the cause of true independence at a time when Spain – having driven out the French with the help of Wellington in 1814–15 – was able to send an expeditionary force of over 10,000 regulars under General Pablo Morillo to reconquer northern South America. By the time Bolívar decided to flee New Granada for Jamaica, his forces had dwindled through desertion and disease from 2,400 to 700.[44]

The arrival of large numbers of disciplined Spanish troops under a competent commander did much to allow the reassertion of royalist control over key areas of both Venezuela and New Granada.[45] But, as in the past, the basic problem for Bolívar and other patriot leaders was that the population was still largely indifferent or hostile to the cause of independence.

This fact was driven home to Bolívar when he mounted an expedition from Haiti in May 1816 predicated on the assumption that his small force would be augmented by the local population on arrival in Venezuela. In fact the people of Carúpano, where he landed, fled the town rather than flock to the patriot banner. Bolívar attempted to counter this by declaring freedom for all slaves on 2 June 1816 – on condition that all males enlist in his army.[46] As always, the Liberator described all this in the best possible light.

The number of ex-slave recruits was 'considerable', and though the Spanish were gathering their forces, 'our small army, animated by sentiment of liberty, will suffice to destroy them'.[47] The reality was that only a few hundred slaves signed on, Bolívar made poor strategic choices, and the expedition collapsed. Bolívar, under ignominious circumstances, set sail for Haiti in July, abandoning his men to their fate.[48]

Undaunted in adversity, Bolívar launched another come-back attempt from Haiti in December 1816, landing first at Margurita island and then moving inland up the Orinoco river. By this point the strategic situation was rather more favourable to the patriot cause. The Spanish expeditionary force, it was becoming clear, had problems. From the start, many Spanish officers and almost all the conscripts had not been eager to serve in South America. At Cádiz they had to be closely guarded before the fleet set sail to avoid desertion, and it was only once the force was at sea that Morillo felt it safe to reveal to his officers that they were heading for what was known to be a region where the climate was hostile and 'war was fought without quarter and with savage ferocity'.[49] Desertion and disease quickly began to take their toll once the force had landed, Americans had to be pressed into the ranks, the cavalry ran short of usable mounts, and morale remained low.[50]

Pacification, furthermore, ran into serious difficulties in the more remote regions, particularly among the *llaneros* of the Orinoco basin. Boves had been killed, and the new chieftain of the plains, José Páez (who, unlike his predecessor, had never been personally insulted by the creole republicans), had continued the rebellion against central authority – which this time happened to be royalist.[51]

This did not mean, however, that the royalist cause was once again on the verge of defeat. For one thing, the patriot chieftain-generals – Santiago Mariño in the east, Manuel Piar in the region of Barcelona in the north-east, Páez along the Apure in the south, and Bolívar on the Orinoco in the south-east – were fierce rivals, usually unwilling to co-ordinate their actions.[52] For another, though benefiting in 1817 from Morillo's rather inept strategy of trying to seek out and destroy his more mobile *llanero* adversaries, the majority of patriot troops usually lacked the discipline to advance under heavy fire and exploit the successes they had achieved.

Bolívar, to be sure, was trying by 1817 to turn those forces under his control into something resembling a regular army. However, asserting primacy by executing a rival patriot leader such as Piar on charges of treason *pour encourager les autres*, or decreeing the creation of a general staff and trying to centralize the distribution of plunder,[53] did not an army make. Strategic goals had to be subordinated to the hard fact that, on and off the battlefield, patriot troops lacked discipline. Behaving like banditti was a positive advantage in guerrilla operations, but when the time came to try and move on the major towns and Caracas itself, Spanish forces, stiff-ened by a core of Peninsular War veterans, usually proved superior to the ill-disciplined patriots. 'Their lack of discipline and their fondness for plunder', O'Leary wrote of the *llanero* cavalry, 'frequently made their cooperation of dubious value and always proved very embarrassing for their general in chief.'[54]

Poor generalship on the part of Bolívar only served to highlight his troops' deficiencies. At the battles of Calabozo and Sombrero in February 1818, Morillo was able to fend off attacks by a force under Páez and Bolívar twice the size of his own, and a month later at El Semen (16 March 1818) completely routed the disorganized enemy in a fierce counter-attack. Repeated attempts by Bolívar to open up the road to Caracas in early 1819 were repulsed with heavy loss.[55]

Patriot troops, meanwhile, lacking pay, clothing, and food, remained prone to desertion if not facing the immediate prospect of booty. During the protracted siege of San Fernando, where Bolívar planned to allow his men to loot, morale quickly slipped and desertion rose. 'The army had almost melted away', Bolívar complained in a letter to Páez in May 1818,

> ... the whole brigade of Colonel Vásquez deserted last night, so that hardly one hundred men remained with him. General Cedeños's division is also beginning to desert, and last night, some troops left from General Monagas'. I cannot send troops after them, for I do not trust those who remain, who would probably follow their example.[56]

In public, the Liberator continued to distort the facts in his favour. Despite the fact that the patriots had been thoroughly defeated at El Semen and had been repulsed from the town of Ortiz in March 1818, the Liberator described the battles as follows:

> It was bloody and stubbornly fought on both sides; but victory remained on our side and the enemy lost one thousand men, counting dead and wounded, as they themselves confess [*sic*]. As I had infinitely fewer infantry and we had fought frequent encounters and I had lost many rifles, I returned to the plains to restore my losses and above all to ask for more arms and ammunition, which I lacked. I organized the army efficiently and I again defeated the Spaniards at Ortiz [*sic*].[57]

In a proclamation to the people of New Granada that August, Bolívar claimed that 20,000 Spanish troops had been killed in all; which was quite a feat when one considers that only 10,000 had been dispatched in 1815.[58]

Privately, Bolívar knew that he was facing a dangerous standoff. Regular Spanish cavalry was disciplined enough to charge in closed squadrons, the shock effect often overcoming the disorganized hordes of *llaneros*. Moreover, as Bolívar explained in a letter to Admiral Luis Brión of the fledgling Venezuelan Navy in May 1818, even when Spanish cavalry was absent 'their infantry is excellent. On the high ground around Caracas they are invincible owing to their *resistance*.'[59] On the plains, the *llaneros* could harass enemy columns to the point of exhaustion, but if defending a specific objective such as Caracas on interior lines, the Spanish could hold out against superior numbers. Owing to lack of firearms and drilling patriot infantry battalions, like the cavalry, tended to close with the enemy rather than exchange fire (the underlying reason for the famous patriot charges). If the enemy was taken by surprise, this could be effective; but if ready and waiting, Spanish regulars could do serious damage to troops who often lacked the discipline to advance under regular volleys of musket and artillery fire.[60]

Bolívar, acutely aware of this, decided that the only solution was to try and recruit regular soldiers from abroad. This was the origin of the units composed of foreign legionaries.

In the mythology of the wars of liberation, the foreign volunteers hold a special place. Chiefly drawn from unemployed English and Irish veterans, these men were portrayed as selfless and courageous idealists.[61] 'During his stay in Angostura', O'Leary related of a visit by the Liberator in February 1819,

> General Bolívar had the satisfaction of witnessing the arrival of some of the foreign volunteers, whose bravery on the battlefield would merit no little praise, for on more than one occasion it would be a deciding factor in victories in the cause they had come to uphold.[62]

What O'Leary and later historians tended to downplay was the behaviour of foreign volunteers *off* the battlefield.

The root of the problem lay in the fact that monetary reward and prestige played a greater role in motivating most veterans to volunteer than did faith in the cause. Luis López Méndez, the republican agent in England, offered generous terms to those willing to cross the Atlantic. Officers would move up one rank; pay would be equal to that in the British Army; travel costs would be met; and sundry other rewards and reimbursements would await volunteers in a paradisiacal Venezuela. At a time when tens of thousands of soldiers were being demobilized in the wake of the Napoleonic wars, such terms had an obvious attraction, and Méndez was besieged with offers of service.

The fact that personal advancement and financial gain loomed larger in most volunteers' minds than a burning desire to free Spanish America would not have mattered much if there had not been such a yawning gap between expectation and reality. The vanity and venality of some of the first foreign officers to organize volunteer regiments did little to aid the situation, but the plain fact was that Méndez had misled prospective freedom fighters as to the true conditions in Venezuela. Firearms, footwear, clothing, and other basic equipment had become extremely scarce in Venezuela, regular pay (at least among the patriots) was unheard of, and the food supply was erratic at best. Camp discipline in the patriot forces, particularly by European standards, was virtually non-existent, and regular drilling very rare. Instead of the land of milk and honey they had anticipated, the volunteers were confronted with tropical diseases such as malaria and yellow fever, wretched living conditions, an indifferent or hostile population, and patriot leaders apparently unwilling (though in truth simply unable) to provide the resources – most especially the pay – promised in London. The sense of shock and disillusionment was profound, and resulted in a number of ugly episodes.

Senior volunteer officers, such as Colonels Hippisley and Wilson, soon began to suspect Bolívar of bad faith, and were genuinely sickened by the slaughter of enemy prisoners (at a time, contrary to patriot propaganda, when prisoners were being spared by Morillo).[63] After acrimoniously trading accusations of treason and disloyalty they returned to England without having fired a shot. Among the legionnaires themselves drunkenness became endemic, sometimes leading to battles with the local population. Mutual hostility grew, as did desertion. There was even a full-scale mutiny within the Irish Legion over poor conditions and absence of pay in 1820. 'I am not surprised', wrote Bolívar. 'One may expect anything of men who will not kill without pay. They are like courtesans who do not give themselves until they have received their money.'[64]

Bolívar, however, did not abandon hope that once the wheat had been separated from the chaff foreign volunteer units could be of great service. More volunteer units were sponsored, and in the end his faith was vindicated; the foreign units became a steadying influence in a number of key engagements. But it is worth noting that in the early days one of his generals, Rafael Urdaneta, claimed that he preferred ten battles to one march with the British legionaries.[65]

Meanwhile, in the first months of 1819, Bolívar carried out what would be lauded as his greatest strategic achievement and a high point of the patriot cause – the crossing of the Andes with an army from Venezuela into New Granada. Amid great climatic hardship and against the odds, the Liberator led his band of committed patriots over the mountains and to ultimate victory, an act of daring comparable with Hannibal or Napoleon crossing the Alps and invading Italy, or (closer to home) the scaling of the Andes and the liberation of Chile by San Martín in 1817.[66]

It was, in truth, a plan of great daring, but it was driven more by necessity than strategic vision, and was far less heroic than subsequent histories (and innumerable paintings) would suggest. The fact of the matter was that Bolívar had few options open to him. The rainy season was about to begin, curtailing mobile operations. That in turn would mean that troops would have to be maintained in quarters, rather than living off the land they passed through. The resources to support the men *in situ* simply did not exist, and as always when not under close supervision, they would tend to desert.[67] Movement was thus almost a goal for its own sake, and given the campaigning limits in Venezuela imposed by the weather, friction with other patriot warlords (not least the powerful Páez), and dangers posed by the forces of Morillo, moving into New Granada was a necessity if Bolívar was to maintain his role as a patriot leader.[68]

Whatever sense is made in terms of keeping the army together and making a name for the Liberator, the crossing was still a tremendously risky task. At the war council Bolívar called with his lieutenants to discuss the plan, he concealed the fact that he intended to use the most difficult route to deceive the enemy for fear of dissent. As for the men themselves, they were deliberately kept in the dark for fear of desertion.[69]

Conditions were much worse than Bolívar anticipated. Flooding seriously impeded the movement of the 21,000 men Bolívar had assembled for the expedition (most of whom found themselves wading rather than marching). There was no protection at all from the elements either in the plains or, once cold became a factor, on the ascent. Men used to a tropical climate, often lacking footwear and almost naked, suffered greatly from the cold and freezing rain once the crossing of the Andes began on 22 June 1819. Fuel was scarce, the weather remained atrocious, and horses, cattle, and eventually hundreds of men began to die from a combination of cold, hunger, and altitude sickness. Discipline disintegrated, officers deserted, and the remaining men had to be lashed forward to prevent them falling by the wayside. By the time the remnants of the army descended into New Granada, all the horses and cattle and – to take the one unit for which losses are known – a quarter of the British Legion under Colonel James Rooke had perished.[70]

If the royalists had been more alert, Bolívar's exhausted and depleted force could have been destroyed piecemeal as it came down the mountains. 'The army', as the commander of the vanguard, General Francisco Santander, put it bluntly after describing the dreadful nature of the crossing, 'was a moribund body.'[71] It was only through a combination of patriot propaganda and luck that royalist forces remained on the defensive, allowing time for Bolívar's men to arrive, rest, and recuperate. After heavy losses incurred during the first major clash of arms at Vargas on 25 July 1819, where the British Legion and *llaneros* cavalry saved the day, the crossing had reduced the patriot army to a grand total of 1,800 men – one-tenth or so of the original expeditionary force.[72] Unlike San Martín, a former regular officer who had planned every aspect of his trans-Andean campaign meticulously, Bolívar, luck on his side, had simply blundered to glory.

As in the past, the peasant population did not flock to the patriot banner, despite the 'enthusiasm' which Bolívar claimed met his men in New Granada.[73] The Liberator solved this problem by declaring martial law and ordering a mass levy of all males between the ages of 14 and 40 within twenty-four hours on pain of death.[74] Bolívar, again as much through luck as skill, managed to manœuvre the royalist commander, Colonel José Barreiro, into a strategically impossible position, where he was decisively defeated at the battle of Boyacá (7 August 1819). 'On a single day Bolívar destroys the fruits of a five-year campaign', Morillo gloomily remarked on learning of Boyacá, 'and in one battle wins back all that we have gained in countless engagements.'[75]

Yet even after the triumph at Boyacá the war in the north as a whole was far from over. In New Granada, lack of public support meant that the army had to live off extortion revenue. As Bolívar explained to Santander in late 1819:

in order to gain a few faithful followers we had to emancipate the slaves; in order to recruit the two armies of last year and this, we had to resort to the terror of martial law; and to obtain the 67,000 pesos which are on their way to Guayana, we had asked and taken all public and private funds within our reach.[76]

Meanwhile much of Venezuela still remained in royalist hands, the patriot leaders were bickering, operations remained uncoordinated, and both arms and manpower were extremely short. Bolívar tried, without success, to obtain arms from the United States.[77] He also once more turned to slaves to swell his ranks; freedom was to be offered in exchange for two years' service. 'We need robust, vigorous men who are accustomed to hardship and fatigue', he explained to Santander, 'men . . . for whom death can have little less meaning than life.' Besides, such a policy would reduce the risk of slave insurrections.[78]

The relative discipline of Spanish troops, moreover, especially in the face of uncoordinated and ill-conducted local campaigns (the assault on Cumaná in August 1819 by General Urdaneta, for example), remained formidable. 'Discipline is the soul of these enemy troops, just as valour is that of ours', Bolívar wrote in January 1820,

and, in the final analysis, the former is of greater help in a pitched battle than the latter . . . . I am responsible for the destiny of eighteen free provinces in my hands and must not chance them on a throw of the dice.[79]

As luck would have it, the risk of defeat was greatly reduced by events in Spain. At the beginning of 1820, just as another major expeditionary force was about to embark for the New World, a liberal government came to power in Spain through a military coup and immediately ordered General Morillo to negotiate a truce with the rebels. The 20,000-man expedition, which would have provided Morillo with the first major reinforcement from Spain since he had landed in 1815, was abandoned.[80]

Morillo had always been pessimistic about the long-term prospects for Spanish rule. The colonies were simply too large, the population too apathetic, and counter-insurgency too expensive in terms of the men and supplies needed to guard territory won back from the rebels. In open battle, Morillo considered only the foreign contingents a potential match for his regulars. But to win the war, he estimated that even a force of 30,000 might not suffice.[81] The collapse of the Cádiz expedition and the truce he was ordered to negotiate, however, made what was likely to happen eventually a certainty in the near future.

The truce, which lasted from November 1820 to April 1821, was of considerable benefit to Bolívar and the other patriot leaders and a disaster for the royalists. Negotiations revealed what should have been obvious to the ministers in Madrid: that the rebels were interested in independence, not a reformed Spanish Empire. The stark fact that Spain had chosen to initiate talks was interpreted, even in hitherto loyal areas, as evidence of weakness (which it was), and constituted a decisive propaganda victory for the patriot cause.[82] 'Public opinion', as O'Leary noted, 'previously unfriendly to the patriots', had swung towards those who would, it was now clear, eventually rule Venezuela: 'this can be considered the greatest triumph won by Colombia during the year'.[83] It is worth noting, however, that even at this stage Bolívar was ordering one of his commanders to 'act speedily and to send us many slaves to re-stock our northern army'.[84]

The royalist army in Venezuela, now under the command of General La Torre, suffered conversely from a sense of hopelessness. Local conscripts, who now made up the vast majority of the army, began to desert in record numbers, and when La Torre finally faced Bolívar at the battle of Carabobo (24 June 1824) his was the smaller army. Once again, though, it was the intervention of the British Legion and also the *llaneros* – whom Bolívar had to control personally for fear of disorder – at critical moments which ensured a complete patriot victory and the final defeat of Spanish power in the north.[85]

Bolívar, however, was far from satisfied. The people of Venezuela and New Granada might have abandoned the royal cause, but – public pronouncements to the contrary – they showed no interest in the Liberator's ambition to move south-west and drive the Spanish out of Ecuador and Peru. The estates of former royalists were sold off to provide funds for the expedition. 'If in this way the requirements of the army are not met', Bolívar plaintively explained in a decree issued in July 1821, 'H[is] E[xcellency] is at a loss to know how he is to keep an army, since the people refuse to lend any help.'[86]

The subsequent series of campaigns once again revealed the true nature of the patriot forces and – his customary luck notably absent – exposed the Liberator's limitations as a general. Recruits, for example, had to be pressed into service *en route* on pain of death because the people of the valley of the Cauca were 'selfish cowards'.[87] The rate of desertion was higher than ever before, insubordination was rife, and as he moved south Bolívar was constantly in need of new conscripts. 'I try to raise three battalions of men in this country', he wrote to Santander in early 1823 from Guayaquil in northern Peru, 'but it will be of no avail, because when a unit is moved from one part to another, they all desert.'

Everything has been violence upon violence. The countryside, the cities have been laid waste to gather 3,000 men and two hundred thousand pesos. I know better than anyone how far violence can go, and all has been used. In Quito and Guayaquil we have taken away every man, in the streets and in the churches, for recruits. Money has been extorted at the point of a bayonet.[88]

Some success was achieved in enforcing discipline and regularizing pay in the 1824 campaign, but desertion to the enemy and even mutiny still occurred.[89]

The patriot armies under Bolívar and his lieutenants did, to be sure, score some important victories, as at Bomboná (7–8 April 1822), Pichincha (22 May 1822), and Junín (5 August 1824), but each time a patriot army teetered on the edge of disaster. Bomboná was a long and confused struggle in which Bolívar lost as many as 800 dead and 1,000 wounded. Pichincha was a clearer-cut victory, but could have turned into a rout if the Albion Regiment (the reconstituted British Legion) had not thwarted a dangerous flank attack by Spanish regulars. As for Junín, a confused cavalry fight, evidence suggests Bolívar was out of touch with events as they unfolded. Even in the wake of victory, moreover, concerns about desertion continued to plague the Liberator.[90]

These were problems which the royalists in Peru also faced, but Bolívar made a point of publicly stressing the selflessness and nobility of his men. The following proclamation issued in August 1824 is fairly typical of the overblown image the Liberator was trying to sustain:

> Soldiers! You are about to finish the greatest undertaking Heaven has confided to men – that of saving an entire world from slavery. Soldiers! The enemies you have to overthrow boast of fourteen years of triumphs; they are therefore worthy to measure their swords with ours, which have glittered in a thousand combats. Soldiers! Peru and America expect from you Peace, the daughter of Victory. Even liberal Europe beholds you with delight because the freedom of the new world is the hope of the universe. Will you disappoint it? No! No! You are invincible.[91]

This was fantasy, yet perhaps a fitting prelude to the gap between rhetoric and reality surrounding the final battle of the war at Ayacucho (9 December 1824).

Ayacucho is usually viewed as the high-water mark of patriot fortunes, the point at which the last Spanish army, filled with regulars, was defeated and Peru finally liberated. The patriot victory, however, was suspiciously easy. The Spanish forces were superior in number (7,000 to 5,700), yet both officers and men – many of whom recognized that Spain was incapable of sustaining them – appear to have fought halfheartedly. The battle lasted only two hours, casualties were light, and surrender came quickly. There exists the possibility that the commanders on each side – General Sucre and the Viceroy – had negotiated an 'honorable defeat' beforehand. How else to explain the long pre-battle fraternization between senior enemy commanders and that 'an army superior in numbers, training and discipline, with at least seven times more artillery, was defeated when it still had 2,000 soldiers who had to surrender after it was fought'?[92]

The heroic image of the war of liberation fostered by the Liberator and his contemporaries, and followed in subsequent histories, is largely a myth. Patriot armies, largely amateur and undisciplined, were motivated more by fear, hope of profit, and (sometimes) personal allegiance than by selfless commitment to the cause. Bolívar, though a man of much greater vision and energy than many of his contemporaries, was a lucky rather than a brilliant general and a leader who – to judge from the press-gang recruiting methods and rate of desertion – does not appear to have inspired his people in the manner traditionally assumed.

There were, to be sure, admirers who truly were driven by his example to deeds of endurance and bravery, particularly among his staff. On the whole, though, the liberation of what would become the rather short-lived Republic of Gran Colombia was accomplished in spite of, rather than because of, the attitude of the people towards *El Libertador*.

The romance of the revolution at arms, however, not least the tendency to equate success with a people's destiny, was by no means confined to Latin America as the nineteenth century progressed. Nor, as it turned out, did a revolutionary force necessarily have to have its ideological roots in the Enlightenment. Fourteen years after the victory at Ayacucho, a bloody encounter between Boers and Zulus halfway around the world in southern Africa would form the basis of a new mythology of arms – one equal in power to that of Bolívar or the French or American Revolutions, yet in spirit much more akin to the stern puritanism associated with the New Model Army two centuries earlier.

5 The Voortrekkers, Blood River, and the Zulu War of 1838–40

A nation of heroes?

[It] pleased the Allhighest (on Whom we called) to deliver [the Zulus] into our hands.

Andries Pretorius, Chief Commandant, December 1838[1]

The first regiment of Zulus attacked at the run. They were shot down like mown grass.

Eyewitness Zulu narrator, *circa* 1860[2]

For generations now the Great Trek has been portrayed by Afrikaner patriots as the central episode in the history of the *Volk*. After all, this large-scale migration of Boer families in the mid- and late 1830s, punctuated by tragedies and triumphs, eventually produced the first independent Boer republic in Natal. And within the drama of the trek itself, no single event looms larger than the battle of Blood River (16 December 1838) when a Boer commando of a few hundred men smashed a Zulu army over twenty times its size. This was the key moment, so it has been said, in defining the destiny of the Afrikaner people.

Writing in reaction to the threat to the Boer identity posed by the growing power and influence of the British in southern Africa, a series of writers in the late nineteenth and early twentieth centuries presented the trek as the apotheosis of Afrikanerdom. To men such as George Theal (Canadian-born author of the first history of the Boers and immensely influential) and G. S. Preller (biographer of two of the leading trekkers and an Afrikaner himself) the trek was an heroic civilizing enterprise.[3] For these chroniclers, and even more so countless ordinary Boers steeped in the Old Testament, the exodus of fiercely independent, self-reliant, and God-fearing trekkers was often associated with the flight from Egypt, and the struggles with the Zulus made akin to the battles between the Israelites and Amalekites. God, indeed, was popularly believed to have intervened directly to ensure a victory against all odds at Blood River as a result of a Covenant Oath sworn by the Boer commando before the battle.[4]

A Chosen People engaged in an heroic civilizing mission was certainly a flattering image, and one which generated enormous resonance by the time of the trek centenary celebrations in 1938. Symbolic wagon treks retracing the routes of the first pioneers generated enormous pride among Afrikaners, and over 100,000 Boers attended the ceremony on 16 December marking Blood River at which the first stone was laid for what would become the massive Voortrekker Monument outside Pretoria.[5]

What had become the orthodox version of the Great Trek was literally carved in stone, on the walls of the Hall of Heroes within the monument, through a series of bas-relief friezes outlining the major points in the journey frame by frame. For patriotic Afrikaners, as National Party leader D. F. Malan put it, 'the Great Trek was the most important, most decisive, and all-overshadowing event in our People's history'.[6]

Once in power, moreover, the National Party in the 1950s, 1960s, and 1970s vigorously promoted trek mythology in the schools and in public ceremonies. School texts portrayed the trek in terms of civilized whites overcoming savage nature and barbarous blacks, while Blood River – sometimes with the Zulus' numerical advantage inflated to as high as thirty to one – was explained in Christian-Nationalist terms: the fruits of a Covenant with God.[7]

Celebrations of the anniversary of the battle, meanwhile, officially known after 1952 as the Day of the Covenant (changed to the Day of the Vow in 1980), became more and more elaborate. The Voortrekker Monument itself, for example, was supplemented by plans for sixty-four life-size bronze wagons constructed at public expense on the restored battle site.[8]

By the 1970s, liberal Afrikaners were beginning to have doubts about the appropriateness of celebrating a victory of white over black.[9] The mainstream message, however, repeated every anniversary by Afrikaner politicians and enshrined in the guidebook to the Voortrekker Monument, remained essentially the same into the 1980s. 'The Monument will arouse the pride of belonging to a nation of heroes', the guidebook explained. '[I]t will arouse and strengthen a love for the country for whose sake so much was sacrificed; and it will strengthen a faith in God in whom the people trust.'[10] In 1983 the Dutch Reformed Church was still maintaining that Blood River was a miracle. Statistically, the monument guide maintained, the Boers only had a 1 per cent chance of winning, thereby 'supporting the belief that this victory was an Act of God'.[11]

Even in the latter 1980s and early 1990s, amidst the collapse of Apartheid and the arrival of black majority rule, right-wingers – especially the fascist-leaning Afrikaner Resistance Movement (AWB) – continued to rally on 16 December and uphold the traditional interpretation by the tens of thousands.[12] Blood River still has great resonance among the faithful.

Few within the Afrikaner historical profession have not been influenced by the prevailing cultural assumptions concerning the trek. Professor H. B. Thom, for example, in a study published soon after the National Party's electoral triumph in 1948, explained Blood River in the following terms:

> a handful of men . . . conscious of the gravity of their task and trusting steadfastly in the God of their fathers, called on the Lord in the hour of

their direst need; . . . they made a solemn covenant with the Lord . . . .
He heard their entreaties, miraculously saved them and gave them a great
victory over overwhelming numbers of their enemy.

'The Covenant was the prayer', Thom concluded, 'and Blood River the
answer.'[13] As late as the 1970s, Professor A. N. Pelzer was asserting that the
victory could only be explained as a 'miracle'.[14]

Attempts by more sceptical South African scholars to investigate some of
the more questionable assumptions about the Great Trek and the victory at
Blood River, meanwhile, have been dealt with severely. G. E. Cory, for
example, the first historian this century to suggest that the much-touted
treaty ceding areas of Natal to the Boers in 1838 was a fake, was forced to
retract his views. Despite the suspicious conditions under which the treaty
was initially discovered – on the bodily remains of Piet Retief almost a year
after King Dingane of the Zulus had signed the treaty and then murdered
the trek leader – to question the orthodox version of events was interpreted
as both treasonous and sacrilegious.[15] Later attempts to suggest that the
significance of the vow had been overstated generated similarly impassioned
criticism; and when the dean of Afrikaner historians, F. A. van Jaarsveld,
dared to suggest in a public forum in 1979 that the traditional version of
Blood River contained too many mythical elements and needed to be
revised, he was literally tarred and feathered by members of the AWB for –
as their leader put it to the press – 'attacking the sanctity of the Afrikaner in
his deepest essence'.[16]

The *Wenkommando* (victory commando), as the force was soon dubbed,
thus remains sacrosanct for many Afrikaners. Pretorius and his few hundred
men, vowing before God that they would annually commemorate His intervention if they won, had gone forth and triumphed against the Zulu hordes.
They were a conservative rather than radical revolutionary force, but a revolutionary force nevertheless, their fighting strength sustained during the
battle of Blood River – despite the enormous odds against them – by their
faith in God's providence.[17] 'The commando resembled an itinerant prayer
meeting rather than a modern army on the march', George McCall Theal
stated in his *History of Boers in South Africa* (first published in 1887,
immensely popular with Afrikaners, and along with his other works the
basis for many twentieth-century textbooks), 'for the men were imbued with
the same spirit as the Ironsides of Cromwell and spoke and acted in pretty
much the same manner.'[18]

Though clung to with great tenacity for over a century, the orthodox
image of Blood River and the Zulu War of 1838–40, based on faith as much
as knowledge, does not stand up particularly well under critical scrutiny.
Rhetoric aside, the conduct of the Boers was neither as pious nor as heroic
as conventionally portrayed.

Even if one is neither an atheist nor an agnostic, interpreting God's hand
in human affairs inevitably ends up being the province of the theologian as

much as – if not more than – that of the historian.[19] The established rules of evidence within the modern historical profession, though, do suggest that the Lord was rather less biased in favour of the Voortrekkers than their descendants came to believe. If the view of the struggle between Boers and Zulus for control of Natal is extended beyond the chronological confines of the morning of Blood River, it appears that God by no means always favoured white over black.

The war began in February 1838 with a pre-emptive strike by the well-drilled Zulu impis (regiments) of King Dingane against the parties of Boers that had made their way over the Drakensberg mountains and were resting at the foot of the passes. For the most part caught unprepared, the Boers – men, women, and children alike – were killed by the hundreds and vast herds of their cattle seized. The first trekker punitive expedition, moreover, a commando of 347 men under the joint leadership of Piet Uys and Andries Potgieter sent to seek out and destroy the Zulu Army, ended in complete failure. The force was lured into a Zulu ambush at the battle of Italeni on 11 April, and it was not until the end of the year that a second, rather more successful, offensive was launched in the form of the commando under Pretorius. Even after the victory of 16 December, furthermore, events did not consistently favour the Boers. Eleven days later, the Zulus once again pulled off a successful trap at the battle of the White Umfolozi (still a source of great pride in Zulu folklore). As J. B. Liebenberg first pointed out in explicit terms, the patchy battle record of the Boers forces the conclusion that, if divine intervention was present, God was on the side of the Zulus much of the time.[20]

The Voortrekkers certainly had no exclusive command of the moral high ground. Twentieth-century Zulu nationalist attempts to rehabilitate the historical image of former kings such as Shaka and Dingane have sometimes produced an image that is as distorted as the one they are supposed to replace.[21] Yet there is no question that nineteenth-century white observers (and later Afrikaner historians) overstated in overtly racist terms the capriciousness and general barbarity of the Zulu royal family.

According to the Afrikaner version of events, the Voortrekker leader Piet Retief had visited King Dingane at emGungunlovu in November 1837 with a straightforward request that the trekkers, having made their way across the Drakensberg mountains, be allowed legal title to unsettled land in Natal. Dingane asked that in return the Boers recover a large herd of Zulu cattle stolen by Sikonyela, a neighbouring Basuto chief. This Retief did, travelling back to emGungunlovu with the herd and fifty-odd men in January 1848. Dingane signed the treaty Retief had drawn up, but then, with typical fickleness and cruelty, suddenly had Retief and his party murdered and then unleashed his impis on the unsuspecting Boer encampments strung out along the tributaries of the Tugela river in February.[22]

Dingane, however, despite being lazy and at times impatient, was not (as many Afrikaners would have it) simply a barbarian despot striking out at a more sophisticated and peaceful people, an uncivilized and unreliable 'monster in human form'.[23] There were logical reasons for him to be extremely suspicious of the Voortrekkers.

In a November 1837 letter accepting Dingane's terms for permission to settle in Natal, the Boer leader made the great mistake of dwelling on a recent and crushing Boer victory over King Mzilikazi of the Matabele. 'The great Book of God', Retief continued, 'teaches us that kings who conduct themselves as Umsilikazi [Mzilikazi] does are severely punished, and that it is not granted to them to live or reign long.'[24] Whether he was consciously attempting to intimidate the Zulu king or just being naïve, Retief, in focusing on a victory over an enemy the Zulus themselves had been unsuccessfully striving to conquer for many years, confirmed Dingane's suspicions that the Boer settlers – already pouring by the hundreds into Natal – posed a great threat. A bad situation was made worse when Retief returned to emGungunlovu in early February 1838. Announcing his arrival by having his fifty-odd men charge round on horseback firing their guns in the air – again interpreted as a threat display – Retief angered Dingane by admitting that he had let Sikonyela go once the latter had met Boer demands, and by refusing to hand over the horses and guns that he, Retief, had extorted from the Basuto chief along with the stolen cattle. From the Zulu king's perspective, the Boers appeared both duplicitous and dangerous: hence the order to 'kill the criminals!'[25]

Whatever side God and Right may or may not have been on, the vow made by Pretorius and his men a week or so before Blood River was probably not as significant to them as was later made out. The orthodox view of a Covenant between God and his Chosen People, as laid out in the Voortrekker Monument and popular accounts, is largely based on the deathbed recollections of Sarel Cilliers, a former member of the *Wenkommando* and a church elder. According to Cilliers, a dying man recalling events over thirty years past, he had persuaded Pretorius that like the Israelites 'we should make a promise to the Lord that if He gave us the victory over the enemy we should observe that day every year as a Sabbath'. Cilliers had then made this vow a collective endeavour at an open-air prayer meeting before the entire commando from atop a gun carriage.[26]

In Cilliers' pious mind the biblical parallel – the Covenant – was quite intentional and meaningful. However, the only two contemporary accounts, read in terms of what we now know of Boer religious observance at the time, suggest a less than epiphanal event.

The Boers in the 1830s undoubtedly held the Bible (the only book known to most families) in great awe, but as highly individualistic farmers on the farthest margins of Western civilization their grasp of basic Christian theology and of themselves as a collective entity – a people – was extremely limited. The idea that the early Boers were full-blown Calvinists, like so much else of the mythology surrounding the trek built up in the last quarter of the nineteenth century, is an *ex post facto* construct.[27]

The chronicle of J. B. Bantjes, secretary to Commandant Pretorius, details the latter's repeated assertion to his men that God was on the side of the Boers, as well as a request he made to his deputies: 'he wanted to make a vow to God Almighty, if they were all willing, that should the Lord be pleased to grant us the victory, we would raise a House to the memory of His great name.' This was agreed to, but instead of assembling *en masse*, as Cilliers remembered, the men of the commando prayed in their constituent groups and the oath – only a promise to build a church, rather than the perpetual day of thanksgiving asserted by Cilliers – was formally taken among the dozen or so men in Pretorius' tent.[28]

This was something less than a full-blown Covenant, yet at the same time – and contrary to the standard view that something of unique significance had taken place – not without precedent outside the pages of the Old Testament. Several times since the turn of the century various Boer leaders had attempted to bind their followers to a particular cause through the swearing of a public oath. Pretorius may well have been emulating other leaders who had attempted through a unifying oath to overcome the notorious fractiousness of Boers trying to act in concert with one another.[29]

Pretorius certainly did little after Blood River to suggest that the vow had been much more than an exercise in forging unity. The official dispatch he wrote after the battle begins with the assertion that 'Our only hope was in God', but says nothing of the vow; nor, indeed, is there any mention of divine intervention. In fact the only reference to the vow Pretorius made was in a follow-up letter, and this rather pro forma and almost in passing.[30]

Whatever its form or intent, the vow itself went unobserved as a day of remembrance in the middle decades of the nineteenth century within the Boer community. Only in the 1880s and 1890s, when the Great Trek became the central focus of the Afrikaner nationalist revival, did it resurface in the guise of Covenant between God and Chosen People.[31]

The vow, though, does suggest that members of the *Wenkommando* were not as calm and confident in God's favour as commonly supposed; the mere fact that Pretorius decided that a formal oath was necessary suggests that morale was not as high as he might have wished.[32] Even more indicative of something other than universal courage and confidence was the fact that several Boers deserted during the advance. Even in the wake of the success at Blood River, Pretorius found himself 'besieged from all sides from persons wanting to ride out' and had to explain in letters to base camps who exactly he had authorized to accompany dispatch riders. 'I must earnestly tell you, Gentlemen', he grimly wrote to one trek party in January 1839, 'that I wish . . . that all bad examples of this kind must be punished with the utmost severity.'[33]

Even more ironic, in view of the twentieth-century racial-cum-cultural Afrikaner mythology surrounding Blood River – a triumph of (white) civilization over (black) barbarism – was the fact that the Boers owed some of their success in the battle to native help. Over 200 natives aided the 470 white men in the commando by looking after the cattle and horses in the laager and using spare muskets alongside the Boers at Blood River.[34]

If, then, the Voortrekkers possessed no obvious moral superiority over their foes and suffered reverses which call into question a preordained victory at Blood River, then what really happened on 16 December 1838? To answer that question we need to examine the circumstances of the battle itself, circumstances which indicate that – once a few key decisions had been taken – the odds were almost entirely in favour of the Boers.

Andries Pretorius, as Commandant-General in charge of the largest commando that the Voortrekkers had yet assembled, is justly credited with an above-average sense of the hurdles confronting a punitive expedition. While doing his best to overcome the constant bickering that plagued all attempts at co-operative enterprise between trek parties, he advanced slowly in five well-protected columns, ignoring possible Zulu traps and making his men laager their wagons at night to counter a surprise attack. On the afternoon of the 15th, after the commando had crossed the Buffalo river, scouts reported a large enemy force in the vicinity: the Zulu army was preparing to give battle.

It was at this point that Pretorius made a fateful decision. Sarel Cilliers and others in the commando were all for riding forth to attack the Zulus. This the Commandant decided against because many of his men were still out in reconnaissance parties and because he correctly suspected that the Zulus were trying to lure him into close and rocky terrain where a musket-armed horseman would lose much of his advantage over a spear-wielding warrior on foot.[35] If he had given in to the urgings of Cilliers, Pretorius might have met the same fate as Uys and Potgieter at Italeni.

As always, the wagons laagered for the night, this time up against a wide section of the Ncome river flanked by a 14 foot (4.25 metre) deep donga (dry streambed). The Zulus might still have achieved a partial victory, since Pretorius by his own account still intended to launch a mounted attack in the open: but by chance the 16th was a Sunday, a day on which the Boers did not fight. The Zulu commanders, Ndlela and Dambuza, however, were probably under pressure from Dingane to stop the Boer advance on the royal kraal, and drew up five impis around the laager on the night of 15/16 December. (The need to build up forces, rather than – as Afrikaner mythology would have it[36] – superstitious fear of the glowing lamps that the Boers had hung out at the end of whip-stocks round the laager, prevented a night attack.) When dawn broke, clear and dry, 'all of Zululand sat there', as one trekker put it.[37]

The precise nature and order of events over the next few hours remains unclear.[38] However, the general pattern and flow is quite discernible. The morning was clear and bright, the ground around the Boer position flat and devoid of cover. Pretorius and his men, armed with muzzle-loading muskets and two or three small cannon, and with plenty of powder and ammunition, were positioned behind laagered wagons, any gaps protected by movable 'battle gates' specially designed for the expedition. The Zulus, numbering around 10,000 and armed almost exclusively with stabbing assagais and protected only by oxhide shields, were arrayed round the laager from the donga to the Ncome river.

Several massed attacks were launched by the Zulus and beaten off with heavy loss, each advance made more difficult by the dead and dying of previous assaults. After about two hours, Pretorius decided it was time to counter-attack. The battle gates were opened, and parties of mounted Boers armed with muskets charged out to try and break up the remaining Zulu formations. 'The Zulus stood our assault firmly for some time', Pretorius recorded, 'but at last, finding their number rapidly decreasing, they fled, scattering themselves in all directions.'[39]

This last stage of the battle was, if anything, even worse for the Zulus than what had come before. Those who fled were hunted down for three hours by horsemen and shot; those who took shelter in a nearby ravine were simply butchered. 'We were endowed with great courage', Cilliers later claimed (without irony), 'and we left the Kafirs lying on the ground as thick almost as pumpkins upon the field that has borne a plentiful crop.'[40] Those who tried to hide along the banks of the Ncome met an equally grim fate, the Ncome itself becoming known as Blood River for the colour the water turned. 'The next day we counted the number of the [Zulu] slain', J. G. Bantjes recorded. 'Those who had been killed about or near the camp, of which some have not been counted, with those who had been overtaken and killed, we found amounted to – the lowest certain number – more than 3,000.' No Boers had died, and only three had been wounded in the chase.[41]

It was the Zulus, rather than the Boers, who needed a miracle to win. Almost all the circumstances of the battle favoured the Voortrekkers. Zulu numbers counted for little given the disparity in arms and protection between the two sides. The impis had no cover other than their shields, which were quite useless in warding off the musket balls and cannon shot that cut down the Zulus at least 20 yards (6 metres) short of the range at which assagais could be wielded. Even if assagais were used as missile rather than stabbing weapons, and the Zulus managed – as was apparently the case – to use some of the muskets taken from Retief's men, the laagered wagons provided excellent protection for the men of the commando. Once the Zulu regiments began their series of suicidal charges, the only real danger the Boers faced was running out of powder or ammunition, a possibility which Retief avoided by wearing the Zulus down and then launching counter-attacks which broke Zulu cohesion and effectively ended the battle. In the open, a man on foot armed with a short spear was no match for a man riding a horse and wielding a firearm. Even the weather helped, keeping gunpowder dry and providing a clear view of the oncoming Zulus. 'It was not a battle', as an uneasy Dutch Reformed Church minister later wrote, 'it was an execution.'[42]

Blood River, in short, was won by the Boers very much on, rather than against, the odds. Paradoxically, however, it may also have been less significant a victory than myth would have it. In the aftermath of battle, Pretorius learned from a Zulu prisoner

that the people of Dingaan had fallen in countless numbers; that they after the defeat inflicted on them by us spread out and fled in disorder; that only one chief with a few people has survived, who stand ready when we approach to flee (if they are able) or to surrender themselves.[43]

That certainly made Blood River appear decisive; unfortunately, as was revealed when this prisoner led part of the commando into a trap at White Umfalozi, the Zulus were far from beaten.

This dangerous overestimation of the effect of Blood River on the Zulu capacity to go on waging war may also have been the result of inflated ideas of just how many Zulus had been killed. All subsequent accounts have taken at face value the estimate made by the victors of over 3,000 Zulu dead.[44] This was certainly possible in rough statistical terms: each armed man within the laager firing one mortal musket shot every twenty minutes could have produced such a figure within the first two hours. There are, however, reasons to doubt that Zulu losses were quite so high.

In many ways Blood River was a repeat performance of the Voortrekker victory over the Matabele on 15 October 1836 (the victory which Piet Retief had so imprudently boasted of to King Dingane). Matabele regiments – estimated to number up to 9,000 men, and just as brave and well drilled as the Zulus – had attacked a Voortrekker laager of fifty wagons protected by about forty men and boys (each able to fire at about three times the normal rate since the women loaded extra muskets and passed them over to their husbands after each shot). The fight was more concentrated in time, the Matabele retiring after an hour of continuous attack in contrast to four Zulu attacks spaced over two hours. Yet the Zulus were supposed to have lost over 3,000 men in the immediate vicinity of the laager while the Matabele lost a mere 350.[45] Even if the Boers had been in the same strength as at Blood River, net Matabele losses would have been only 1,313 – well under half of what the Zulus were supposed to have suffered. It seems unlikely that the three small cannon and cavalry charges at Blood River made so great a difference.[46]

An even more damning indication that the victors of Blood River may have been blowing their trumpet a little too hard (or simply made rather too loose an estimation as they surveyed the battlefield) were Zulu losses against the British in the war of 1879. At Isandhlwana, approximately 600 British infantrymen armed with accurate breech-loading rifles able to fire at several times the rate of a muzzle-loading musket had inflicted approximately 2,000 casualties on the attacking Zulus over a period of about three hours before running short of ammunition and being overwhelmed. At the more successful defence of Rorke's Drift, when 140 infantrymen firing from behind an improvised perimeter wall of mealie bags and boxes strung between a few buildings (not unlike a laager) had held off a series of fierce attacks by two Zulu impis (4,000 men) spread over nine hours, 20,000 rifle rounds were fired, but only about 500 Zulus were killed.[47]

Blood River, in short, may not have been as comprehensive a massacre as is often assumed. It certainly did not break the back of Zulu resistance. The impis recovered sufficiently almost to trap Pretorius at the White Umfalozi; and it was in fact a victory over Dingane by the forces of Mpande (a rival claimant to the Zulu throne who allied himself with the Boers) on 30 January 1839 which brought the war to an end. Zululand became a vassal state under the wing of the newly established Republic of Natal, but only until 1843, when Natal was bloodlessly annexed by the British.[48] It was left to the British themselves, after initial reverses, to conquer successfully the Zulu people forty years after the last shots had been fired at Blood River.

The *Wenkommando* was clearly not the righteously decisive force – revolutionary in an almost biblical sense – that so many Afrikaners have been taught to believe. The Zulu defeat at Blood River was part of a continuum of successive native encounters with superior European military technology, rather than being a singular, divinely sanctioned moment of truth in the history of white and black in South Africa.

Westerners, however, among whom one can number the Boers, were to have no permanent monopoly on recasting the past in the non-Western world. Once Western concepts of linear time and progressive historical development began to influence the outlook of Asian intellectuals in later decades, past events would come to be reinterpreted in light of Western concepts.[49]

In both China and India, as the next two chapters demonstrate, twentieth-century independence movements would seek to create their version of the nineteenth-century past in opposition to that of the imperial powers. This would in turn elevate mid-century revolts into the status of anti-imperialist revolutions – albeit premature ones – complete with patriot armies.

6 The armies of the Heavenly Kingdom and the Taiping Rebellion in China, 1850–68

Holy soldiers?

> Resolved to serve the state, they happily resist aggression; Covered with courage they enjoy launching frontal attacks.
>
> Yang Hsiu-ch'ing, Taiping Chief of Staff, 1854[1]

> In every engagement [new conscripts] fight in the front rows, while the [Taiping] rebels send men carrying swords and shields to march behind them. If they turn back or run away they are killed.
>
> Tseng Kuo-fan, Hunan local corps organizer, 1853[2]

That the Taiping Rebellion quickly assumed major historical significance in the eyes of contemporary observers as well as historians of modern China is hardly surprising. It was, after all, a civil war of truly cataclysmic proportions. By the time it was over, much of the fertile and prosperous Yangtze valley had been devastated and depopulated so thoroughly that a century later it had not fully recovered. A conservative estimate puts the number of Chinese who were killed or who starved to death as a result of the struggle at 20 million; the true figure may be closer to 47 million.[3]

The sheer scale of destruction, however, was not the only feature which distinguished the Taiping Rebellion from the dozens of other popular revolts which wracked nineteenth-century China. There was also the ideological dimension to consider.

Most popular uprisings lacked any clear programme beyond a burning desire to throw off the yoke of Ch'ing oppression and (in some cases) establish a new ruling dynasty along traditional lines. The Taipings, on the other hand, fought to overturn not only the Manchus but also the entire Confucian-based social order. Though fuelled like many other rebellions by racial friction and peasant discontent over increasingly onerous tax burdens and general corruption, the *Taiping Tienkuo* ('Heavenly Kingdom') movement possessed a unique ideological agenda based on the messianic teachings of its spiritual leader, Hung Hsiu-ch'üan.

A humble schoolteacher in Kwangsi province who had tried and failed several times to pass the civil service entrance examination, Hung had suffered a nervous breakdown during which he had visions that he later interpreted – largely on the basis of a highly moralistic evangelical Christian tract he read in 1843 – to mean that God wished him to convert the people of China to the true path of monotheistic righteousness and slay all 'demons'. Initially the 'demons' that Hung and his first disciples attacked were merely village idols, and the Society of God-worshippers a purely religious enterprise. By 1850–1, however, friction between the growing number of converts and the ranks of the unconverted had led to open warfare with the local authorities and the evolution of the movement into a militant revolutionary force bent on exterminating 'demons' now seen to be the ruling Manchus.[4]

The nature of this force, as codified in a series of decrees issued after the first Taiping victories had enabled the God-worshippers (now numbering in the tens of thousands) to break out of their first base at Chin-t'ien and seize the city of Yung-an in the autumn of 1851, was militantly radical. In essence, Taiping society was to be run along military lines, with the sexes separated, barracks set up, and people – all said to be equals, brothers and sisters without reference to family or class – organized into work brigades according to function. Private property and personal ownership were abolished, with the state taking responsibility for the distribution of needed goods and services. A series of prohibitions and regulations were also issued defining godly behaviour (no smoking, plenty of group prayer, and no licentiousness – i.e. fraternization between men and women even if married).

It was all certainly a far cry from traditional Chinese society, which other rebels had sought to control rather than destroy. A highly complex and hierarchical social and political order that had evolved over a millennium under the influence of Confucian philosophy was being repudiated in the name of a radically new theocratic order, a curious mixture of egalitarian and totalitarian elements. The Taipings even looked different, a decree having been issued by Hung ordering his men to go about without a pigtail and without shaving the upper forehead (the outward marks of subservience decreed by the Manchus).

The purely evangelical aspect of the movement was not something with which later generations could identify (though Western missionaries in the 1850s were understandably intrigued – at least until they discovered that Hung claimed to be the younger brother of Jesus and to have travelled to Heaven and back). The idea of traditional Chinese society reshaped and harnessed to throw off the shackles of alien oppression, however, had an enormous degree of resonance among nationalists of the twentieth century seeking a new order for China. For by the time they were organizing themselves at Yung-an in 1851–2 in preparation for the campaign that would eventually take them to the old imperial capital at Nanking in 1854, the Taipings were making no secret of their basic aim: the overthrow of Manchu imperialism, the destruction of the 'Imps' and all they stood for, and the creation of a truly Chinese regime. Clashes between the Taipings and European forces around the treaty ports in the 1860s only added to their appeal among later generations of Chinese revolutionaries. Anti-imperialism, then, coupled to a greater or lesser degree with elements of Taiping society, made the Taiping Rebellion seem a natural precursor to later, more successful efforts at overthrowing the existing order.

Dr Sun Yat-sen, venerated as the father of modern Chinese nationalism, was far from unique among the nationalists of the early twentieth century in seeing the Taiping programme as a premature attempt at reordering China along modern lines. Decrees pointing towards the equal distribution of wealth, state control of the means of production, the need for a China run by the Chinese, all seemed to be an early version of the socialist–nationalist programme Sun and others believed China should follow. Both before and after the 1911 Revolution which overthrew the imperial regime, the Taipings were heroes in nationalist circles. The young Chiang Kai-shek, for example, praised them as a 'revolutionary army', and down to the mid-1920s the rebellion was officially celebrated by the Kuomintang (KMT).[5]

It was the Chinese communists, however, who developed the greatest degree of admiration for the Taipings. Given the key role the peasantry played in the revolutionary thinking of Mao Tse-tung, this was entirely predictable. Since according to Mao the peasantry 'formed the real motive force of historical development' in China, it was only natural to celebrate 'the glorious revolutionary tradition and splendid historical tradition' of the Taipings and other peasant rebels.[6] In the latter 1930s and early 1940s, Mao drew a number of explicitly favourable parallels between his movement and the Heavenly Kingdom.[7] Once the communists came to rule all of China after 1949, peasant uprisings in general and the Taiping Rebellion in partic-ular became by far the most intensely studied aspect of Chinese history.[8]

The central theme of the large number of works on the subject published in China in the 1950s and 1960s was the close resemblance between the Taiping movement and Maoist communism. The movement's roots among the peasantry, its dynamism, the emphasis on collectivism and equality, even the rigorous moral code were seen as early versions of communist practices. The class-conscious Taipings had staged a premature revolution – rather than a mere rebellion – aimed at overthrowing both domestic and foreign tyranny in the name of the people. The ultimate failure of the movement was due to contradictions within the Taiping leadership – a tendency to give way to luxurious living and squabbling once the Taipings had reached Nanking. It was in this respect (higher organization and leadership) that the Chinese Communist Party was far superior.[9]

In the political upheavals of the 1960s and 1970s, to be sure, changes occurred in the prevailing interpretation of particular aspects of the Taiping movement. Suggestions in the early stages of the Cultural Revolution that Taiping General Li Hsiu-ch'eng (hitherto considered a revolutionary hero) had in fact been a traitor were used by radical factions as a means of attacking more conservative leaders within the CCP.[10] Similarly, after the death of Mao and the swing away from radicalism in the latter 1970s and 1980s, subtle comparisons were drawn between the despotic tendencies of Hung Hsiu-ch'üan and Mao Tse-tung while questions were raised concerning the revolutionary nature of the peasantry.[11] Overall, however, the Taipings have at all stages since 1949 been considered in a positive light. Through films, museum exhibits, and indirect comparisons with contemporary events as well as written histories, the Taiping Rebellion continues to serve an exemplary function, not least among those who believe that the CCP has become akin to the Ch'ing dynasty.[12]

The military aspects of the movement's success, and comparisons with the People's Liberation Army of a century later, have ranked among the most prominent points of discussion among Chinese communist historians. Evidence is cited, for example, of the good order and high morale maintained among Taiping troops, their consistent bravery, the links between civil and military administration, propaganda efforts, and the essential uprightness of soldiers in dealings with the peasants – all of which are said to have 'won the hearts of the people'.[13] Contrary evidence is dismissed as 'slanderous' imperial or later bourgeois propaganda.[14]

Particular attention, moreover, has been focused on the Taipings' use of guerrilla tactics by leading historians such as Lo Erh-kang and Hua Kang. Both in the early years (1851–3) and in the last years after the fall of Nanking (1864–8), the Taipings are said to have practised a form of warfare which emphasized mobility, speed, and surprise at the expense of set-piece sieges and engagements. They were, in short, employing the kind of guerrilla tactics that were said to have brought victory to Mao over the KMT in the following century.[15]

Historians outside China, unconstrained by the dictates of ideological orthodoxy, have called into serious question some of the more sweeping claims concerning the progressive nature of the Taipings. Yet a number of the leading figures have in fact reinforced the idea of a revolutionary Taiping army through reference to the major feature of Taiping ideology that the communists tend to downplay – religious zeal.

Jen Yu-wen, for example, a Western-trained authority on the Taipings and the sympathetic author of a vast multi-volume history of the movement, consistently referred to Taiping warriors as 'holy soldiers'. In his view the Taiping religious code of conduct transformed them 'into an obedient, fanatically loyal, and spiritually united revolutionary army that would rank as one of the bravest in Chinese history'.[16]

To some British observers and historians, moreover, the evangelical fervour and puritanical aspects of Taiping Christianity suggested an obvious parallel: the Taiping forces were cut from the same cloth as the New Model Army. In both cases strength of faith allowed soldiers to press onward against adversity while maintaining strict discipline. Thomas Meadows, for instance, an interpreter who had an opportunity to observe the Taipings at first-hand in the 1850s and later wrote the first history of the rebellion, made much of this.[17] Over a century later Jack Gray, writing the volume of the *Short Oxford History of the Modern World* on China, argued that the rebellion was a situation in which ' "decayed tapsters and serving men" [the

Manchus] faced men who "knew what they fought for and loved what they knew" [the Taipings]'.[18]

From a variety of perspectives, in short, the Taiping Army has been viewed as revolutionary in nature. Ultimate defeat, it is usually stated or implied, was due to failure of leadership at the top, not through any flaws in the fighting troops themselves. A rereading of the available evidence, however, suggests that the army of the Taipings was neither as fanatical nor as tactically innovative as is often supposed.

That observers should conclude that the Taipings developed a consciously mobile form of warfare, quite distinct from the slow, static style of war practised by their adversaries, is understandable. In the early years they did indeed move quickly, were well organized, and struck hard.

Between 1851 and 1853, on their march northward from Chin-t'ien to Nanking, the Taipings paid little heed to baggage trains and lines of communication. As a group of former Taiping warriors explained to a French officer, they had been a society on the move, living from day to day, unencumbered:

> When we had money we spent a lot. When we didn't, we managed as best we could but didn't complain. The days of distress followed the days of opulence and we found it all quite natural. It was just that which made us superior to the imperial troops. When they camp, they need big installations. They have to have fortifications, tents, and so on. We went straight on. If there were houses, we stayed there, if not, we slept under the stars.[19]

Even when the Taipings did on occasion stop to rest in a city they had taken, and found themselves surrounded by imperialist besiegers, they always managed to break out successfully and resume their march. 'They cut their way through their enemies', Meadows noted admiringly, 'inflicting far greater damage on the latter than they themselves incur, and move to another position.'[20]

The Taipings, moreover, were more than a mobile peasant host. Growing in size as success followed success and recruits poured in, the Taiping Army was organized along sound theoretical lines. An army corps (13,155 officers and men) consisted of five divisions, each division possessing five brigades, each brigade made up of five companies, and each company holding four platoons. Even the Taipings' great nemesis, Tseng Kuo-fan, admired this system.[21]

The aggressive qualities of the Taipings in battle on their way to Nanking were also noted by contemporary observers, not least by disconcerted imperial officials. 'The rebels generally are powerful and fierce', lamented Governor Chou T'ien-chüeh of Kwangsi in 1851, 'and cannot by any means be likened to a disorderly crowd; their regulations and laws are rigorous and clear.'[22]

It would be dangerous, however, to conclude from all this that the Taipings in the first phase of the rebellion were operating on a coherent plan, or that they were unstoppable. Luck and the nature of the enemy had more to do with their military success than novel strategy and tactics.

Though blessed with natural military leaders such as Yang Hsiu-ch'ing, effectively the Commander-in-Chief during the march, the Taiping leaders – Hung and the other *wangs*, or kings, that he appointed – more often than not reacted to events and operated through force of circumstance. How long a position was occupied, and what route was taken on the march, seemed to depend very much on enemy activity rather than farsighted planning.

Meadows perceptively recognized that there was a curious pattern to the campaign between 1851 and 1853. The Taiping Army would seize a city, and then expend a lot of energy fortifying it. Meanwhile, pursuing imperial troops would come up and concentrate, eventually hemming in the Taipings. Direct assaults on the occupied position failed, but after a time – a matter of weeks or months – the Taipings would begin to feel the pinch of blockade. Then 'the Tae pings, strained by want of provisions, are compelled to break out', moving on to a new city, where the pattern eventually repeated itself.[23]

The circuitous routes often chosen for marches, furthermore, were the result of enemy action rather than a conscious choice to stick to the hills and use terrain as a weapon in guerrilla fashion. In the spring of 1852, for instance, after wasting time trying to take the Kwangsi provincial capital, Kuei-lin, the Taipings were forced to take to the hills in order to avoid contact with the imperial forces that were concentrating. Similarly, a disastrous encounter with a corps of local militia in June of the same year diverted the Taiping Army away from a thrust directly northward by river through Hunan and towards a winding march on foot along the hilly border region between Hunan and Kiangsi.[24]

The Taiping Army that marched and fought its way to Nanking – hailed as revolutionary in terms of structure, tactics, and above all discipline and morale – also needs to be put in perspective. At first glance, it certainly appears as a revolutionary force, much as it did to many contemporary Western observers, but closer inspection reveals a rather more ambiguous picture.

There can be little doubt that the original band of true believers from Kwangsi province who battled their way out of Chin-t'ien were inspired by religious fanaticism and consequently fought with unusual vigour.[25] But there were only from 3,000 to 7,000 warriors in the early years, many of whom would have been killed in the course of the march to Nanking (especially at their first great reverse at the So-li ford ambush in June of 1852, where 2,000 were said to have perished[26]). By 1853–4, to be sure, as many as 140,000 Taiping soldiers may have been in the field; success brought in new recruits by the thousands as the army travelled through Hunan, Hupeh, and Anhwei.[27] The quality and discipline of these troops, however, may not have been up to the high standards of the original God-worshippers.

Some of the new recruits, to be sure, were oppressed peasants bitter at Manchu rule and more than willing to join the rebellion if not always to believe truly in the new faith. Others, however, were simply deserters from the imperial forces (which, as we shall see, were usually of low quality); there were also a fair number of bandits and other riff-raff, as well as – in uneasy partnership – contingents from the Triads and other secret societies.[28] The original Taiping units were, it seems clear, obeying strict instructions to win over the peasantry by drawing what they needed only from Ch'ing officials and other 'Imp' supporters.[29] The new arrivals, though, often appear to have been less scrupulous.

Lacking the inner conviction of the original long-haired rebels, the new men were not averse to plunder and destruction of all kinds at the expense of the local peasantry. The fact that Hung Hsiu-ch'üan, the self-styled Heavenly King (*T'ien Wang*), several times issued edicts on the march to Nanking forbidding such practices – 'I earnestly beseech you to obey the heavenly commands, and not to offend again' – and that penalties if caught were severe, suggests that his troops were becoming less rather than more well disciplined.[30] The most supportive of the foreign missionaries in China admitted that there were bad elements who had joined 'to enrich themselves by rapine' and cared little for the Taiping cause as such.[31]

Yet even with the addition of these rather dubious troops, the battlefield drain on Taiping manpower became a major source of concern. In consequence, as early as 1853 the Taipings were introducing general conscription in the areas they controlled.[32] Those unwillingly pressed into service, needless to say, lacked much positive motivation.

By 1853 the standard practice was to keep conscripts under guard until their hair had grown long enough to identify them as Taiping troops (thus making it more difficult to slip away unnoticed).[33] The ongoing separation of the sexes was a further incentive to loyalty. Wives, sisters, and daughters forced to live in separate camps were in essence hostages to good behaviour by their menfolk. Interestingly, this was a deterrent to cowardice thought necessary not only for the new recruits but also for the older long-haired rebels – which in turn suggests that faith alone was not always enough of an incentive to fight fiercely even for some of the God-worshippers.[34] As for the conscripts, they were often placed ahead of the veteran soldiers in order to prevent them from running away in the face of the enemy.[35]

The conduct of the Taipings once they had established themselves at Nanking, moreover, did not inspire confidence within the population at large. In time-honoured fashion, the Taiping soldiers were allowed to loot the city for about three days. Killing was not indiscriminate, but as one resident noted, even by the notorious standards of the Ch'ing armies, the rebels 'plunder and despoil to a degree that makes one's hair stand on end'.[36] Taxes imposed on the common people were initially lower than under the imperial regime, but this was counter-balanced by the tendency arbitrarily to confiscate property and food in the name of the state.[37] The separation of the sexes and organization of the civilian population into heavy work battalions was far from popular, and disrupted local patterns of agricultural and other production. 'It is not without reason that the country-people fear the insurgents', the Reverend Joseph Edkins of the London Missionary

Society wrote after a visit to Taiping territory in 1861. 'They are obliged, without pay, to work for them as carriers of burdens, returning when their tasks are done to their own employments, till it is their turn again to labour for these hard masters.'[38]

Suicides – especially among women – went up, as did efforts among both soldiers and civilians to escape from Taiping territory. The separation of the sexes and the women's work battalions were more or less abandoned in 1855, but the tendency to view the civilian population as simply an auxiliary labour pool persisted.[39]

If all this was so, though, why did so many observers comment on the positive qualities of the Taiping Army in the 1850s? In essence because the standard point of reference was the army of the Ch'ing dynasty – which by the middle of the nineteenth century was a force so abysmal in every respect that it made anything else look good by comparison.

The standing army of the Ch'ing dynasty consisted of two types of troops: the Manchu bannermen, garrisoning the major cities, and the native Chinese Green Standard forces. By the mid-nineteenth century, both suffered from a myriad of problems. Pay, which had remained fixed for centuries amid inflation, was quite inadequate – a situation made worse by the tendency of officers to supplement their income with money supposedly destined for their men. Desertion was rife and discipline slack, and soldiers – especially on campaign – became little better than bandits, preying on the peasant population ruthlessly to survive. Looting, arson, rape, and murder were the rule rather than the exception.

Meanwhile the command structure created by the Manchus, though politically expedient, showed itself increasingly ineffective in time of military crisis. Lines of authority were kept deliberately vague and ambiguous, thereby preventing any one general or governor from assuming enough power to present a potential threat to the dynasty, but also making it virtually impossible to organize and run campaigns with any efficiency. Utter failure in the First Opium War (1839–42) against the British highlighted the degree to which the Manchu military system had fallen into a state of utter decay and decrepitude.[40]

Under these circumstances it should hardly come as a surprise that the imperial response to the Taiping Rebellion in its early years was slow, poorly organized, and ineffectual. Quite by chance three of the better Ch'ing generals died *en route* to Kwangsi, leaving the job of suppression in the hands of regional governors and officials totally unsuited to the task. As for the troops at their disposal, their lethargy – a stark contrast to the briskness of the Taipings – was well described by a French missionary, Dr L. G. Delaplace, in November 1852:

> For the equipment of a few soldiers, it is incredible what a number of families have to be troubled; for it must not be imagined that the Chinese foot soldier will go on foot: no, no; he must be provided with a car [i.e.

sedan chair]. The cavalry-man, likewise, would be too much fatigued were he to go on horseback; he must also have a car. Indeed, the war-steed himself cannot carry his saddle. To transport his harness, cars must be employed; so that last week, in the town of Choui-Tcheou-Fou, two leagues hence, a thousand men were required to transport the equipment of three hundred soldiers.[41]

Slow in movement, caring more about themselves than their duty, and led by timid and often incompetent commanders, such troops did not perform well in combat. Indeed, imperial generals were loath to follow the rebels closely and engage in pitched battle for fear of the consequences. Though usually outnumbering the rebels – and indeed eventually encircling them in the cities they occupied – imperial soldiers fought with little enthusiasm and even less discipline once Peking had made it impossible for generals to offer any more excuses for delay. 'Our troops have not a tincture of discipline', Governor Chou T'ien-chüeh lamented in April 1851, 'retreating is easy to them, advancing difficult; and, though again and again exhorted, they always remain as weak and timorous as before.'[42]

Plundering the civilian population was a far less dangerous and more profitable enterprise than fighting the Taipings, and imperial troops – regardless of orders – if at all possible kept their distance from the enemy. 'They [the rebels] have captured one town after another', the Peking court circular fumed in 1852, 'as if the country was undefended.... If the rebellion is allowed to spread in this way, how can it ever be suppressed?'[43]

In comparison with their adversary, therefore, the Taipings could hardly not appear to be a revolutionary force – even though their supposedly innovative army structure was based on a Chou dynasty model dating from the fourth century BC.[44] Moreover, despite their initial successes, the Taipings ultimately failed to topple the Ch'ing, and were themselves eventually defeated.

Most historians date the military decline of the movement from the strategic errors and in-fighting of the mid-1850s. The attempt to conquer the west as well as the north simultaneously with expeditions from Nanking was certainly a grave mistake, since neither force proved strong enough to succeed. Within the capital, the bloody massacres associated with the struggle for power that broke out between the Heavenly King and the other leading *wangs* in 1856 deprived the movement of some of its best generals and tens of thousands of veteran God-worshippers.[45] Yet the decline in Taiping military fortunes, evident from the mid-1850s and accelerating precipitously in the 1860s, can be traced to weaknesses masked to a great extent by the far greater problems of the imperial forces but nevertheless present almost from the start of the rebellion.

Losses, for one thing, necessitated further efforts to rope in as many volunteers and conscripts as possible, regardless of their commitment to the

Taiping cause. Hung Hsiu-ch'üan might claim that 'my Heavenly soldiers are as limitless as water', but the truth was that the Taiping Kingdom was chronically short of men.[46]

In 1857, for example, the Reverend R. S. McLay noted that at the battle-front at Fu-chou (Kiangsi province) a force of 10,000 Taipings appeared to contain only about 2,000 true believers. 'The rest of the army', he wrote in a letter to the *Hong Kong Register*, 'was made up of natives of the Province, whom prospect of plunder, good pay, or fear had driven to the rebel camp.'[47] In some cases the dynamism of Taiping commanders – most notably Li Hsiu-ch'eng – could offset the quality problem.[48] But, in overall terms, Taiping forces were becoming more like imperial troops in outlook and behaviour, often with negative results. As early as October 1853, in the initial phase of the unsuccessful Northern Expedition (1853–5), Taiping troops, despite orders to the contrary, massacred the population of the city of Ts'ang-chou – over 10,000 people – after a hard-fought siege.[49]

Yung Wing, an American-educated observer who visited Nanking in 1859, made the following observation of this army in subsequent months:

> In their victorious march through Hunan, Hupeh, Kiang Si and part of An Hwui, their depleted forces were replenished and reinforced by fresh and new accessions gathered from the people of those provinces. They were the riffraff and scum of their populations. This rabble element added no new strength to their fighting force, but proved to be an encumbrance and caused decided weakness. They knew no discipline, and had no restraining power to keep them from pillage, plunder and indiscriminate destruction.[50]

As the years passed the problem became worse.

During the brief Taiping occupation of Ningpo (Chekiang province) in early 1862, a British observer, F. W. Harvey, noted that the ranks were being swelled by 'all the bad characters of the districts they pass through', and that pillaging captured towns was now routine. 'Why should I not like it?' an evidently typical Taiping soldier answered Harvey on being asked if he enjoyed being in the army. 'I help myself to everything I choose to lay my hands upon; and if interfered with, I just cut the man's head off who interferes.'[51]

The Taipings also continued to round up conscripts and force them into battle. 'The corps which attacked and captured Ningpo', Harvey later reported,

> might have had one old rebel in ten in its formation, the veterans serving principally to keep in a proper state of submission the younger volunteers or pressed men, as well as to inspire courage to those who might recoil from their duty.[52]

Even Augustus Lindley, an avid supporter who actually worked for the Taipings for a time, admitted that he had seen 'the rear-rank men carrying drawn swords to decapitate any who might attempt [to flee]'.[53]

Highlighting the widening gap between the myth and the reality of the Taiping revolutionary army were the defeats it began to suffer at the hands of the enemy. To an increasing degree by the late 1850s and early 1860s, orthodox imperial forces were supplanted by new, unorthodox formations built from the ground up. Regional armies, created from local gentry-run militia formations, later supplemented by European-model formations armed, trained, and led by Westerners, were what eventually defeated the Taipings.

As guardians of the Confucian order from which they benefited the Chinese gentry, as a class, had a great stake in upholding the existing socio-cultural structure and, by extension, the political status quo. Taiping ideology, so radically different from the existing order and adhered to by rebellious peasants and other marginal elements, was anathema to most gentry. And with the imperial government patently failing to contain the threat, leading members of the gentry – in a fashion reminiscent of earlier crises – began to develop militias to protect their localities.

The authorities in Peking were far from happy at this development, fearing that it would eventually threaten Manchu control of China. Yet as the devastating ambush set by the militia organized by Chiang Chung-yuan in southern Hunan had demonstrated in 1852, such forces – based on a mixture of conservative patriotism and personal obligation that gave them far greater coherence and reliability than the crumbling units of the corrupt and bureaucratic Banner and Green Standard armies – appeared an obvious way of containing what was fast becoming a critical threat.[54]

It was for this reason that in January 1853 the Emperor appointed a senior Peking official, Tseng Kuo-fan, to oversee the development of the Hunan militia. Luckily for the Ch'ing dynasty, Tseng, though not a Manchu, turned out to be not only loyal but also a brilliant organizer and a patient strategist.[55]

Often without revealing to Peking the full extent of what he was doing, Tseng slowly but surely created a new force – the Hunan Army – out of scattered militia units. Choosing his commanders with care, Tseng built up a complex and effective hierarchy of personal relationships and loyalties among his officers. As for the ordinary volunteer recruits, Tseng developed unorthodox but eventually quite effective strategies to raise money for regular pay, and did his best to train and equip them properly.[56]

The Hunan Army suffered reverses as well as successes through the mid- and late 1850s, and eventually began to be afflicted with the same problems of poor discipline and low morale as the more orthodox imperial forces. But Tseng – placed in overall command of suppression efforts in 1860 – was patient, and despite several major setbacks slowly but surely drew a noose around the Taiping capital, culminating in the capture of Anking, a key transport and communications centre, in 1861. Moreover, just at the point where the Hunan Army was showing signs of having worn itself out, Tseng authorized one of his principal lieutenants, Li Hung-chang, to raise a new army along similar lines in Anhwei province – the Huai Army – to counter the last great Taiping offensives eastward towards Shanghai and the coast in the early 1860s.[57]

Well-trained regional armies, then, composed of volunteers and led by officers whose first loyalties were to their commanders rather than to the Manchus, caused the Taipings increasing (and ultimately fatal) difficulties. Moreover, in their advance eastward towards the coast, Li and other generals encountered even more revolutionary locally raised forces – small armies raised, equipped, and trained by Westerners.

Neither side in the rebellion was particularly keen to see a greater Western presence in China. The Manchus bitterly resented the Western treaty-port enclaves and other concessions forced upon them by defeat in the Opium War and later threats of military action.[58] As for the Taipings, they were more prepared to deal in a friendly manner with fellow Christians – as long as the Heavenly King's divine status and overlordship were acknowledged.[59] This was as naïve as the Manchu hope (born of xenophobic desperation) that the foreigners could simply be talked into going away. Both sides, at root, operated on the same assumption: that China was the only seat of civilization, beyond which lay barbarians who by rights ought to acknowledge China's inherent superiority and certainly had no business interfering in internal affairs.[60]

There was, however, an important difference between the attitudes of Peking and Nanking. The Manchus concluded more quickly than the Taipings that the potential benefits of allowing in Western military advisors and weapons outweighed the risks of diminishing indigenous authority over the armed forces.

Never having seen modern firearms in action, and quite able to combat Banner and Green Standard forces similarly equipped with a mixture of spears, swords, primitive matchlocks, and cannon, the Taiping generals initially expressed little interest in obtaining foreign weapons or adopting Western tactics. Thomas Meadows, the interpreter on the first official British expedition to Nanking in 1853, commented on the fact that 'while there was a great demand among the Tae ping soldiers for swords, they seemed to take little interest in guns'. A Taiping commander explained why:

> Lo [the commander] said that his people did not understand the use of them, and that they were valueless when the supply of ammunition ran out or the spring went wrong. Swords and spears, he said, seldom got out of order, were easily repaired, and he found that his people could beat the Imperialists with them.[61]

The Taipings were also worried that modern weapons would necessitate employing foreign instructors to teach their men modern tactics and possibly even command them in battle. 'A thousand [foreign] devils would lord it over ten thousand of our men', the T'ien Wang argued, 'and who would stand for that?'[62]

Even Hung Jen-kan, by far the best-educated and most cosmopolitan of the Taiping leaders, and a man who as premier in the latter 1850s made a valiant attempt to reform and revitalize the Taiping Kingdom, seemed unenthusiastic about trying to arm and train troops along Western lines. When in 1859 a Yale graduate, Yung Wing, enthusiastically offered his services in organizing a Taiping army 'on scientific [i.e. Western] principles', complete with a training school for officers, Hung Jen-kan politely indicated that the Taiping leadership would be unable to agree on such a radical idea.[63]

Tens of thousands of muskets were, to be sure, smuggled from Shanghai from 1853 onward. But there appear to have been only a few dozen Westerners serving as mercenaries in Taiping service at any one time, and these mostly deserters and other riff-raff who were given little authority and could not provide much help in the way of organizing the proper use and maintenance of firearms.[64]

Hence observers continued to report on how poorly equipped the Taiping forces seemed. 'All the rebel soldiers we saw were badly armed', Garnet Wolseley, the future field marshal, commented after a trip into Taiping territory in the autumn of 1860, noting that most were armed with spears or swords, and only a small number with 'old muskets, matchlocks or pistols' plus a few 'fowling-pieces and rifles'.[65] Two years later the testimony of two more British observers from Shanghai indicated that the situation had not improved very much. Modern weapons were in evidence among nearby Taiping troops, including some Enfield rifles, but only one man in ten had a firearm of any kind.[66] Whatever else it may have been, the Taiping Army was reactionary, rather than revolutionary, in its attitude to weapons.

This might have mattered less if the imperial forces had been equally orthodox in their attitude to Western arms. Unfortunately for the Taipings, this was not the case by the 1860s – the period in which the Taiping Kingdom was in gravest danger.

Manchu officials had no great love for Westerners. But the inability of imperial forces in 1859–60 to stop an Anglo-French force from penetrating from the coast to Peking in order to force further concessions on the Emperor had underlined the superiority of Western arms. Hence, when the Taipings began to move towards the coast and took Soochow, no real attempt was made to stop fearful Shanghai merchants from sponsoring a 'Foreign-rifle corps' in 1860; indeed Li Hung-chang eventually assumed responsibility for it.

Initially a rather rag-tag affair run by the American adventurer Frederick Ward (later killed in action), this unit of a few thousand men evolved into a force to be reckoned with. Armed, trained, and led by Europeans into battle, the well-drilled Chinese volunteers of what was officially dubbed the 'Ever-Victorious Army' showed that adopting the Western way of war could yield significant results. Though the Ever-Victorious Army was something of a misnomer, and relations between senior Chinese officials and the European officers were often fraught with mutual suspicion and acrimony, this experimental effort at 'Westernizing' Chinese troops was successful. Ningpo was recaptured and the Taipings repulsed from Shanghai in early 1862, and in concert with the Huai Army of Li Hung-chang the Ever-Victorious Army – under the command of the inspirational Charles ('Chinese') Gordon – pushed the Taipings out of Taitsang, Kunshan, and Soochow in the course of 1863.[67]

The advantages of fielding Chinese forces trained and equipped along Western lines against the Taipings was so obvious, indeed, that in 1862 the Peking government authorized the raising of a second army to the north in Chekiang – this time Franco-Chinese rather than Anglo-Chinese in character. Though smaller and less famous than the Ever-Victorious Army, the 1,000-man Ever-Triumphant Army also scored notable successes against the Taipings between 1863 and 1864.[68]

Though the role of the Ever-Victorious Army in the final defeat of the Taipings was greatly exaggerated by nineteenth-century British historians – the new model regional armies were much more important overall – there was no doubt that the imperial government, albeit unwillingly and under the pressure of circumstance, had taken a revolutionary step which greatly aided their suppression efforts. The Taiping commander in the east at this time, Li Hsiu-ch'eng, wrote in disgruntlement after his eventual capture that Li Hung-chang and the Huai Army would not have taken Soochow and later Hangchow without 'the efforts of the foreign devils'.[69] But that was precisely the point: Li and other senior Ch'ing officials, unlike their adversaries, had accepted that they could not do without Western arms and experience.

'Although I have no great faith in foreign doctrines, even when they might be of some benefit', Li Hung-chang wrote to his mentor, Tseng Kuo-fan, in February 1863, 'I cannot help being concerned at the inferiority of our armaments. I, therefore, daily exhort my generals and men to be humble and ready to learn some western techniques, in order to improve our combat force.'[70] According to Gordon, if the Taipings had taken the trouble to build up a supply of modern weapons, 'the tables would have been turned'.[71]

As it was, by the time the Taipings woke up to the need to re-equip their forces with modern arms when faced with the Ever-Victorious Army, it was too late. The Western powers, having decided by 1860 at the latest that a Taiping victory would not serve their purposes (especially now that the imperial government had given in to their demands), sold weapons and offered aid only to the government forces, forcing the desperate Taipings to rely on the few poor-quality pistols and muskets that smugglers offered at exorbitant cost and on the technical knowledge of captured Europeans to operate and repair them.[72]

By the early 1860s, moreover, there were signs that, to a greater extent than ever before, many Taipings were motivated less by revolutionary zeal than by a desire to survive. A live-and-let-live system, including trade, could develop between imperial and Taiping troops in areas where local commanders were disinclined to press matters. What fighting did occur in such areas seemed, at least to Western eyes, rather artificial and intentionally indecisive.

Laurence Oliphant, a member of the 1859 British expedition up the Yangtze river under Lord Elgin, recorded in his diary the following account of a 'battle' he witnessed on 24 October some way upstream from Nanking:

> bodies of [Taiping] men were marching in gallant array down the park-like slopes, to meet their foe in the plains beneath. The Imperialist position was upon the flat ground upon the river margin. Here they erected straw screens and temporary earth-works, behind which a few small guns were placed, which were keeping up an apparently harmless fire upon the enemy. Now and then groups of men carrying gingalls [a primitive blunderbuss] would advance from the hostile ranks, and approach to within two or three hundred yards of each other, fire their gingalls, and retire amid a great waving of banners. We could not wait to watch the issue of the battle, which might last forever, if they continued to fight on the same principle.[73]

Travelling up the Yangtze and passing Anking in March 1861 – admittedly a few weeks before each side began seriously to wrestle for control of the city – Garnet Wolseley wrote in amazement of how military affairs were conducted between the imperial siege army and the Taiping relief force encamped around them.

> Several shots were exchanged by the belligerent parties whilst we were passing, but there did not seem to be any energy or bustle in the ranks of either side. . . . I never saw less impassioned combatants. . . . Their fighting consists in discharging occasionally a few guns, which are frequently unshotted. . . . They [both sides] have nothing to gain by victory, and so prefer doing nothing to exposing themselves to the risk of death or wound.[74]

There is a danger, of course, of making too much of the fleeting observations of Westerners unfamiliar with Chinese military traditions; a way of war which emphasized reason over passion and – in contrast to much of the Western military inheritance – viewed battle as something to be undertaken only under the most favourable circumstances, and certainly not as an end in itself.[75] Still, in the early years of the rebellion, Western commentators had almost always stressed how unusually *aggressive* the Taipings were in battle, something which by the 1860s, it would seem, could not always be assumed to be the case.

An even clearer indication that the Taiping forces lacked true faith in their cause was the steady rise in desertion to the enemy. As far back as the mid-1850s there had been instances of Taiping officers and men trying to change sides. In some cases the men involved were converts under duress whose ultimate loyalty still lay with the Ch'ings, but in others jealously of the Kwangsi old guard combined with old-fashioned greed inspired several unsuccessful mutiny plots.[76] By the early 1860s, moreover, despite efforts by the Heavenly King to ensure loyalty through wholesale distribution of princely titles, cases of generals changing sides – and taking their men with them – were multiplying.

Tung Jung-hai defected in the summer of 1862; Lo Kuo-chung early in 1863; and Ku Lung-hsien towards the end of 1863.[77] Then, in December 1863, four senior officers in the besieged garrison of Soochow – Kao Yung-k'uan, Wang An-chün, Chou Wen-chia, and Wang Hua-pan, all with many years' service in the Taiping Army – murdered their commander and, as agreed in secret meetings with the enemy, handed the city and the garrison over to Li Hung-chang and the Huai Army. 'Within the city', Li drily observed, 'the rebel soldiers had all shaved off their [long] hair.'[78] Unfortunately for the turncoats, Li decided that their numbers still posed a threat, and the generals along with 'over two thousand of the fiercest rebels' were massacred.[79]

Despite the Soochow massacre, Taipings continued to change sides. Though the imperial forces tended to distrust very senior generals and the old die-hards from Kwangsi, recruits from other provinces were generally spared. At the end of 1863 Li Hung-chang reported that 10,000 former Taipings were in his hands, among whom the officers 'are being temporarily retained to assist us in campaigning'. Li was all in favour of a lenient policy towards an enemy whose morale was clearly disintegrating – 'it seems to me that they ought to be pardoned and rewarded in order to encourage others to surrender'.[80]

In April 1864 yet another Taiping general, Teng Kuang-ming, switched sides and along with his 4,000 men became a valued adjunct to the Ever-Triumphant Army. 'He is a sly old fox', Prosper Giquel, a senior French officer, wrote in his diary, 'who surrendered in time to safeguard the three hundred thousand taels that he had earned in his position as a principal Taiping chief.' A native of Hunan, Teng Kuang-ming was pardoned without much fuss and placed 'in the position of rendering the services which have already earned him the rank of brigade general'.[81] As the year progressed, moreover, more and more deserters came in, including 'thoroughgoing rebels' with ten or more years with the Taipings.[82]

In the summer of 1864, as Nanking lay besieged, the T'ien Wang grew increasingly paranoid over the possibility that senior officers would betray him – as indeed a number attempted to do unsuccessfully.[83] The death by suicide of Hung Hsiu-ch'üan in June and the fall of Nanking the following month (accompanied by the massacre of its population) marked the end of the Taiping Kingdom. A further indication that religious zeal – whatever the true extent of its influence among the original God-worshippers in the early 1850s – had ceased to play a role in people's thoughts was the complete absence of any attempt to keep Taiping Christianity alive. Despite the survival of many former Taipings, the religion vanished without trace once it was no longer an official faith.[84]

Still, for those who hold the Taiping Rebellion to have had revolutionary potential in the military sphere, the period after the fall of the Taiping Kingdom, the years between the fall of Nanking in 1864 and the final suppression in the north in 1868 of the Nien Rebellion (a more traditional secret-society revolt going on since 1851), do not go unnoticed. For it was in these years, as in the early 1850s, that the Taipings were practising 'mobile warfare' of a kind that could be connected to Maoist guerrilla operations. Senior historians such as Lo Erh-kang and Hua Kang argued in the 1950s that Lai Wen-kuang, a Taiping commander who fled north after 1864, created a mobile and very effective guerrilla force after combining his troops with the Nien rebels.[85]

According to Lo, who developed this thesis to its full extent in his *Mobile Warfare of the New Taiping Kingdom* (1955), the Nien were converted to Taiping ways (titles, flags, ideology, etc.) and along with Taiping remnants reorganized into a highly motivated mounted guerrilla force that ran rings around imperial forces for four years. 'I was surprised to discover', Lo explained in the preface,

> how the new army led by the Taiping rebel Lai Wen-kuang had utilized a strategy of the weak defeating the strong, the inferior force subduing the superior in the course of its struggles against the Hsiang and Huai Armies headed by the traitor Tseng Ku-fan.[86]

Unfortunately, this interpretation, which even some other mainland historians apparently thought was going too far,[87] is not borne out by the facts. The Nien and Taipings had been in contact at various points in the mid-1850s, but co-operation had been sporadic and limited by ideological incompatibility. The Nien rebels, with their roots in traditional secret-society behaviour, had little time for Taiping moral strictures, and – in Taiping eyes at least – lacked discipline. Though the Nien over time adopted certain Taiping titles and ranks, they continued to do as they pleased. After the fall of Nanking it was the northern remnants of the Taipings who were absorbed by the Nien rather than the other way round (though Lai was acknowledged to be a great commander by all). If Taiping titles were still used, the religious ideology underlying the cause had been killed off in 1864. Moreover, the hit-and-run warfare of the Nien was really that of 'primitive rebels'[88] simply fighting as they knew how rather than a conscious, thought-out strategy that they adopted. In addition, having been driven from their original fixed bases and constantly pursued, these troops really had no choice but to keep moving. Despite some victories, the Nien–Taiping forces, under constant pressure, eventually split into two groups and were defeated in detail in the summer of 1868.[89]

At virtually no point, therefore, does the modern image of the Taiping Army, fostered by nationalist and ideological affinity, fully correspond to the historical record. The past, of course, always tends to be viewed through the prism of the present. Where the emotive subject of revolution or rebellion is concerned, however, the gap between subjective interpretation and objective reality often appears particularly wide. Lo Erh-kang, indeed, was at times so enthusiastic about the Taiping Revolution that he claimed its influence extended beyond China's frontiers. Thousands of miles to the west, Lo argued, news of the success of the Taiping Kingdom had helped spark the Indian Mutiny of 1857.[90]

7 Sepoys in the Indian Mutiny, 1857–9

Martyrs to *swaraj*?

'Advance, Heroes, for you have gained the victory!'
Recommended cry to sepoys, Awadh, July 1857[1]

'How much longer am I to pay the sepoys for doing nothing?'
Begam of Awadh, December 1857[2]

Though the phrase 'Indian Mutiny' is often frowned upon on the subcontinent these days (it is thought to be morally and descriptively misleading), the dramatic events with which it is associated most emphatically are not. Rather, the great wave of military and civil disturbances in 1857–8, which for a time swept away the British *Raj* from large sections of northern India, are widely celebrated as a First War of Independence.

The reasons for this are easy to understand. Just as nationalists in China sought to appropriate the Taiping Rebellion for the anti-imperialist cause, so twentieth-century Indian nationalists under British rule drew inspiration from the events of 1857–8 when tens of thousands of native troops and countless civilians rose up in rebellion.

Based largely on a selective reading of English memoirs, edited collections, and the works of nineteenth-century British historians such as Malleson and Kaye (the rebels themselves having left little in the way of a written record), patriotic Indian writers, both before and since independence, have constructed a view of the mutiny which has more than met Indian needs for a usable past.[3] The revolt of 1857, rather than being a mindless, reactionary, and xenophobic spasm directed against enlightened British rule – the popular nineteenth-century British view – was in fact a conscious and planned revolutionary war of liberation fought with great skill and heroism against a cruel and bloodthirsty English foe.

The basic pattern was set forth fifty years after the end of the mutiny with the publication of *The Indian War of Independence of 1857* by the poet and militant nationalist agitator V. D. Savarkar. This book soon became an immensely influential underground classic after being banned in British India as subversive literature.[4] Later Indian writers, particularly the more thoughtful professional historians in the post-independence decades, tended to try and distance themselves from some of Savarkar's more obvious factual errors and flights of imaginative fancy, but many of the basic assumptions underlying this highly popular polemic – which in the meantime appeared in several languages and was published in India as soon as the British left in 1947[5] – were upheld in their own works.[6]

The efforts of the Indian government to celebrate the centenary of the mutiny only added to the weight of what had become by the early 1960s the orthodox Indian view of the mutiny as a war of independence, with new commemorative monuments being added to the new histories in order to counter those left by the British.[7] As the state itself has begun to fracture under the pressures of sectarian and other animosities in the decades since the 1970s, most of the contending parties have incorporated the mutiny into their own heroic tradition.[8]

Some historians, to be sure, notably S. N. Sen, maintained a high degree of detachment in researching and writing about the mutiny, and R. C. Majumdar was openly sceptical of the romantic nationalist aura that was being built up around the rebellion and its leaders. The one or two critical voices, however, have largely been drowned out by the nationalist chorus – who have not only attacked their scholarship but have also called into question their patriotism.[9] Whether on a national, regional, or ethnic basis, the war of 1857 clearly remains for many 'one of the most memorable and inspiring episodes in the history of Indian people'.[10]

Moreover, beneath the influence of the written word on educated opinion in India, a folkloric oral tradition celebrating the semi-mythical exploits of famous rebel leaders, such as the Rani of Jhansi, continues to thrive. Aided by the popular biographical pictures made by the Indian film industry, oral tradition reinforces among rural Indians a view of the mutiny as 'a glorious war fought by passionate heroic patriots'.[11]

Heroism, self-sacrifice, and valour are central to the popular image of the mutiny in India, an image which often assumes among other things the existence of a sophisticated plot to overthrow the British extending into sepoy ranks, a unified and co-ordinated rebel command structure, and a proto-nationalist determination amongst ordinary Indians to throw off the shackles of alien rule and regain cultural and political autonomy.[12] Countless unknown patriots as well as famous heroes were engaged in a desperate battle for liberty against a well-trained, well-armed, and blood-thirsty foe.

Almost invariably campaigns by the 'revolutionaries' or 'nationalist forces' against the British and their native allies are described in terms of 'fierce battles', 'severe engagements', and 'tough fights'.[13] Rebel victories such as the battle of Chinhat (30 June 1857) and the deaths of prominent British officers are celebrated at length, and great stress laid upon how 'fearful' the British authorities became in the face of rebel actions.[14] Rebel defeats, conversely, are glossed over or minimized through reference to heroic acts of resistance in the face of overwhelming odds.[15]

Fighting in freedom's cause inspired great deeds within rebel ranks – not least among the 100,000 or so infantrymen (sepoys), cavalrymen (sowars), and artillerymen from the mutineer regiments, the ultimate key to success or failure. 'The sepoys were undoubtedly the mainstay of the rebellion', as nationalist agitator Asoka Mehta put it.

> They bore the brunt of the struggle to break the coils that imprison India. They prevented the wave of wrath against the Government from dispersing into a spray of futile gestures. They gave backbone to the resistance, became its shield and spear.[16]

The sepoys, playwright Uptal Dutt made clear in a 1973 play on the Mutiny revived in the mid-1980s, were 'warriors for freedom'.[17] The native regiments had been trained and equipped along European lines, and could thus in theory match the skills of similarly trained and equipped British units deployed against them. As V. D. Savarkar had been the first to explain rhapsodically, 'the glorious ideal of Swaraj had filled the sepoys with a new inspiration and a new courage which discounted all odds'.[18]

Moreover, when the tide of battle eventually turned against the rebellion in early 1858, heroes such as Tatya Tope, Kunwar Singh, and Khan Bahadur Khan and their troops engaged in a highly successful guerrilla war against the British which lasted into 1859. Only through death or treachery were these guerrilla fighters eventually neutralized.[19]

Yet when all was said and done, as even the most enthusiastic nationalist writer has had to admit, the rebellion failed – and failed in spite of an initial advantage over the British in terms of trained troops in northern India of about seven to one.[20] Given the emphasis placed on the moral strength and unity of the revolutionary forces, some face-saving explanations were clearly in order.

One of the most common nationalist excuses for defeat concerned the timing of the rebellion. Supposedly a general rising had been planned for 31 May 1857. On that day a co-ordinated, simultaneous series of revolts would free all strategic points and overwhelm the British. However, the 'premature' mutiny on 10 May at Meerut – native soldiers driven beyond the point of endurance by British efforts to punish them for their beliefs – threw this carefully laid plan into turmoil. The British now had more time to react as stations rose up one after another through the summer rather than all at once. The throwing off of the timetable of revolt, therefore, was partially responsible for later failures.[21]

Another key factor was the extent to which the British were helped by 'traitors' to the cause of freedom. The Gurkhas and the Sikhs to the northwest, as well as various Indian princes further south, opportunistically declared themselves loyal to the British and actively fought against their Indian brethren. 'The defeat was chiefly due to the treachery of those men who had not sense enough to understand [the alien threat]', Savarkar observed, 'and of those who had not the honesty or patriotism to refuse to give help to the foreigner against their own countrymen.'[22]

An additional explanation for defeat concerned British superiority in weapons and equipment. Especially once British Army reinforcements from overseas began to arrive, rebel superiority in numbers was more than offset by British technological advantages. As well as possessing the telegraph, which eased communications problems, the British had an ace up their sleeve in the form of the Enfield rifle – a weapon considerably more accurate and with a much greater range than the Brown Bess muskets still used by the sepoys (not to mention the more primitive matchlocks of rebel irregulars). 'If they [the rebels] had better arms', as Mehta reflected in his history of the mutiny, 'the Rebellion would perhaps have ended differently.'[23]

Yet as even many nationalists conceded, these hindrances were not sufficiently powerful to explain fully how swiftly incipient victory turned into utter defeat for the rebels. Savarkar himself had to admit that there were problems with rebel military leadership and organization. Expecting a swift *coup d'état* rather than a series of campaigns, the revolutionary leadership lacked enough seasoned generals and administrators successfully to direct the revolutionary energies of the sepoys and people through a prolonged war.[24] This factor, though, tends not to be dwelt on at any length, and is implicitly minimized through the lavish attention devoted to the heroic efforts the rebel leaders made to correct structural weaknesses and lead by example in their territory.[25]

Defeat, therefore, did not to any significant extent undermine the popular image of self-sacrificing leaders and followers standing firm in defence of Indian independence. There is reason to believe, however, that the natural desire among Indian nationalists to view the events of 1857–9 in the best possible light has created a somewhat mythical image of the revolt in general and the fighting in particular.

Many of the popular Victorian and Edwardian explanations for the rebel defeat, full of *Boys' Own* patriotism and social Darwinist assumptions – a few brave and gallant Englishmen overcoming hordes of shiftless and faithless natives – against which Indian nationalists such as Savarkar were reacting, needed to be challenged and now appear embarrassingly xenophobic.[26] Yet a close examination of the events of 1857–9, unencumbered by nationalist sentiment (either British or Indian), suggests that the Indian view of the 'War of Independence' is possibly as overdrawn as that of the 'Deeds that won the Empire' school of Victorian England.

A survey of the scenes of major action in the period when the outcome was still in doubt – around Delhi and the Kanpur–Lucknow axis between the summer of 1857 and the spring of 1858 – illustrates the full extent of rebel military failure, and thereby calls into question some of the nationalist assumptions concerning rebel combat motivation (as well as the reasons posited for ultimate defeat).

As everyone realized at the time, Delhi, as the ancient Moghul capital, possessed immense psychological significance. It was the natural rallying point for the rebellious sepoys, and its recapture was consequently among the highest priorities of the beleaguered British. Hence as rebel units made their way to the ancient seat of the Moghuls in the summer of 1857, so too did the Delhi Field Force, composed of whatever British and loyal native units could be scraped together and hastily dispatched from Simla and points further afield to retake what had been lost.

In theory the defenders of Delhi ought to have been able to deal quite easily with the troops sent against them. Indeed, the tiny Field Force sent down from Simla to retake Delhi might well have been defeated before it even arrived. Rebel attempts to block the advance of the Field Force towards Delhi, however, badly miscarried.

On 30 May 1857, the Field Force advance guard of 700 men met and routed an approaching force of over 4,000 sepoys at the Hinden river, capturing five guns in the process. Nine days later the performance was repeated at the battle of Badli-ki-Serai, where a frontal attack by less than 2,500 infantry, supported on the flanks by cavalry but with only light artillery support, drove off a 3,000-man rebel force holding a strong defensive position with lots of cannon.[27]

In early June 1857, when the Field Force established itself on a ridge opposite Delhi, it numbered under 3,000 men as against well over 4,000 trained sepoys inside the city.[28] The arrival of new batches of mutineers, moreover, consistently outstripped efforts to reinforce the Field Force through the summer.[29] The *de jure* besiegers, indeed, were often the *de facto* besieged, never able to invest the city and spending much of their time fighting off rebel attempts to destroy them. By the time the British finally launched an assault on the city, the Field Force could still only deploy 8,748 effectives (over 5,000 of whom were from loyal native units) as against 16,000 mutineers.[30] Efforts to dislodge the British from the ridge, however, always ended in failure, as did the few attempts at cutting British communications.

In August, for example, a strong rebel force (two infantry brigades accompanied by eighteen guns) sent out from Delhi to prevent the arrival of the British siege train, was attacked by a column under Brigadier John Nicholson of just over 2,000 cavalry and infantry, also with eighteen guns, dispatched from the Field Force to intercept it. Despite holding strong defensive ground, the rebel force was routed at Nujufghur on the 25th.[31] This marked the last major rebel attempt to foil a general assault on Delhi, successfully undertaken by the British in September 1857. Clearly, rebel numerical strength had been cancelled out by significant weaknesses in other areas.

The same was true of the extended campaign for Lucknow and Kanpur. Both when attacking the small British enclaves hastily established in each city as the mutiny spread in late May and early June 1857 – the Lucknow Residency and Wheeler's entrenchment at Kanpur – and when attempting to foil British efforts to recapture these strategically important cities, rebel military efforts were almost invariably defeated.

In Lucknow over 6,000 trained native troops, plus thousands of volunteers, supplied with ample artillery and enjoying cover from nearby build-ings, were positioned to attack 1,700 soldiers and civilians under Sir Henry Lawrence trapped inside an improvised perimeter around the Residency in June.[32] At Kanpur the odds appeared even more in favour of the rebels. In order to allay sepoy suspicions of mistrust, Major-General Sir Hugh Wheeler had constructed only a rather flimsy earthen entrenchment near the native lines as a place of temporary refuge for Europeans if the troops rose. Contrary to expectations, when the garrison mutinied on 4 May it remained in Kanpur rather than marching on Delhi and invested the entrenchment. Thus 400 British infantry, protected only by a mud wall and low on supplies, faced a siege by 3,000 well-provisioned and armed mutineers and other rebel troops.[33]

Yet despite the odds, and the immense hardships suffered by the besieged, both enclaves were able to beat off repeated rebel assaults (as were other small defending forces at later points).[34] Wheeler held out for twenty days, only surrendering – the entrenchment battered but still intact – in the hope of saving civilian lives when it was clear that supplies of water, food, and ammunition were going to run out before relief arrived. The Residency at Lucknow, reinforced by troops brought in under General Sir Henry Havelock in September 1857, withstood a prolonged siege until an army under Sir Colin Campbell arrived at Lucknow in November and evacuated the place.[35]

Rebel failures, however, were by no means confined to an inability to assault British enclaves successfully. As in the struggle for Delhi, attempts at engaging in open battle undertaken by rebel armies against British field forces along the Lucknow–Kanpur axis almost always met with defeat and often complete disaster.

Attempts to hinder the movement of the relief force under Sir Henry Havelock advancing from Allahabad towards Kanpur and Lucknow were uniformly unsuccessful. At the battle of Fatehpur on 12 July 1857, a surprise attack by well over 3,000 rebel soldiers accompanied by twelve cannon was met and overcome by a force of only 1,000 infantry, six guns, and a few cavalry.[36] The battle that decided the immediate fate of Kanpur occurred 7 miles (11 kilometres) outside the city where Nana Sahib had arrayed a mixture of sepoys and local levies (5,000 men in all), along with some formidable artillery pieces, in a very strong defensive position astride the Grand Trunk Road and anchored by walled villages. Despite geographical and numerical advantages (the relief force still numbering just over 1,300 men), on 16 July 1857 the rebels' left flank was turned and the Nana's army put to flight.[37] Continuing his initial advances towards Lucknow, Havelock and his small army met and continued to defeat rebel blocking forces. Only the attritional effects of exhaustion, cholera, and incremental battle losses eventually left Havelock with no alternative but to return to Kanpur with under a thousand fit men.[38]

When the British advance on Lucknow was renewed in September 1857 with 3,179 men, and a major rebel force (over 11,000 sepoys and levies) attempted to halt the advance on 23 September at the Alambagh, the walled pleasure garden of the kings of Awadh, it was soon in full retreat.[39] The rebels were given another chance, however, when substantial losses in the fight in Lucknow itself caused Havelock's weakened forces to become a reinforcement to, rather than a relief for, the Residency. Yet despite the building of some good entrenchments reinforcing the defensive strength of walled buildings on the outskirts of the city, when a second relief force of 3,400 men under Campbell arrived from Kanpur in November 1857 it successfully fought its way to the Residency and evacuated the garrison (despite being outnumbered twenty to one).[40]

Tatya Tope, meanwhile, had moved back into Kanpur while Campbell was occupied at Lucknow accompanied by a 20,000-man rebel army which included the British-trained Gwalior Contingent, but once again, when Campbell's army closed with Tatya Tope's army outside the city on 6 December 1857, the result was decidedly unfavourable to the rebels despite some desperate resistance. Well directed by Campbell, the British force of 8,000 men defeated a rebel army of 25,000 deployed in a strong defensive position.[41] Lucknow was still in rebel hands, but in March 1858 Campbell, now commanding an army of over 20,000 men, engaged in a step-by-step assault on the city. The rebel defenders, numbering over 100,000 in all (including almost 30,000 mutineers), were well entrenched and well supplied with artillery – yet were unable to hold Lucknow against Campbell's attack, suffering over 3,000 casualties as against British losses of 127 killed and 595 wounded.[42]

There were, of course, as nationalist historians point out, some British defeats. When Henry Lawrence on 30 June 1857 sent out a force from Lucknow of 470 infantry and 120 cavalry with ten guns towards Chinhat, expecting to meet and disperse only a small enemy force but instead blundering into 5,500 rebel infantry and 800 cavalry, the British were quickly forced into headlong retreat back to the Residency.[43] The same fate befell a column of over 1,000 men under Major-General C. A. Windham near Kanpur on 24 November 1857 when he tried a similar pre-emptive thrust against what turned out to be the main rebel force under Tatya Tope (20,000 men) rather than just an advance party.[44]

Yet what is striking is not that the British suffered occasional reverses, but that they did not suffer them more frequently and at greater cost. Hastily built on an *ad hoc* basis from whatever troops were on hand or could be sent later – European units of varying form raised in India, regular and irregular native infantry and cavalry regiments, as well as Queen's troops – the Delhi Field Force and the columns operating along the Kanpur–Lucknow axis rarely performed according to plan when all but the most straightforward operations were attempted. British commanders, with the exception of Campbell and one or two others, were brave but indifferent generals commanding poorly integrated units. In terms of the running of unnecessary risks and failure to follow up successes, the British effort in the Indian Mutiny can be compared with the notoriously inept campaigns of the Crimean War fought only a few years before.[45]

The pattern, therefore, in spite of staff blunders, was for inferior numbers of British and loyal native troops to take the initiative against, and defeat in battle, superior numbers of mutineer sepoys and other rebel troops. This was as true of the lesser actions as it was of the main campaigns in 1857–8.

Why, then, especially given the numerical odds, was the rebel battlefield performance so disappointing? In light of the repeated stress on nationalism (*swaraj*) uniting and inspiring the revolution, and the soft pedalling of military failure – 'severe engagements' and 'terrific battles' are among the common terms used to describe lost battles while ingenious attempts are made to explain tactical defeats as strategic victories[46] – are the explanations for failure put forth by the more zealously patriotic Indian historians sufficient?

There is, to be sure, some merit to the nationalist interpretation of defeat. There is absolutely no question that the passive or active assistance of loyal princes and native soldiers was crucial to British survival in 1857. If the recently conquered Punjab had risen in revolt, or elements of the Bengal Army as well as the entire Madras and Bombay armies – 187,000 men combined – had not remained loyal to their officers (or at least quiescent), thoughtful British observers admitted that the game would soon have been up.[47] There remains, however, a tendency among nationalists to overstate or distort some of the other factors mentioned, and as we shall see there are serious problems with the central assumption that a well-planned rising went unexpectedly awry.

The Enfield rifle, certainly, had definite advantages over the Brown Bess musket and other less advanced shoulder arms. Nationalist historians, however, tend not to point out that the number of British troops armed with the Enfield was quite small, and that there were problems with the new weapon. Only about one-tenth of Havelock's force, for example, used the Enfield in battle, the rest using the Brown Bess. Those with Enfields, moreover, found that the ammunition for the rifle 'used very often to "jam" in a dreadful and disappointing manner'.[48]

Moreover, the damage done by the Enfield – and by other British weapons the sepoys had not previously encountered (certainly at the receiving end) such as rockets and exploding shells – was as much psychological as physical. After the rebel defeat at the battle of Fatehpur, for example, General Havelock wrote that '[t]he rifle fire, reaching them at an unexpected distance, filled them with dismay'.[49] A sepoy spy, reporting on the fighting at Lucknow on 6 November, commented to a British intelligence officer that 'the musket balls of the Europeans reach the rebel entrenchment and kill people', while 'the rebels' matchlock balls do no harm to the Europeans'. As a result, 'all [in the rebel lines] were frightened'.[50] Whooshing rockets and deafening explosive shot – 'those great iron fire balls' – also appear to have significantly undermined enemy morale during the final British assault on Lucknow.[51] This is not the stuff of heroic legend, and suggests that rebel faith in the cause was not quite the stiffening factor often supposed.

There are also problems with the nationalist presentation of the idea that the rebels lost in part because they lacked experienced leaders. The difficulty here is one of emphasis. General allusions are indeed made to problems of inexperience and administrative confusion in military affairs, yet the supposed achievements of rebel heroes – Nana Sahib, Tatya Tope, the Rani of Jhansi, Kunwar Singh, and others – are praised at much greater length. This tends to downplay the significance of poor generalship.[52]

In point of fact the majority of rebel military leaders were quite ignorant of the task they faced, possessed little or no strategic vision, and could almost never co-ordinate their actions until it was too late. Once British rule had been overthrown in a particular region, the greater and lesser chiefs often appear to have believed that the British *Raj* was gone for good and that attention could now be devoted to restoring real or imagined dynastic glories – Mughal, Maratha, Rajput, etc.

The dispossessed prince Nana Sahib, for instance, after taking nominal command of the rebellion in Kanpur in June 1857 and declaring himself Peshwa, fully indulged his taste for ceremonial pomp and issued proclamations claiming – among other things – that France and Russia were at war with Britain and that a British relief expedition had already been completely destroyed in Egypt by the Sultan. In fact, Havelock was already well on the road to Kanpur.[53]

In Delhi, meanwhile, Bahadur Shah, the pensioned-off heir to the throne of the Mughal Empire, hailed as Emperor of Hindustan by the rebel sepoys, had handed over command of the rebel garrison first to his incompetent and avaricious sons, and then to Bakht Khan – a native battery commander who, while possessing greater organizational skills than his predecessors, cared much about pomp and appearances and pestered Bahadur Shah for a royal title while delaying action against the British.[54] As for the Emperor himself, a court proclamation was issued in his name in August in which it was claimed that the British (despite having been on the ridge opposite the city for three months) were already defeated – the astrological signs were apparently good and a British army was said to have been crushed by the Afghans.[55]

Other regional warlords made equally naïve and spurious claims – which they often appear to have believed themselves to judge by their complacent inertia – concerning enemy fortunes. In Bareilly, for instance, another pensioner, Khan Bahadur Khan, assuming the title of Nawab Nazim of Rohilkhand, put the situation thus in a proclamation dated 29 March 1858: 'the [mutinous] soldiery ... began killing the English [in 1857], and slew them wherever they were found, and are now considering means for slaying the few still alive here and there'.[56] Bareilly had been free of British rule for many months, leaving Khan Bahadur to play out the role of local ruler (with debatable results[57]), but this hiatus was due to the fact that subjugating Awadh was a higher political priority for the British than reconquering Rohilkhand. At the very point Khan Bahadur Khan was claiming that only mopping-up operations remained to be undertaken against the infidels, four British columns were about to converge on Bareilly.[58]

Common misapprehensions, moreover, were not accompanied by united action. Their strategic vision circumscribed by the boundaries of their fief-doms, the major figures thrown into prominence by the revolt did not co-operate beyond a few purely rhetorical claims of allegiance to the Mughal Emperor. At no point, for instance, did Nana Sahib consider taking his forces (including four regiments of sepoys) to raise the siege of Delhi, seat of his supposed overlord Bahadur Shah.[59]

Even when forced to abandon their passive attitudes and flee from their capitals, leading rebel figures still found it difficult to co-operate actively and think ahead. In late March 1858, for example, a British expeditionary force of 2,000-odd men under Sir Hugh Rose found itself in great peril while attempting to lay siege to the fortress of Jhansi. Rose was menaced by the approach of a 20,000-man rebel army under Tatya Tope, and risked annihilation when he split his force to watch Jhansi and at the same time attack Tatya Tope on 1 April. The rebels were utterly defeated, whereas they would almost certainly have won if the 10,000-man rebel garrison of Jhansi had taken the opportunity to sally forth and attack a force that was only one-tenth its size.[60]

One of the few successful instances of concerted strategic action, when the shattered forces of Rao Sahib and the Rani of Jhansi linked up with Tatya Tope and captured Gwalior on 1 June 1858, was immediately followed by failure. The usual false sense of security immediately took hold of the rebel leaders once in Gwalior, who – with the possible exception of the Rani – devoted their time to pomp and celebration until British expeditionary columns were within a few miles of the city two weeks later. No thought had been given, or preparations made, to meet the inevitable British counter-thrust, and last-minute efforts to defend or flee from Gwalior met with disaster.[61]

Rebel leaders, in short, even those who occasionally displayed flashes of strategic insight such as Tatya Tope, were often quite myopic both in thought and action, especially in light of their supposed role in the formulation of a pan-Indian, nation-wide plot. Even if the mutiny had not begun as planned, the poor military performance of rebel leaders goes beyond being taken partially by surprise or lack of experience. For the most part their actions – or lack thereof – suggest a psychological attitude to unfolding events at odds with the conventional nationalist view.

Before exploring this issue further, however, or concluding – as do Indian Marxists – that it was such 'feudal elements' who were to blame for defeat,[62] it is worth stressing that the mutineers themselves bear a good deal of responsibility. For, despite the nationalist image of hard-fighting commitment and selflessness, sepoy behaviour was far from being a shining example of altruistic dedication to corporate action on behalf of ordinary Indians. Plundering the property of civilians and quarrelling with their leaders (and each other) characterized mutineer actions off the battlefield, while when faced with an actual fight the sepoys were rarely able to stand and fight successfully either in the open or in strongly fortified positions against smaller British forces. Again, a survey of events at Delhi, Kanpur, and Lucknow is instructive.

Delhi, seat of the great Moghul emperors, was a natural focus of rebel allegiance. Tens of thousands of mutinous sepoys – beginning with the first two mutinous regiments from Meerut on 11–12 May – made their way to Delhi in the spring and summer of 1857 to place themselves as 'complainants seeking justice' under the protection and direction of Bahadur Shah, their Emperor.[63] Yet it quickly became apparent that the sepoys seemed to care very little about either justice or hierarchy.

Extortion and plunder became a way of life for the sepoys in Delhi under the pretext that – despite having often already enriched themselves from the treasuries and other buildings of the stations where they had mutinied – the soldiers were not being adequately paid or compensated.[64] Quarrels over the apportioning of loot between units were acrimonious in the extreme, as were debates over how much more rebel soldiers should receive than the (admittedly miserly) Rs 7–9, minus deductions, they had been paid in the Bengal Army.

A far from atypical entry from the diary of Mushi Ali Jeeluan Lal, a minor Delhi court official, dated 28 May 1857, illustrates the kind of bickering, confusion, and general lack of order such attitudes and actions produced:

> deductions were ordered [by the Court] to be made on account of the sums already paid to [the soldiers]; nine [rupees] for the sowars and seven for the infantry were fixed. A great uproar ensued. The cavalry demanded Rs. 30 for their pay, and no deduction for charges paid. The subhadars [native officers] of the Delhi Regiment accepted Rs. 7 as their pay. A violent, abusive altercation followed between the Meerut cavalry and the mutineers of the Delhi regiments. The Meerut sowars accused the Delhi regiments of having enriched themselves by plunder. . . . The foot sepoys replied that the Meerut men were rebellious and utterly bad. . . . Fierce passions were so raised, that at one time there was every probability of a serious encounter.[65]

Declaring with a mixture of rage and despair that 'it was no use giving orders, as they were never obeyed, and he had no one to enforce them', the old King of Delhi became an object of familiarity and scorn rather than veneration among soldiers eager to extract concessions in return for service.[66]

Naturally enough, such conditional service did not lend itself to unity, good order, and unqualified determination in the face of the enemy. 'They only acquire numbers', as a British officer reflected in his diary on 15 June after reading spies' reports on the goings-on in Delhi,

> and there is jealousy between the old and the new mutineers; the former are gorged with plunder, and think they have done enough, and wish to leave the hard work to the new arrivals, but have no inclination to give them a share of the spoils.[67]

New arrivals over the summer were indeed forced to attack the British on the ridge as a rite of passage before being allowed into Delhi, but rarely struck with sufficient strength, vigour, or clearness of purpose to threaten the enemy position seriously. 'They get beaten in detail', as one puzzled British officer recorded in his diary, 'and apparently fight without any defined object.'[68] Such skirmishes almost became a ritual for both sides. 'There were daily accessions to the ranks of the rebels', a native resident of Delhi later recalled, 'and daily attacks on the English position; daily the rebels were driven back until this became the recognized rule.'[69]

As the Bahadur Shah constantly lamented, planned expeditions against the British in greater strength with a definite object in mind – forcing the British to withdraw from in front of Delhi – were rarely undertaken, and when they were, after a good deal of argument and squabbling, plans always seemed to miscarry. 'Their characteristic is to do the wrong thing at the wrong time', as one British observer reflected.[70]

Poor command arrangements were part of the problem, but so too was rebel behaviour under fire. There were certainly many instances recorded by British observers of individual mutineers and even entire formations behaving with exemplary coolness and heroism.[71] Some of the skirmishes and full-scale battles in the Delhi campaign, indeed, involved very bitter fighting by all concerned. Yet there were also instances where rebel officers were unable to drive their men to attack,[72] and even in the most hard-fought engagements the sepoys always broke and retreated back into Delhi amidst mutual recrimination between different contingents and the jeers of the city population.[73]

Sustained British rifle and artillery fire was certainly disheartening, but what often appeared to precipitate complete collapse – pell-mell flight back to the safety of Delhi – was a British bayonet charge. At the first encounter between rebel and British forces at the Hinden river, for instance, artillery fire followed by a direct assault of a battalion of the 60th Rifles caused the rebels to abandon their cannon and flee back to Delhi in disorder. 'Inquiries were made about the behaviour of the Sepoys', Lal noted in his diary. 'It was admitted that as soon as the rebels received a volley from the English, they lost heart, and began to return to the city.'[74]

Similarly, at the battle of Nujufghur, the defensively deployed mutineer column sent out to try and intercept the British siege train was charged by an infantry force with fixed bayonets supported by artillery. 'Only a few of the rebels fought with any pluck', one participant noted.[75] According to a more senior officer, the enemy simply 'fled in panic stricken confusion', having lost thirteen guns and 800 men as against 100 British casualties.[76]

By the time of the storming of Delhi in September 1857, when despite being swept from the wall at the point of the bayonet the rebels still had an opportunity to defeat the British attacking columns in house-to-house fighting, sepoy morale was not up to the task. After the initially quite bitter resistance within the city streets which lasted several hours on 14 September, the remaining rebels slipped away where they could.[77] The Delhi fighting did not, in short, really match Savarkar's claim that the 'brave sepoys', heroes all, fought 'a splendid fight', a prolonged campaign 'befitting a high and noble principle!'[78]

The Kanpur–Lucknow campaigns were little different in terms of sepoy behaviour. As at Delhi, bickering, looting, extortion, and (at best) variable levels of determination and endurance in battle were characteristic.

In Kanpur, the regiments which mutinied immediately set to plundering the treasury and engaging in arson (as was always the case at stations where the troops rose). But instead of marching on Delhi, thereby bringing anarchy to a close in the immediate vicinity, the Kanpur sepoys stayed to deal with Wheeler's *ad hoc* entrenchment and the few hundred civilian and military personnel taking shelter there. In consequence, plunder and extortion of the native civilian population went on.[79] There were also quarrels between units over the sharing of the loot.[80] Nana Sahib, who complained that the sepoys would not obey his orders, sought to win the loyalty of his new army by promising massive pay increases. A newly elected colonel, for example, was to receive over 100 times his former pay and allowances.[81] 'Let your minds be at rest', he uneasily assured mutineer officers in early July 1857, 'all promises made will be fulfilled.'[82]

Meanwhile, as the sepoys enriched themselves, rather desultory efforts were made to deal with Wheeler's entrenchment. Conditions for the trapped British were indescribably bad, but this was as much the result of poor preparation by Wheeler as enemy action. Heavy guns were brought up to bombard the entrenchment, but plans to launch an infantry assault were abandoned (apparently through fear that the British would blow themselves up and the sepoys with them if they were overrun). 'The rebels fired daily about 400 [artillery] rounds', a native observer noted, 'but did not dare make an attack.'[83] Wheeler, meanwhile, launched a sortie on 11 June which managed to spike one of the sepoys' heavy artillery pieces.[84] It is as indicative of the difficulty the sepoys were having in taking the entrenchment as it was of the awful physical conditions the women and children inside were enduring that Nana should offer, and Wheeler accept, liberal surrender terms on 26–27 June.[85]

Nor did the mutineers under Nana particularly distinguish themselves in the first battle of Kanpur outside the city against Havelock's advancing column on 16 July. Despite five-to-one odds in favour of the rebels, a strong defensive position, accurate artillery fire, and a good attempt at a rally, the steady advances by the 78th Highlanders and 64th Foot completely routed the rebel infantry (who appear in most cases to have fled at the prospect of crossing bayonets).[86] The sepoys, fleeing back to Kanpur, then vented their fear and frustration on the captive women and children who had survived the massacre of Wheeler's surrendered force at the Suti Chaura Ghat on 27 June (also possibly against orders).[87]

All in all it is difficult not to agree with the assessment arrived at by Lieutenant-Colonel G. Williams after investigating the circumstances of the massacres in late 1859:

> The Nana and his Court possessed little or no authority over the rebel troops who, it is evident, did just as they pleased – manned the attacking batteries and joined in the assaults [on the entrenchment] or not as they deemed fit – the greater portion taking their ease, lounging in the bazaars and on the banks of the canal, plundering the provisions as they were brought into the city. The distribution of the promised rewards and of pay occasioned much wrangling and bitter speeches against their nominal ruler, whom they even threatened to depose.[88]

The situation in Lucknow was, if anything, even more anarchic. After the victory at Chinhat the sepoys and other rebels ran wild, looting, burning, and killing almost at random for over a week. Then the usual squabbles over the apportioning of the spoils began.[89] The general lack of order was only exacerbated by in-fighting among contenders and members of an elected military council over who exactly should command the rebels in Awadh and its capital. Only in early August 1857 was the Begam Hazrat Mahal formally acknowledged as regent in the name of her 10-year-old son (heir-apparent to the throne of the King of Awadh deposed by the British). And even then the troops themselves, according to British spies, continued to boast 'of being the *Alpha* and *Omega* of the whole administration'.[90]

The Begam herself thought that sepoys' churlishness and arrogance meant in essence that she was 'under their orders' rather than the other way round. 'On the one side, I had the British as enemies', she gloomily recalled in early 1859 while trying to flee into Nepal, 'on the other, the troops made us as goats.'[91]

The deterioration in the military situation only made things worse in Lucknow. By the last months of 1857 intrigue, insubordination, and general lack of confidence were rife. Sepoys, their loot having all been spent, clamoured for better pay; different contingents came to blows with one another over who deserved and was responsible for what; orders from the Begam to attack the British were disobeyed; and morale in general sank lower and lower with news of rebel defeats at Delhi and elsewhere.[92] 'The whole army is in Lucknow, but it is without courage', the Begam fumed in front of her principal army chiefs. 'Why does it not attack . . . ? Is it waiting for the English to be reinforced, and Lucknow to be surrounded?'[93]

The Lucknow mutineers, though heavily reinforced by volunteer levies from the Awadh countryside, did not distinguish themselves particularly in battle. From the futile attempts to take the Residency to the last battle against Campbell, the rebel military effort was characterized by general lassitude occasionally punctuated by individual acts of great tenacity and bravery.

Though the constant rebel artillery bombardment of the Residency was quite effective, rebel infantry assaults were only launched periodically (the landowners from the countryside then often proving more courageous than the sepoys).[94] This was probably not a conceived strategy. One of the besieged inhabitants of the Residency noted in his diary on 14 July the typically abortive nature of some actions.

> A grand attack to-day all round, that is, the enemy is shouting *ad infinitum*, and sounding the advance at the bugler's discretion. Great guns and musketry are loaded and fired as fast as they can be, but that is all. Every hostile battery, every house, vomits forth fire in some shape or other, but not a man appears. Jack Sepoy evidently will not come to the scratch. He is no doubt of Falstaff's way of thinking, that discretion is the better part of valour.[95]

Those attacks which *were* pressed home were admittedly worrisome. Of the grand assault on the Residency on 20 July, for instance, the same diarist noted that the rebels 'displayed in the attempt more courage than we had given them credit for', while Private Henry Metcalfe remembered that they came on 'like so many demons in human forms'.[96] Mounting losses, however, combined with disappointment that predictions of imminent British collapse were untrue, led to such attacks dwindling in number.[97]

By the end of 1857 it was the Lucknow insurgents who were on the defensive, trying to thwart British efforts to retake the city. Despite entrenchments and other works which bolstered naturally strong walled enclosures, and a great rebel numerical edge, Campbell, choosing his approaches wisely, usually managed to flank the most dangerous positions. The actual fighting for Lucknow took on a pattern: the rebel forces fighting fiercely ('they fought like devils' as one Highland sergeant recalled of the first battle for Lucknow[98]) but then losing their cohesion and scattering where they could ('flying before us as fast as their legs could carry them'[99]) in the face of heavy artillery fire, rifle volleys, and – above all – fierce charges by British infantry. 'When we make an attack you must come to close quarters as quickly as possible', Campbell explained to the 93rd Highlanders. 'Keep well together and use the bayonet.'[100]

The main rebel armies, in short, did not perform well. But what of the assertion – especially attractive amidst a series of successful Third World wars of national liberation in the 1950s and 1960s – that by the latter stages of the revolt the remaining sepoys had become seasoned guerrilla fighters? Here again the reality proves rather more prosaic than the nationalist image.

It is certainly true that the British were sometimes inconvenienced when sepoys or other rebels, acting alone or in loose groups, engaged in harassing fire against exposed troops from within the safety of bamboo thickets and other cover which made it difficult for their opponents to root them out.[101] It is also true that it was often difficult to pin down the small forces accompanying Tatya Tope and other rebel leaders that avoided battle, kept on the move, and hid themselves in jungle or other hard-to-negotiate terrain in the latter part of 1858 and early 1859. Moreover, a general order from Khan Bahadur Khan was captured which might suggest that this was part of a conscious strategy. 'Do not attempt to meet the regular columns of the infidels', he advised,

> because they are superior to you in discipline and blunderbuss, and have big guns; but watch their movements, guard all the ghauts on the rivers, intercept their communications, stop their supplies, cut up their daks and posts, and keep constantly hanging about their camps; give them no rest.[102]

However, as one British participant in the mutiny put it, 'nothing came of it'.[103] Khan Bahadur Khan evidently decided not to take his own advice, being defeated by Campbell in a set-piece battle for control of Bareilly.[104] Groups of sepoys sniping from cover and keeping their distance in the battles for Delhi, Lucknow, and other places almost certainly did so on their own initiative as opportunity offered rather than because they were instructed to. Their actions were likely a natural reversion to a more individualistic 'primitive rebel' form of fighting as it became more and more difficult – for reasons to be discussed shortly – to adhere to regimented European formations and tactics.[105]

As for national heroes such as Tatya Tope, it must be remembered that while eluding capture for many months, they were always under pressure and on the run to avoid encounters with pursuing British columns. It was the British who held the initiative, not they and their followers. And this, naturally enough, had a bad effect on morale. Rebel bands, often lacking supplies and hope, showed less and less stomach for any fighting. Bitter recriminations, desertion, and a penchant to question authority were common.[106] 'In consequence of the different opinions of the troops', Tatya Tope wrote to Nana Sahib quite early in 1858, 'I shall be obliged first to try to make them all unanimous and then write to you what measures may be adopted.'[107]

In early 1859 Tatya Tope was finally caught, by then virtually in rags and accompanied only by a few loyal followers. His trial deposition makes it clear that to view his actions over the previous months as those of a guerrilla leader is grossly to romanticize a rather sordid outlaw existence. The latter parts are a sad litany of ongoing defeats, squabbles, and betrayals, as are the depositions of other captured rebel leaders.[108]

Rebel behaviour, then, either among the leaders or among the sepoys, did not in fact live up to the high standards of selfless heroism and sacrifice set by later generations of Indian nationalists. This was due in part to the fact that the basic premiss of the nationalist case is fundamentally unsound.

Hard evidence for a nationalist plot simply does not exist. Indeed, there is every reason to conclude, from the available documents and leaders' actions, that the representatives of the old regime such as Bahadur Shah and Nana Sahib who accepted princely titles thrust upon them by the sepoys did so out of a mixture of fear and opportunism rather than as part of a plan.[109] The senior rebels, unexpectedly taking on roles which they had not been prepared for, and for which – given the nature of the task – a traditional upbringing was a liability rather than an asset, naturally enough pursued traditional dynastic goals in the context of general ignorance concerning the true extent of British power. The resulting lack of strategic coherence has already been outlined. Yet if there was no planned national crusade, then what motivated the sepoys to revolt on so wide a scale – and why did it not prove a sufficient spur to better performance?

Muslim and Hindu sepoys, already holding grievances over low pay and poor promotion prospects, had become progressively more concerned that the British were undermining the orthodox social and cultural order in India. In particular, there was a gnawing worry that the East India Company was intent on spreading Christianity. Hence the instant credibility lent to the rumour that the British, in order to sever the sepoys' ties with their faith, had coated the paper cartridges for the new Enfield rifle with cow and pig grease (the cow sacred to Hindus, the pig unclean to Muslims).

Attempts to enforce regulations which were seen as sacrilegious had precipitated mutinies in the past, and it was the effort to punish soldiers for refusing to handle the new cartridges which sparked off the initial mutiny at Meerut in May 1857. Through luck as much as skill, serious insubordination over the cartridge issue had been contained earlier in the year at Berhampure and Barrackpore, and it was chance and poor leadership which created a situation in which the Meerut native soldiers were able to mutiny and then flee to Delhi. It was the winning over of the native garrison at Delhi, and the slow British response to this event, that in turn encouraged other units all across northern India to revolt.[110]

There was a good deal of spontaneity to it all, as the varying reactions of sepoys to the choice of breaking salt or risking damnation attest. A unit could swear its allegiance one day – and mean it – and the next be in open mutiny; some elements of a regiment could remain loyal while others joined the rebels; individual soldiers could help their officers escape before themselves joining their mutinous comrades; some sepoys came to regret their initial impulsiveness and wished that they had not been led astray, while others – though the reverse was made impossible by the British policy of executing known mutineers – thought better of their initial loyalty to the British and deserted to the rebel camp later on.[111]

Religious faith, of course, can be a powerful spur to action. 'If the religion of a Hindu or a Mussalman is lost', as a fugitive band of sepoys petitioning to enter Nepal in 1859 put it, 'what remains in the world?'[112] The battle cries heard most often among attacking sepoys and other rebel forces were *Deen! Deen!* and *Ja Allah!* (for the faith),[113] and even those British soldiers most contemptuous of the sepoys admitted that they did persevere in trying to best their foe in combat, and that there were those among them who stood their ground, 'loading and firing with the greatest delibera- tion'.[114] When cornered, moreover, sepoys could and did fight with savage determination, as in the hand-to-hand struggles for the fortified enclosures and buildings on the outskirts of Lucknow.[115]

And yet, as we have seen, the overall behaviour of the sepoys was less than impressive. As one loyal native officer recalled of the fighting after the relief of Kanpur,

> in no fight that I was in – and they were not a few – did I ever see the mutineers . . . ever make a good stand and fight. Usually they stood the first discharge and then took to flight – if they could not find shelter behind walls or trees.[116]

Indian nationalism as such was not present (or where it was in limited form – as in the recently annexed state of Awadh and its capital Lucknow where the people rallied around the *ancien régime* – still appears to have had little impact on discipline).[117] Common religious fears did not either produce responsible action behind the lines or ensure corporate unity (as opposed to individual acts of heroism) under battlefield stress. Even when mitigating circumstances are taken into account, the sheer number of sepoy mutineers – armed and trained along European lines to behave in a highly disciplined manner both on and off the battlefield – ought to have made a better showing than they did. What, then, was the problem?

In a sense, rebel motivation became irrelevant. Whether inspired by reli- gion, loyalty to the old order, or fear of retribution, sepoys could not adequately deal with the individual freedom they now possessed. Like all armies, the Bengal Army had operated through a clearly defined command structure backed up by the threat of coercion (punishment for those who did not perform according to regulations in and out of battle). When they mutinied, the sepoys cut themselves loose not only from British authority but also from the structures that had made them effective as soldiers.

Initially mutineer units appear to have maintained at least the outward appearance of discipline. Despite the absence of British officers, regiments marched in step, accompanied by regimental colours and bands playing traditional British airs.[118] 'When we first came [to Delhi] all was quiet', a former trooper recalled of the arrival of the 3rd Light Cavalry from Meerut, 'and the regiment did exactly as if they were in cantonments.'[119]

Moreover, after some days sepoys started to elect from among themselves new commanders to replace their British officers. These men, however, propelled directly from very junior non-commissioned ranks to the giddy heights of senior regimental or brigade command, lacked experience. Furthermore, as elected representatives they lacked coercive authority.

With the coercive element removed from their lives, sepoys could and did begin to question authority, dispute orders, make demands, and as we have seen allow their baser instincts to rule their actions. Religious concerns had been enough to generate revolt, but they were not enough to maintain disciplined cohesion. As Bruce Watson has observed, 'the very act of mutiny dislodged the traditional roles and organizational framework that had brought them into being and sustained them'.[120]

This absence was particularly critical in battle. Despite the ability (born of long practice) to deploy in line and deliver volley fire, the rebel sepoys could not manœuvre in as co-ordinated a manner as their foes and could not stand their ground when faced with heavy fire and/or direct assaults by British troops. Individual courage or belief in the cause had little to do with this; what mattered was that the sepoys no longer possessed some of the crucial elements – experienced officers and regulations backed by coercive threats – which had bound them together in effective fighting units.[121] Regular defeat in battle only made the situation worse. As morale declined residual cohesiveness began to wear off, as mounting desertion, communal bickering, and the discarding of uniforms and other symbols of corporate identity attest.[122] The morale problem – and hence in part the cohesion problem – was made worse by the naïvety of the sepoys. Many, not unlike their leaders, appear to have believed after they rose up that the British were, *ipso facto*, beaten. Any British troops that the sepoys themselves had not encountered were thought to be merely mythical.[123] It therefore came as a pronounced shock, for example, when news of the approaching Field Force reached Delhi.[124] Attributing British success to 'magic' or enchantment, and attempting to ward off rifle bullets with charms and recitations, only made matters worse.[125]

The sepoys' corporate military identity, in short, gradually disintegrated. This meant that instead of serving as a professional stiffener to the large number of ill-armed and untrained native levies in some of the main rebel armies (at Lucknow and Kanpur, for instance), the sepoys over time simply became part of a vast, ill-organized, and poorly armed host that was even less able to confront the much more professional British Army.[126]

Indian nationalists, in trying to fit the mutiny into the mould of a modern war of independence, err on a number of counts. Neither the principal rebel leaders, nor the sepoys nominally under their control, saw themselves as nationalist freedom fighters: their world-view was essentially premodern, and their actions were determined by a mixture of chance, circumstance, and concerns that had more to do with dynastic hopes, religion, personal safety, and profit than with any Western-based notion of national unity. Furthermore, even if nationalism *had* been the principal motivating force behind a planned uprising, it would have ultimately made little difference in terms of sepoy performance. British troops still would have possessed the crucial advantage of corporate coherence in battle.

Powerful myths, of course, are remarkably resilient. Indeed, it is likely that the casting of the Indian Mutiny as the First War of Indian Independence – or regional variations on the same theme – will last as long as there is a contemporary need for this kind of past.

It is worth noting, though, that the mystique surrounding such 'revolutionary' armies in the twentieth century is not necessarily a purely national affair of varying political flavour. The following chapters seek to show how, at least up until the end of the Cold War and the supposed 'end of history' à la Fukiyama, transnational ideologies have also had a role to play.

8   The International Brigades in the Spanish Civil War, 1936–9

No pasaran?

> According to our theories, because the men of our side were inspired by a high ideal, we should be stronger than soldiers who were pure mercenaries.
>
> British volunteer on brigade strategy at battle of Jarama, January 1937[1]

> We were set up, goddam it. Lambs for the slaughter. No pasaran! They pasaranned all over us.
>
> American volunteer on battle of Belchite, August 1937[2]

Almost sixty years since the last shots were fired, the Spanish Civil War continues to hold a unique place among the wars of modern times. Both during the fighting and ever since, the Spanish Civil War has been portrayed by participants, observers, and even well-qualified historians in terms both partisan and passionate. The struggle between the armies of the Madrid government and the armies of Franco is very often presented as a battle between the forces of light and darkness, democracy versus Fascism. To the majority of committed intellectuals of the day, and many writers and historians since (excepting of course those in Franco's Spain[3]), the Spanish Civil War was a pre-eminently moral conflict. Though the loyalists were eventually defeated, support for the Republic – even posthumous support – meant or implied an identification with what (rather wistfully) became known as the Last Great Cause.[4]

As the decades have rolled by, to be sure, the ideological and moral lines drawn so confidently in the 1930s have become somewhat blurred and increasingly complex. Especially since the 1960s, it has become increasingly apparent that to view the conflict in terms of democracy versus Fascism is to oversimplify vastly. It is now widely recognized that the war in Spain was in many ways a uniquely Spanish historical event, and certainly far more politically and morally complex than a straightforward and unambiguous battle between democracy and Fascism. It has gradually become apparent to the more dispassionate observers that such value-laden ideological abstractions, derived from the interwar European experience beyond the Spanish frontier and artificially imposed on the Iberian peninsula, do not adequately represent the convoluted and largely unique reality of 1930s Spain.[5]

Even so, the Good Fight mentality remains quite prevalent,[6] and on one subject virtually sacrosanct. For while some aspects of the civil war experience have been open to revision and critical analysis, attitudes towards the volunteers who flocked to Spain to join the International Brigades continue to be fiercely partisan.[7]

The International Brigades, after all, represented a way in which the Spanish Civil War clearly appeared an idealistic and international struggle between good and evil. In all, 32,000 volunteers from fifty countries had served in the five international brigades (XI to XV), selflessly making their way to Spain to be part of the anti-Fascist cause.[8]

The heroic image of the International Brigades has remained remarkably consistent. What was written at the time by sympathetic observers, and subsequently recorded in memoirs and unit histories, has been perpetuated in much of the secondary literature. Four assumptions in particular, all interrelated, have been passed on virtually unaltered.

The first assumption is that the initial volunteers, the German and Italian political *émigrés*, the French, Belgian, and other European anti-Fascist elements of the XI and XII International Brigades, were crucial in saving Madrid from Franco's advancing columns in November 1936. During the war itself many accounts, written by pro-loyalist foreign journalists and observers, either implied or stated outright that without the timely arrival of these first two International Brigades – thereby boosting morale and shoring up crumbling defences – the capital might well have fallen.[9] Memoirs and histories (often by former brigaders themselves) published subsequently repeated this assertion, and it became an established fact in much of the secondary literature.[10]

The second assumption, also fostered by wartime reports and later memoirs, is that the International Brigades served both as a shield and as a model for the new People's Army being built by the Republic.[11] At Madrid the example of the men of the XI Brigade showed raw Spanish militiamen the virtues of using cover and conserving ammunition.[12] Then and in later battles the brigades – replete with picked volunteers who had combat experience or some form of military service which the Spanish lacked – shielded the new Spanish units and demonstrated the virtues of intensive training and disciplined commitment.[13] Only when the People's Army was fully operational were the volunteers withdrawn, their task completed.[14]

The third assumption concerns the training the brigaders received. Several contemporary brigade sources and later accounts often stress that even those volunteers without military experience received intensive tactical instruction in and around the brigades' base at Albacete, especially in the latter stages of the war.[15]

These sources do sometimes concede that the exigencies of the military situation meant that recruits often received only a minimum of training.[16] Yet in much of the literature the case is also made – again perpetuating opinion dating from the war – that anti-Fascist political conviction inspired the volunteers to unparalleled feats of endurance and bravery.[17] This is the fourth assumption.

Unlike conventional armies each battalion of the International Brigades had a commissar, part of whose job it was to explain to the men the military and political significance of the tasks before them. Thus even when enthusiasm might flag, the commissar would be there to put things in perspective and remind volunteers what they were fighting for. These commissars, according to memoir accounts and unit histories (in which the brigades are often compared with the forces of Cromwell and the soldiers of the American and French Revolutions[18]), often did their job superlatively well. Hence political education, along with the personal determination of the men themselves (all of whom had after all volunteered to fight the Good Fight), made up for limited training and equipment. John Gates, the last political commissar of the XV Brigade, succinctly summed up this view: 'it would be difficult to explain how poorly armed men could fight a much more powerful army for so long and so well, if it were not for their political convictions.'[19]

Whatever the conditions the International Brigades always fought on, suffering very high casualty rates in virtually every engagement but always stopping the enemy in his tracks. Whether it was fierce Moroccan mercenaries, foreign legionnaires, or Italian blackshirts that the internationals were facing, they always saved the day for the loyalist cause.[20]

Even what might appear at first glance to be costly disasters could be presented as having furthered the republican war effort. If the enemy was halted, then an 'at all costs' attack or 'hold to the last man' defence – however bloody – had been justified. In many sources, indeed, the higher the losses the greater the admiration for particular units in the brigades. Political commitment had found its ultimate expression.

On 13 November 1936, for example, in one of several bloody engagements around Madrid, elements of the XII International Brigade had assaulted Cerro de los Angeles, a hill on top of which stood a monastery occupied by the enemy, as part of a republican counter-offensive. The assault was very poorly co-ordinated, the brigaders were driven off, and losses among the men of the Garibaldi Battalion particularly severe. Yet this was hailed as a strategic victory amid tactical defeat, since – it was thought – it had diverted rebel troops from attacking elsewhere.[21]

In one day of the Madrid fighting in January 1937 holding actions and counter-attacks on the village of Las Rozas by the Thaelmann and Edgar André Battalions of the XI International Brigade (1,500 mostly German volunteers) produced horrendous casualties. The Thaelmann alone – which refused to retreat under fire – lost two entire companies to a man, and overall the brigade lost around 900 killed and wounded.[22] But since the enemy had stopped advancing in this sector, this was interpreted by Hans Kahle (the Edgar André Battalion commander) as a success: 'even though the battle has meant the sacrifice of our best men, the fascist drive has been stopped. . . . They didn't pass and they shall not pass.'[23] Accounts of the battle by other contemporary and later observers tend to mirror this admiration for heroic sacrifice.[24]

The battle of the Jarama in February 1937, in which the nationalists launched a surprise attack across the Jarama river in a bid to encircle Madrid, was an equally costly experience for the International Brigades. Caught off guard, elements of the André Marty Battalion (Frenchmen in the XI International Brigade) fought bravely but were surrounded by Moroccan cavalry and massacred to a man.[25] In the course of republican efforts to contain and roll back the nationalist tide, the new XV International Brigade was thrown into the fray in piecemeal holding actions and counter-attacks and suffered heavy losses. The British Battalion lost 275 of 400 men in its first day of action (2 February) defending a position that became known as 'suicide hill'.[26] An over-the-top counter-attack by 263 Americans of the new Abraham Lincoln Battalion on 27 February produced 113 casualties and had to be abandoned.[27] Casualties among the other battalions of the XI, XII, and XIV International Brigades engaged at Jarama were also high, often exceeding 50 per cent. In all, 5,550 of the 8,700 internationals involved were lost.[28]

Yet Jarama too was presented both then and later as a real (if tragic) victory. The enemy offensive had been contained, if not actually rolled back. 'Franco's assault', as the first official historian of the Lincoln Battalion explained,

> which had aimed to cut the vital Madrid–Valencia motor highway and thus isolate Madrid from the rest of Loyalist Spain, had been so decisively stopped that never again, until the day the Spanish war ended, were the enemy to advance a single pace on this vital sector.[29]

The military skill and sheer guts of the internationals in both attack and defence, their willingness to suffer appalling losses in order to hold or retake ground, had so impressed and intimidated the 'crack troops' of the enemy army that they gave up their offensive.[30] And, as the commander of the Lincoln Battalion reflected after the attack of 27 February, 'losses must be suffered for gains achieved'.[31]

During the battle of Brunete in July 1937, the first major republican offensive, the British Battalion lost 268 men out of 300 effectives over nineteen days of fighting for key villages and ridges. The Lincoln and Washington battalions, 900 men in all, lost 620 men over three weeks. Other nationalities in the XV Brigade were also hard hit, the 6th of February Battalion (French) losing 272 of 360 men, and the Dimitrov Battalion (Slavs) 272 of 450. The brigade as a whole went from a strength of 2,500 men down to under 600 effectives.[32]

The Brunete offensive did not succeed in its strategic objectives but was the scene of much heroism among the volunteers, and was therefore a 'moral' victory. It showed the world that the republican forces were capable of launching a large-scale attack, and also demonstrated, when the enemy counter-attacked, that the legendary International Brigades could still stop the Fascists in their tracks: *¡No pasaran!*[33]

Paradoxically, 'Fascist' sources could be cited in support of the fighting quality and overall importance of the International Brigades. Some of Franco's generals and later historians found it convenient to blame the volunteers – portrayed as well-trained, well-equipped, and well-led Red fanatics – when trying to explain nationalist setbacks. Thus just as Madrid was about to fall in November 1936, 'the International Brigades, perfectly trained and equipped, with foreign professional cadres, supplied with very modern and abundant materiel, hurl themselves into the struggle'.[34] The *Caudillo* himself even got in on the act, proclaiming in a 1949 speech that the brigaders ('the shock troops of international communism') had borne the brunt of the fighting in Spain.[35]

If even the enemy acknowledged the fighting quality of the volunteers, how could they not have been everything that wartime propaganda made them out to be? That is, politically motivated, well trained, and above all tremendously effective on the battlefield?

Thus the wartime rhetoric surrounding the International Brigades has been perpetuated, and the saga of the volunteers time and again presented in terms of a crusade, the Last Good Fight, in which Fascism might have been defeated if it had not been for the unlimited material support given to Franco by Mussolini and Hitler and the democracies' criminally negligent policy of non-intervention.[36] At the very least 'Franco's rebellion might have succeeded in a matter of months but for the decisive intervention of the IBers'.[37] They were always in the thick of the action, played a 'pivotal role' as inspirational shock troops, and – or so Herbert Matthews argued – if they had *not* been withdrawn prematurely then the civil war might have gone on long enough for Spain to be caught up in the wider world war (the Republic thereby becoming one of the Allies).[38]

However, the tendency to carry on the Good Fight in print – with brigade veterans themselves writing, sponsoring, and commenting on much of what has been written and spoken about their force – has not been an entirely positive phenomenon. Criticism of anyone or anything connected with the brigades, however indirect or muted, has tended to be met by fierce denunciation and even (on occasion) attempts at censorship.

In 1952, for example, when the Veterans of the Abraham Lincoln Battalion were sponsoring an anthology of writings on the civil war, anything by Ernest Hemingway was deliberately excluded because the author had dared to criticize André Marty (the Chief Administrator of the International Brigades) in *For Whom the Bell Tolls* (1940).[39] Even the most honoured of historians, such as Hugh Thomas, author of the best-selling *The Spanish Civil War* (1961), could be criticized by veterans for being politically incorrect (daring to suggest that the war was more than a simple contest between democracy and Fascism).[40] Suggestions that the International Brigades were badly run unleashed storms of fierce denunciation.[41] Former brigaders who wrote memoirs critical of their experience drew heavy fire, and even in one case a threat of legal action.[42] The war of words, though becoming less vituperative with each passing year, continues.[43] Meanwhile the heroic aura surrounding those who sacrificed themselves has been reinforced in the English-speaking world through dozens of memorials as well as in commercial films ranging from *For Whom the Bell Tolls* (1943) to *Land and Freedom* (1995).[44]

The belief that the moral strength of a particular cause for which men or women fight makes a positive and vital difference in battle is deceptively easy to accept. Alas, the history of the International Brigades in Spain, stripped of a priori moral assumptions and viewed dispassionately, is one of ideological analysis confronting a reality which did not match theoretical expectations.

Though often presented in terms of spontaneous and classless anti-Fascism and broadly left-wing, popular front-style politics,[45] the International Brigades were very much a communist affair. It was the Comintern, under the watchful eye of the Kremlin, which from the autumn of 1936 onward ran the requisite network of semi-clandestine recruiting stations and smuggled somewhere in the region of 32,000 enthusiastic volunteers from all over Europe to Iberia. It was also the Comintern that appointed party figures from various nations to organize and take command of the volunteers – themselves mostly working class and at least 50 per cent communist[46] – once in Spain.[47] Without this channelling of popular left-wing sentiment in favour of the Republic the International Brigades would not have existed as such. But while a marvellous feat of organization and a tremendously impressive anti-Fascist symbol, the brigades were more effective in the political sphere than they were efficient in the military arena.

There is no gainsaying the fact that, like all loyalist forces, the International Brigades suffered from a crippling shortage of standard modern arms and equipment. Owing to the arms embargo imposed by the declared policy of non-intervention by the Great Powers, the brigades had to make do with a mixture of rifles and machine guns of mixed calibre and variable vintage and provenance.[48] Though arms shipments from the USSR allowed for a certain degree of uniformity, and even qualitative superiority at times, the People's Army (into which the brigades were incorporated in September 1937) suffered from such poor logistical arrangements that weapons often did not make their way to those who needed them.[49]

Though there is perhaps a tendency in memoirs and unit histories to dwell on the crushing superiority of Fascist arms – immediately followed by a condemnation of the non-intervention policy – without acknowledging the logistical failings of the Republic, one cannot in all fairness place responsibility for arms shortages on brigade organization. Propaganda aside, equipping the internationals involved true miracles of improvisation. Unfortunately the problems encountered by the International Brigades in the field went far beyond a shortage of arms and ammunition.

According to several orthodox accounts, the volunteers were carefully screened before being sent to Spain on the basis of previous military experience as well as general health and suitability. And to be sure, those from the states of Continental Europe with compulsory national service usually possessed at least a rudimentary knowledge of matters martial. Some had also seen service in the Great War.[50] Yet in practice the brigades were far from being composed mainly of experienced veterans.

To begin with, there were plenty of recruits without any true military experience at all. Volunteers from Britain, the United States, and Canada – as well as other states without peacetime military service – could often claim only cadet training at school or university (if that), and even among men from the Continent there were plenty lacking the requisite skills.[51] Some of them bent the truth or simply lied about physical disabilities or lack of military experience.[52] In theory all but a tiny fraction of volunteers were motivated by political idealism. In practice motives were often more complex, involving a desire for personal fulfilment, excitement, and paid employment as well as the 'official' goal of combating Fascism.[53] There were even those who claimed that they were not voluntary recruits at all – they had been lied to or bundled off to Spain while too drunk to know what they were doing.[54]

And whether idealists or not, recruits were understandably anxious to assume the role for which they thought themselves best suited – and they sometimes lied to get it. As one Belgian recruit recalled of his early days at Albacete:

> A clerk then read out the list [of names] and asked if there were officers, non-commissioned officers, cooks, stenographers, artillerymen, and machine-gunners among us. The answers were what one would have expected because there being no control there was no need to be bashful and each one ranked himself according to his own private ambitions.[55]

This was by no means a unique occurrence.[56]

Then there was the question of what constituted valuable experience. With uncomfortable frequency party cadres seem to have regarded party pedigree as the best test of soldierly qualities among potential recruits. Membership of communist paramilitary squads and street fights with riot police, however, were not equivalent to combat between armies equipped with modern weapons.[57] Service in a national army, moreover, was not always that helpful. Parade-ground skills learned in peacetime many years previously, and even fighting in the Great War, did not necessarily translate into effective battlefield performance in Spain.[58]

When the Thaelmann Centuria, which would form the core of the German battalion, was formed in the autumn of 1936 the antiquated nature of the officers' military service was such that the men were being ordered to fire by volley, apparently in close order.[59] As late as July 1937, during the Brunete offensive, the Thaelmann Battalion was observed advancing in the open in lockstep, stopping only to fire by numbers.[60] Elements of the XI International Brigade were first taught to move forward in an impressive but impractical 'V' formation, while another new battalion advancing on open ground became a perfect artillery target after being ordered by its Italian commander to form a hollow square.[61]

The Lincoln Battalion, initially commanded by a former US Army sergeant, was taught to advance in tight diamond formations, as was the later Washington Battalion. The last of the international units, the Mackenzie–Papineau Battalion of the XV Brigade, received four months of training in the summer of 1937, and consequently had the reputation of being the best prepared of the internationals. But this training was largely in imitation of American practice, and when the Mac–Paps first went over the top on 13 October 1937 – after first mistakenly shooting at the Lincolns – they lost a quarter of their strength.[62] No thought was apparently given to practising the particularly vital skill of digging in. This was one of several reasons for the huge losses at Jarama and Brunete.[63]

Lack of adequate training, despite partisan claims then and later,[64] was one of the chief difficulties new brigaders faced. Efforts were made from the first by individual battalions to set up training programmes for newly arrived men, but these were hampered by the lack of truly experienced officers and by the more or less constant pressure to plug gaps in the ranks at the front. The result was that the initial training period, set at a totally unrealistic fifteen to twenty days, was often reduced to a couple of days of marching, a few lectures, and one or two mock attacks.[65]

Men of the XI and XII International Brigades often went into action at Madrid in November 1936 only having fired their rifles once or twice, and in some cases without any idea of how to load them. The same was true of the British and American battalions of the XV Brigade at Jarama in February 1937, and even the Mac–Paps in October of the same year.[66] Apologists have suggested that training grew longer and improved over time,[67] and there is some evidence to support this. The American writer Alvah Bessie, for example, who arrived in Spain in January 1938, received five weeks of intensive instruction.

> We marched and counter-marched to toughen our muscles; we trotted and ran; we ran and fell with our rifles, learning how to fall without hurting ourselves or damaging our arms. We practised close order drill . . . and we practised infiltrating over the terrain – advancing by squads and platoons and sections; seeking cover, advancing, charging. We dug various types of fortifications: fox holes, firing pits, dugouts, and we learned how to camouflage them. We received instruction in musketry – dry firing, triangulation, target practice, fire and also movement. We learned how to strip and clean our arms and reassemble them, even in the dark. We were taught how to take cover from various types of fire – artillery, machine-gun, rifle, airplane.[68]

More often than not, however, a crisis at the front would take precedence over training. Losses among the British at Brunete in the summer of 1937, for instance, led to men being drafted to the front within a week of arrival in Spain.[69] Basic training remained minimal at best, and shortages meant that live firing practice remained severely limited.[70]

This does not appear to have bothered terribly much recruits without combat experience. Idealism, faith in the anti-Fascist cause, would see them through.[71] Indeed, one of the problems faced by the organizers of the brigades was a tendency on the part of new volunteers to believe that, in a classless people's army such as the International Brigades, orders should only be carried out after they had been explained and a vote taken. 'Harry's Anarchists!' a frustrated Wilfred MacCartney, the first British CO, exclaimed one day in late 1936 (referring to the British Communist Party leader Harry Pollitt). 'That's my name for this battalion! All deputations and opinions and little Soviets discussing each order before they obey it, or don't obey it.'[72] Petty disobedience, particularly drunkenness, was not uncommon behind the lines; and at one point during the battle for Madrid in December 1936 virtually the entire André Marty Battalion, then in reserve, spontaneously went absent without leave in order to visit the fleshpots of the capital.[73]

Exhortations from Marty and others to adopt a more disciplined approach were only partially successful, field training (such as it was) being regarded by some at least as something of a lark. On 20 January 1937 MacCartney – who had seen active service in the Great War – wrote worriedly to the military commandant at Albacete that:

> Discipline is still backward, too much drinking, and too much arguing, when orders are given by group and section commanders.
>
> The lack of discipline expresses itself in erratic military performance. One day the battalion does its work well, indeed very well, and the commander begins to flatter himself that great progress is being made, but the next day the battalion behaves badly, is slack and indifferent, even conveys the impression of incompetence.[74]

'The war was still a long way off,' as one British veteran recalled, 'and it was all rather fun.'[75] The result was, more often than not, a sudden slaughter of the innocents, many naïve enthusiasts discovering too late that political commitment – manifest in such forms as a desire to fight in the open rather than taking cover[76] – was an inadequate substitute for military proficiency. As one British volunteer recalled: 'we were convinced that we possessed an invincible armament of spirit, and that in the eyes of the world and the angels, we were on the right side of this struggle.' Alas, 'We had yet to learn that sheer idealism never stopped a tank.' As another volunteer bluntly put it, 'we were totally unprepared for what was going to happen to us'.[77]

The effects of lack of time to train and a somewhat cavalier attitude to learning military skills among new recruits might have been mitigated if the quality of junior leadership within the newly formed brigades had been less variable. Relatively few of those with military experience had previously served as officers, and at least some idealists had trouble adjusting to the conventions of hierarchical command. 'It seemed to me that it would take ten years to learn all this bullshit', recalled Ben Goldstein, an American volunteer who resigned from the brigade officer training school in disgust in the summer of 1937. 'It was like a bourgeois army, not like a people's army.'[78]

In any event, the selection and promotion of officers and commissars, whether elected or – as was increasingly common after the first few months – appointed, seems largely to have been based on political rather than military qualifications. In terms of organizing recruitment and running administrative machinery a reliance on experienced party cadres was not necessarily a bad thing, but at the front even the most respected party stalwarts did not always do well under fire. Quite apart from military inexperience leading to errors in timing and location, several officers and commissars had to be quietly removed after displaying signs of hysteria and cowardice in battle.[79]

The test of combat, to be sure, is one that even the most highly trained professional soldiers sometimes fail. And there were certainly those among the officers of the International Brigades who proved to be born leaders in battle. (Even if, like the English officer George Nathan or the Italian commander Randolfo Pacciardi, they were not always those with the best political credentials.)[80]

Political considerations, however, continued to influence who was and was not promoted throughout the war, and not always with positive results. Some of the better field officers were removed for questioning the powers of commissars in military decision making.[81] Men of more average military capacity were promoted above their ceiling if they possessed the right political credentials or if they had some particular propaganda value.[82]

Many of the officers, moreover, tended to get wounded or killed setting an example to their men (casualty rates among officers being higher than among those they commanded). This was not always effective, since without officers to lead, squads and platoons could lose what cohesion and direction they might have in the midst of an operation and act strictly on impulse.[83]

If anything, political factors were even more pervasive and problematic at the higher levels of command. In appointing commanders for the five International Brigades, the Comintern sought to mesh military requirements with political expediency. The most obvious possibility – importing trained Red Army commanders – was out of the question. While Soviet officers could and did serve in Spain as staff and technical advisors, it was important to avoid giving the impression that the International Brigades were run from the Kremlin. Soviet aid of too blatant a character would run counter to Soviet claims to be adhering to the non-intervention agreement, and might also undermine propaganda efforts to make the brigades appear a spontaneous manifestation of international anti-Fascism.[84] The remaining alternative was to deploy supernumerary officers of various foreign nationalities: mostly former POWs of the Central Powers who had converted to communism and fought against the Whites in the Russian Civil War and subsequently been recruited into the Comintern intelligence apparatus.[85] Given pseudonyms and impressive revolutionary fighting records for propaganda purposes,[86] these men rapidly acquired an aura of exotic mystery in the sympathetic Western press but were in reality sometimes in above their heads as commanders of brigades (or even battalions).

Again, the question of training and experience is pertinent. Men such as the Hungarian 'General Lukács' (Máté Zakla) placed in command of the XII Brigade, or the German 'General Gomez' (Wilhelm Zeisser), put in charge of the XIII Brigade, had little experience of the complexities of modern war. The most famous, 'General Kleber' of the XI Brigade, the so-called 'saviour of Madrid', had undergone formal military academy training, but the others appear to have had little more knowledge of war than what their time as soldiers or junior officers in the wartime Austro-Hungarian or German Army, and civil-war Red Army, had given them.[87]

Apart from a certain amount of somewhat studied exoticism – the Hungarian 'General Gal' (Janos Galicz) of the XV Brigade, for instance, liked to remind his headquarters staff that he had once been a budding opera star by singing famous arias – the one thing most of these Comintern imports had in common was an acute awareness of the political implications of their actions. Service in Spain brought opportunities, but was also fraught with peril.

The Moscow show trials and political purges engineered by Stalin had been under way since 1935, and by the summer of 1937 the Great Terror had extended into the highest ranks of the Red Army.[88] Any contact with the outside world raised suspicions of treasonous activity, which could only be allayed – if at all – by slavish obedience at any cost. For the émigré commanders the need to avoid the very slightest hint of dissent (which would be read as 'Trotskyism' by the NKVD) meant that obeying directives to the letter usually overrode all other considerations, including an operation's likely cost and chances of success.

It is these factors which help explain the peculiar penchant in brigade headquarters for the 'to the last man' defence and 'at all costs' attack – even when it became clear that these operations were virtually suicidal. Appearances were more important than results. Optimistic situation reports could be used to disguise battlefield failure of anything other than monumental proportions, and in the latter case a less culpable scapegoat could be found. (A bungled attack on Lopera at the end of December 1936 by the XIV International Brigade, for example, was blamed on the non-communist commander of one of the French battalions, Gaston Delasalle, who was executed for treason.)[89] The slightest hint of a willingness to reflect independently and adapt orders to circumstance must have seemed a death warrant to anyone aware of the climate of terror in Stalin's Russia. Hence the almost hysterical reaction when junior officers unfamiliar with the realities of the Soviet Union chose to modify or disobey inappropriate orders.

During the battle of the Jarama in February 1937, for example, Tom Wintringham (then the British Battalion commander) was ordered several times by General Gal to advance or hold ground despite his protests that promised support on the flanks had not arrived. The only response of Gal and his minions to any questioning of these orders was to threaten a court martial. When Wintringham independently conducted a withdrawal from Suicide Hill without asking permission, one of the brigade staff officers went berserk. 'To retire?' he screamed. 'You have not the right! It is General Gal's order that you hold at all costs.'[90] Wintringham's instructions were overridden by an order to the men on the hill direct from brigade HQ to 'hold at all costs'. Only 125 of 400 men survived among the three British companies.[91]

Two weeks after the British baptism of fire at Jarama the new Lincoln Battalion was ordered to launch an attack which was supposed to be made possible by a synchronized preparatory artillery and air bombardment and flank support by the Spanish XXIV Brigade. 'Plan good and sounded like good use of all arms', Robert Merriman, the American Battalion commander, optimistically wrote in his diary after Gal had explained it to him.[92] Unfortunately most of the promised support failed to materialize on the morning of 27 February, and a worried Merriman telephoned XV Brigade HQ to explain the situation. The shouted response he got from Vladimir Čopić, the brigade commissar, was that the Lincolns had to go over the top 'at all costs'. Fifty-eight per cent of the American officers and men were killed or wounded in the subsequent attack.[93]

This sort of thing continued throughout the Jarama battle, and was repeated at Brunete, Belchite, and elsewhere. The assault by the Mac–Paps and the rest of the XV Brigade on Fuentes in October 1937 was a study in command failure. Traffic jams and lack of co-ordination created a three-hour delay, and it was only at noon that the promised air support arrived. An hour later, by which time the nationalists had recovered, assaulting republican tanks with Spanish infantry clinging on roared forward so fast that they were cut off and proved unable to support the Mac–Paps as they advanced in formation across a mile of open ground. The delays ought to have alerted the brigade or even divisional staff to the fact that the plan was unravelling, yet no attempt was made to call it off. Čopić blamed such failures on poor marksmanship and indiscipline among the troops, but in reality these factors were secondary to poor staff work and political considerations.[94]

Either because they were convinced of the need to endure more sacrifice or through ignorance, officers and men were persuaded by commissars and brigade staff to obey such orders.[95] Among the émigré brigade commanders only Lukács – who was killed by a shell – appears to have had much humanity.[96] Ironically, the hard-line approach of Gal and Čopić did not save them from execution after their return to Moscow.[97]

There were also more direct communication problems. In theory unity in a common cause and ever-present translators allowed brigade officers to exchange information and send and receive orders effectively. In practice, especially in the heat of battle, language problems were common. Efforts were made to assign volunteers to battalions and brigades on the basis of a common tongue, but this took time. The linguistic nightmares that occurred in the Chapiev ('21 Nations') Balkan Battalion of the XIII International Brigade or the 'Nine Nations' Battalion of the XIV International Brigade, both formed at the end of 1936, can well be imagined. Attempts at transmitting instructions in the polyglot XI International Brigade in the initial fighting for Madrid made it appear a legion of Babel. The brigades, even after reorganization, always contained more than one language group, which in turn affected communications and also led to friction between contingents (as when German volunteers mistakenly 'captured' a group of Fascists who turned out to be Italian IB volunteers).[98] Jason Gurney, a British volunteer who served as a runner between battalion and brigade HQ at Jarama, later recalled what this meant in practice.

> Theoretically the common language of the [XV] Brigade was French, a language which none of the Brigade staff nor any of the battalion commanders spoke with any real fluency, except for those of the Franco-Belge Battalion. To make matters worse, the bad French spoken by a Russian or a German is quite unlike the bad French spoken by an Englishman or an Italian. People could just about make themselves understood in ordinary life but in the heat of battle, over an inadequate telephone line, there was virtually no communication at all.[99]

Matters were not made easier by the increasing number of local recruits drafted into the brigades as the war progressed, since very few of the internationals spoke Spanish.[100]

According to several secondary studies and memoirs, the very heavy losses sustained by the International Brigades did not seriously affect morale. Though a few 'bad elements' might have whined and even deserted, the vast majority of brigaders were sustained in adversity by anti-Fascist determination.[101] The Lincolns, according to the American John Tisa (editor of the XV Brigade newspaper *Volunteer for Liberty*), after the importance of their sacrifice on 27 February 1937 had been explained to them on 1 March, were as eager to fight as ever. 'We were now anxious to rush back to our positions', he states in his memoirs.

> Morale took a great leap forward. We returned quickly to our lines, singing on the way up, joking, whistling, cursing the bloody fascists, and pledging revenge for our fallen comrades, proud and secure in the knowledge that our efforts and our losses were not in vain.[102]

This was not in fact the case. It was true that many of the idealists showed remarkable endurance, fighting on grimly until the very end.[103] But not all the volunteers *were* idealists, and even among the most committed there were those who found that the realities of modern war – at least as experienced by the International Brigades[104] – could not be borne for ever.

The initial encounters of the internationals with Franco's forces produced a good deal of shock among the more green troops who imagined fighting Fascism would be a matter of good (democracy) triumphing, *ipso facto*, over evil (Fascism). The Moroccans of the Army of Africa, for instance, quickly demonstrated to the British Battalion at Jarama that seasoned professional mercenaries could more than match even the most enthusiastic amateurs.

> There must have been three battalions of Moors [advancing] and their movement was amazingly skilful. Bobbing up and down, running and disappearing again, while all the while maintaining a continuous accurate fire. . . . It was terrifying to watch the uncanny ability of the Moorish infantry to exploit the slightest fold in the ground that could be used for cover, and to make themselves invisible. . . . The effect of these brown, ferocious bundles suddenly appearing out of the ground at one's feet was utterly demoralizing. There appeared to be thousands of them popping up and disappearing all over the place, but seldom visible for long enough for anyone to get a shot at them.[105]

Amid the confusion of their first battle, with unseasoned officers and poor communications, some men under artillery, machine-gun, and rifle fire, sometimes cut off, surrounded by the incredible din of war, seeing comrades fall dead or wounded screaming, discovered that they simply could not take it. At Jarama one English company commander, unable to stand the pressure, abandoned his command. Some men ran away and had to be rounded up at pistol point. Between fifty and a hundred men from the British Battalion stole away the first night and hid in an underground wine vault, and only came out under threat of being shot.[106] As one volunteer (who then ran off) put it to one of his fellows in an earlier, equally bungled, action: 'This isn't war, it's bloody massacre . . . I've had enough.'[107]

Those who fought on and survived such bloodbaths were often both shocked and furious, and engaged in protest that verged on mutiny. After the events of 27 February, for example, the Lincolns marched out of the line *en masse* demanding that they be given proper training and that someone be held accountable for the disaster. Contrary to the rather rosy interpretation of the subsequent mass meeting given by Tisa, other participants suggest that though they returned to the line the Lincolns remained surly and mutinous for weeks. A similar situation existed among the British volunteers after Brunete, at least sixty of whom demanded repatriation or refused to return to the line after recovering from wounds.[108] And, needless to say, the Canadians were furiously angry after their débâcle at Fuentes del Ebro in October, as some of their officers made clear in a post-action meeting with a senior Spanish general.[109]

For undertrained men engaged for the first time in heavy fighting such reactions were to be expected. Immediate rest and reorganization might well have allowed the men to come to terms with the realities of combat and return to the line as determined as ever but wiser. Unfortunately, at brigade level and above, faith in what has been termed the 'Marx + Courage = Success' formula remained absolute.[110] The answer to grumbling in the ranks was more political education work by the commissars, more visits by prominent party figures.[111] Only when a brigade had been reduced by death and wounds to about 20 per cent of its initial strength was it removed from the line for rest and refitting – a period which could last less than twenty-four hours in an emergency.[112]

In theory, political commitment ought to have allowed the volunteers to stand the stresses of battle indefinitely. 'Where soldiers don't have any real interest in the war they're fighting, shell shock can and must exist as a scientific fact', Steve Nelson, a popular American commissar, explained. 'But in this army – our army – it's different. Our boys know what they're fighting for. They're here because they want to be here. They came to Spain because they understood what this war is about.'[113] In practice, however, either the shock of real war or battle fatigue over time can take hold of anyone. As George Nathan more realistically admitted, 'it might take six months, it might take two years but the nerves would let one down in the end'.[114]

The best of the commissars at least implicitly recognized that morale was best sustained through catering to the fighting men's immediate concerns: sleep, food, cigarettes, and news from home.[115] Alas, too often the political perspective took precedence. Sid Quinn, a British volunteer, angrily recalled an episode during the Brunete offensive which graphically underlined the limits of this approach to morale.

> Then we had a really bizarre happening – only the communists could do it. We were told Frank Pitcairn [the *Daily Worker* journalist Claud Cockburn] was going to speak to us, he would hold a meeting. A meeting! We were under a perfect barrage of artillery and snipers when Pitcairn came up. . . . He told us Eden [the British foreign secretary] was going to drop his non-intervention policy. The stupidity of it, the awful stupidity. He wasn't even right in what he said, and there we were holding a meeting under shell-fire. Sixteen men were *killed* at that meeting, the snipers just picked them off one after another.[116]

Even among the idealists day-to-day concerns about survival often made the most rousing of speakers impotent.[117] New, idealistic recruits were often shocked by the apathy and cynicism they found among veteran volunteers.[118]

Overly long spells in the line without relief, combined with bloody battles, led to further desertions and even units suddenly cracking up completely. At Jarama, a company of the Thaelmann Battalion (previously one of the most reliable units) broke and ran after being badly cut up.[119] After the first days of fighting at Brunete, the XIII Brigade refused to go on without some rest.

The commander, 'Kriegger' (Vincenzo Bianco), tried to drive them back at pistol point, but when he shot one soldier the entire brigade rose in open revolt and marched towards Madrid. Though the mutineers were surrounded and disarmed by loyalist forces, the XIII Brigade had to be broken up completely.[120]

Lack of leave also became a problem, especially for the volunteers who were not political exiles from their home countries. The brigade authorities were understandably keen to prevent men from simply going home whenever they felt like it. 'If [we] let all the sick and dispirited leave Spain', Peter Kerrigan, the British commissar at Albacete, explained to Stephen Spender, 'then others might want to return as well. It [is] difficult to withdraw one man without discouraging the rest.'[121] But even the concept of rotational home leave was anathema to zealots like André Marty, who claimed that calls for leave were simply a justification for cowardly, if not actually Fascist, behaviour. Party figures feared that if volunteers were allowed to go home they would never return, and might even complain about their treatment to the Western press, as a number of deserters – branded as cowards and Fascist agents – had already done by the summer of 1937.[122] Only the most trusted party members were allowed to return home to promote the cause, which did nothing to improve the morale of those left behind. Even those crippled in action were left to wander about Albacete.[123]

Requests for leave or repatriation were therefore received with great hostility. Commissars, often men ordered to go to Spain by the Comintern to restore morale, usually took a tough line. They stressed that 'the struggle' took precedence over the individual, even accusing the men concerned in one case of being cowards.[124] Those who pressed the idea of leave were treated as *agents provocateurs*.[125]

Not all recruits, of course, were true idealists (especially as time went on and news of losses made it harder to attract volunteers in 1937–8).[126] Even among the more politically committed, moreover, men suffering from battle fatigue did not respond well to berating sessions by commissars.[127]

Desertion and self-inflicted wounds, which had initially been confined to the more faint hearted, became a more general problem as the battles of 1937 took their toll. During and after Brunete in particular the number of deserters from battalions climbed into the hundreds.[128] Fleeing men tried to get help from their nearest national consulate, or independently attempted to cross the Pyrenees or stow away on ships. The French consul at Valencia helped 400 deserters, while the British consulate provided assistance for at least a few of the almost 300 British volunteers who made their way home.[129]

Much to their credit, the more humane party apparatchiks advocated a less callous approach towards the many deserters who were caught in Spain. A special rehabilitation centre was set up at Albacete in 1937 for captured soldiers, where – apparently through persuasion rather than coercion – at least some of the several hundred men incarcerated changed their minds and returned to the front.[130] There was even some talk (which spread like wild-fire within the brigades) of repatriating men who had served six months in combat.[131]

Unfortunately the efforts of those who advocated rehabilitation were increasingly undermined as the war continued by those who thought they should be shot. Those sent back to the line sometimes found themselves placed repeatedly in the most exposed positions, a virtual death-warrant. The rehabilitation camp itself was eventually closed, and most of its inmates simply disappeared.[132] André Marty, whose paranoia quickly rivalled that of his idol Stalin, pressed commissars to execute deserters despite opposition within the brigades – orders which were at least in some cases carried out.[133] Indeed, anyone who even complained and was informed on ran the risk of being 'removed' by agents of the NKVD or the in-house *Servicio Investigacion Militar* (SIM).[134] When called to account after the war, Marty admitted to French communist authorities that he had ordered the execution of 500 'Trotskyists' (i.e. deserters and other troublemakers within the brigades).[135] As many as 10 per cent of the volunteers may have lost their lives this way.[136]

Needless to say, this did no more to boost morale than the realization that repatriation only applied to party cadres.[137] Mounting losses also took their toll: by the autumn of 1938 somewhere between 16 per cent and 30 per cent of the internationals had been killed and an even larger proportion wounded.[138] Most battalions had more Spanish conscripts than foreigners in the ranks by this point, which helps explain why withdrawing the volunteers was not (at least in statistical terms) a major blow to the Republic.[139] On the other hand, as one senior commissar explained, by late 1938 mounting fatigue and demoralization brought into question the further usefulness of the internationals.[140]

The one great military asset which the brigades possessed until the end was the capacity of many of the men (who over time became professionals by default) to endure. Sadly, dispassionate examination of the evidence reveals that neither at Madrid, Jarama, nor at any other major battle were the blood sacrifices made by the brigades the key to nationalist setbacks. Nationalist weaknesses and the effect of other republican units – the brigades never accounting for no more than about 6 per cent of republican forces at most – had a more significant impact.[141]

Even their symbolic value, the effect they had on loyalist morale in Madrid and elsewhere, may have been overstated. 'Ours was not a triumphant entry', one member of the XI International Brigade recalled of the supposedly morale-raising march into Madrid in November 1936. 'I thought that the hurrying people on the pavements looked at us as if we were too late and had come to die.'[142] Though there was much cheering in Barcelona and elsewhere, relations between the internationals and the Spanish were not always cordial. Foreign intervention, however well inten-tioned, sometimes offended national pride. For their part, some of the volunteers suspected (and not without reason) that Spaniards saw them as cannon fodder, useful only in order to save as many natives as possible from the hazards of battle.[143]

Yet the internationals, despite their many problems, *did* possess greater staying power than many early Spanish militiamen and later Spanish conscripts, and were consequently less likely to break when faced with better-armed and trained nationalist forces engaged in a campaign of methodical annihilation.[144] This capacity to 'take it', rather than skill as shock troops, was why the volunteers were thrown into every major battle from Madrid to the Ebro until they had virtually ceased to exist.

The price of endurance among those who stuck it out, however, was high. Casualty rates were far greater in the International Brigades than in the Allied armies in the Second World War (or indeed the Italian Expeditionary Forces fighting with Franco). Even the worst days of the First World War did not compare.[145]

Many sources see such casualty rates as proof of the internationals' commitment, their willingness to die for the cause.[146] There were hundreds, possibly even thousands, though, who sooner or later reached the limit of their physical and psychological endurance. And the huge number of volunteers killed, wounded, and unaccounted for in battles that (despite wishful thinking) were never really won, serves better as tragic testimony of the reality that amateur enthusiasm by itself – however great – is no substitute for professional competence.

The International Brigades, though, would not be the only transnational force held up as an ideal amid the great upheavals and ideological clashes of the twentieth century's middle passage. The onset of the Second World War within months of the last shots being fired in Spain would herald the rise of another international army – though this time one of the Right rather than the Left.

9 The Waffen-SS in the Second World War, 1939–45

Europe's *Übermenschen*?

I believe that we succeeded, despite difficulties, in producing a new type of soldier rarely equalled in the history of warfare.

Werner Ostendorff, Commander, 17th SS Panzer-Grenadier Division
Goetz von Berlichingen[1]

I can tell you, we had no desire to go to the Eastern Front at all.

Hans-Jürgen Welle, 1943 Recruit, 1st SS Panzer Division
Leibstandarte Adolf Hitler[2]

'As the Spanish Civil War was an international conflict on both sides', neo-conservative German historian Ernst Nolte has written, 'so also was the German war against the Soviet Union an international war.' In his mind the multinational Waffen-SS fighting on the Eastern Front represents the mirror image (the ideological polarity reversed) of the International Brigades in Spain. Both were militant expressions of the ideas underlying a twentieth-century European civil war between Left and Right.[3]

The validity of this frame of reference is, to say the least, debatable. Yet in some ways at least the comparison is quite apt. Whatever each force represented in reality, there can be little doubt that both the International Brigades and the Waffen-SS are seen by their respective champions (left leaning on the one hand, right leaning on the other) as embodying the soldierly qualities of commitment to the ideals of a transnational cause. Solidarity, idealism, physical courage, self-sacrifice, strength in the face of adversity: these are all virtues which have been attributed to both forces.

Moreover, while the image of the International Brigades undoubtedly enjoys a far greater degree of public empathy in the Western democracies (progressives having generally outnumbered those on the extreme right), the Waffen-SS possesses a surprisingly wide cult following among military buffs. The status of a military elite within the German armed forces, the camouflage uniforms worn by the men, the impressive combat record and aura of toughness that surrounded the force: all hold enormous fascination for modellers and collectors alike – as the huge volume of postwar photographic and illustrated material relating to the Waffen-SS attests. As one of the more perceptive purveyors of popular war history put it, the 'glamour which that service undoubtedly had for the Germans of Hitler's day has by no means been dissipated by the passage of time'.[4]

The origins of what might be termed the Waffen-SS mystique lie in the way in which the force was portrayed within the Third Reich. In the latter 1930s the nucleus of what would become the Waffen-SS, the first few regiments of *SS-Verfügungstruppe* and the *Leibstandarte Adolf Hitler* (the Führer's bodyguard unit), had been vigorously promoted as an elite force. Though the number of regiments was kept small – Hitler deferring to the generals who feared that Reichsführer-SS Heinrich Himmler was trying to build an alternative army[5] – it was widely known that the SS-VT took in only the best men and was far more innovative and challenging than the Wehrmacht.

Physical fitness, speed, toughness, and ruthless aggressiveness were all emphasized in addition to weapons training. A conscious effort to eradicate traditional class-based barriers between officers and men was made, certain ex-Reichswehr officers such as SS-Sturmbannführer Felix Steiner wanting to recreate both the *Kamaradschaft* and tactics of the 1918 Stormtrooper battalions and the later Freikorps. 'NCOs and officers taught us the great value of two things', one prewar recruit recalled, '–speed and comradeship.'[6]

The profile of the Waffen-SS (named in 1940) as a revolutionary force grew stronger as the war progressed. Hitler, always distrustful of aristocratic Wehrmacht generals, from 1941–2 onward grew increasingly suspicious of men who questioned his orders or might even disobey them. In his own mind the constant carping on the difficulties in the East, the repeated requests to withdraw, only exposed the cowardice and disloyalty of Wehrmacht generals. The Waffen-SS, on the other hand, especially those units led by old party comrades like Josef 'Sepp' Dietrich, commander of the *Leibstandarte*, could be relied upon to do their duty. 'In sharp contrast to the leading gentlemen of the Army', propaganda minister Josef Goebbels noted in his diary in January 1942, '[for] the leaders of the Waffen-SS . . . difficulties exist only to be overcome.'[7]

Aggressiveness when on the attack, tenacity when holding ground, and above all a willingness to obey the Führer's orders were rewarded by promotions, well-publicized awards of decorations, and a massive expansion of the Waffen-SS in the latter half of the war. From a strength of five divisions in 1941 the force would expand exponentially until by 1944–5 over thirty-five divisions existed. And it was in this expansion phase that the image of the Waffen-SS as a 'European army' can be first discerned.

Even before the war efforts had been made by Heinrich Himmler as Reichsführer-SS to recruit suitable 'Germanic' volunteers outside the borders of Germany, and in the wake of the conquests of 1940, Danish, Dutch, Norwegian, as well as German volunteers formed the nucleus of what would become the *Wiking* division. In addition, restrictions imposed on the manpower of the Waffen-SS that could be drawn from within the Reich imposed by the Army led SS-Brigadeführer Gottlob Berger, the

Machiavellian chief of Waffen-SS recruiting, to encourage volunteers from among the *Volksdeutsche*, the millions of ethnic Germans living in neighbouring countries.[8]

It was the Nazi attack on the Soviet Union in June 1941, however, that really precipitated the transformation of the Waffen-SS into a multinational force. Proposals were quickly made by a number of far-right parties in occupied Europe to raise volunteers to fight in an anti-Bolshevik crusade – offers which were accepted and resulted in the creation of Dutch, Flemish, Norwegian, Finnish, and Danish legions which fought in the East and eventually were transformed into divisions. As the manpower problems of the Reich grew more acute the net was cast even wider, and nationals previously considered insufficiently Germanic were invited to join over a dozen new volunteer units (brigades and divisions) between 1943 and 1945.

By the end of the war the Waffen-SS had created units composed of Frenchmen, Belgians, Dutchmen, Norwegians, Danes, Italians, Hungarians, Ukrainians, Latvians, Estonians, Russians, and even Bosnian and Albanian Muslims. Of the total of thirty-eight Waffen-SS divisions that had been established by May 1945 (at least on paper), twenty-one were based on foreign contingents.[9]

As was to be expected, much was made of the foreigners' contributions by the Nazi propaganda apparatus. Racial issues were played down in favour of European unity in the face of Asiatic barbarism. Those decorated for valour, such as the Dutch volunteer Gerdus Mooyman (who won the Knight's Cross), became symbols of the strength of the New Europe.[10]

Such efforts cut no ice with anti-Nazis. As Albert Camus put it to the occupiers in an underground French Resistance newspaper issued in April 1944: 'You never spoke this way until you lost Africa.'[11] Moreover, when the time of reckoning arrived at Nuremberg in the late summer of 1945, SS-Oberstgruppenführer Paul Hausser and other Waffen-SS witnesses were unable to convince the Allied tribunal that the Waffen-SS was an elite, multinational force that had fought honourably and had been in no way connected with the activities of the regular SS. The Waffen-SS was condemned along with the rest of Himmler's former SS empire as a criminal organization, and well-known figures such as Sepp Dietrich and SS-Brigadeführer Kurt 'Panzer' Meyer served lengthy prison terms for war crimes.[12]

If this was not sufficient humiliation for those who believed that they had been fighting for a cause that would within a few years bring the West together under the North Atlantic Treaty Organization – making Waffen-SS men 'premature anti-communists' – there was also the way in which veterans were treated in their own country. As the Federal Republic began to take shape, the SS became 'the alibi of a nation',[13] onto which all responsibility for past crimes could be shifted. As former members of a Nazi organization, Waffen-SS veterans were denied the war pensions issued to members of the Wehrmacht in 1951. Those Waffen-SS men who wished to join the new Bundeswehr when it was formed in the mid-1950s found the political screening process was quite discriminatory, especially towards ex-officers. By September 1956, only 33 of 1,310 applications by former Waffen-SS officers had been accepted (making them 0.4 per cent of the new officer corps), as compared with 270 of 1,324 applications by former NCOs and 195 of 462 applications by enlisted men.[14]

These were bitter pills to swallow, and the more aggressive chose to fight back. As early as the summer of 1951 Otto Kumm, last commander of the *Leibstandarte*, had established the *Hilfsgemeinschaft auf Gegenseitigkeit der ehemaligen Angehörigen der Waffen-SS* (HIAG), an organization of Waffen-SS veterans, to lobby Bonn and in general work to restore the tarnished image of the force. Through rallies, meetings with political figures of the centre and right, a magazine, and a flood of memoirs and detailed unit histories, HIAG achieved its initial goal when in 1961 the Bundestag partially restored pension rights to Waffen-SS veterans.[15] The wider aim of complete rehabilitation proved harder to achieve, in part because some of the more enthusiastic members of HIAG sounded alarmingly Nazi in their pronouncements.[16] Only the extreme right – most recently in the form of the Republikaner Party led by ex-Waffen-SS man and TV personality Franz Schönhuber – has made no bones about embracing the HIAG version of history, and it has never attracted more than slightly over 7 per cent of voters.[17]

Yet while HIAG itself continues to decline as members die off, the positive image of the Waffen-SS the organization has promoted has taken root – and by no means only in Germany. In an era of Cold War between the Soviet Union and the West, senior Waffen-SS personnel were not shy about suggesting that *they* had once organized and led a NATO-like army (and an elite one at that).

Memoirs and histories by former SS generals, bulky 'official' unit histories (often in several volumes), as well as a few lavishly illustrated coffee-table books, have poured forth from Munin Verlag in Osnabrück and Plesse Verlag in Göttingen in a steady stream since the 1950s. These volumes, which constitute the single largest and most detailed body of work on the subject, invariably portray the Waffen-SS men as misunderstood idealists who fought honourably and well (and had nothing to do with the concentration camps). Testimonials by former Wehrmacht generals praising the fighting qualities of the Waffen-SS are prominently displayed in these volumes.

Steiner and Hausser, for example, each wrote books defending both themselves and the Waffen-SS, once in the 1950s and again, for good measure, in the 1960s. The titles of the latter two books cut to the essence of how HIAG saw the Waffen-SS being treated and what its members believed was the truth: *Army of Outlaws* (1963) and *Soldiers Like Any Others* (1966).[18] A brief review of the first two books, among the first HIAG-sponsored volumes to appear, will suffice to indicate the tone and thrust of the corpus as a whole.

Hausser was first off the mark in 1953 with *Waffen-SS im Einsatz*, which had the double lightning bolt SS runes and motto ('my honour is loyalty') printed on the cover. The much-admired Wehrmacht panzer General Heinz Guderian was persuaded to endorse the Waffen-SS in a special foreword as 'courageous troops' who did their duty like other soldiers and were in addition 'the first realization of the European idea'. Hausser himself went on to detail the growth of the Waffen-SS into a multinational force where foreign volunteers, including 'our Muslims', fought and died heroically to the bitter end 'as a militant example of the great European idea'.[19]

Steiner went even further in *Die Freiwilligen* five years later. The Waffen-SS, it appeared, was nothing less than the ultimate expression of the kind of youthful and restless idealism which had caused men from distant lands to fight with Byron in Greece in the 1820s, Garibaldi in Italy in the 1850s, and Pilsudski in Poland in the 1920s. The foreign volunteers were men of spirit who, like their German comrades, saw the 'diabolical' threat to Western civilization posed by Bolshevism and 'fought like lions' against it under the banner of the Waffen-SS.[20]

The memoirs of Steiner and Hausser, along with those of other high-profile field commanders such as Meyer (12th SS Panzer Division), were only part of a quadruple publishing effort. The HIAG journal, *Der Freiwillige*, propagated the same basic themes year after year, former SS personnel such as Ettore Vernier contributing articles with titles like 'Volunteers for Europe' into and beyond the mid-1970s.[21] Glossy books such as *Waffen-SS in Pictures* (1957), *Scattered are the Traces* (1979), and *Panzer Grenadiers of the 'Viking' Division in Pictures* (1984), all replete with propaganda photographs of Aryan-ideal volunteers from all over the Continent, blended elitism with pan-European idealism. 'From all European lands', it was stated in the 1957 volume, 'came volunteers as genuine comrades-in-arms. They fought for their Fatherland against Bolshevism.'[22] And, last but not least, there were the unit and formation histories: full of reprinted operational orders, letters of praise from Wehrmacht commanders, tales of valour and heroism by officers and men of the unit, and condemnation of treatment at the hands of both the Russians and the Allies. The older or more famous the unit, the larger the work – to the point where no less than five volumes and well over 2,000 pages were devoted to the doings of the 2nd SS Panzer Division *Das Reich*.[23]

Adding to this chorus of self-justification were a smaller number of foreigners who had once served in the Waffen-SS. As among the German veterans, there were one or two foreign volunteers who were surprisingly frank about their wartime motives and actions;[24] their voices, however, were swamped by the volume and dogmatic persistence of true believers. Léon Degrelle, for example, the Belgian leader of the fascistic Rex Party who had risen to command the 29th SS Volunteer Grenadier Division *Wallonien* and escaped to Spain at the end of the war, has given many interviews and written several highly partisan accounts of the Waffen-SS that were subsequently published in several languages.[25]

This portrayal of the Waffen-SS as an idealistic band of brothers, as comrades-in-arms engaged in a noble crusade, was by no means acceptable to all in West Germany. Yet the prevailing tendency, at least until the 1980s, was to try and forget the past – to view the end of the Third Reich as 'zero hour'. This allowed Germans to evade the question of collective guilt, but at the same time also meant that instead of being a counter-memory fighting an uphill battle against a prevailing orthodoxy the vision propounded by HIAG was to some extent filling a void.[26]

As the older generation of Waffen-SS scribes has died off, a new, postwar cadre of writers has done much to perpetuate the image of the force as a revolutionary European army. The degree of admiration and acceptance of the HIAG version of events varies, but an overall tendency to accentuate the positive lives on (and has indeed grown stronger as the war continues to recede into history).

The most extreme admirers are, not surprisingly, to be found on the fringes of the far right. In the United States the single most prolific author on the Waffen-SS has been Richard Landwehr, who issues his own magazine on the subject (*Siegrunen*) and has published a volume on just about every foreign Waffen-SS formation through Legion Bibliophile Books. The basic thrust is always the same: a pan-European crusade fought by noble idealists with unprecedented valour against a cruel and remorseless foe. 'They spoke different languages', Landwehr has written, 'but they shared a common commitment: a love of their continent and a hatred of communism and international capitalism. Motivated by the call of conscience, they chose voluntarily to do battle against these predatory enemies.'[27] The Waffen-SS was an international phenomenon 'unprecedented in history'.[28] In his view the men of the Waffen-SS – 'a truly international European Army' fighting for 'Western Civilization'[29] – were far superior in every respect to the 'terrorist' Resistance in occupied Europe.[30]

Hinting of grand conspiracies to cover up the true facts and taking the same confrontational attitude to mainstream history as the revisionist tracts of the *Barnes Review* and *Journal of Historical Review* (published by the neo-Nazi Institute for Historical Review), the works of Landwehr and other pro-Nazis have not achieved wide distribution or much academic acceptance (though it is worth noting that many colleges and universities have his volumes on their shelves).[31] Yet many of the postwar generation of writers who are not quite as overtly sympathetic to National Socialism have accepted the idea of the Waffen-SS as an idealistic European army. Chief among these fellow-travellers, and the most prolific author of all – well over fifty books – is Jean Mabire, a French paratrooper turned popular writer who has specialized in elite forces in general and *la Waffen SS européenne* in particular. In over a dozen works published since the 1970s Mabire has presented the officers and men of the Waffen-SS as comrades-in-arms from across Europe, and clearly sees the force as having been a premier fighting elite. Though not as dogmatic as Landwehr,

Mabire also reproduces in large part the HIAG version of the Waffen-SS at war.[32]

England also has had its share of admirers, the focus here being more on the qualities of the German units. In the 1990s two popular writers, Gordon Williamson and Edmund L. Blandford, sought to restore the tarnished moral reputation of the Waffen-SS in the West and reiterate its superb fighting qualities by letting veterans tell their own stories. The results are predictably positive. While Williamson approaches his subjects with at least a degree of scepticism, Blandford is unquestionably partisan. He appears to believe that the Waffen-SS has been unjustly maligned and its revolutionary achievements as a 'New Model Army' underplayed.[33]

Then there are the large number of English and American popular historians who – though less willing to try and relativize Waffen-SS war crimes and often somewhat critical of the European army idea – appear to have been partially or even wholly seduced by the mystique of the premier German SS units. In the early 1970s, for instance, John Keegan – shortly to become the most famous military historian in the English-speaking world – wrote in a volume of the popular Ballantine war series that the best (or, to use the favoured term, 'classic') panzer units of the Waffen-SS altered the course of the war and were 'faithful unto death and fiercer in combat than any soldiers who fought them on western battlefields'.[34] As one astute observer summed up in 1974:

> It is not really the hard evidence of the SS that constitutes a problem, as much as the spread of its image through fiction, films, and folklore as tough, select, dedicated bands of men who stood off the world in spite of the foot-dragging of an apathetic or disloyal Wehrmacht. The SS upstaged the French Foreign Legion as a popular image of military elitism. Its fame has outlasted many of the forces that brought it down, and it continues to gain respectability as the generation who felt the direct horror of Nazism fades away. It may well have a delayed impact, a deferred inheritance of the Thousand Year Reich. The tree was cut but the seeds are still on the wind.[35]

To judge by what has appeared since then this prediction was spot on.

The opinions of James Lucas and Bruce Quarrie, popular authors who each wrote a series of books dealing with the Waffen-SS in the 1980s and early 1990s, are indicative of prevailing trends. The Waffen-SS, Lucas has asserted, was 'revolutionary' in terms of tactics, social inclusiveness, and supranational qualities. A 'unique bond of comradeship between all ranks' developed, along with a 'warrior spirit' which allowed the force to achieve 'spectacular victories'.[36] To Quarrie the elite units of the Waffen-SS deserved to be compared with the Israeli Defence Forces for sheer toughness, innovation, and courage. In his view 'a much closer camaraderie existed between officers and men than was possible within the Wehrmacht'; which, alongside a stress on aggressiveness and initiative, created a force which altered the course of the war. Moreover, Steiner and other Waffen-SS visionaries 'were trying to create something like a pan-European precursor of the North Atlantic Treaty Organization'.[37]

Meanwhile, in the Reich itself, the rehabilitation of the Waffen-SS indirectly achieved greater success in the latter 1980s through the tacit support of right-wing academics, leading journalists such as Nolte, and mainstream politicians seeking a usable past for Germany. In 1986 Andreas Hillgruber, a respected conservative academic historian, published a slim volume in which he appeared (among other things) to be arguing that both the Army and the multinational units of the Waffen-SS had been fighting desperately in 1945 to uphold a 'European concept' against the ravages of a barbaric Soviet enemy.[38] Two years later Hillgruber – by then a central figure in the *Historikerstreit* that had broken out over the meaning of the Holocaust[39] – almost wistfully admitted that efforts to achieve a pan-European partnership during the war had been rendered useless by Hitler's 'depraved' racial ideas.[40]

The debate over the relativization of the German past in the latter 1980s was fierce and the outcome far from inevitable, as the furore surrounding President Reagan's visit to a war cemetery at Bitburg (which included graves of Waffen-SS men) indicated.[41] Nevertheless, ideas which had previously been confined to the margins of popular culture have entered mainstream academic and political discourse. The unreconstructed war memoirs of Schönhuber, in which the Waffen-SS is portrayed as a misunderstood European 'military elite', went through eight printings in under a year.[42] Nolte's book *The European Civil War* – a quote from which opens this chapter – became an instant best-seller that went through three printings in as many months.[43]

The Waffen-SS, in short, has achieved varying degrees of acceptance. Though large-scale atrocities continue to tarnish its image and judgements concerning the European army concept are sometimes qualified, the 'classic' divisions are commonly treated as a revolutionary fighting elite.

These images of the Waffen-SS, like those of other forces supposedly embodying some form of revolutionary idealism, cannot be dismissed out of hand. As their adversaries were the first to admit, the SS panzer divisions were far from easy to overcome in battle, often fighting with great tenacity and skill.[44] Foreign volunteers, moreover, did indeed come from many countries to fight against the Soviet Union. SS men are known to have behaved with generosity and chivalry on occasion; and, as the more fervent admirers point out, opposing forces were not entirely free from the charge of mistreating POWs.[45] In every respect, however, there is ample reason to call into question the various elements of the Waffen-SS mystique.

The idea that the men of the Waffen-SS were 'just like other soldiers' in terms of behaviour towards prisoners and foreign civilians is the least credible of the several claims made on behalf of the force. Rather ironically, recent scholarship conclusively indicates that on the Eastern Front the

Wehrmacht was just as brutal as the Waffen-SS.[46] Yet in the West, at least, the notoriety of the force was entirely justified. Soldiers in all armies occasionally disregard the laws of war, but neither the Allied forces nor the Wehrmacht carried out reprisals with the same kind of systematic ferocity as the Waffen-SS.

During the invasion of France in the spring of 1940 elements of the 1st SS *Leibstandarte* and 3rd SS *Totenkopf* divisions, acting under orders in two separate incidents, shot in cold blood over 100 British POWs from the Norfolk and Warwickshire Regiments.[47] Four years later the 12th SS Panzer Division *Hitlerjugend* was responsible for a similar shooting of Canadian prisoners in Normandy, while the 2nd SS Panzer Division *Das Reich* engaged in the mass execution of the civilian population of Oradour-sur-Glane in southern France. In the Ardennes offensive later in 1944, seventy-one American POWs were gunned down near Malmédy by *SS Kampfgruppe Pieper*.[48] And, all protests to the contrary, there was undoubtedly a significant number of transfers between SS units that guarded the concentration camps or manned the *Einsatzgruppe* death squads and the front-line formations.[49] By no stretch of the imagination can the Waffen-SS be said to have fought a clean war, whatever veterans may claim.[50]

Rather more seductive is the idea that the Waffen-SS was a precursor to NATO, an army united by pan-European idealism. Here too, however, wartime realities clash with postwar mythology.

Even Hillgruber admits that Hitler was less than enthusiastic about the possibility of a European union under German auspices. What the Führer wanted was a Greater Reich in which neighbouring countries were either assigned minor satellite status or simply eliminated.[51] While quite content to see those of Aryan extraction brought into the Waffen-SS fold, he was less than pleased to learn of efforts to build units of Slavic *Untermenschen* and other foreign racial inferiors. Himmler was equally loath to see non-Aryans in SS uniform, and until manpower considerations forced him to reconsider his position in the latter part of the war he was willing to let the Wehrmacht supervise all Eastern and French volunteer units.[52] And though the Reichsführer-SS changed his tune in public utterances, his basic world-view remained no different from that of his master, as was revealed when he told assembled SS commanders in April 1943 that Scandinavia and the Low Countries would be incorporated and that foreign volunteers were expected to 'subordinate your national ideal to a greater racial and historical ideal, to the German Reich'.[53] It is hardly surprising, therefore, that even the most enthusiastic collaborationist leaders found to their dismay that raising men for an anti-Bolshevik crusade did not entitle them to any say in determining their country's future as an independent state. Like the units they helped sponsor, they became pawns rather than partners.[54]

Hitler himself remained adamantly opposed to Slavic SS units in particular, and a certain amount of subterfuge was necessary to get them established. When the Führer learned of their existence he was far from pleased. 'I have just heard for the first time, to my amazement', he exclaimed at a war situation conference in March 1945, 'that a Ukrainian SS-Division has suddenly appeared.' If the war had continued it is likely that Hitler would have made good his threat to disband such units and hand over their arms to newly raised German divisions.[55]

Xenophobic attitudes, moreover, were by no means confined to the political leadership. The staff of German military training schools found it difficult to adjust their methods to volunteers of a different (and, *ergo*, inferior) language and culture. To the Germans, the foreigners often appeared unfit for service in every sense. They were dim, slovenly, and lacking in discipline. Racial slurs and even physical abuse directed at the men in the ranks were not uncommon. The Flemings, for example, found themselves subject to beatings and referred to as 'a nation of idiots', 'filthy people', and 'gypsies'.[56] The Nordic volunteers, often coming from a higher social class than their SS trainers, were far from amused at the contempt in which they seemed to be held. Lacking the paramilitary training German recruits received in the Hitler Youth (HJ) and Reich Labour Service (RAD), and often not fluent in German, foreigners often found themselves handled with complete disdain. Even officers from foreign armies arriving with their legions commonly seem to have been thought to be incompetent, and were often replaced by Germans (or German pawns) while in training or at the front. Such moves, along with insistence on using the SS uniform and a tendency to assign foreign nationals arbitrarily to whatever Waffen-SS unit needed replacements, may have been justified on military grounds, but they also served to heighten nationalist friction. Several Dutch officers of the *Freiwilligen-Legion Niederlande*, for instance, resigned in protest at the high-handed manner in which they were being treated.[57]

Complaints from foreign Nazi leaders such as Staff de Clerq (Flanders) and Anton Mussert (Holland) led Himmler to order some overdue reforms in early 1942. The Waffen-SS officer school at Bad Tölz was opened up to foreign recruits, and cultural orientation sessions were made mandatory for German personnel involved with the volunteer legions. These changes, however, were not sufficient to convince collaborationists that they were involved in a true partnership and that their nationals were not mere cannon fodder. The technical services and senior ranks of most foreign units remained overwhelmingly German down to 1945, trained replacements from Bad Tölz being too few to keep up with demand even at the lower levels of command.[58] Even Steiner, commander of the most successful of the 'mixed' Waffen-SS units (*Wiking*) and a leading postwar promoter of the European army idea, admitted that integrating foreign nationals was 'not easy'.[59]

Xenophobia and military necessity aside, however, the SS training staffs had a point in complaining about the foreign units. Used to dealing with the most dedicated of German volunteers, they were shocked to find that many foreigners were not always committed to the cause. The collaborationist parties did their best to drum up support, and recruiting was fairly brisk (especially after the Nazi attack on the Soviet Union prompted the creation of national legions). There were, however, only so many Nazi sympathizers and anti-communists willing to risk their lives for their convictions – especially once it became clear that the Soviet Union would not be easily defeated. In occupied Europe joining the Waffen-SS, either directly or through one of the legions, carried with it the stigma of consorting with the enemy. In September 1941, for instance, volunteers from the *Freikorps Danmark* on a month's leave in Copenhagen were shocked to discover that they were treated with disdain rather than adulation by the city populace.[60] In December 1943 Himmler himself admitted that a third of foreign volunteers had been disowned by their families.[61] Despite some rather spurious attempts to suggest a mass movement, only a tiny fraction of national populations (0.057 per cent at most) chose to don a German uniform.[62]

As early as May 1940 some of those who volunteered for the SS Regiment *Westland* did so under the impression that they were signing on for a six-month sport course or joining the police.[63] Of the 875 Flemish volunteers for the *Flandern* Legion on the books by January 1942, 500 claimed to have signed on for labour service, not the Waffen-SS.[64] Other foreign volunteers from the West came forward for such non-idealistic motives as avoiding compulsory labour service, a desire for adventure, steady pay, or to escape sticky domestic situations or even prison terms. (Berger, perhaps making a virtue out of necessity, took the view that criminals often made effective soldiers.[65]) POW and foreign labour camps in the Reich, along with concentration points for collaborators fleeing the Allied advance in the West in 1944–5, became a key pool of recruits for the thinning ranks of the foreign SS units, and physical requirements were consistently lowered.[66] One or two men had even served in the International Brigades.[67]

Postwar studies of active collaborators in the Netherlands and Denmark revealed that while there was a hard core of politically committed volunteers, they were outnumbered by the rest. Among the Dutch volunteers, those who enlisted for food and adventure were over three times as numerous as idealists and committed Nazis. Among the Danes, an average of 16 per cent of volunteers were unemployed, and an average of 25 per cent had criminal records (the yearly percentages increasing over time as the war continued).[68] Faced with recruits such as Jutte Olafsen who decided 'I would join this [*Freiwilligen-Legion Norwegen*] rather than go to work in Germany', little wonder that one exasperated German NCO should complain that such men were 'a bunch of mercenaries only interested in their pay'.[69]

If there were motivational problems with recruits from the West, they were nothing compared with those of the men from the East. Though outnumbering the volunteers from Western Europe at least two to one, these men owed even less ideological allegiance to the German cause. The Bosnian and Albanian Muslims joined the Waffen-SS in order to pursue their time-honoured struggle with the Christian Serbs; the Finns, Estonians, and Latvians were pushing out those who had invaded their lands a year or so previously (or, in the later stages, were simply conscripted); Ukrainians, Turkomens, Cossacks, and other peoples under Russian control for longer periods fought for ethnic rejuvenation; and the Russians themselves, mostly recruited from POW and labour camps, donned German uniforms in order to avoid death by starvation and disease. Others, such as members of the notorious Kaminski Brigade, were simply bandits in uniform.[70]

All these motivational factors – plus limited equipment – had an effect on combat performance. This varied from unit to unit and over time, but rarely rose over the adequate and was often very poor indeed.

East European units (with the exception of the Baltic and Finnish volunteers fighting on their home ground) proved of distinctly limited fighting value. Balkan units employed on anti-guerrilla duties proved capable of carrying out spontaneous civilian massacres but incapable of adopting the discipline necessary to combat partisans successfully. The 13th *Waffen-Gebirgsdivision* der SS Handschar mutinied while in training and was later disbanded in 1944. A similar fate awaited the two other Muslim units, the 21st *Waffen-Gebirgsdivision der SS Skanderberg (alban. Nr. 1)* and the 23rd *Waffen-Grenadierdivision der SS Kama (kroat. Nr. 2)*, after high desertion rates quickly made them hollow shells. The Hungarians of the 25th and 26th *Waffengrenadier* Divisions formed at the end of 1944 proved so eager to go over to the Red Army that they had to be disarmed. Other units from the Balkans and points further east were either not committed to battle – for fear they would collapse – or were swiftly decimated in combat with the Red Army.[71] The so-called Russian Army of Liberation, which included former SS units, had the unique distinction of fighting its first and last battle against the Germans in Budapest (in the vain hope that this would expiate the volunteers' sins in the eyes of the oncoming Red Army).[72]

West European units were perhaps less prone to complete collapse, but still had serious problems. Morale in most of the legions took a plunge when the realities of life on the Eastern Front became apparent. Not always trained to the same standard as German formations, and certainly not equipped as first-line units, the legionaries – many of whom thought they would only arrive in time for the Moscow victory parade – were both physically and psychologically unprepared for winter fighting with the Red Army. Combat performance varied, with the *Freikorps Danmark* faring best and the French LVF worst. In almost all cases, however, German senior officers involved with the legions believed they had cause for complaint.

The LVF, it appeared, could not even keep up march discipline or take preventative action against frostbite. 'Working with the staff of Regiment [*sic*] *Niederlande*', according to a senior formation report dated February 1942, 'is very difficult, as officers fail to appreciate the tactical situation.' The operations officer of the *Legion Flandern* noted in early March of the same year that attacks suffered because of poor reconnaissance and a tendency for men to halt in their tracks if the German officer or NCO leading them was killed. As for the *Legion Wallonien*, the operations section of the 17th Army noted in January 1942 that the corps to which they were attached was complaining of behaviour 'bordering on treason'.[73] To the intense mortification of the German authorities, a Norwegian and a Dane actually deserted to the enemy from the *Nordland* Regiment in early 1942.[74] Field police began to be placed on troop trains to prevent volunteers on their way to the Eastern Front from acting on second thoughts.[75]

Combat performance improved over time as experience was acquired, but by then plenty of the volunteers had had enough. Without having fired a shot in anger, 500 of 1,000 Dutch volunteers in the *Nordwest* Regiment declined to join the *Niederlande Legion* when it was formed in July 1941, forcing the German authorities to close down *Nordwest* for lack of men.[76] When enlistments expired, many men simply wanted to go home. In the *Norwegen* Legion, for instance, only 20 per cent of the survivors re-enlisted in January 1943. New recruits often proved even less enthusiastic. The commander of the *Nordland* Regiment complained in March 1942 that the Danes and Norwegians he was getting 'cry like babies'.[77] As late as April 1945, when supposedly only hard-core fighters remained, about 50 per cent of the remnants of the French *Charlemagne* Division chose to opt out when given the opportunity to do so.[78]

There were, of course, both individuals and units that performed well and fought on to the bitter end. But it is worth noting that even in cases such as Knight's Cross winner Mooyman or the much-admired *Wiking* Division the reality does not match the rhetoric. Mooyman became a hero almost in spite of himself. Very much a juvenile and not a particularly enthusiastic soldier, he was sulking in his dugout when Soviet tanks attacked the *Niederlande* Legion south of Lake Ilmen on 13 February 1943. Virtually thrown out of his dugout by a German officer, Mooyman was furious and took out his frustrations on the enemy – knocking out thirteen tanks in the process.[79] As for the *Wiking* Division, there is no doubt that it was among the half-dozen best Waffen-SS formations. It was not, however, particularly foreign in composition. Of the 19,377 men on strength in June 1941, only 1,564 were Danes, Norwegians, or Dutch.[80]

Indeed, as the war dragged on and non-Germans came forward in fewer numbers even the more foreign formations were increasingly made up of Germans. The III SS Germanic Armoured Corps, for instance, which included the *Nordland* and *Niederland* Divisions, was only 26 per cent foreign by December 1943.[81] Overall, in fact, the non-German (neither *Reichsdeutsche* nor *Volksdeutsche*) contribution to the Waffen-SS was quite small. Steiner claimed that there were about 113,000 West Europeans in the force; the true number may have been as low as 63,000. This was roughly the equivalent of 10 per cent of the Waffen-SS at its peak strength in June 1944.[82]

The Waffen-SS had not, after all, 'practically created a supranational soldiery' dedicated to 'the dream of a united Europe'.[83] But to some enthusiasts this does not affect the level of homage due to the force. The *real* elite were the fighting men of the 'classic' German divisions: 1st *Leibstandarte*, 2nd *Das Reich*, 3rd *Totenkopf*, 5th *Wiking*, 12th *Hitlerjugend*, with opinion divided on the merits of two or three others. It was these formations which time and again saved the day for the wavering units of the Wehrmacht and fought doggedly to the end. To many observers the fighting record of the dedicated German volunteers in these units is incontrovertible proof of their revolutionary nature.[84]

That these units often fought with great tenacity cannot be doubted, as any Allied or Russian soldier unfortunate enough to be facing them could attest. Yet there are several indications that even the 'classic' Waffen-SS was not quite the army of supersoldiers it was made out to be.

To begin with, it needs to be remembered that a very large number of 'German' wartime recruits for the Waffen-SS were *Volkdeutsche* (racial Germans from abroad). This allowed Berger and Himmler to get around army restrictions on the number of men from within the Reich they could recruit and engage in an expansion programme from 1941 onward. But it also meant taking in men who might be part of the *Volk* by blood but in terms of habits, culture, and language were entirely separate.

Theodore Eicke, the commander of the *Totenkopf* Division, complained in 1942 that:

A large number of the racial Germans can only be described as intellectually substandard. Many can neither read nor write German. They do not understand the words of command and are inclined to be insubordinate and malingering. Orders issued are generally not carried out, the excuse being that they did not understand what their officer wanted. This is an invitation to cowardice.[85]

Many ethnic Germans, like other foreigners, resented the high-handed manner in which they were treated by *Reichsdeutsche* officers and NCOs. Friction grew so great that in 1942 the SS journal, *Das Schwarze Korps*, had to remind its readers several times that *Volksdeutsche* truly were German and should not be treated with condescension.[86]

Matters were not helped by the fact that some racial Germans signed on for what they thought was labour service in the Reich and then found themselves in uniform. As early as August 1941, *Volksdeutsche* were being conscripted directly into the Waffen-SS.[87] Not surprisingly, their combat performance was not always very good.[88] Senior commanders soon began to judge the worthiness of Waffen-SS units by the number of *Volksdeutsche* they contained: the higher the proportion of racial Germans, the less effective the unit.[89] This is particularly revealing when it is remembered that by the end of 1943 a quarter of the entire Waffen-SS was made up of *Volksdeutsche*.[90]

As one would expect, the hard cores of the classic divisions were volunteer *Reichsdeutsche*. Yet even here motivation was not always based on altruistic idealism. Becoming an SS combat leader offered the prospect of faster promotion for army officers. The high physical standards and 'Black Guard' mystique of the SS before the war held considerable inverse snob appeal, and it is worth remembering that service in the SS-VT counted towards fulfilment of the universal military service obligation. 'I must say that if I had a choice', one German veteran candidly observed, 'I would not have joined any of the forces at all, it was only conscription which forced me into it [choosing the Waffen-SS].'[91]

To be sure, the prewar SS recruits were by and large well motivated, and in the early years of the war developed a well-deserved reputation for dash and energy in the field. As the force expanded, however, entry standards and commitment tended to decrease. As early as December 1938 the creation of new units meant that recruits lacking several teeth, those with varicose veins, bone abnormalities, and co-ordination problems were standing alongside the earlier examples of perfect Aryan manhood.[92] The huge wartime expansion of the Waffen-SS meant that standards had to be lowered even further: 'funny sort of SS men, this crowd', as one veteran *Wiking* officer recalled of the very young and overage recruits he was leading by March 1944.[93]

Moreover, the fierce reputation that the Waffen-SS gained soon came back to haunt the recruiting effort within the borders of the Reich. Many parents were not, it turned out, all that eager to see their sons become martyrs. Nor were Germany's young men necessarily willing to sacrifice themselves. In March 1942 the SS security service was reporting to Himmler that there was talk of Waffen-SS men being 'recklessly sacrificed'. Recruiting centres reported in early 1943 that many young men and even more parents were 'anti-Waffen-SS'. The general attitude, one report stated, was: 'if I am conscripted I can do nothing about it, but volunteer I will not'.[94]

Given that the Waffen-SS prided itself on being an all-volunteer force, this was extremely worrying. In an effort to keep up a façade of voluntarism, Berger tried hard to strong-arm young Germans into joining up. A few men 'volunteered' as an alternative to a prison sentence.[95] Recruiting officers sent out among the Hitler Youth and to RAD camps, facing apathy and outright hostility from parents and offspring alike, bullied and sometimes beat youths into signing on from 1942 onward. Some were simply tricked: having volunteered for the Wehrmacht, they found themselves in SS uniform.[96] By 1943 the voluntary response had become so weak that to form the new 9th and 10th SS Divisions, RAD men had to be conscripted wholesale (forming 80 to 90 per cent of all recruits). Outright conscription – which included underage youths – became the norm in the last years of the war.[97] After the failed attempt on his life in July 1944 had completely destroyed Hitler's faith in the reliability of the Wehrmacht, Himmler was even allowed to incorporate 50,000 men from Luftwaffe field units into Waffen-SS divisions – a move which 'aroused much dissatisfaction' among the personnel concerned.[98]

Conscription, of course, in and of itself does not mean that those drafted into units with existing cadres of battle-hardened SS personnel would not fight well. There is much evidence to suggest, in fact, that many conscripts absorbed the battle ethos of elite divisions like *Das Reich* and *Hitlerjugend*.[99] Yet it is worth bearing in mind that even the best of the German formations included reluctant or low-quality soldiers in the latter stages of the war.[100]

In both the 2nd and 12th SS, when opportunities for men to avoid danger to life and limb by accepting Allied inducements to desert presented themselves, a number of men (albeit small) took advantage.[101] There were also cases of self-inflicted wounds, desertion in the face of the enemy, men being driven forward at gunpoint, defeated battle groups of several hundred men surrendering *en masse* to smaller British forces, and even – by the end of the Normandy battle – something approaching terrified flight.[102] In the hard-fought battle for Arnhem in September 1944, green conscripts of the 9th SS under attack by British paratroopers attempted to fade away to the rear or even cross over to the enemy and surrender. Some at least took the view that 'it's all useless anyhow, they'll simply overrun us'.[103]

Such scenes, though rather less evident to the Allies than the fanatical resistance of the majority of Waffen-SS men fighting in the West, were nevertheless symptomatic of the wider morale problems of the final stages of the war. The very last division in the Waffen-SS order of battle, the 38th Panzer-Grenadier Division *Niebelungen*, scraped together from the personnel of SS training schools and assorted other odds and ends in April 1945, never really got off the ground. 'We had no materials', an SS man transferred from the *Wiking* Division lamented, 'and morale in the ranks was poor . . . . After a hopeless few days, we sent everybody home, and the *Niebelungen* Division collapsed.'[104] In the final days of the Third Reich some Waffen-SS men fought to the bitter end, but even among the elite units like 'Wiking' other men were caught trying to desert or convicted of cowardice in the face of the enemy and summarily executed (including SS-Obergruppenführer Hermann Fegelein, who had served as Waffen-SS liaison officer at the Führer's side).[105] 'Don't be a hero', one SS-man advised another in the 9th SS. 'The war is lost.'[106]

What, then, of the oft-cited revolutionary training methods of the Waffen-SS? What of the class-free nature of all ranks, the lack of social distinction between officers and men, the status as an elite comradeship-in-arms? Once again the available evidence suggests a more complex situation than is often suggested.

To begin with the class issue, there is no doubt that the senior ranks of the Waffen-SS included men of humble background who would never have risen to field rank – or even been commissioned – in the old Imperial Army or the Reichswehr of the 1920s. For old Nazi fighters such as Theodore Eicke (the stationmaster's son who led the *Totenkopf* Division) and Sepp Dietrich (the one-time butcher who eventually commanded the 6th Panzer Army), the SS offered avenues of advancement that would almost certainly have been blocked in the status-conscious regular army.[107]

The prewar SS, indeed, made it a point to avoid setting educational qualifications at a level accessible only to the privileged few (as was the case in the Reichswehr).[108]

Moreover, the kind of bluff and informal mateyness that Dietrich fostered in relations with the troops under his command, the effort to eradicate the traditional social gulf between officers and men, was consciously fostered at SS training schools and within units by officers like Felix Steiner, disciples of the kind of *Frontgemeinschaft* echoed in the works of (among others) Ernst Junger. In this sense the Waffen-SS really was a career open to talent in which officers, NCOs, and men mixed (eating together, for example) and spoke easily, and forged a disciplined unity of effort based on respect rather than fear or status.[109]

Many personal accounts stress the degree to which this culture of comradeship was fostered within the combat SS, and how much it helped instill a sense of mission. Other accounts relate the way in which Dietrich, say, went out of his way not to take on superior airs, to visit his men, and to speak bluntly in all circumstances. The contrast with Prussian *Junker* manners was quite striking, as a witness to a conversation between Field Marshal Ewald von Kleist and Dietrich in April 1942 observed.

> I remember . . . that the Field Marshal had a rather haughty manner. His thin lips never moved, except when this was strictly necessary. Fat old Dietrich, on the other hand, waved his arms about and talked a lot. He looked rather like a shopkeeper doing a deal with a customer.[110]

This sort of absence of social consciousness, the focus on proven ability in leadership as a qualification for promotion, along with the bonds forged in the heat of battle once the war began, confirmed for many SS men the sense that from top to bottom the Waffen-SS was a classless band of brothers. 'A mutual respect existed', as an NCO of the *Wiking* division recalled. 'Many commanders radiated a certain charisma and their troops would follow them to hell and back.'[111] As Hitler himself admiringly noted of Dietrich (in a remark that could also have applied to many other SS officers), 'what care he takes of his troops!'[112]

A number of qualifications need to be raised about this image of 'all for one and one for all' (as one veteran put it).[113] First, as the Waffen-SS massively expanded during the war and simultaneously suffered heavy losses, the tight ties of community began to unravel. 'So much is said about the special comradely relationship between officers and men in the Waffen-SS', one lance-corporal observed,

> but I have to say that it wasn't always so. In the [16th SS Panzer-Grenadier] Reichsführer-SS Division, for example, I didn't even know that SS-Gruppenführer Max Simon was my divisional commander until after the war had ended. Sometimes we didn't even know who our company commander was.[114]

As in the army, high casualties on the Eastern Front in particular meant that units saw such a high turnover that group identity became problematic.[115]

The second caveat concerns the assumption that social mobility and officer–man relations in the Waffen-SS were more advanced than in the regular armed forces. To be sure, in the Reichswehr of General Hans von Seeckt educational and other qualifications were stringent enough to prevent promotion from the ranks, and many younger army officers saw better prospects for advancement in the armed SS of the early 1930s.[116] Once Hitler began to rearm Germany, however, and the Wehrmacht began to balloon in size – from 100,000 soldiers in 1933 to 730,000 men under arms by 1939 – promotion prospects and social mobility in the army dramatically improved. The war, of course, only increased opportunities. By 1945, eight of the Wehrmacht's generals had risen from the ranks.[117] Moreover, the classlessness of the Waffen-SS should not be overstated, especially at the senior level. The majority of Waffen-SS generals had transferred from the army in the 1930s or during the war, and very few of them came from a lower-class background. Of the sixty-nine SS-Brigadeführer to SS-Oberstgruppenführer officers who served in armed formations, fifty-two had been career officers in the Imperial Army – as against only seven former NCOs.[118] Despite being high profile, commanders like Dietrich were the social exception rather than the rule.

As for the revolution in officer–man relations within the SS, here too the case has been overstated in relation to the army. As early as May 1934 General Werner von Blomberg had issued orders that officers should mix with enlisted men at social functions, while (as always) looking after the physical and emotional well-being of the troops under their command. Two years later the German officer was told 'to find his way to his subordinates' hearts and gain their confidence by understanding their feelings and their thoughts'.[119] During the war US Army interrogators found that captured German soldiers 'usually remarked that their officers felt genuine interest in the welfare of their men'.[120] The Waffen-SS, moreover, was by no means free of the fanatical attention to order and neatness that British soldiers would term 'bull'.[121]

Then there is the supposedly elite nature of Waffen-SS training. Without a doubt it was tough, emphasizing sports, teamwork, initiative at all levels, and a great deal of aggressiveness. But this was also true of the army.

In both cases, for example, training infantry to deal with enemy tanks sometimes involved forcing men to dig and hide in holes before an oncoming vehicle rolled over them.[122] Nor should SS training be perceived as necessarily tougher than in other armies. 'How hard was it?' a member of the *Wiking* Division reflected in an interview. 'I can state quite categorically that the training I went through in the Danish Cavalry was tougher than anything I later encountered in the Waffen-SS.'[123]

As for speed and aggressiveness, von Seeckt himself had stressed this in the 1920s, and the emphasis was carried over into the 1930s. 'The officer who demonstrates cold-bloodedness, determination, and courage in front of the enemy', a 1936 instruction ran, 'pulls the troops along with himself.'[124]

The similarities between the two forces were not coincidental: the regulations for SS-VT training were patterned on those of the army, and the personnel and the tactical curriculum of the SS Junkerschule at Bad Tölz was virtually interchangeable with the army officer training school at Munich.[125] Not surprisingly, therefore, army officers also tended to lead from the front once war began.[126]

In addition, just like army formations, Waffen-SS units had to make do with low-quality replacements with increasingly limited training as the war progressed. The resulting decrease in SS combat effectiveness was first demonstrated in July 1941, when policemen drafted into *SS Kampfgruppe Nord* simply panicked and ran in the face of a Soviet counter-attack at Salla. Himmler could hush up this affair, but by the last years of the war training was increasingly a problem.[127] 'Nearly all the men in my *Kampfgruppe* are new recruits', as one officer noted in reference to the state of the *Wiking* Division in March 1944. 'It's difficult to make them camouflage themselves properly. The platoon commanders have to shout orders and give warnings almost all the time.'[128] Six months later, elderly replacements for the *Das Reich* Division were lucky to get ten days' training before going into action – with predictable results.[129] During the Ardennes offensive in December 1944, SS-Oberrtsturmbannführer Joachim Peiper found that after heavy fighting only the threat of being shot prevented the crews of some of the tanks in his *Kampfgruppe* – spearheading 1st SS – from retreating when they were supposed to be advancing.[130]

The Waffen-SS did, however, have one crucial advantage over the army, especially in the last years of the war: it got more and better equipment. Its reputation in the latter stages of the war as Hitler's 'fire brigade' was due at least in part to the elite Waffen-SS units receiving more and better equipment than army divisions. By the end of 1943, seven of the thirty panzer divisions and six of the seventeen panzer-grenadier divisions were Waffen-SS, despite the fact that the force then only made up 5 per cent of armed forces' strength.[131] At the battle of Kursk that year, the SS panzer divisions possessed two to three times more tanks than the army panzer divisions, and nearly all the newest models.[132] By the autumn of 1944 a typical SS panzer divison had forty more tanks and assault guns, 4,000 more men, and a much larger motorized component than a typical army panzer division.[133]

This helps to explain, among other things, the incredible success of SS panzer divisions against entire Soviet corps and armies in 1944–5. The apparent disparity in strength between a division and a corps or army has sustained the myth of a Waffen-SS David fending off a Red Army Goliath. The difference in actual numbers of tanks and men, however, was by no means as great as the titles 'division', 'corps', or even 'army' would suggest, the Soviet forces – especially rifle regiments – being often considerably understrength. An up-to-strength SS panzer division in 1944, for example, had approximately double the number of tanks possessed on paper by a Soviet tank brigade, and sixty-five per cent of the tanks and tank destroyers allocated to an entire Soviet tank corps. Only a Soviet tank army possessed the five-to-one superiority in armour considered necessary for any chance at a breakthrough.[134]

The qualitative advantage was more evident in the West, where German Tiger and Panther tanks, though few in number, massively outclassed British Cromwell tanks and the hordes of American-built Sherman tanks both in armour and armament. The results could be devastating for British, Canadian, and American crews, and leave SS men feeling like supermen. 'A thing like that', a section leader of the 2nd SS Panzer Division reflected on an episode where his Panthers had knocked out four Shermans and halted an American attack in Normandy, 'puts you at an unbelievable emotional level. . . . You feel like Siegfried, that you can dare to do *anything*.'[135]

Nevertheless the Waffen-SS did not, overall, perform better than the German Army. Statistical analysis of dozens of operations has shown that German formations, *whether Waffen-SS or not*, inflicted 50 per cent more casualties on British and American formations than they incurred. The same appears to have been true of the war in the East.[136] The Waffen-SS, it is worth noting, won no more Knight's Crosses than the army relative to the size of each force.[137] In the West the tendency to portray the Waffen-SS as virtual supermen may in part be due to a disinclination to accept Allied failures in staff work and field training.[138]

Yet the men of the Waffen-SS did differ from the soldiers of the German Army in one crucial respect that had nothing to do with equipment or fighting power. Strength and casualty figures for both forces vary, depending on the source, and HIAG has vehemently denied claims by army generals that the Waffen-SS suffered heavier losses.[139] Even the most conservative calculations, however, show that the Waffen-SS suffered 5 per cent more fatalities than the army, a figure which may in reality be much higher.[140]

In part this may have had to do with the sheer level of death-defying aggression fostered within the elite SS units. Arrogantly confident in their own superiority and (like all German youth but perhaps to an even greater degree in an SS environment) caught up in the Nazi creed of heroic sacrifice for the Fatherland, Waffen-SS men tended on first acquaintance to hurl themselves at the enemy.[141] Army officers took note of the high casualties SS units suffered as early as the 1939 campaign in Poland, a trend also noticeable in France in 1940.[142] In May 1940 the commander of *Totenkopf* argued that if an objective was achieved 'losses made no difference', a comment that applied equally to holding positions to the last man (literally) rather than withdrawing if the Führer had so ordered. The Waffen-SS was always to the fore, but also constantly suffering from high casualties – losses brought about in part by a refusal to adapt to reality. Even in training the Waffen-SS was willing to accept significant losses.[143]

Survivors of the early battles tended to be more cautious: 'listen my lad', as one veteran put to an overeager newcomer in 1941, you're going to cop it in double-quick time if you go on like this. You don't have to fight as if you were a knight in the Crusades; just kill Russians, that's all. Very brave of you, and all that, but it's not good enough.[144]

In one celebrated episode Kurt Meyer had to drive veterans of his *Leibstandarte* battalion forward into enemy fire during the 1941 campaign in Greece by throwing a hand grenade at them.[145]

But arrogance, tenacity, and aggressiveness in battle remained part of the Waffen-SS creed even in the latter years of the war. 'Often the SS soldiers went into battle even though they were severely wounded', a volunteer in the *Leibstandarte* remembered proudly of his service in 1943–4. 'Doing otherwise never crossed their minds.'[146]

Kurt Meyer, the archetype of the dashing young Waffen-SS commander, later admitted that the kind of attritional warfare being waged against both the Russians and the Allies 'was the very antithesis of all we had learned and believed in'.[147] Yet he himself, like other SS officers, could not always adapt to the new reality. On 6–7 June 1944, for example, Meyer was so confident that the British and Canadians were 'little fishes' compared with the men of the 12th SS that he launched a counter-attack that left many dead and the surviving youths of the *Hitlerjugend* Division crying tears of frustration.[148]

A few months later, during the battle for Arnhem, a disastrous attempt to retake the bridge was made by a group of 9th SS armoured cars and personnel carriers under the command of SS-Hauptsturmführer Viktor Graebner (recent winner of the Knight's Cross and a typical armoured swashbuckler) who was apparently under the impression that British paras would be unable to withstand crack SS panzer-grenadiers.[149] 'Young fanatics [of the 10th SS]', claimed 30 Corps commander General Brian Horrocks, 'had even advanced into battle sitting on the outside of their tanks shouting, "I want to die for Hitler".'[150] Field Marshal Albert Kesselring, commanding Army Group G, was afraid that some SS men would refuse the order to surrender in May 1945. The cease-fire order was obeyed, though some Waffen-SS volunteers went on to emulate their late Führer by choosing to shoot themselves rather than fall into Russian hands.[151]

Yet in all probability it was the senior officer corps of the Waffen-SS – especially the old fighters – which constituted the larger problem leading to high casualties. While admiring the dash and fortitude of SS men, some army generals had serious doubts about the competence of officers such as Eicke and Dietrich. As early as the summer of 1940 staff officers were claiming that in France the Waffen-SS had 'suffered tremendous losses' in attacks launched without thought or skill, the result of 'foolhardy and inexperienced leadership'.[152] General Erich Hoepner of the 16th Panzer Corps had called Eicke a 'butcher' to his face in the course of the campaign. Erich von Manstein, one of the great panzer generals of the Eastern Front, had serious reservations about the leadership of the *Totenkopf* division. 'It is not to be denied that many SS commanders gave proof of outstanding bravery nor that their troops often won great tactical successes', noted General Siegfried Westphal (Chief of Staff in the West in 1944), 'but at what appalling cost were they bought!'[153]

The basic problem was that while good leaders of men the type of officer whom Goebbels fondly described as 'an old Party warhorse' did not possess the staff skills for senior command positions.[154] Though the influx of middle-class professionals into the SS after 1933 and the transfer of ambitious army officers raised the educational standard of the officer corps, over 40 per cent of senior men (Obergruppenführer to Brigadeführer) possessed only a primary or middle school certificate.[155] The best SS generals, like Hausser, had undergone senior staff training in the Reichswehr or Wehrmacht. But the old political fighters, including Dietrich and Eicke, were much more at a loss in high command.

The rise of such men owed as much to their political record – helping eradicate the SA leadership in 1934, for example – as it did to their military skills. Eicke, for instance, who hated the army, became a divisional commander simply because *Totenkopf* was initially composed of concentration camp guards then under his direction.[156] Dietrich, who rose from leading Hitler's bodyguard in the early 1930s to command the 6th Panzer Army by late 1944, enjoyed the complete confidence of the Führer through his plain speaking and bluff optimism. 'The role of Sepp Dietrich is unique', Hitler enthused in January 1942. Perhaps no other single figure enjoyed as much lavish publicity, as many decorations, and as rapid a series of promotions as Dietrich, a man whom Hitler (perhaps naïvely) considered a simple but loyal fighting soldier.[157] Conversely, Hitler disliked Hausser – 'a wise guy [who] gives the impression of a weasel' – who behaved too much like the aristocratic army generals he distrusted.[158]

Unfortunately the SS men to whom Hitler warmed often lacked the expertise for high command. At the same time, they tried to showcase their talents and those of their men by thrusting forward even when ordered not to do so. Though killed before he could be promoted in 1943, Eicke displayed signs of incompetence even at the divisional level. In May 1940 he led the *Totenkopf* Division across the line of advance of Army Group B, creating huge traffic jams. In February 1943, in an effort to speed up the pace, Eicke led the motorized elements of the division off a road and, as the ground thawed, into a sea of mud where they got stuck.[159] Manstein complained that 'I repeatedly had to come to the division's assistance'.[160]

Dietrich was luckier in the gambles he took, but the Armed Forces High Command (OKW) was less than pleased when in November 1941 he sent the *Leibstandarte* Division 'charging into Rostov' without orders 'purely to gain a prestige victory'.[161] Once he was promoted to command a corps in the summer of 1943 Hitler's favourite was at least assisted by a competent Chief of Staff transferred from the army: yet 'burning with zeal', according to Manstein's ADC, Dietrich yearned 'to become the reconqueror of Kharkov, and Manstein had to take some pains to prevent him from making a frontal attack on the big town'.[162] By 1944 there were clear signs that he had been elevated above his ceiling. Field Marshal Erwin Rommel, in charge of Army Group B in the West, did not trust him to co-ordinate an attack by I SS Panzer Corps in Normandy and placed him under General Geyr von Schweppenburg of Panzer Group West.[163] Field Marshal Gerd von Rundstedt, C-in-C West, regarded Dietrich as 'decent but stupid' and was especially critical of his handling of the 6th Panzer Army in the Ardennes. Many other generals agreed; even his principal staff officer conceded that Dietrich 'was no strategic genius', while an angry POW from the 6th Panzer Army snarled to an interrogator that 'Sepp Dietrich is not even fit to be a good butcher'.[164]

Reputedly neither Eicke nor Dietrich had been taught how to read a military map,[165] and they were by no means the only SS field generals to be criticized for headstrong incompetence. Von Kleist radioed to *Wiking* HQ in the summer of 1942:

> The commander of the 'Viking' division is 1: to be informed that the Army will not have positions occupied contrary to orders; 2: to report how it comes about that, without reporting the fact, he has occupied a position other than that expressly ordered by Corps headquarters.[166]

Herbert Gille, commander of *Wiking* and later of IV SS Panzer Corps, was in some ways a bumbler, and Brigadeführer Theodor Wisch, leading the *Leibstandarte* in Normandy in 1944, expended copious amounts of Panther ammunition in shooting up dozens of British tanks on the night of 18 July that had already been hit and abandoned.[167] Even Hausser appears on one occasion to have succumbed to the Waffen-SS predilection to charge forward, inflicting unnecessary casualties on I SS Panzer Corps by driving straight into Kharkov against orders in March 1943 (evidently the feat Dietrich had wished to repeat that summer).[168]

In sum, therefore, the Waffen-SS was a powerful but flawed instrument. By the last years of the war, as SS-Untersturmführer Hans Woltersdorf (*Das Reich*) conceded, the fierce reputation of the force was largely a myth: the men merely 'living on the laurels earned by its very first volunteers'.[169] Waffen-SS successes, sometimes overrated, were achieved at a high price in men and material denied to the army. Relations between the two forces were sometimes very sour indeed, soldiers displeased at the way the Waffen-SS was being built up at its expense and the men of the Waffen-SS suspecting that army commanders were using them as cannon fodder.[170] Extreme unit loyalty made it more difficult for SS men to form the kind of *ad hoc* battle-groups that the Wehrmacht used to effect after orthodox formations had been mauled. On the Eastern Front, *Landser* penal units were apparently used by Waffen-SS officers as expendable human shields for SS personnel engaged in anti-partisan operations, and there is at least one recorded instance of a front-line Waffen-SS man shooting down in cold blood a Wehrmacht supply officer who got in his way. Not surprisingly, there was considerable 'bad blood' between the Wehrmacht and Waffen-SS as a result of such actions.[171]

The Waffen-SS possessed both the strengths and frailties of the German Army, but also weaknesses of its own making. Its multinational component was not by any stretch of the imagination a prototype for the European Community, and the supposedly revolutionary *Frontkameradschaft* and driving aggression can be seen to be either unexceptional or self-defeating in nature.

Like that of the International Brigades – though in the multinational context to an even greater extent – the collective portrait of the Waffen-SS built up since the end of the war is a distortion of the truth. Yet, as with revolutionary armies whose image and fame are purely national in character, it was those involved in both the International Brigades and the Waffen-SS who actively promoted the development of a mythology. There was, however, one further possibility concerning the genesis of such mythologies that needs to be explored. As we shall see in the next chapter, it was even possible for *the enemy* to be the main source of support for an army's 'revolutionary' credentials.

10 The Viet Cong in the Second Indochina War, 1960–75

Legs of brass and shoulders of steel?

... defeat material force with moral force, defeat what is strong with what is weak, defeat what is modern with what is primitive, defeat the modern armies of the aggressive imperialists with the people's patriotism and determination to carry through a thorough revolution.

General Vo Nguyen Giap on NLF strategy, December 1964[1]

Now wait a minute. You don't have to explain anything to me. I'm tired of the damn Vietcong and have come over to the government side. Just ask me anything you want.

Viet Cong defector on turning himself in, January 1966[2]

In many ways the military accomplishments of the military wing of the National Front for the Liberation of South Vietnam (NLF), more commonly known as the Viet Cong, appear unique. The Vietnamese communists, after all, had managed to force the withdrawal from Indochina of the most powerful nation on earth by 1973, thereby presenting the world with an image of a David-and-Goliath struggle in which ideological strength and endurance had triumphed over modern military technology.

To be sure, the roots of guerrilla warfare can be traced back to ancient times. Furthermore the Viet Cong, one among many freedom-fighter movements in the era of the Cold War and decolonization, were to a considerable extent following the path of revolutionary development first charted by Mao Tse-tung in China's civil war in the 1930s and 1940s.

The basic pattern of Maoist-style peasant revolt – which the Vietnamese followed with their own variations in both the First Indochina War against the French from 1945 to 1954 and in the Second Indochina War against the Americans in the 1960s – involved several stages of revolutionary activity. First, a revolutionary movement would establish itself in the hinterland, working patiently and methodically to gain the support of the rural population. Second, guerrilla fighters would seek to weaken the enemy army through hit-and-run attacks and ambushes. Finally, sometime after many years of protracted struggle, a third and final stage would be reached in which the enfeebled regime would be toppled through a mixture of guerrilla and conventional military action.[3] The Viet Cong, therefore, were not themselves creating a new way of war.

Nevertheless in some ways the Viet Cong victory has seemed more complete than those of similar forces engaged in rural 'wars of national liberation'. VC weaknesses, for one thing, have not been subsequently exposed for all the world to see, as was the case with the Cuban guerrilla movement under Castro or the *mujahidin* of Afghanistan.

The obvious inability of Che Guevara to organize a *foco insurreccional* in Bolivia in the mid-1960s has indicated to all but the faithful – in marked contrast to what had been thought at the time – that a few hundred brave *Sierra guerrilleros* were not in fact the primary force behind the 1959 Cuban Revolution as Castro had claimed.[4] As for the *mujahidin*, evidence of the vicious internecine squabbling that delayed victory over the Najibullah regime by at least a year in the late 1980s (and has created a state of near chaos in Afghanistan ever since) has tarnished the Western propaganda image created in the early 1980s of bands of freedom fighters intent only on throwing off the Soviet yoke.[5] The People's Republic of Vietnam, in contrast, continues to try to avoid providing the outside world with evidence of dissension involving the VC (and, if anything, has tended to play down the role of the VC in achieving unification).[6]

Moreover, no other revolutionary force had successfully faced the full might of the American military machine. Red China, to be sure, squared off against US forces in the Korean War, but even the People's Liberation Army found itself in difficulties when continuous contact with superior US firepower had generated criticism of Maoist reliance on revolutionary willpower and brought many front-line PLA units to the point of despair by the time of the 1953 armistice.[7] The Vietnamese, on the other hand, learned from their mistakes and simply fought on and on against the Americans, eventually bringing to fruition Ho Chi Minh's prediction that it would be the enemy who would lose the will to continue the fight.

To many, especially Americans, the VC – to a greater extent than their northern brethren in the NVA[8] – continue to appear as the toughest, most dedicated of unconventional opponents. They were stealthy masters of the night; experts at camouflage; men (and women) who lived in jungles or tunnels, set ambushes, and made every effort to remove their dead and wounded from the battlefield; people of courage and conviction who could overcome great physical hardship and constant danger; fighters who could subsist on only a few grains of rice a day, supported by only the most primitive of medical facilities; expert guerrillas who could blend in with and control the population; underdogs in the war who made the best possible use of their inferior weaponry and could manufacture a host of booby traps. In short, the VC are viewed as opponents of almost superhuman ingenuity, dedication, endurance, and skill. In metaphorical terms, 'the individual Viet Cong guerrilla was the rock on which the American enterprise in Vietnam foundered'.[9]

Not surprisingly, this is a picture which many former VC find congenial. Too much applause for the southern war effort is frowned upon in Hanoi, but low-level former guerrillas and more senior former VC now living in the West have made their feelings clear. 'Although the guerrillas were short of food and often sick', Troung Nhu Tang (a senior political official associated with the NLF) recalled in his memoirs, 'they maintained the kind of esprit and comradeship that animates people who are fighting for a common purpose in which they believe with all their hearts.'[10] The VC moved 'like black ghosts' at night, an anonymous Main Force ex-VC fighter reminisced.[11] 'General Westmoreland', one former village guerrilla explained gleefully to an American friend, 'thought he was fighting a traditional army. Ha!'[12] Or as a VC village cadre put it to a US correspondent towards the end of American involvement with evident pride: 'we have no airplanes. We have no tanks. All we have are men with legs of brass and shoulders of steel.'[13]

Yet to a very great extent it is the former enemy, the Americans, who have built up the cult of the VC. And to understand properly the ways in which external reality may have been confused with products of the imagination, the wartime roots of the American image of the Viet Cong must be examined.

Though US military advisors had been assisting the Army of the Republic of Vietnam (ARVN) since 1959, few among the growing number of American combat troops sent to Vietnam from 1965 onward – reaching a peak strength of over 500,000 men in 1968 – had much understanding of either Vietnam or the VC (beyond a somewhat hazy belief that communist invaders had to be stopped). The language and culture of Vietnam was entirely foreign, and even intelligence officers had to rely for the most part on interpreters.[14] Vietnamese behaviour patterns, not least those of the VC, were confusing and frustrating. Confident in their equipment, training, and weapons, American troops arrived expecting to fight off successfully waves of Asian communists in the manner of the Korean War. Instead, they found themselves searching for, but as often as not failing to make contact with, a very elusive enemy in an alien environment amidst a peasant population whose loyalties remained a closed book.[15]

Whether as individual guerrillas or in full-blown units up to regimental or even on occasion divisional strength, 'Victor Charles', or more commonly 'VC' or just plain 'Charlie', seemed able to escape village sweeps or big search-and-destroy missions while planting mines and booby traps and choosing the perfect moment to ambush an isolated American platoon or company. Peaceful farmers by day could turn into stealthy guerrillas by night, and a booby trap or ambush might await daylight American foot patrols or even men relaxing within supposedly secure camp perimeters. Charlie was always 'out there', watching and waiting, but keeping his distance unless he had the advantage; and when he did engage in battle, he rarely stayed around long enough to be caught and destroyed. 'Charlie's an enemy that is nowhere', a soldier in the 101st Airborne explained to a fellow paratrooper in 1966, 'but at the same time everywhere.'[16]

This was stressful. 'You were never "out of it" in Vietnam', a lieutenant of the 173rd Airborne Brigade remembered of his tour in Binh Dinh province in 1971–2. 'You could never let your guard down.'[17] The VC 'would watch you all the time', a staff sergeant stationed at Tuy Hoa in 1967–8 related to an interviewer. 'They knew your pattern.'[18]

It was also frustrating. 'We had been out [on patrol] for nearly two months', Lieutenant Colin Powell later wrote of his experiences as an ARVN advisor in 1963. 'I had seen men hurt. I had seen men die. But I had yet to see the enemy.'[19] A junior officer in the 11th Light Infantry Brigade, Americal Division, described to a journalist the effect of such a situation on the men of C Company in 1968.

> At seven each day, we would start out through the villages to reconnoiter them . . . we were sniped at. We never learned who by, though . . . and the Vietnamese [villagers] told us, 'we don't know either.' It frustrated us, it hurt our morale. . . . We had been in Vietnam three months: we were losing men, we were being nickel-and-dimed away, we were being picked off. We were in Vietnamese villages daily, and we still hadn't seen one VC.[20]

Watching yet rarely seen – even dead bodies vanished after the enemy withdrew from a firefight – the VC might begin to take on different shapes in the minds of Americans.

To Lieutenant Philip Caputo, among the first wave of US Marines to serve in Vietnam in 1965 and the author of one of the most highly acclaimed Vietnam memoirs, the VC became like 'wraiths' or 'djinns', apparently able to vanish at will yet willing to fight to the death when they chose.[21] Others described them as 'devils', 'phantoms', or 'ghosts'.[22] Zen-like metaphors also popped up. A good VC, according to one long-range patroller, was at one with nature and thereby 'master of the sinuous, floating art of guerrilla war'.[23]

The VC could thus appear as something more than mortal flesh. An army manual published for infantry officers lamented the fact that the VC had become swathed in a 'haze of myth and legend', and that it was 'often forgotten that he is a human being'.[24] Marines interviewed for a book in 1966 told tales of peaceful villagers who at night turned into deadly guerrillas 'as readily as Clark Kent into Superman'.[25] The sheer invisibility of the enemy could be disconcerting. 'I don't know where these guys go to when you kill 'em', a baffled 25th Infantry Division veteran later mused. 'It's just that they just vanish. Somewhere. I don't know. Maybe the Twilight Zone.'[26] Troops in training at Fort Polk in 1968 chanted a mock nursery rhyme that seemed to place the enemy in the same category as the more malevolent characters in a Grimms' fairy tale: 'Vietnam, Vietnam, every night, while you're sleepin', Charlie Cong comes a-creepin'.'[27]

The VC could also seem something less than human. 'The VC is almost never seen close up', veteran French observer Bernard Fall reported in October 1965 with the clinical air of an enthusiastic zoologist studying a particularly dangerous big cat; 'he lives a shadowy existence in deep forests and grottoes, displays no unit insignia . . . carries no dog tags . . . manages to bury his weapon before he is found dead . . . [and] remains faceless and nameless.'[28] The hunting-a-dangerous-animal metaphor was implicit also in descriptions of impossible feats of endurance and mortally wounded VC who either kept on coming or crawled away to die. A VC fighter, according to one veteran, was 'the smartest animal there is'.[29]

Some US soldiers, to be sure, reacted with undiluted contempt towards an invisible enemy who used civilians as a shield or (worse yet) were civilians by day and fighters by night: 'dinks', 'slopes', or 'gooks' who refused to stand and fight like real men. 'I had no respect for the sneak-around, hide-in-the-bushes Viet Cong guerrilla', a Marine staff sergeant recalled. Norman Schwarzkopf, who served as a battalion commander in the 23rd Infantry Division in 1970, labelled them 'opportunistic brigands'.[30] 'Why do you and the other correspondents pick on the 173rd [Airborne Brigade] and print nothing but stories about the VC's elusiveness?', Brigadier General Ellis W. Williamson complained to Peter Arnett in August 1965. 'Don't you know that the VC are cowards, they fight only at night and when we catch a bunch of them together they run away?'[31] The VC 'were . . . very lousy, pitifully stupid fighters – period', the (1968) commanding general of the 25th Infantry Division replied angrily when asked his view of the enemy long after the war.[32]

Others, hating yet also fearing the enemy, began to treat all Vietnamese as potentially hostile; indeed to treat all locals as if they were the enemy and behave with great brutality as a psychological release from the anxieties of constantly lurking but unseen danger. The massacre of well over 100 women and children in My Lai 4 in 1968 was only the largest and most well-documented case of American troops turning on the people they had been told they were there to protect. At least some combat soldiers could empathize with Lieutenant William Calley's assertion that 'these people, they're all the VC'.[33]

Yet the majority of US servicemen at all levels seem to have developed at least a healthy respect and often a sneaking admiration for the apparently indefatigable VC. 'I dunno, Charlie's up to something', was a fairly typical Grunt point of view. 'Slick, slick . . . *so* slick. Watch!'[34] Elaborate tunnels for secrecy and infiltration purposes were said to be everywhere, and when the sun went down Charlie 'owned' the night – so much so that some units eventually either avoided or faked night contacts with the enemy.[35] This was all in marked contrast to the South Vietnamese forces, which came to be regarded as cowardly and incompetent. 'There are only two lots of good soldiers in Vietnam', as one Australian private put it. 'Us and the Viet Cong . . . let's get together and do the rest over.'[36] Many American soldiers began respectfully to refer to the enemy as 'Mr. Charles' or 'Sir Charles'.[37]

Junior officers, too, came away from Vietnam impressed by the enemy. The VC 'would do anything to win. You had to respect that. They believed in a cause', according to a Marine platoon leader who served in 1968–9.[38] 'I had a great deal of respect for the Viet Cong', a captain in the 1st Cavalry Division who served two tours in Vietnam admitted. 'They were trained and familiar with the jungle. They relied on stealth, on ambush, on their personal skills and wile, as opposed to firepower.'[39]

The views of two battalion-level commanders, both veterans of Korea decorated for bravery and highly outspoken concerning US failures they observed in Vietnam, are particularly revealing. 'I had a great deal of respect for the fighting capabilities of the Vietnamese [VC/NVA] troops', Lieutenant-Colonel Anthony Herbert recalled when looking back at his time with the 173rd Airborne Brigade in 1968–9. Colonel David Hackworth, who commanded a battalion of the 9th Infantry Division in 1969, agreed. 'Charlie was a most worthy opponent.'[40]

Even many of those at the top conceded in retrospect that initial perceptions of an easy US victory were flawed. 'The enemy was tough, versatile, tenacious, and cunning', according to Lieutenant-General Willard Pearson, a brigade commander in the 101st Airborne Division in 1966.[41] General William E. DePuy, chief operations officer at Military Assistance Command Vietnam (MACV) under General William Westmoreland in the mid-1960s, looking back thirty years on, thought that the VC were 'motivated patriots' and that their battles 'were planned, prepared, and executed in minute, careful detail in such a manner that almost guaranteed success'.[42] Of over 100 generals polled in 1974, only 6 per cent thought the VC were not worthy adversaries – 57 per cent going so far as to agree that they were 'skilled and tough fighters'.[43] Westmoreland himself (grudgingly) went on record to admit that his foes had been 'wily, tenacious, persevering, and courageous to the point of fanaticism', while former Defense Secretary Robert S. McNamara in retrospect realized that the VC were 'an elusive and deadly enemy'.[44]

War correspondents, lacking face-to-face contact with the VC in the field, might also unconsciously build a largely mythical picture of the opposition. 'I had thought of these guerrillas as shadowy jungle fighters who moved on the edge of reality', an Austrian writer admitted.[45] The sheer weight of American firepower – bombs, shells, napalm, chemical defoliants – made their (unseen) survival seem all the more remarkable. 'They displayed more courage than I imagined within me to summon', *Los Angeles Times* correspondent Jacques Leslie recalled; 'I was awed.'[46] Moreover, after several years of US involvement the constantly upbeat claims made at the daily MACV press briefings (the so-called 'five-o'clock follies') began to lose their credibility in the face of continuing enemy resistance.[47] And, unlike the generals, the press were free to speak their minds to the American public.

The huge scale of the surprise 1968 Tet offensive, in which the VC suddenly attacked all over the country and tried to stage a mass uprising to topple the South Vietnamese army government, seemed to indicate conclusively that the enemy remained undefeated. '[A]fter two years of massive military intervention in Vietnam', Joseph C. Harsh intoned in an ABC television report on 1 February, 'the enemy has been able to mount and to launch by far the biggest and boldest and most sophisticated offensive of the whole war.' The VC were 'ready and willing to die', Frank McGee stated in an NBC special report. Other correspondents spoke or wrote of the VC's tenacity, courage, boldness, daring, their 'power to make themselves invisible', and their extreme dedication unto death. 'The Vietcong proved they could take and hold almost any area they chose', a CBS reporter stated.[48] With VC sappers having even made it into the US Embassy compound in Saigon, it seemed as if the VC had achieved dominance. 'Vietnam was a dark room full of deadly objects', Michael Herr remembered; 'the VC were everywhere and all at once like spider cancer . . . they didn't seem depleted, let alone exhausted.'[49]

In point of fact the VC had been hurt badly in Tet '68 and had failed to smash the GVN, but this outcome was overshadowed by the post-Tet erosion of the political will in Washington to fight on to victory and by the growing mystique surrounding an enemy who apparently never gave up. This mystique did not diminish as US forces in Vietnam undertook a gradual withdrawal from 1969 to 1973; nor did the successful invasion by the North in 1975 dissipate the sense that the VC possessed enviable soldierly attributes. Military analysts draw parallels with the ragged Continentals and militia in the American War of Independence, and the memoirs already cited began to appear.[50] 'Charlie was not lousy opposition', a former US Marine stated emphatically twenty years after the American withdrawal. 'He was good, damn good.'[51]

The aura surrounding the VC, indeed, grew stronger as the American public began in the latter 1970s and the 1980s to develop a picture of the Vietnam War largely based on Hollywood movies.[52] 'Charlie didn't get too much [relaxation]', Captain Willard reflects in *Apocalypse Now* (1978). 'He was dug in too deep, or moving too fast. His idea of USO was cold rice, and a little rat meat. He had only two ways home: death . . . or victory.' Though most films concentrated on American soldiers and neither the enemy nor the Vietnamese in general are shown in any detail, the VC were always lurking in the wings. 'Right under us, at this very second', a soldier in the film version of *Casualties of War* (1989) explains tensely to another Grunt at night, 'could be VC tunnels as far as the eye can see.' Even in the movies which stressed realism, the enemy could be portrayed as a crawling jungle menace closing in on unsuspecting GIs.[53]

Barring the racial subtext, there is a good deal of substance to the image of the VC as an elusive, tenacious, and well-organized revolutionary army. Detailed analyses of NLF activity at the time and subsequently revealed that the VC in the early 1960s methodically built up a politico-military infrastructure in villages throughout South Vietnam through a mixture of persuasion and intimidation. Southern cadres reinfiltrated from the North highlighted the corruption and injustices of landlords and GVN (South Vietnamese) officials, demonstrated in word and deed that the NLF was for the people, and engaged in a highly effective campaign of selective assassination of GVN officials in rural areas. Coupled with progressively bolder guerrilla actions against South Vietnamese security forces, this campaign had by 1964–5 wrested control of much of the countryside from the Saigon regime.[54]

The VC infrastructure, moreover, was sufficiently deep rooted and flexible, and VC cadres so motivated and resourceful, that the National Liberation Front was able to weather the storm of direct US intervention in the latter 1960s. With part-time local, and full-time regional and main force units operating in secret in the villages and jungles, the VC managed most of the time to avoid battle except on its own carefully planned terms. In conjunction with NVA units operating in the border regions, VC fighters managed to avoid complete destruction while inflicting a steady stream of casualties on American soldiers through booby traps and ambushes. Life in the NLF forces grew harder, but the system of political indoctrination and group solidarity fostered through self-criticism sessions, combined with the selfless dedication of many cadres, was generally quite effective in keeping the VC a going concern.[55]

Yet at the same time there can be little doubt that certain factors have combined to inflate the justifiable military attributes of the VC into the realm of fantasy. Quite apart from the racial issue and the elusiveness of the enemy, there is the fact that the United States clearly lost the war – something only a truly outstanding adversary could have accomplished in the minds of many Americans. 'It is a symbiotic relationship', a veteran who served with a long-range reconnaissance unit between 1967 and 1969 reflected; 'if we were good . . . then they must be good too.'[56]

Vietnam remains in many ways a closed society, and frank discussion of the war, let alone free access to important documents, is not encouraged. Nevertheless, enough evidence exists through published material and recollections to call into question the scale of the VC mystique.

To begin with, the David-versus-Goliath nature of the struggle between the US Army and the VC can be overrated. It is true, of course, that American units could call down massed artillery fire and air strikes to assist them, and that armoured vehicles and above all helicopters allowed infantrymen to be deployed in the field at great speed and in comparative safety. The VC had almost no heavy artillery, no air support, and were not airmobile. On the other hand, the VC possessed certain advantages that often negated American mobility and firepower.

Artillery and air bombardment, above all B-52 strikes, were undoubtedly frightening and potentially quite lethal. However, the VC quickly learned to 'hug' the enemy or withdraw from their initial positions, so that artillery or air strikes either could not be called in at all for fear of hitting GIs or struck at abandoned positions.[57] Armoured vehicles were largely road bound, and vulnerable to ambush by VC equipped with rocket-propelled grenades or captured recoilless rifles.[58] Helicopters firing into the jungle were often shooting blindly, and were themselves vulnerable to ground fire when approaching landing zones (cleared areas which became prime targets for ambushes).[59]

Even the feared B-52s could be countered. In VC sanctuaries in Laos and Cambodia, taking shelter was made possible by advanced warning from spies and Soviet intelligence ships. And at least initially, troops on the move could anticipate the linear bomb pattern of B-52s and choose the best direction in which to run. A CINCPAC (Commander-in-Chief Pacific) study in 1969 indicated that even as B-52 raids had increased five times over between 1965 and 1968, the number of VC killed in these strikes had declined by 80 per cent.[60]

Nor, man for man, was the VC in an inferior position. American strength in Vietnam did grow by 1968 to a total of 543,000 men; which, with the ARVN and allied troops added, gave the United States a theoretical numerical advantage of anywhere from 3-to-1 to 6-to-1 over the enemy. But of these, only about 80,000 were combat troops.[61] This reduces the ratio for 1968–9 to about 1.6 to 1, a figure which does not take account of the real – as opposed to paper – field strength of many US combat units in Vietnam.

In 1966, Marine battalions in Vietnam were found to be operating with only about half their allocated manpower. Three years later, the 173rd Airborne Brigade (10,000 men) could only deploy 3,000 infantrymen in five rifle battalions. A check on the 9th Infantry Division in 1968 showed that battalions supposed to be able to send out 157 men were in fact fielding only 65 to 70 men.[62] Whether due to the ever-present 'call of the rear', disease, or the need to create and maintain an adequate support infrastructure, the number of American soldiers in the field was quite small.

Just how large the VC was in the years of American involvement remains a matter of sharp dispute.[63] Nevertheless it was the US Army, not the VC, which was in the weaker numerical position in the field. If MACV was correct in its conservative estimates (280,000), then US field forces in 1968 were outnumbered 3.5 to 1 by the VC. If the more comprehensive estimates of the CIA are used (600,000), then the Americans were outnumbered 7.5 to 1.[64]

US forces were, to be sure, much more concentrated and mobile than the VC, who were spread around the country and moved on foot. In areas of US offensive operations in 1967 it was estimated that the ratio of combat infantrymen on each side was roughly equal.[65] The VC, however, rarely allowed themselves to be put in a position of numerical equality in battle, let alone inferiority. General Westmoreland (one of whose ancestors had reputedly fought at Naseby for the King[66]) pursued a strategy of attrition, hoping to find, fix, and destroy main force VC and NVA regiments in large, multi-battalion search-and-destroy operations in remote areas, making maximum use of airmobility and firepower.[67] Yet time and again, operations like ATTLEBORO (September–November 1966), CEDAR FALLS (January 1967), and JUNCTION CITY (February–April 1967), as well as their smaller brethren, failed in their purpose because the VC avoided all but minimal contact while withdrawing to sanctuaries in Cambodia and Laos.

What fighting there was almost always was the result of VC initiatives – usually ambushes of one sort or another – against semi-isolated US units. A national security study at the end of 1968 revealed that three-quarters of all battles were conducted at a time, place, and duration of the enemy's choosing.[68] (Armour was particularly vulnerable to surprise attack: army figures showed in early 1967 that 88 per cent of all firefights by armoured troops with the enemy were begun at the latter's behest.)[69] VC casualties in what fights there were could be heavy, but the loss rates could always be controlled.[70]

Nor were the VC necessarily inferior to American soldiers in terms of food and arms. The VC did not enjoy the incredible wealth of supplies available to US troops, but they rarely went without enough food in a land that produced enormous amounts of rice. Food supply dumps captured and destroyed by the enemy could be replaced within five to ten days by taxing the local peasantry.[71] As for arms, by 1967 main and regional force units were quite well equipped with Chinese AK-47s, mortars, and RPGs sent down the Ho Chi Minh trail or shipped through Sihanoukville.[72] US battalions were generally still heavier, but this was by no means necessarily an advantage. Once dropped at the landing zone, US infantry units had to sweep areas on foot. 'Humping in the Boonies', as it was known, was extremely fatiguing, the effects of a tropical climate made worse by the need to carry up to 60 pounds (27 kilograms) or more of equipment (helmet, rifle, grenades, flak jacket, extra ammunition, radios, and sundry other items). Stealth was also harder to achieve. 'The Americans were like elephants', one VC fighter recalled, 'especially when moving through the jungle.'[73] In contrast VC soldiers in one fairly well-equipped main force battalion carried, on average, only 27 pounds (12 kilograms) of weapons and ammunition, wore the lightest of clothing and webbing, and used conscripted civilian porters for long marches.[74]

Added mobility, moreover, could mean more time on operations, especially early on. The 173rd Airborne, for example, was redeployed half a dozen times for various major missions between May 1965 and January 1966. The men were exhausted.[75] Based on over 200 in-depth interviews with POWs and defectors, a RAND study covering the 1966–7 period showed that the VC soldier on average only engaged in battle a mere 2.32 times over a twenty-six-month span. As more and more US forces arrived in Vietnam in 1967–8, this rate grew to two to three times every six months – still far below the contact average for US field troops (especially when contact with booby traps, accounting for up to 25 per cent of US casualties,[76] is included as a form of combat). Serious efforts, moreover, were made to rest VC troops after severe engagements.[77]

Furthermore, whereas the VC often learned from their mistakes, the US Army did not. Generals who fought in Vietnam in retrospect recognized that both in terms of strategy and tactics the right lessons had not been learned.[78]

In terms of strategy, Westmoreland from 1964 to the end of 1968 doggedly attempted to seek out VC and NVA main force units, convinced that the VC infrastructure and guerrillas could be left to the South Vietnamese. Given that the main force VC and NVA regiments could and did avoid contact by retreating over the border into Cambodia or Laos, and that bureaucratic bungling and corruption within the GVN consistently undermined village pacification efforts (which the VC resisted fiercely), this was a strategy that consistently played to enemy strengths.[79]

Efforts to switch the focus away from big-unit search-and-destroy operations or sweeps in favour of small-unit counter-insurgency tactics were always sidelined. The Marines, for example, initiated a quite promising system of Combined Action Platoons in early 1966, whereby small units consisting of a mixture of Marines and local South Vietnamese militia were stationed in lowland villages. Westmoreland, fearing that such small units ran the risk of being overwhelmed and seeing the big enemy formations along the border areas as the real threat, successfully pushed for this strategy to be watered down to the point where 95 per cent of all combat units in the second half of the year were involved in search-and-destroy operations. In June of the following year, despite the fact that 90 per cent of all VC operations had taken place in the populated coastal plains, 86 per cent of all MAVC battalion operations were still dedicated to search-and-destroy missions elsewhere.[80] 'Our effort belonged where the people were', Marine General Walt Krulak complained in reference to Westmoreland's overruling the Marine approach, '*not* where they weren't.'[81]

By the time Westmoreland had been replaced by the more flexible Creighton Abrams in late March 1968, it was already clear that the United States was going to pull out of Vietnam. Though Abrams made some effort at moving away from search-and-destroy missions, in the last years of US involvement the dwindling number of American soldiers and their declining willingness to fight limited what could be done.[82]

There were also failures at the tactical level. Partly because of institutional inertia and partly because of the rotation system which placed officers in-country for only a few months and the soldiers for twelve, the lessons of combat in Vietnam had to be constantly relearned. Making matters worse was the fact that the manpower demands of the war, combined with the political necessity of avoiding a call-up of the reserves, meant that the quality and training of junior officers, NCOs, and men had seriously deteriorated by the late 1960s. Hence the famous quip that the United States did not fight in Vietnam for ten years, but one year ten times over.[83]

Moreover, the US emphasis on firepower was extremely wasteful and often self-defeating. Artillery fire and air strikes took an enormous toll on civilian life and property, and generated millions of refugees.

US officials admitted that in 1968 alone 27,200 civilians had been killed by friendly fire, a figure which is almost certainly far too low.[84] The infamous VC/NVA body count used to help determine the success rate of US units encouraged soldiers to be quite liberal in choosing who to shoot at.

As early as November 1966 McNamara was worried that since 'the VC/NVA apparently lose only about one-sixth as many weapons as people', it seemed likely that 'many of the killed are unarmed porters or bystanders'.[85] Perhaps as many as one-third of all casualties listed as VC were in fact civilians.[86] In a brigade of the 9th Infantry Division, for example, the kill ratio shot up to over 1,000 to 1 in March 1969 (up from the 1968 average of 4.3 to 1) when rules of engagement were in effect loosened to the point where troops could shoot at virtually anyone.[87]

Needless to say this kind of thing did not tend to win the hearts or minds of the rural peasantry.[88] Furthermore the emphasis on mass firepower, combined with poor training, created a situation where by 1969 15 to 20 per cent of all American casualties were caused by friendly fire or accidents.[89]

In short, American material superiority was not as marked as is often assumed. On the other hand, it is equally misleading to assume that the VC were all highly motivated freedom fighters who always knew how to fight well.

The core of the NLF, those tens of thousands of dedicated party members who had either fled north in 1954 (and had been secretly sent back south from 1959 onward) or remained in place, were undoubtedly willing and able to endure a great deal in the ongoing struggle for liberation and unification.[90] Moreover, grievances among the poorer peasantry against landlords and local officials, combined with appeals to nationalist sentiment, generated a good deal of popular support for the VC in the countryside.

In the early 1960s, as the Saigon regime grew weaker and the NLF stronger, the VC also attracted many of the more uncommitted peasants who were told, not without reason, that the puppet regime would shortly collapse. Hatred of local officials, expectations of a rapid victory, a desire for adventure and advancement, and a wish to avoid being drafted into the ARVN (which – unlike the VC at this stage – forced recruits to serve away from their home localities), all played a role in swelling the ranks of the active VC to over 50,000 fighters by the end of 1964.[91]

In part because of strategic miscalculations, the opportunity to topple the Diem regime before US ground forces could be committed in 1965 was lost. General Nguyen Chi Thanh (commanding the southern theatre) and others within the Central Office for South Vietnam (COSVN) nevertheless remained confident that the plan for the 1965 winter–spring campaign, which had been formulated prior to American intervention, was still sound. The imperialists and their puppets would be engaged fiercely, and out of a protracted struggle would come a general offensive and uprising that would topple the puppet regime and force the United States to withdraw.[92]

VC fighters, convinced through propaganda and battlefield success against the ARVN that they were invincible and that victory was just around the corner, were in for a shock. US tactics were far from subtle, but the combination of heavy firepower and a willingness to fight generated huge losses among VC and NVA units committed to battle in 1965–6. Morale within the VC was shaken, and although the infrastructure displayed remarkable resilience, there were signs that the newer recruits were having second thoughts about their active commitment to the NLF now that the end of the war was no longer in sight and the risk of death had significantly increased.[93]

Even before direct US intervention difficulties had arisen. The shift towards a full-scale offensive strategy in 1964–5 had led the NLF to impose total mobilization on the countryside, including three years' compulsory military service for men 18 to 35 years of age. The prospect of being drafted into the regional or main forces and being sent to fight elsewhere, however, was not met with much enthusiasm among the peasantry. The setbacks of 1965 simultaneously increased VC manpower and materiel demands on the villages and the peasants' reluctance to serve. Subterfuge and blackmail had to be employed by VC cadres, and desertion became a major problem. In one village in Dinh Tuoung province 80 per cent of the youths drafted in the first half of 1965 ran away.[94]

The big American offensive operations of the mid-1960s only made things worse. Though allowing the VC to return to the villages after the Americans had passed through, big sweeps were unsettling and disruptive, causing the loss of stores and hideouts and forcing VC units to move more often and live under highly unpleasant conditions in remote jungles or underground (neither of which the Vietnamese liked any better than Americans).[95] Villagers began to become more circumspect in supporting the NLF as prospects for short-term victory receded and manpower and other demands increased. Even allowing for body-count exaggeration and VC efforts to drag away and hide bodies – designed to deceive VC troops as well as the enemy about the true extent of losses – it became more and more obvious that losses were increasing into the hundreds each month.[96]

Morale was maintained at an acceptable level within the VC through rigorous indoctrination and denial. Enemy losses were exaggerated, VC losses minimized or ignored. The lessening of enthusiasm among the villagers, moreover, was met by greater coercion and even terror. Overall, indeed, the VC remained strong as the draft was expanded in scope and enforced with greater rigour. Gullible or reluctant youths of both sexes were tricked, blackmailed, and even kidnapped outright to swell the ranks of the main force units at a rate of over a thousand recruits per week.[97]

The proportion of volunteers among recruits, however, had as early as the middle of 1965 declined to under 20 per cent.[98] Furthermore, holier-than-thou calls for personal sacrifice for the sake of the cause did not always work too well with draftees. The gap between NLF claims and the reality of life in the VC could not always be bridged, and claims that homesickness or illness were evidence of moral failure were sometimes alienating. 'Being in the communist ranks', one ex-VC complained, 'is almost like being a priest.'[99]

Moreover, though the VC did learn from their mistakes (avoiding direct confrontation with large US units after 1966, for example), there were inherent problems that could not be easily overcome. Though meticulously planned, ambushes and night assaults could go disastrously wrong if (as often happened) enemy resistance was tougher than expected or co-ordination broke down. For the sake of security the VC often could only train in small groups. In a force largely made up of simple peasants bravery was stressed over initiative and adaptiveness, with the result that the more complex an operation the greater the chances for something to go seriously awry – especially since the VC had to operate at night (a matter of necessity rather than choice). Limited live-firing exercises, furthermore, meant the VC were often very poor shots.[100] Even when total surprise was achieved, in attacks on US positions the VC on average lost five times as many men as did the Americans, in part because once an attack was under way it could not be altered. On those occasions where American commanders learned to anticipate VC moves and caught the enemy by surprise, the ratio increased to twenty-five to one.[101]

When they themselves became subject to surprise attack, the VC (especially in cases involving the semi-trained local and village forces) often made their situation worse than it might have been through carelessness and lack of knowledge. The local VC, a Marine of a Combined Action Platoon in Thu Luong in 1965 recalled, 'didn't move in a military manner, they talked while moving at night, smoked cigarettes, and didn't know what to do when caught in an ambush'.[102] This was not an isolated case. 'One night an enemy column walked right into the position of one of my machine guns', General Williamson remembered. 'The entire column continued walking to their deaths out of sheer ignorance.'[103]

Disasters of this sort did little to improve morale. Despite stringent efforts to prevent it, tens of thousands of VC ran away when the opportunity arose. Ideology played little or no role in this. Just as many fighters had joined up for reasons other than the cause, so too many men and women – especially young conscripts – chose to leave for non-ideological reasons. Above all else, the dangers and sacrifices of guerrilla or main force life made either going home or changing sides quite attractive. 'We used to joke that life was hard at home,' one fighter remembered, 'but that life in the Viet Cong was ten times worse.'[104] A constant refrain among ralliers was 'I couldn't stand the hardships any longer'.[105]

At American urging the South Vietnamese government had set up a programme (*Chieu Hoi*) in 1963 to entice VC to switch sides. Despite its lack of priority – until 1965 a single ARVN captain ran the whole thing – the *Chieu Hoi* programme was a great success. Very few North Vietnamese regulars defected, but among the VC, as one hard-core guerrilla admitted, 'a lot of people switched sides'.[106] In 1964, when the Saigon regime seemed about to collapse, there had been 5,000 ralliers. In 1965, when US troops intervened, the number jumped to 11,000. In 1966, there were 20,000 ralliers, and 27,000 more in 1967.[107] Even more of a problem for the VC were those who went home. CIA and RAND calculations in 1966 suggested that anywhere from 50,000 to 100,000 VC were deserting annually.[108]

Many of these deserters and ralliers were, to be sure, low-level draftees, and a few were *agents provocateurs*. Yet cadres and party members also turned themselves in, including in 1966 a lieutenant-colonel who turned out to be Deputy Chief of Staff to the VC 5th Infantry.[109] NVA soldiers had to be infiltrated to make up the shortfall in numbers.[110]

The NLF viewed the *Chieu Hoi* programme with some alarm – 'loyalty was something the Viet Cong always worried about'[111] – and made serious efforts to persuade VC fighters that the safe-conduct leaflets dropped from aircraft could not be trusted.[112] But a striking indication that VC fighters were – at the very least – seeking an insurance policy was the discovery after one engagement that 90 per cent of those killed and captured by American forces were carrying *Chieu Hoi* safe-conduct passes (a punishable offence).[113] 'These defectors have denounced our activities to the enemy', an outraged VC cadre in Phu Yen province complained in reference to an engagement in June 1967 where over four times as many guerrillas had rallied than had died in action, 'thus at present the enemy knows our operating procedures and is creating many difficulties for us.'[114]

Some stabilization did occur after the shock of US intervention began to wear off.[115] The VC, however, already under considerable strain despite American mistakes, was almost destroyed in 1968 as a result of strategic errors.

The goals of the VC/NVA war effort that year were ambitious. Impressed by anti-war demonstrations in the United States and given a false sense of the extent of support for the VC among the southern populace, the Hanoi leadership began to plan a general offensive and uprising that would, if all went well, end the war. US units would be drawn to remote regions such as Khe Sanh through NVA demonstrations and other deception measures. Then, during the lunar new year celebrations – traditionally a period of truce – the VC with NVA help would attack with everything it had. The population would rise up, the ARVN would collapse, and the United States *ipso facto* would be forced to withdraw.[116]

The Tet offensive was a military disaster. American intelligence failed to anticipate fully the scale of the first wave of attacks, so a fair degree of surprise was achieved. Almost everything else went wrong. Assaults were poorly co-ordinated, the population did not rise up, the ARVN did not collapse, and by coming into the open the VC exposed itself to the full effects of American firepower. As General Tran Van Tra (commanding VC forces in the Mekong Delta region) admitted, planners 'did not fully realize that the enemy still had considerable capabilities and that our capabilities were limited, and set requirements that were beyond our actual strength'.[117] By the end of February 1968, amidst the heavy fighting that so impressed reporters, the communists lost as many as 37,000 fighters killed in action (24,000 of them VC) and COSVN was admitting failure.[118]

Things only got worse in the wake of Tet. Colonel Houng Van Ba, commanding the E268 Regiment, remembered that after the failure of the campaign near Saigon 'we didn't have enough men left to fight a major battle, only to make hit-and-run attacks on posts. So many men had been killed that morale was low.'[119] The number of deserters and defectors soared as, once again, the prospect of imminent NLF victory receded. A follow-up offensive in May 1968 collapsed in disarray, in part because the plans had been betrayed by Colonel Tran Van Dac, the deputy political commissar for military region 4 who had defected in April.[120] Attacks between February and July 1969 generated huge casualties to little effect. In 1969 the annual number of ralliers, including an unusually high proportion of cadres, peaked at 47,000.[121]

Moreover, the often successful efforts by the VC to rely on persuasion rather than generalized terror in winning over the population were severely undermined by the mass executions carried out during the Tet offensive in Hue by overzealous political cadres. This served to stiffen anti-communist resolve: an NLF victory, it now seemed, would produce a bloodbath.[122]

At the same time, rural pacification – which Giap later asserted was 'a threat to the progress of the war' even before Tet[123] – was becoming more effective through the new CORDS (Civil Operations and Revolutionary/Rural Development Support) organization.[124] Though subject to the usual problems of corruption and statistical manipulation, the joint CIA–GVN effort to target the VC infrastructure – the Phoenix Program – also caused difficulties for an organization very much on the defensive.[125] 'There's no doubt 1969 was the worst year we faced, at least the worst year I faced', a VC village organizer in Long Kahn province recalled. 'There was no food, no future – nothing bright.'[126] The US/ARVN incursion into Cambodia in 1970 only added to NLF woes, and by 1972 the total number of ralliers since 1963 had reached 890,000.[127]

It is important to bear in mind that though mauled, the VC were by no means destroyed in the latter 1960s. The Tet offensive, though a military failure, had helped swing public opinion in the United States in favour of American withdrawal from Vietnam, and as units were progressively withdrawn from 1969 to 1973 US Army performance deteriorated. The GVN and the South Vietnamese security forces were better organized and more effective than in the past, but this did not make up for the fact that without direct US military support South Vietnam was still too unstable, corrupt, and fractious to overcome the full-scale enemy offensive in 1975.[128] (In this sense the war may have been lost for Saigon in the early 1960s when the NLF first established itself in the countryside, victory only being postponed in the years of US direct intervention.)[129]

Nevertheless, the VC after 1968 played a smaller and smaller role in the war against the Saigon regime. They suffered net losses, and new main force recruits lacked crucial training and experience – leading to further losses. 'At night the VC usually strolled in single file and created as much, if not more bedlam than we did', one former US infantryman noted of his time in-country in 1969. 'They'd utter aloud, cluster into groups, and often employ a flashlight to consult maps.'[130] Increasingly what replacements there were came from the north – making up an estimated 75 per cent of some units[131] – and in both the 1972 Easter offensive (which failed) and the 1975 spring offensive (which succeeded) it was the NVA which played the major role. Until disbanded in the wake of victory the remnants of the VC soldiered on, but as Lieutenant-General Ely R. Roberts, the commander of the 1st Cavalry Division, asserted: 'By late 1969 the VC as such was not a force to be reckoned with.'[132]

Overall, therefore, the VC do not live up to the more far reaching of the claims made by admirers. They were neither jungle supermen nor natural troglodytes, and their dominant motives both for joining and leaving the NLF usually involved individual or family hopes and fears rather than abstract principles. Despite a well-organized infrastructure, a viable long-term strategy, and an excellent system of controlling behaviour and attitudes within units, the VC leaders time and again were mistaken in believing that people could withstand any hardship and that offensives and uprisings would succeed because 'it is possible . . . to defeat the most modern weapons with a revolutionary spirit'.[133] There was, in short, a fair amount of clay mixed in with the brass and steel.

Conclusion

The cult of heroic sacrifice on the battlefield has weakened in the wake of the sheer destructiveness of the world wars. The romanticism associated with idealistic conceptions of fighting righteously and gloriously has not stood up well to the mechanistic and rather sordid realities of total war.[1]

Yet even in the context of a general sense of disillusionment and disenchantment, revolutionary armies have to a considerable extent maintained their hold on the collective imagination. The battle of Naseby may not loom very large today in English consciousness, but the Ironsides remain a model of stern determination and commitment that crops up repeatedly (especially in a comparative context) and continue to serve a foundation-myth function for the British Left. Those who joined the ranks of the Continentals, especially the first minutemen who sprang to arms in 1775, have always been portrayed as the very essence of the unchanging values of the United States, a symbol of heroic self-sacrifice and moral uprightness still used to promote everything from life insurance to ICBMs. As the 1989 bicentennial celebrations indicated, the men of the *levée en masse* are still central to the republican image of the French Revolution. In northern South America, those who followed the icon Bolívar continue to enjoy the status of *libertadores*. Though in retreat in the 1990s, hard-core Afrikaner nationalists go on celebrating Blood River; and in spite of changing politics the memory of the Taiping and Bengal Army rebels continues to be a source of inspiration to elements in China and India respectively.

Nor is this simply a matter of drawing on the past to compensate for the lack of heroic idealism in the twentieth century. Participants in wars fought within the last sixty years or so, such as the fighters of the International Brigades and their *alter egos* in the Waffen-SS, have striven to control the dominant collective memory of their struggle: the former with more success than the latter (though this may be changing). In the case of Vietnam, usually portrayed in terms of collective disillusionment in the United States, the stereotypical image of unwavering political commitment and military success has been a constant presence – only this time displaced onto the enemy.

Perhaps the most telling indicator of the strength of the belief that 'the

Cause maketh the Soldier' is the double standard applied to victory and defeat. Victory for a revolutionary army is often taken as a sign of the relative moral strength of the two sides. (This is true even in the case of the American view of Vietnam: Colonel Kurtz's assertion in *Apocalypse Now*, for example, that the Viet Cong possessed the stronger will to win.) The converse, however, does not necessarily apply. The Taipings, the Indian mutineers, the International Brigaders, and the men of the Waffen-SS were all on the losing side, but this is explained away through reference to betrayals. The cause of the Chinese peasant was betrayed by some of the leaders and by imperialist intervention; the rebels in India were let down by the Sikhs and the princes; the power of the International Brigades in Spain was undermined by the non-intervention policy of the liberal democracies and by the anarchists; and the Waffen-SS fought the Good Fight against Bolshevism while Wehrmacht generals engaged in anti-state plots and the British and Americans refused to recognize the Red threat that they themselves would confront in the following decade. Being on the losing side apparently only adds the cachet of martyrdom to the cause.

Moreover, individual mythologies are often used to support one another. Observers of past revolutionary situations have tended to distil events into what they regard as the dynamic essence of revolution. This in turn has led them to explain particular phenomena in one age through reference to apparently similar phenomena in another.

Allusions to the New Model Army are a case in point. Chaplains in the England of the 1640s are said to be akin to the commissars of the type found in the International Brigades;[2] the men of the *Wenkommando* are supposedly 'imbued with the same spirit as the Ironsides of Cromwell';[3] while the Taipings are comparable with the troopers at Naseby in that they 'knew what they fought for and loved what they knew'.[4] The overall effect of such comparisons is to legitimize interpretations of particular armies by placing them within a comparative context that in turn implies a common set of variables, centring on faith in a moral cause,[5] that constitute a form of *deus ex machina* for successful revolutionary armies.[6]

This tendency towards comparative reinforcement, furthermore, is by no means confined to *ex post facto* academic discourse. Those observing revolutions at the time also often sought to understand what was happening in familiar terms. For Englishmen of the mid-nineteenth century, for example, the New Model Army was the natural precedent within their own national experience to draw upon in trying to explain the rise of the Heavenly Kingdom.[7] Similarly, late twentieth-century Americans have contextualized their understanding of the patriots of the War of Independence as a means of understanding contemporary revolutionary armies ranging from the International Brigades to the Viet Cong.[8]

It may well be that conflicts between nation states and conventional wars of national liberation are becoming a thing of the past now that the colonial empires are gone and the Cold War is over.[9] Many of these particular revolutionary armies, focused as they were on particular socio-political phenomena, may eventually lose their power as exemplars. Yet even if warfare does indeed continue to devolve into terrorist/freedom-fighter struggles over ethnic and religious identity (in which professional armies organized along state-versus-state lines may be comparatively useless), both those warring and those who later interpret the fight will continue to present the conflict in moral terms and establish and perpetuate myths of martial foundation.

In most myths, furthermore, the layers of intuitive projection interacting with the known facts are by their very nature plastic enough to accommodate a fair degree of remodelling as the needs of the present change. The capacity of some of the more chronologically distant armies such as the New Model to be integrated into new ideologies suggests that some at least will continue to resonate in the future. The past may indeed be a foreign country, but history – i.e. attempts to comprehend and impose order on the past – will remain crucial to group identity.

Whatever the utilitarian nature of the recovered past, in open societies it remains the task of the historian to distinguish as far as possible what really happened from what we would like to believe happened. War is indeed too serious a business to be left entirely to the professionals, but there is no gainsaying the fact that – the myriad historical examples of professional military incompetence notwithstanding – success in campaigns has always required more than courage and commitment.

This book, in essence, is an attempt to cast a cold eye on death. The picture drawn of revolutionary armies is not particularly uplifting, but it does, hopefully, help to indicate the extent to which those who fight often do so for a variety of non-altruistic motives, the degree to which chance and the actions of the enemy can influence outcomes, and – last but not least – the all-too-human tendency to draw positive meaning from chaos and destruction.

There were, of course, soldiers in all these armies whose performance and motives matched the idealistic collective portrait painted at the time and subsequently. But if history is to have any utilitarian value, it needs to be on an objective basis, recognizing (to paraphrase Cromwell's instructions on the composition of his portrait) the 'warts and all' quality of life. War is also too serious a business to be left to the romantics.

Notes

INTRODUCTION

1 J. Adelman, *Revolution, Armies and War: A Political History*, Boulder, CO, 1985; J. Ellis, *Armies in Revolution*, New York, 1974; K. Chorley, *Armies and the Art of Revolution*, Boston, 1973 edn.

2 On the equivocal nature of the word 'revolution', see e.g. R. Koselleck, *Futures Past: On the Semantics of Historical Time*, Cambridge, MA, 1985, p. 40.

3 D. Lowenthal, *The Past is a Foreign Country*, Cambridge, 1985, p. 224.

4 See e.g. G. Martel, 'Toynbee, McNeill, and the Myth of History', *International History Review*, 1990, vol. 12, pp. 330–48.

5 M. Halbwachs, *On Collective Memory*, Lewis A. Cosner (trans.), Chicago, 1992 edn; M. Foucault, *Power/Knowledge*, Colin Gordon (trans.), New York, 1980; see P. H. Hutton, *History and the Art of Memory*, Hanover, VT, 1993; J. Fentress and C. Wickham, *Social Memory*, Oxford, 1992; A. M. Alonso, 'The Effects of Truth: Re-Representations of the Past and the Imagining of Community', *Journal of Historical Sociology*, 1988, vol. 1, pp. 33–57. On the problems many historians have in coping with subjectivity and theory, see e.g. the Arthur Marwick–Haydn White debate in *Journal of Contemporary History*, 1995, vol. 30 and 1996, vol. 31.

6 See G. M. Cuthbertson, *Political Myth and Epic*, New York, 1975, pp. 11, 14, 156; Fentress and Wickham, op. cit., p. 129; R. W. Brockway, *Myth from the Ice Age to Mickey Mouse*, Albany, NY, 1993, appendix; see also S. Ausband, *Myth and Meaning, Myth and Order*, Macon, GA, 1983, ch. 7, p. 115.

7 On the role of such myths – i.e. distortions of recorded human events rather than 'classical' mythologies involving gods, etc. – in relation to states see T. Brennan, 'The National Longing for Form', in *Nation and Narration*, H. K. Bhabha (ed.), London, 1990, p. 45; J. T. Marcus, 'The World Impact of the West: The Mystique and the Sense of Participation in History', in *Myth and Mythmaking*, H. A. Murray (ed.), New York, 1960, pp. 221–3, 230, 232–3.

8 C. von Clausewitz, *On War*, M. Howard and P. Paret (eds), Princeton, NJ, 1984, p. 187.

9 On the importance of myth in making sense of the world, see S. C. Ausband, *Myth and Meaning, Myth and Order*, Macon, GA, 1983, p. 118. On the importance of symbolic representation, see J. Lukács, *Historical Consciousness: The Remembered Past*, New Brunswick, NJ, 1994 edn, pp. 167–9.

10 From T. Clark (ed.), *The Anabasis of Xenophon*, Bk III, ch. I, p. 185 ('whichever army goes into battle stronger of soul, their enemies generally cannot withstand them') to B. Montgomery, *Memoirs*, London, 1958, p. 77 ('the morale of the soldier is the greatest single factor in war') soldiers have argued the case for the

primacy of moral factors in determining success. In practice, however, excessive faith in morale has created problems: e.g. the disastrously mistimed belief in the *furia français* enshrined in much of the professional literature in France before 1914. See M. Howard, 'Men against Fire: The Doctrine of the Offensive in 1914', in *Makers of Modern Strategy: From Machiavelli to the Nuclear Age*, Peter Paret (ed.), Princeton, NJ, 1986, pp. 510–36; A. Gat, *The Development of Military Thought: The Nineteenth Century*, Oxford, 1992, pp. 134–72.

11 Fentress and Wickham, op. cit., p. 40; D. A. Segal, 'Nationalism, Comparatively Speaking', *Journal of Historical Sociology*, 1988, vol. 1, pp. 317–18.

12 Postmodern attempts at 'faction' narratives by the likes of Simon Schama have proven problematic. See D. Samuels, 'The Call of Stories', *Lingua Franca*, May/June 1995, pp. 35–43; see also K. Windschuttle, *The Killing of History*, Sydney, 1994, ch. 8. The latter author, in highlighting in a somewhat Doomsday manner some of the problems of recent theory-driven approaches to history, makes the point that even those authors consciously trying to break with the empiricist tradition tend to employ empirical evidence to support their conclusions.

13 'Revolution' here being defined in broad terms to include regimes and armies which are thought to have marked a definite break with the past, rather than the more narrow progressive definition associated with the French Revolution and its progeny. See D. Close, 'The Meaning of Revolution', in *Revolution: A History of the Idea*, D. Close and C. Bridge (eds), London, 1985, pp. 2–3, 7, 13; see also n. 2.

14 The armies of the French Revolution, for instance, have traditionally been celebrated in terms of nameless common soldiers while the armies involved in the liberation of northern South America have always been linked to the heroic image of Simón Bolívar. See Fentress and Wickham, op. cit., pp. 130–1.

15 See e.g. Shu Guang Zhang, *Mao's Military Romanticism: China and the Korean War, 1950–1953*, Lawrence, KS, 1996; see also A. J. Gregor, 'The People's Liberation Army and China's Crisis', *Armed Forces and Society*, 1991, vol. 18, p. 21.

16 See e.g. Ellis, op. cit., ch. 4. For the traditional Soviet account of the Red Army, see e.g. *History of the Communist Party of the Soviet Union (Bolsheviks), Short Course*, New York, 1935, p. 245. Echoes of the old heroic image, however, can still be found in overtly left-wing studies (e.g. T. Cliff, *Revolution Besieged: Lenin, 1917–1923*, London, 1987, p. 204) and even some popular textbooks (e.g. M. K. Dziewanowski, *A History of Soviet Russia*, Englewood Cliffs, NJ, 1993 edn, p. 104).

17 T. Stoppard, *Rosencrantz and Guildenstern are Dead*, New York, 1967, p. 41.

1 THE NEW MODEL ARMY IN THE ENGLISH CIVIL WAR, 1645–6

1 W. C. Abbott, *The Writings and Speeches of Oliver Cromwell, Vol. 1, 1599–1649*, New York, 1937, p. 248.

2 H. G. Tibutt (ed.), *The Letter Books of Sir Samuel Luke*, HMSO, 1963, p. 311.

3 See J. Kenyon, *The Civil Wars of England*, London, 1988, ch. 7.

4 W. D. Hamilton (ed.), *Calendar of State Papers, Domestic Series, Charles I, 1645–1647*, HMSO, 1891, p. 155.

5 Abbott, op. cit., p. 248.

6 Ibid., pp. 258, 256.

7 Ibid., p. 256.

8 B. Whitelocke, *Memorials of English Affairs*, Oxford, 1853 edn, vol. 1, p. 72;

David Masson (ed.), *Camden Society, new ser., XII: The Quarrel between the Earl of Manchester and Oliver Cromwell*, London, 1875, pp. 72, 74.

9   R. Baxter, *Reliquiae Baxterianae*, M. Sylvester (ed.), London, 1696, vol. 1, p. 51.

10 Abbott, *Special Passages*, 9–16 May 1643.

11 Whitelocke, op. cit., p. 209; Baxter, op. cit., p. 98.

12 See I. Gentles, *The New Model Army in England, Ireland and Scotland, 1645–1653*, Oxford, 1992, pp. 94–5.

13 J. A. Sprigge, *Anglia Redivia: England's Recovery: Being the History of the Motions, Actions, and Successes of the Army under the immediate conduct of His Excellency Sir Thomas Fairfax*, Oxford, 1854 edn, pp. 331–2.

14 Cromwell to Walton *re* Marston Moor, 5 July 1644, in Abbott, op. cit., p. 287. On the debate over the relative importance of Fairfax and Cromwell in the New Model Army, see G. Foard, *Naseby: The Decisive Campaign*, Whitstable, 1995, pp. 68–71, 339–40.

15 C. H. Firth, *Cromwell's Army: A History of the English Soldier during the Civil Wars, the Commonwealth and the Protectorate*, London, 1902, chs 12–13.

16 G. M. Trevelyan, *England Under the Stuarts*, London, 1925, p. 265.

17 F. C. Montague, *The History of England: From the Accession of James I to the Restoration (1603–1660)*, London, 1925 edn, pp. 307–8.

18 T. S. Baldock, *Cromwell as Soldier*, London, 1899, p. 298.

19 C. Hill, *God's Englishman: Oliver Cromwell and the English Revolution*, New York, 1970, p. 79; id., 'The English Revolution and Patriotism', in *Patriotism: The Making and Unmaking of British National Identity: Volume I: History and Politics*, R. Samuel (ed.), London, 1989, p. 165; id., *The World Turned Upside Down: Radical Ideas during the English Revolution*, London, 1972, p. 20.

20 B. Manning, *The English People and the English Revolution 1640–1649*, London, 1976, p. 251.

21 J. L. Malcolm, *Caesar's Due: Loyalty and King Charles 1642–1646*, London, 1983, p. 99.

22 J. R. Adelman, *Revolution, Armies, and War: A Political History*, Boulder, CO, 1985, p. 26, *passim*; see J. Ellis, *Armies in Revolution*, New York, 1974, p. 20; G. Bonnet, *Les guerres insurrectionelles et révolutionnaires de l'Antiquité à nos jours*, Paris, 1958, p. 22.

23 Adelman, op. cit., pp. 22–4.

24 See B. Schwartz, ' "The People" in history: The Communist Party Historians' Group, 1945–56', in *Making Histories: Studies in history-writing and politics*, R. Johnson *et al.* (eds), London, 1982, pp. 79, 90; R. Hutton, *The Royalist War Effort 1642–1646*, London, 1982, pp. xii–xiv. For a highly critical analysis of the Whig tradition, see C. Parker, *The English Historical Tradition since 1850*, Edinburgh, 1990. For a fuller treatment of the historiographical context of writings on the English Civil War, see R. C. Richardson, *The Debate on the English Revolution Revisited*, London, 1988 edn. The continuing resonance of the English Civil War for the Old Left in Britain can be gathered from the 1996 reprinting (with a new foreword by Christopher Hill) of D. W. Petergorsky's *Left-Wing Democracy in the English Civil War*, London, 1940. See also S. Raphael, 'British Marxist Historians, 1880–1980', *New Left Review*, vol. 120, 1980, pp. 26–8.

25 On the place of this film in the context of twentieth-century views of Cromwell, see P. Karsten, *Patriot Heroes in England and America: Political Symbolism and Changing Values over Three Centuries*, Madison, WI, 1978, p. 160. To be fair this is, in essence, only an exaggeration of the kinds of attitudes towards the New Model and other armies contained in many contemporary secondary

works. See e.g. D. Underdown, *Somerset in the Civil War and Interregnum*, Newton Abbot, 1973, pp. 93, 100–6, 115.

26 L. B. Smith, *This Realm of England, 1399 to 1688*, Lexington, MA, 1996, p. 285.

27 See M. A. Kishlansky, *The Rise of the New Model Army*, Cambridge, 1979, ch. 2; Gentles, op. cit., ch. 1.

28 See Kishlansky, op. cit., pp. 38, 40–1. According to G. E. Aylmer, Fairfax was 'about as upper class a commander-in-chief as could have been chosen'. G. E. Aylmer, *Rebellion or Revolution? England, 1640–1660*, Oxford, 1986, p. 73.

29 C. Holmes, *The Eastern Association in the English Civil War*, Cambridge, 1974, pp. 177, 198–9; Kenyon, op. cit., p. 133.

30 Sprigge, op. cit., p. 39; see Kenyon, op. cit., p. 143.

31 Kishlansky, op. cit., p. 43.

32 Gentles, op. cit., pp. 16–19; Kishlansky, op. cit., pp. 40–5.

33 R. Temple, 'The Original Officer List of the New Model Army', *Bulletin of the Institute of Historical Research*, 1986, vol. 59, p. 53.

34 Gentles, op. cit., p. 14.

35 *Journal of the House of Lords, 1645–6*, vol. 8, p. 268; see C. Carlton, *Going to the Wars: The Experience of the British Civil Wars, 1638–1651*, London, 1992, pp. 68ff.

36 *Calendar of State Papers, Domestic Series, Charles I, 1644–45*, vol. 7, pp. 411, 420, 426, 437.

37 Abbott, op. cit., vol. 4, p. 471.

38 *Journal of the House of Lords, 1644–5*, vol. 7, p. 461; see Carlton, op. cit., p. 68; Gentles, op. cit., pp. 32–3.

39 Gentles, op. cit., pp. 32–3, 40.

40 R. Baillie, *Letters and Journals*, Edinburgh, 1841, vol. 2, p. 265.

41 Malcolm, op. cit., p. 110; Carlton, op. cit., pp. 67ff.

42 Gentles, op. cit., p. 34.

43 Malcolm, op. cit., pp. 100–1.

44 Holmes, op. cit., pp. 177, 198–9.

45 Abbott, op. cit., vol. 1, p. 256; id., vol. 4, p. 471.

46 Id., vol. 1, p. 256; see R. Ashton, *The English Civil War: Conservatism and Revolution 1603–1649*, London, 1978, p. 223.

47 Abbott, op. cit., vol. 1, p. 231.

48 P. Young, *Naseby 1645: The Campaign and the Battle*, London, 1985, ch. 8.

49 Samuel Luke to Oliver Luke, 10 June 1645, in Tibbutt, op. cit., p. 311; see Kishlansky, op. cit., p. 65; Gentles, op. cit., pp. 106–7.

50 Kishlansky, op. cit., p. 69.

51 Gentles, op. cit., pp. 106–7, 116; Kishlansky, op. cit., pp. 65–6; Kenyon, op. cit., p. 134.

52 Kishlansky, op. cit., pp. 71–2; see R. P. Stearns, *The Strenuous Puritan: Hugh Peters 1598–1660*, Urbana, IL, 1954, p. 249.

53 Carlton, op. cit., p. 127.

54 Id., p. 82.

55 P. A. Scholes, *The Puritans and Music in England and New England*, London, 1934, p. 272.

56 Ashton, op. cit., p. 409, n. 30; M. van Cleave Alexander, *The Growth of English Education, 1348–1648: A Social and Cultural History*, University Park, PA, 1990, p. 234.

57 Carlton, op. cit., p. 93; Gentles, op. cit., p. 107.

58 Gentles, op. cit., p. 94.

59 Kenyon, op. cit., p. 133; Young, op. cit., chs 3–4; Carlton, op. cit., p. 21; P. R. Newman, *The Old Service: Royalist regimental colonels and the Civil War,*

1642–46, Manchester, 1993, pp. 71–3, 80, 126, 127–30; id., 'The Royalist Party in Arms: The Peerage and Army Command, 1642–1646', in *Politics and People in Revolutionary England*, C. Jones *et al.* (eds), Oxford, 1986, pp. 85, 90, 92.

60 Carlton, op. cit., p. 125.

61 See Hutton, op. cit., ch. 10; Gentles, op. cit., p. 40.

62 A detailed discussion of the likely number of men at Naseby on both sides is contained in Foard, op. cit., pp. 197–207. See R. Spalding (ed.), *The Diary of Bulstrode Whitelocke 1605–1675*, Oxford, 1990, p.167; Sprigge, op. cit., pp. 37, 45.

63 As was the case in most field engagements. See S. Peachey, *The Mechanics of Infantry Combat in the First English Civil War*, Bristol, 1992, p. 21.

64 See F. Kitson, *Prince Rupert: Portrait of a Soldier*, London, 1994, p. 244.

65 In the mid-seventeenth century the mechanisms for effective behind-the-lines command simply did not exist. Between the colonels of regiments and the commanders of Foot and Horse, not to speak of the general-in-chief, there existed no chain of command worthy of the name. A simple battle plan might be explained to unit colonels the night before, but the only way for commanders to influence events once the fight was joined was by sheer physical and moral presence. Being amongst the men, on the spot, leading by personal example, was as crucial to the outcome of a battle in the English Civil War as it had been in the days of Alexander the Great. To be sure, if a cavalry or infantry commander was killed or wounded the effect could be disastrous. However, 'being there' undoubtedly helped morale and allowed for at least some control over the course of events in the immediate vicinity.

66 See Okey's account in H. G. Tibbutt, *Colonel John Okey, 1602–1662*, Streatly, 1955, pp. 10–11.

67 See Foard, op. cit., p. 265.

68 See n. 66.

69 Carlton, op. cit., pp. 144–5.

70 On the lure of the baggage train see B. Denton, *Naseby Fight*, Leigh-on-Sea, 1991, pp. 39–43.

71 Firth, op. cit., p. 144.

72 Ibid., pp. 142, 144.

73 'A True Relation and Account of a Victory. . . . ', reprinted in Young, op. cit., p. 373; see Sprigge, op. cit., p. 47.

74 The most recent and detailed analysis of the course of the battle – of which my own account is a mere sketch summary derived from a number of accounts – can be found in Foard, op. cit., chs 8, 10.

75 Abbott, op. cit., vol. 1, p. 360; see C. and W. Whetham, *A History of the Life of Colonel Nathaniel Whetham*, London, 1907, p. 102; Tibbutt, *Colonel Okey*, pp. 10–11. See also Foard, op. cit., p. 265.

76 With the exception of the hard-core Ironsides.

77 Only four of the twenty-four regiments showed evidence of being seriously influenced by Leveller doctrines, and it is striking the extent to which support for the Levellers within these four collapsed in the face of personal intervention by Cromwell and promises by Fairfax to redress arrears in pay. See Gentles, op. cit., pp. 221–5; Aylmer, op. cit., pp. 74, 89–90. Left-wing commentators have sometimes asserted that the collapse of radical agitation was the result of a generals' plot to divide and conquer. See F. Brockway, *Britain's First Socialists: The Levellers, Agitators and Diggers of the English Revolution*, London, 1980, p. 53; H. N. Brailsford, *The Levellers and the English Revolution*, London, 1961, p. 291. There were, however, practical difficulties in assembling the army in one place. See A. Woolrych, *Soldiers and Statesmen: The General Council of the Army and its Debates, 1647–1648*, Oxford, 1987, pp. 266–7.

78 Sprigge, op. cit., p. 13.
79 Kishlansky, op. cit., pp. 52, 50.
80 Young, op. cit., p. 28.

2 THE CONTINENTAL ARMY IN THE WAR OF AMERICAN INDEPENDENCE, 1775–82

1 Quoted in E. Robson, *The American Revolution in its Political and Military Aspects*, London, 1955, p. 158.
2 J. C. Fitzpatrick (ed.), *The Writings of George Washington from the Original Manuscript Sources, 1745–1799*, Washington, DC, 1931–44, vol. 6, p. 107.
3 See e.g. n. 1.
4 L. H. Cohen, *The Revolutionary Histories: Contemporary Narratives of the American Revolution*, Ithaca, NY, 1985, p. 222, *passim*; C. L. Albanse, *Sons of the Fathers: The Civil Religion of the American Revolution*, Philadelphia, 1976; C. Royster, *A Revolutionary People at War: The Continental Army and the American Character, 1775–1783*, Chapel Hill, NC, 1979, pp. 3–24.
5 The origins of these views may well date back to the first contact between colonial troops and British regulars during the French and Indian War. See F. Anderson, *A People's Army: Massachusetts Soldiers and Society in the Seven Years War*, Chapel Hill, NC, 1984, ch. 4; Douglas Edward Leach, *Roots of Conflict: British Armed Forces and Colonial Americans, 1677–1763*, Chapel Hill, NC, 1986.
6 See D. Higginbotham, 'The Military Institutions of Colonial America: The Rhetoric and the Reality', in *Tools of War: Instruments, Ideas, and Institutions of Warfare, 1445–1871*, J. A. Lynne (ed.), Urbana, IL, 1990, p. 131; C. Royster, 'Founding a Nation in Blood: Military Conflict and American Nationality', in *Arms and Independence: The Military Character of the American Revolution*, R. Hoffman and P. J. Albert (eds), Charlottesville, VA, 1984, pp. 26, 28–9, 32–5; J. K. Martin and M. E. Lender, *A Respectable Army: The Military Origins of the Republic, 1763–1789*, Arlington Heights, IL, 1982, pp. 65–6; see also M. Olansky, *Fighting for Liberty and Virtue: Political and Cultural Wars in Eighteenth-Century America*, Wheaton, IL, 1995, pp. 147–8.
7 See L. D. Cress, *Citizens in Arms: The Army and Militia in American Society to the War of 1812*, Chapel Hill, NC, 1982; R. H. Kohn, *Eagle and Sword: The Federalists and the Creation of the Military Establishment in America, 1783–1802*, New York, 1975, ch. 1; M. Cunliffe, *Soldiers and Civilians: The Martial Spirit in America 1775–1865*, Boston, 1968, pp. 31–42; J. T. White, 'Standing Armies in Time of War: Republican Theory and Military Practice During the American Revolution', Ph.D. Thesis, George Washington University, 1978, chs 1–2, *passim*; J. M. Dederer, *War in America to 1775: Before Yankee Doodle*, New York, 1990, ch. 8.
8 See B. Schwartz, *George Washington: The Making of an American Symbol*, New York, 1987, pp. 164–5; Royster, *Revolutionary People*, pp. 43–6, 146–51, 255–60; see also L. H. Cohen, *The Revolutionary Histories: Contemporary Narratives of the American Revolution*, Ithaca, NY, 1980, *passim*; W. R. Smith, *History as Argument: Three Patriot Historians of the American Revolution*, The Hague, 1966, *passim*.
9 D. Higginbotham, 'American Historians and the Military History of the American Revolution', in *War and Society in Revolutionary America: The Wider Dimensions of the Conflict*, Columbia, SC, 1988, pp. 242–5.
10 J. Hawthorne, *World's Best Histories: United States*, J. Schouler and E. B.

Andrews (eds), New York, 1898, pp. 387–8. See also e.g. J. T. Peck, *The History of the Great Republic*, New York, 1868, p. 217; G. Bancroft, *History of the United States from the Discovery of the American Continent*, Boston, 1834–74, vol. 5, p. 190, vol. 8, pp. 62–4.

11 C. K. Bolton, *The Private Soldier Under Washington*, New York, 1902, pp. 13, 235, 238.

12 Cress, op. cit., pt 3.

13 E. Upton, *The Military Policy of the United States*, Washington, DC, 1904; see Higginbotham, 'American Historians', p. 250; see also S. E. Ambrose, *Emory Upton and the Army*, Baton Rouge, LA, 1993 edn.

14 L. Wood, *America's Duty as Shown by Our Military History: Its Facts and Its Fallacies*, Chicago, 1921.

15 On the problems of military history see C. Reardon, *Soldiers and Scholars: The U.S. Army and the Uses of Military History, 1865–1920*, Lawrence, KS, 1990. On the durability of Washington as a symbol within the overall mythology of the Continental Army and War of Independence, see Schwartz, *passim*; Karsten, *Patriot-Heroes of England and America: Political Symbolism and Changing Values over Three Centuries*, Madison, WS, 1978, pp. 94–5. On the Revolution as break with the past, see M. Kammen, *A Season of Youth: The American Revolution and the Historical Imagination*, New York, 1978.

16 A. Nevins and H. S. Commanger, *A Short History of the United States*, New York, 1966 edn, p. 95; id., *A Pocket History of the United States*, New York, 1967, p. 82.

17 E. S. Morgan, *The Birth of the Republic 1763–89*, Chicago History of American Civilization, D. J. Boorstin (ed.), Chicago, 1979 edn, p. 79.

18 H. H. Peckham, *The War for Independence: A Military History*, Chicago History of American Civilization, D. J. Boorstin (ed.), Chicago, 1958 (sixth impression 1965), pp. 204; see Olansky, op. cit., ch. 6.

19 H. M. Ward, *The American Revolution: Nationhood Achieved, 1763–1788*, New York, 1995, p. 212.

20 S. M. Wanoff and M. Matloff (eds), *American Wars and Heroes: Revolutionary War through Vietnam*, New York, 1985 edn, p. 60; see M. Matloff (ed.), *American Military History*, Washington, DC, 1969, p. iii.

21 D. Higginbotham, *The War of American Independence: Military Attitudes, Policies, and Practice, 1763–1789*, Boston, 1983, p. 57. See also Martin and Lender, op. cit., p. 68.

22 J. R. Morris, *America's Armed Forces: A History*, Upper Saddle River, NJ, 1995 edn, pp. 18–19; see also S. Conway, *The War of American Independence, 1775–1783*, London, 1995, pp. 173–5. Both Morris and Conway, however, do at least mention countervailing tendencies.

23 B. W. Tuchman, *The First Salute: A View of the American Revolution*, New York, 1988, p. 194. See A. R. Millett, 'Whatever Became of the Militia in the History of the American Revolution?', in *Three George Rogers Clark Lectures*, Lanham, MA, 1991, p. 41. See H. S. Commanger and R. B. Morris (eds), *The Spirit of 'Seventy-Six: The Story of the American Revolution as told by Participants*, Indianapolis, 1958 (reissued 1976), vol. 1, p. vii.

24 See F. J. Wetta and S. J. Curley, *Celluloid Wars: A Guide to Film and the American Experience of War*, New York, 1992, pp. 57–8, 213; M. R. Pitts, *Hollywood and American History*, Jefferson, NC, 1995, *passim*; E. T. Linenthal, *Sacred Ground: Americans and Their Battlefields*, Urbana, IL, 1991, ch. 1; D. Lowenthal, *The Past is a Foreign Country*, Cambridge, 1985, pp. 121, 343; see also M. Wallace, 'Visiting the Past: History Museums in the United States', in

Presenting the Past: Essays on History and the Public, S. P. Benson *et al.* (eds), Philadelphia, 1986, pp. 137–61.

25 See M. Frisch, 'American History and the Structures of Collective Memory: A Modest Exercise in Empirical Iconography', *Journal of American History*, 1989, vol. 75, pp. 1130–55.

26 K. Chorley, *Armies and the Art of Revolution*, Boston, 1973 edn, p. 63. Jonathan Adelman, in *Revolution, Armies and War: A Political History*, Boulder, CO, 1985, does not discuss the War of Independence at all, while John Ellis in *Armies and Revolution*, London, 1973, ch. 3, takes an uncharacteristically anti-revolutionary stance when dealing with the nature of the Continental Army.

27 For example, the war as 'a military victory won by free men', T. Fleming, 'George Washington, General', in *America at War: An Anthology of Articles from MHQ: The Quarterly Journal of Military History*, C. L. Christman (ed.), Annapolis, MA, 1995, p. 38. The image of the Revolution as a whole has, of course, also undergone modification to fit the times. See Kammen, op. cit., *passim*. A sense of the strength of the War of Independence in American consciousness can be gathered from the number of articles appearing in the highly popular magazine *American Heritage*. See J. A. Garraty (ed.), *American Heritage 35-Year Chronological Subject Guide, December 1954–December 1989*, New York, 1990, pp. 18–21.

28 It has been suggested that Washington was not entirely free of self-promotion in this respect. See P. K. Longmore, *The Invention of George Washington*, Berkeley, CA, 1988.

29 As General Galvin has suggested, even at Lexington and Concord the reality was somewhat different from the myth. The minutemen and colonial militia who assembled that day had been training for a year for precisely this contingency, and therefore did not, as myth would have it, spontaneously leap to arms in defence of their homes. J. R. Galvin, *The Minute Men: The First Fight: Myths and Realities of the American Revolution*, Washington, DC, 1989 edn. The British, meanwhile, had not been expecting a full-scale conflict and were reluctant to shoot indiscriminately. See ibid.; J. Shy, *Towards Lexington: The Role of the British Army in the Coming of the American Revolution*, Princeton, NJ, 1965, pp. 375–424; T. Hayter, *The Army and the Crowd in Mid-Georgian England*, London, 1978, pp. 14, 166, *passim*.

30 See Martin and Lender, op. cit., pp. 36–7; Royster, *Revolutionary People*, pp. 59–60; White, 'Standing Armies', pp. 96–8.

31 Letter by Benjamin Thompson, 4 November 1775, in Commanger and Morris, *Spirit of 'Seventy-Six*, pp. 153–4; see letter by William Emerson, 17 July 1775, in ibid., p. 153; letter by a British surgeon, 26 May 1775, in ibid., p. 152; R. K. Wright, *The Continental Army*, Washington, DC, 1983, pp. 20, 44; White, 'Standing Armies', ch. 4.

32 Royster, *Revolutionary People*, pp. 59–63; Wright, op. cit., p. 39.

33 Fitzpatrick, op. cit., vol. 3, p. 433.

34 Anderson, *passim*; Wright, op. cit., p. 44.

35 Fitzpatrick, op. cit., vol. 6, p. 108.

36 See D. Higginbotham, 'The American Militia: A Traditional Institution with Revolutionary Responsibilities', in *Reconsiderations on the Revolutionary War*, D. Higginbotham (ed.), Westport, CT, 1978, pp. 90–1, 95–9; J. Shy, 'A New Look at the Colonial Militia', in *People Numerous and Armed*, ch. 2; Millett, op. cit., pp. 53–4.

37 See id., 'Charles Lee and the Radical Alternative', in *People Numerous and Armed*, ch. 6.

38 Fitzpatrick, op. cit., vol. 6, pp. 106–16; see D. Higginbotham, 'Reflections on the War of Independence, Modern Guerrilla Warfare and the War in Vietnam', in *Arms and Independence: The Military Character of the American Revolution*, R. H. Hoffman and P. J. Albert (eds), Charlottesville, VA, 1984, pp. 8–9.
39 Wright, op. cit., pp. 30–2, 36, 39.
40 Id., p. 55.
41 Fitzpatrick, op. cit., vol. 6, p. 106; ibid., pp. 4–5.
42 R. K. Showman (ed.), *The Papers of Nathanael Greene*, Chapel Hill, NC, 1976, vol. 1, p. 303.
43 For the evolution of Congressional thinking on the gap between Whig rhetoric and the realities of war, see White, 'Standing Armies', ch. 4.
44 See M. E. Lender, 'The Enlisted Line: The Continental Soldiers of New Jersey', Ph.D. Thesis, Rutgers University, 1975, pp. 110–39; id., 'The Social Structure of the New Jersey Brigade: The Continental Line as an American Standing Army', in *The Military in America*, P. Karsten (ed.), New York, 1980, pp. 27–44; id., 'The Mind of the Rank and File: Patriotism and Motivation in the Continental Line', in *New Jersey in the American Revolution III: Papers presented at the Seventh Annual New Jersey History Symposium, 1975*, W. C. Wright (ed.), Trenton, NJ, 1976, pp. 21–35; J. R. Sellers, 'The Common Soldier in the American Revolution', in *Military History of the American Revolution: Proceedings of the Sixth Military History Symposium, USAFA*, S. J. Underdal (ed.), Washington, DC, 1976, pp. 151–61; R. Middlekauf, 'Why Men Fought in the American Revolution', *Huntington Library Quarterly*, 1980, vol. 43, pp. 135–48; E. C. Papenfuse and G. A. Stiverson, 'General Smallwood's Recruits: The Peacetime Career of the Revolutionary War Private', *William and Mary Quarterly*, 1973, 3rd ser., vol. 30, pp. 117–32; J. Shy, 'Hearts and Minds in the American Revolution: The Case of "Long Bill" Scott and Peterborough, New Hampshire', in *A People Numerous and Armed*, pp. 172–3; P. Maslowski, 'National Policy Toward the Use of Black Troops in the Revolution', *South Carolina Historical Magazine*, 1972, vol. 73, pp. 379–95; B. Quarles, *The Negro in the American Revolution*, Chapel Hill, NC, 1961, pp. 58–9, 60, 69, 71–2.
45 Wright, op. cit., p. 92.
46 Fitzpatrick, op. cit., vol. 6, p. 110.
47 Royster, *Revolutionary People*, pp. 85–6.
48 See Martin and Lender, op. cit., pp. 108–9. In the end Congress granted pensions of seven years in 1778.
49 See Wright, op. cit., p. 49, ch. 6; Dederer, op. cit., p. 110; J. M. Palmer, *General von Steuben*, New Haven, CT, 1937.
50 See I. D. Gruber, 'The Anglo-American Military Tradition and the War for Independence', in *Against All Enemies: Interpretations of American Military History from Colonial Times to the Present*, K. J. Hagan and W. R. Roberts (eds), Westport, CT, 1986, ch. 2.
51 For American logistical efforts and difficulties, see E. W. Carp, *To Starve the Army at Pleasure: Continental Army Administration and American Political Culture*, Chapel Hill, NC, 1984; J. A. Huston, *Logistics of Liberty: American Services of Supply in the Revolutionary War and After*, Newark, NJ, 1991. For British problems, see R. A. Bowler, *Logistics and the Failure of the British Army in America, 1775–1783*, Princeton, NJ, 1975.
52 See R. F. Weigley, 'Generals Building an Army: American Military Command in the War of Independence', in *Three George Rogers Clark Lectures*, Lanham, MA, 1991, pp. 6–7.
53 P. E. Russell, 'Redcoats in the Wilderness: British Officers and Irregular Warfare in Europe and America, 1740 to 1760', *William and Mary Quarterly*,

1978, 3rd ser., vol. 35, pp. 629–52; Conway, op. cit., pp. 246–7; see also P. Paret, 'The Relationship between the Revolutionary War and European Thought and Practice in the Second Half of the Eighteenth Century', in *Reconsiderations on the Revolutionary War*, D. Higginbotham (ed.), Westport, CT, 1978, pp. 150–1. For the origins of the view that Redcoats were unable to adapt to North American conditions, see Dederer, op. cit., pp. 138–9.

54 Higginbotham, *George Washington*, p. 44; Gruber, op. cit., pp. 22–3.

55 G. F. Scheer, 'Washington and His Lieutenants: Some Problems in Command', in *Military History of the American Revolution: Proceedings of the Sixth Military History Symposium, USAFA*, S. J. Underdal (ed.), Washington, DC, 1976, p. 142.

56 Higginbotham, *George Washington*, p. 16.

57 P. Mackesy, *The War for America 1775–1783*, London, 1964, pp. 33–4; see I. D. Gruber, 'For King and Country: The Limits of Loyalty of British Officers in the War for American Independence', in *Limits of Loyalty*, E. Denton III (ed.), Waterloo, Ontario, 1980, pp. 23–40; id., 'The Origins of British Strategy in the War for American Independence', in *Military History of the American Revolution: The Proceedings of the Sixth Military History Symposium, USAFA*, S. J. Underdal (ed.), Washington, DC, 1976, p. 43.

58 See R. Atwood, *The Hessians: Mercenaries from Hessen-Kassel in the American Revolution*, Cambridge, 1980, pp. 29, 31–2, *passim*; L. Kennett, *The French Forces in America, 1780–1783*, Westport, CT, 1977; Wright, op. cit., ch. 6; S. F. Scott, 'Foreign Mercenaries, Revolutionary War, and Citizen-Soldiers in the Late Eighteenth Century', *War & Society*, 1984, vol. 2, p. 42.

59 Mackesy, op. cit., pp. 4–7. On efforts to avoid plundering, see Atwood, op. cit., p. 173; Frey, op. cit., p. 75; Higginbotham, *George Washington*, pp. 54, 99, *passim*. On protests, see e.g. Washington to Howe, 13 January 1777, in Fitzpatrick, op. cit., vol. 7, p. 3. On officer exchanges, see L. G. Bowman, *Captive Americans: Prisoners During the American Revolution*, Athens, OH, 1976. This is not to suggest that no animosity existed, or that prisoners were not sometimes treated with apparent vindictiveness by either side. See e.g. Bowman, *passim*, and H. C. Rice and A. S. K. Brown (eds), *The American Campaigns of Rochambeau's Army*, Princeton, NJ, 1972, vol. 1, pp. 64, 151.

60 See e.g. W. B. Willcox, 'Too Many Cooks: British Planning Before Saratoga', *Journal of British Studies*, 1962, vol. 2, pp. 56–90; id., 'The British Road to Yorktown: A Study in Divided Command', *American Historical Review*, 1946, vol. 52, pp. 1–35; id., 'British Strategy in America, 1778', *Journal of Modern History*, 1947, vol. 19, pp. 97–121. For a recent summary of British mistakes, see W. Seymour, *The Price of Folly: British Blunders in the War of American Independence*, London, 1995.

61 See Scheer, op. cit., pp. 139–50.

62 Royster, *Revolutionary People*, pp. 86–93.

63 Middlekauf, op. cit., p. 136.

64 Frey, op. cit., pp. 75–6; Atwood, op. cit., p. 173.

65 Fitzpatrick, op. cit., vol. 6, pp. 46–7; see Higginbotham, *George Washington*, p. 54.

66 Frey, op. cit., p. 72; A. Bowman, op. cit., p. 72.

67 W. Johnson, *Sketches of the Life and Correspondence of Nathanael Greene*, Charleston, SC, 1822, vol. 2, p. 220; see Atwood, op. cit., ch. 9; L. G. Bowman, op. cit., pp. 94–7; Frey, op. cit., p. 73; C. Berger, *Broadsides & Bayonets: The Propaganda War of the American Revolution*, San Rafael, CA, 1976 edn, ch. 5.

68 Frey, op. cit., pp. 73–4; see J. Prebble, *Mutiny: Highland Regiments in Revolt, 1743–1804*, London, 1977.

69 See Martin and Lender, op. cit., pp. 161–4; C. van Doren, *Mutiny in January:*

The Story of a Crisis in the Continental Army, New York, 1943; Frey, op. cit., p. 171, n. 14.

70 See Royster, *Revolutionary People*, p. 306; Higginbotham, *War of American Independence*, p. 404; Kennett, op. cit., pp. 83–4; Prebble, op. cit., *passim*.

71 J. K. Martin, ' "A Most Undisciplined, Profligate Crew": Protest and Defiance in the Continental Ranks, 1776–1783', in *Arms and Independence: The Military Character of the American Revolution*, Charlottesville, VA, 1984, p. 136; Prebble, op. cit., pp. 209–10.

72 See Royster, *Revolutionary People*, pp. 306–7, appendix; Middlekauf, op. cit., pp. 147–8.

73 See Higginbotham, 'American Militia', pp. 95–6; Shy, 'Hearts and Minds', pp. 174–8; id., 'The Military Conflict Considered as a Revolutionary War', in *A People Numerous and Armed: Reflections on the Military Struggle for American Independence*, New York, 1976, pp. 211–17; R. F. Weigley, *The Age of Battles: The Quest for Decisive Warfare from Breitenfeld to Waterloo*, Bloomington, IN, 1991, p. 237. On the subsequent problems of making effective use of loyalist sentiment in the colonies, see P. H. Smith, *Loyalists and Redcoats: A Study in British Revolutionary Policy*, Chapel Hill, NC, 1964.

74 G. A. Billias commentary on D. R. Palmer, 'American Strategy Reconsidered', in *Military History of the American Revolution: Proceedings of the Sixth Military History Symposium, USAFA*, S. J. Underdal (ed.), Washington, DC, 1976, p. 69.

75 Billias, op. cit., pp. 69–70.

76 Cohen, op. cit., pp. 57–8. To be fair to the American cause, those who fought Burgoyne were a rude shock to the British after previous encounters. 'The courage and obstinacy with which the Americans fought were the astonishment of everyone', as a member of the expedition put it, 'and we now become fully convinced they are not the contemptible enemy we had hitherto imagined them.' T. Anbury, *With Burgoyne from Quebec*, S. Jackman (ed.), Toronto, 1963, p. 175.

77 Billias, op. cit., p. 70. For assessments of American strategy and the reasons for victory, see J. Ferling (ed.), *The World Turned Upside Down: The American Victory in the War of Independence*, Westport, CT, 1988; R. F. Weigley, 'American Strategy: A Call for a Critical Strategic History', in *Reconsiderations on the Revolutionary War*, D. Higginbotham (ed.), Westport, CT, 1978, ch. 3; D. R. Palmer, *The Way of the Fox: American Strategy in the War for America 1775–1783*, Westport, CT, 1975.

78 Higginbotham, *George Washington*, pp. 71–5.

79 See Cress, op. cit., pt 3; Kohn, op. cit., *passim*; Cunliffe, op. cit., *passim*.

80 For a useful corrective to the selflessness myth surrounding the American Revolution, see N. Gelb, *Less Than Glory*, New York, 1984; see also P. Gerster and N. Cords, *Myth in American History*, Encino, CA, 1977, pp. 40, 41–5.

81 See O. T. Murphy, 'The American Revolution and the Concept of the *Levée en masse*', *Military Affairs*, 1959, vol. 23, pp. 13–20; S. Schama, *Citizens: A Chronicle of the French Revolution*, New York, 1989, ch. 1; D. Ocheverria and O. T. Murphy, 'The American Revolutionary Army: A French Estimate in 1777', *Military Affairs*, 1963, vol. 27, pp. 1–7, 153–62; Berger, op. cit., ch. 7.

3 THE ARMIES OF THE FRENCH REPUBLIC AND THE WAR OF THE FIRST COALITION, 1792–7

1 Quoted in V. Dupuis, *La Campagne de 1793 à L'Armée du Nord et des Ardennes: De Valenciennes à Hondschoote*, Paris, 1906, p. 312.

2 Quoted in C. Rousset, *Les Volontaires, 1791–1794*, Paris, 1892, Vieusseux to Brissot, 15 May 1792, pp. 54–5.

3 'Campagne in Frankreich', in *Goethes Werke, Band X: Autobiographische Schriften, Zweiter Band*, Hamburg, 1959, p. 235.

4 J.-P. Bertaud, *The Army of the French Revolution: From Citizen-Soldiers to Instruments of Power*, R. R. Palmer (trans.), Princeton, NJ, 1988, pp. 39–40; J. A. Lynn, *The Bayonets of the Republic: Motivation and Tactics in the Army of Revolutionary France, 1791–94*, Urbana, IL, 1984, p. 44.

5 *Archives parlementaires*, vol. 36, p. 607.

6 Quoted in J. A. Lynn, 'En Avant! The Origins of the Revolutionary Attack', in *Tools of War: Instruments, Ideas, and Institutions of Warfare, 1445–1871*, J. A. Lynn (ed.), Urbana, IL, 1990, p. 154.

7 J. A. Lynn, 'French Opinion and the Military Resurrection of the Pike, 1792–1794', *Military Affairs*, 1971, vol. 41, pp. 51–5.

8 Quoted in Bertaud, *Army*, p. 66.

9 Ibid., pp. 192–3.

10 F.-A. Aulard (ed.), *Recueil des actes du Comité de salut public, avec la correspondance officielle des représentants en mission et le registre du Conseil exécutif provisoire*, Paris, 1889–1933, vol. 14, pp. 473–5, vol. 13, pp. 101–2; see Rousset, op. cit., p. 205.

11 Quoted in Lynn, 'En Avant!', p. 170.

12 Quoted in S. Lytle, 'Robespierre, Danton, and the *Levée en Masse*', *Journal of Modern History*, 1958, vol. 30, pp. 327–8. On the newspapers, see Lynn, *Bayonets*, ch. 6.

13 M. Countanceau, *La Campagne de 1794 à l'armée du Nord*, Paris, 1903–8, pt 1, vol. 1, p. 404.

14 A. Forrest, *Soldiers of the French Revolution*, Durham, NC, 1990, p. 190.

15 Quoted in Bertaud, *Army*; see e.g. J. Michelet, *Histoire de la Révolution Française*, Paris, 1952 edn, vol. 1, p. 1132.

16 See e.g. A. Mathiez, *Victoire en l'an II*, Paris, 1916. On the limited influence of Marxism, see E. J. Hobsbawm, *Echoes of the Marseillaise: Two Centuries Look Back on the French Revolution*, London, 1990, *passim*.

17 A. Mathiez, *The French Revolution*, C. A. Philipps (trans.), New York, 1962, p. 221.

18 G. Lefebvre, *The French Revolution: From its Origins to 1793*, E. M. Evanson (trans.), London, 1962, p. 261.

19 A. Soboul, *Les Soldats de l'an II*, Paris, 1959, p. 6.

20 See Bertaud, *Soldiers*; id., *La vie quotidienne des soldats de la Révolution, 1789–1799*, Paris, 1985; id., *Valmy, la démocratie en armes*, Paris, 1970; Lynn, *Bayonets*; B. Deschard, *L'armée et la Révolution: du service du Roi au service de la Nation*, Paris, 1989.

21 On the complex evolution of state symbols and occasions associated with the Revolution, see P. Nora, *Les Lieux de Mémoire: La République*, Paris, 1984. On the overall place of the Revolution in French consciousness and its co-option by the state, see R. Gildea, *The Past in French History*, New Haven, CT, 1994, chs 1, 7.

22 K. Chorley, *Armies and the Art of Revolution*, Boston, 1973 edn, p. 195.

23 J. R. Adelman, *Revolution, Armies, and War: A Political History*, Boulder, CO, 1985, p. 50. See J. Ellis, *Armies in Revolution*, London, 1973, ch. 4.

24 G. E. Rothenberg, *The Art of Warfare in the Age of Napoleon*, Bloomington, IN, 1980, p. 11. See e.g. T. Ropp, *War in the Modern World*, New York, 1962 edn, p. 110; J. Gooch, *Armies in Europe*, London, 1980, ch. 2; R. A. Preston *et al.*, *Men in Arms: A History of Warfare and its Interrelationships with Western Society*, Fort Worth, TX, 1991 edn, pp. 159ff. More cautious and nuanced assessments, emphasizing aspects of continuity with warfare in the Age of Reason, can be found in J. Black, *European Warfare, 1660–1815*, New Haven, CT, 1994, pp. 168ff.; R. F. Weigley, *The Age of Battles: The Quest for Decisive Warfare from Breitenfeld to Waterloo*, Bloomington, IN, 1991, p. 280, ch. 12.

25 F. R. Scott, *The Response of the Royal Army to the French Revolution: The Role and Development of the Line Army 1787–93*, Oxford, 1978, p. 106.

26 Id., 'The Regeneration of the Line Army during the French Revolution', *Journal of Modern History*, 1970, vol. 42, pp. 311, 325. The outbreak of war only increased the likelihood of desertion.

27 Bertaud, *Army*, pp. 47–9.

28 Ibid., p. 47; Scott, *Response*, pp. 151–3, 155, 160–1.

29 Ibid., pp. 155, 147–8.

30 P. Paret, 'Conscription and the End of the Ancien Régime in France and Prussia', in *Understanding War: Essays on Clausewitz and the History of Military Power*, P. Paret (ed.), Princeton, NJ, 1992, pp. 57–61.

31 Forrest, *Soldiers*, pp. 61–2; id., *Conscripts and Deserters: The Army and French Society during the Revolution and Empire*, New York, 1989, p. 21; Scott, *Response*, p. 157.

32 Bertaud, *Army*, p. 66.

33 Ibid., p. 67.

34 Forrest, *Conscripts*, pp. 22–4.

35 Scott, *Response*, pp. 166–7; id., 'Foreign Mercenaries, Revolutionary War, and Citizen-Soldiers in the Late Eighteenth Century', *War & Society*, 1984, vol. 2, p. 54.

36 D. Berlemont, 'Le militaire est-il un modèle de citoyen?', M.A. Thesis, University of Paris I, 1987, p. 42; Forrest, *Conscripts*, pp. 26–7.

37 Forrest, *Soldiers*, pp. 69–74; id, *Conscripts*, pp. 26–30. On resistance to the levy in the West, see P. M. Jones, *The Peasantry in the French Revolution*, Cambridge, 1988, pp. 224ff.

38 Forrest, *Soldiers*, p. 80; Bertaud, *Army*, p. 127.

39 Forrest, *Soldiers*, pp. 78–9.

40 Bertaud, *Army*, pp. 108, 117.

41 Mathiez, *La Victoire en l'an II*, p. 102; see also P. Thiebault, *Mémoires*, R. Lacour-Gayet (ed.), Paris, 1962, p. 31; M. Reinhard, *Le Grand Carnot*, Paris, 1952, vol. 2, pp. 99–100.

42 Forrest, *Soldiers*, p. 168.

43 B. Deschard, *L'Armée et la Révolution: Du service du Roi au service de la Nation*, Paris, 1989, p. 130; Bertaud, *Army*, pp. 259–60; A. Corvesier, *Armies and Societies in Europe, 1494–1789*, A. T. Siddall (trans.), Bloomington, IN, 1979, p. 71.

44 Forrest, *Conscripts*, pp. 64, 94–5.

45 Bertaud, *Army*, p. 125.

46 Ibid., p. 128.

47 Ibid., p. 129.

48 Ibid.; Forrest, *Conscripts*, p. 170.

49 Ibid., pp. 128–9. The rate of desertion, moreover, appears to have been considerably higher than in some foreign armies, especially the Russian, in the same period. Compare Bertaud, *Army*, pp. 259–60, with, for example, E. K. Wirtschafter, *From Serf to Russian Soldier*, Princeton, NJ, 1990, p. 111.

50 Forrest, *Soldiers*, pp. 169–70.
51 G. Sangnier, *La désertion dans le Pas-de-Calais de 1792 à 1802*, Blangemont, 1972, p. 89; Forrest, *Conscripts*, pp. 106, 114, 170.
52 Bertaud, *Army*, pp. 151–2.
53 *Mémoires du Général Baron Godart (1792–1815)*, Paris, 1895, pp. 8–12.
54 Quoted in Lynn, *Bayonets*, p. 94.
55 See ibid., p. 98. On the disciplinary problems of the *armées révolutionnaires*, many of which applied equally to the more radical of the volunteer battalions at the front, see R. Cobb, *The People's Armies*, M. Elliot (trans.), New Haven, CT, 1987, p. 511.
56 Quoted in Bertaud, *Army*, p. 57.
57 G. Bodinier, 'L'armée de la Révolution et ses transformations', *Histoire militaire de la France*, vol. 2, J. Delmas (ed.), Paris, 1992, p. 237.
58 See e.g. Lynn, *Bayonets*, p. 98; Bertaud, *Army*, p. 159.
59 Scott, *Response*, p. 116; R. W. Phipps, *The Armies of the First French Republic, I: The Armée du Nord*, Oxford, 1926, p. 78.
60 Scott, *Response*, pp. 116–17; Phipps, op. cit., vol. 1, p. 81.
61 Phipps, op. cit., vol. 1, pp. 84–7.
62 Deschard, op. cit., p. 213.
63 Rothenberg, op. cit., p. 33; see also T. C. W. Blanning, *The French Revolutionary Wars, 1787–1802*, London, 1996, pp. 76–7.
64 See A. Chuquet, *Jemappes et la conquête de la Belgique*, Paris, 1890, pp. 92–102; C. F. D. Dumouriez, *Life of General Dumouriez*, London, 1796, vol. 3, p. 436; Le Comte de Jonquière, *La Bataille de Jemappes*, Paris, 1902, pp. 201–2, n. 1.
65 See A. Chuquet, *Les Guerres de la Révolution, XI: Hondschoote*, Paris, 1896.
66 Rousset, op. cit., pp. 261, 258–63; see Phipps, op. cit., vol. 1, pp. 256–7.
67 See G. E. Rothenberg, *Napoleon's Great Adversaries: The Archduke Charles and the Austrian Army, 1792–1814*, Bloomington, IN, 1982, pp. 34, 36; S. T. Ross, *Quest for Victory: French Military Strategy, 1792–1799*, Cranbury, NJ, 1973, pp. 27–8, 74ff.; Blanning, *French Revolutionary Wars*, pp. 80–1.
68 See e.g. Lynn, *Bayonets*, p. 90, ch. 4, *passim*.
69 S. Wilkinson, *The French Army before Napoleon*, Oxford, 1915, p. 199.
70 Mathiez, op. cit., pp. 36, 27.
71 Bertaud, *Army*, pp. 144–7; Lynn, *Bayonets*, pp. 227, 239–41. Military historian John R. Elting estimates that of the twenty generals executed between May 1793 and July 1794, only two or three were guilty. J. R. Elting, *Swords Around a Throne: Napoleon's Grande Armée*, New York, 1988, pp. 36–7.
72 M. Lyons, *Napoleon Bonaparte and the Legacy of the French Revolution*, New York, 1994, p. 13.
73 Quoted in Lynn, *Bayonets*, p. 87.
74 See R. R. Palmer, *Twelve Who Ruled: The Year of the Terror in the French Revolution*, Princeton, NJ, 1989 edn, pp. 93ff.
75 J. Colin, *Correspondance générale de Carnot*, E. Charavay (ed.), Paris, 1892–1907, vol. 3, p. 314.
76 Quoted in Palmer, op. cit., pp. 82–3. For a detailed analysis of the patronage and political in-fighting which hindered efficiency at the top, see H. G. Brown, *War, Revolution, and the Bureaucratic State: Politics and Army Administration in France, 1791–1799*, Oxford, 1995.
77 Palmer, op. cit., p. 183.
78 See Rothenberg, *Art of War*, p. 112; J.-P. Gross, *Saint-Just: Sa politique et ses missions*, Paris, 1976, pp. 191–4, *passim*; V. Dupuis, *Les Opérations militaires sur la Sambre en 1794, Bataille de Fleurus*, Paris, 1907, p. 184.

79 Le Général Philebert (ed.), *Le Général Lecourbe, d'après ses archives, sa correspondance et autres documents*, Paris, 1895, p. 86.
80 Elting, op. cit., p. 37.
81 Colin, op. cit., vol. 2, pp. 299–302.
82 Reinhard, op. cit., p. 50.
83 Forrest, *Conscripts*, pp. 187, 178–9; Lynn, *Bayonets*, p. 107.
84 On the rationalization of army administration, see Brown, op. cit., pp. 124ff.
85 Lynn, *Bayonets*, p. 109.
86 Bertaud, *Army*, pp. 259–60. The desertion rate rose again, however, when the supply situation deteriorated over the next few years. Ibid., p. 275.
87 Forrest, *Soldiers*, pp. 82–3.
88 G. Saint-Cyr, *Mémoires sur les campagnes des Armées du Rhin et de Rhin-et-Moselle de 1792 jusqu'à la Paix de Campo-Formio*, Paris, 1829, vol. 1, p. 4.
89 See e.g. Bertaud, *Army*, chs 11–14; J. A. Lynn, 'Toward an Army of Honor: The Moral Evolution of the French Army, 1789–1815', *French Historical Studies*, 1989, vol. 16, p. 159.
90 See O. Connelly, 'A Critique of John Lynn's "Toward an Army of Honor" ', *French Historical Studies*, 1989, vol. 16, p. 177.
91 Forrest, *Soldiers*, p. 123; see also Blanning, *French Revolutionary Wars*, pp. 118–19. Arguments to the effect that Jacobin propaganda emphasized loyalty to the Republic rather than to individual government figures are not, to my mind, entirely convincing. See J.-P. Bertaud, *La vie quotidienne des soldats de la Révolution, 1789–1799*, Paris, 1985, p. 217.
92 *Correspondance de Napoléon Ier, publiée par ordre de l'Empereur Napoléon III*, Paris, 1858, vol. 1, p. 107. These exact words were probably not used – they were transcribed on St Helena – but there is no doubt that Napoleon used personal gain rather than collective sacrifice as his main plank in building morale.
93 For a summary of the course of the war, see Ross, op. cit.; Blanning, *French Revolutionary Wars*. Luck, indeed, played a key role in the successes of Napoleon himself, who committed a series of errors in Italy which might well have led to his downfall if exploited. See O. Connelly, *Blundering to Glory: Napoleon's Military Campaigns*, Wilmington, DE, 1987, ch. 2.
94 Lynn, *Bayonets*, ch. 11.
95 R. S. Quimby, *The Background of Napoleonic Warfare: The Theory of Military Tactics in Eighteenth-Century France*, New York, 1968; A. Gat, *The Origins of Military Thought from the Enlightenment to Clausewitz*, Oxford, 1989, p. 52; though see also D. B. Bein, 'The Army in the French Enlightenment: Reform, Reaction and Revolution', *Past and Present*, 1979, vol. 85, p. 95.
96 Lynn, 'En Avant!', p. 162.
97 See P. Paret, *Yorck in the Era of Prussian Reform*, Princeton, NJ, 1966, pp. 29ff., 34, 41–2, 45, 55, 70–1; Rothenberg, *Art*, p. 116.
98 Quoted in E. G. Léonard, *L'armée et ses problèmes au XVIII siècle*, Paris, 1958, p. 235.
99 Quoted in Lynn, 'En Avant!', p.161.
100 P. Longworth, *The Art of Victory: The Life and Achievements of Generalissimo Suvorov, 1729–1800*, London, 1965, pp. 312–13; B. W. Menning, 'Russian Military Innovation in the Second Half of the Eighteenth Century', *War & Society*, 1984, vol. 2, pp. 29–30, 37. That such a form of attack was specifically Russian became an article of faith among many Russian military theorists in the nineteenth century. See W. Pinter, 'Russian Military Thought: The Western Model and the Shadow of Suvorov', in *Makers of Modern Strategy: From Machiavelli to the Nuclear Age*, P. Paret (ed.), Princeton, NJ, 1986, ch. 13.

101 Quoted in Paret, *Yorck*, p. 72.
102 See Paret, *Yorck*; G. A. Craig, *The Politics of the Prussian Army, 1640–1945*, Oxford, 1955, pp. 38–52.
103 It has even been argued that the eventual defeat of Napoleon by his major adversaries indicates that his campaigns were ultimately no more 'decisive' than those of the eighteenth century, and were indeed very much part of a continuum. See R. F. Weigley, *The Age of Battles: The Quest for Decisive Warfare from Breitenfeld to Waterloo*, Bloomington, IN, 1991. A case for continuity can also be found in Black, *European Warfare*.
104 C. Falls, *The Art of War*, Oxford, 1961, p. 34.
105 Blanning, *Origins*, p. 174.
106 On the evolution of the Austrian Army, see C. Duffy, *The Army of Maria Theresa: The Armed Forces of Imperial Austria, 1740–1780*, New York, 1977; Rothenberg, *Adversaries*.
107 Archduke Charles certainly thought so (see Gat, op. cit., pp. 99–100), but even he may have overstated the case. See Rothenberg, *Art*, p. 168.
108 Even if one takes into account later, more serious Austrian defeats at the hands of the French emperor like Ulm (1805) and Austerlitz (1805), it is worth bearing in mind that, under good generals, the essentially eighteenth-century Austrian Army was eventually able to triumph as a key member of the 1813–14 coalition.
109 Blanning, *French Revolutionary Wars*, p. 119.
110 See Palmer, *Twelve Who Ruled, passim*. Mobilization, however, was not without its problems. See Brown, op. cit.
111 Lynn, *Bayonets*, p. 65.
112 Forrest, *Soldiers*, pp. 157–8; Bertaud, *Vie*, pp. 212–16.
113 T. C. W. Blanning convincingly suggests that it was the ability of the regime to generate huge forces that allowed it to absorb defeats. Blanning, *French Revolutionary Wars*, p. 120.
114 It is difficult, for example, to give much credence to the claim by two representatives dispatched to the Army of the North in the spring of 1793 that 'We can guarantee that for the last fifteen days [i.e. since their arrival] the army without being increased in number has been doubled in strength.' Rousset, op. cit., p. 205.
115 See e.g. P. M. Jones, *The Peasantry in the French Revolution*, Cambridge, 1988, ch. 7; G. Bordonove, *La vie quotidienne en Vendée pendant la Révolution*, Paris, 1974; G. Lewis, *The Second Vendée: The Continuity of Counter-revolution in the Department of the Gard, 1789–1815*, Oxford, 1978.
116 Forrest, *Soldiers*, pp. 164–5, 167.
117 Lyons, op. cit., p. 56.
118 See e.g. A. Forrest, 'Regionalism and Counter-Revolution in France', in *Rewriting the French Revolution*, C. Lucas (ed.), Oxford, 1991, ch. 7. A century later the same linguistic and cultural gulf between capital and provinces, urban and rural France, and between regions was still quite evident. See E. Weber, *Peasants into Frenchmen: The Modernization of Rural France, 1870–1914*, Stanford, CA, 1976. Fernand Braudel has argued that such diversity, even micro-regionalism, is characteristic of French historical development over the long term. (*The Identity of France, Volume One: History and Environment*, S. Reynolds (trans.), London, 1988, ch. 1.)
119 See M. Howard, *The Franco-Prussian War: The German Invasion of France, 1870–1871*, London, 1962, chs 6–10.

4 THE ARMIES OF BOLÍVAR AND THE WAR FOR THE LIBERATION OF GRAN COLOMBIA, 1811–24

 1 Quoted in S. Madariaga, *Bolívar*, London, 1952, p. 245.
 2 Ibid., p. 248.
 3 See G. Masur, *Simón Bolívar*, Albuquerque, NM, 1969, pp. 488–9.
 4 See G. Carrera Damas, 'Simón Bolívar, el Culto Heroico y la Nación', *Hispanic American Historical Review*, 1983, vol. 63, pp. 107–45; id., *El Culto a Bolívar*, Caracas, 1973 edn.
 5 L. Yañez-Barnuevo in preface to I. L. Aguirre, *Bolívar*, Madrid, 1983, p. 7; see also e.g. A. U. Pietri prologue to *Simón Bolívar: The Hope of the Universe*, UNESCO, Paris, 1983, p. 9.
 6 V. Lecuna, *Bolívar y el arte Militar*, New York, 1955; id., *Crónica Razonada de las Guerras de Bolívar* (3 vols), New York, 1950, e.g. vol. 1, p. 24.
 7 J. Miller, *Memoirs of General Miller in the Service of the Republic of Peru*, New York, 1973 edn, p. 107; see D. F. O'Leary, *Bolívar and the War of Independence*, Robert F. McNerney (trans. and ed.), Austin, TX, 1970, p. 4.
 8 See e.g. A. B. Alvarez, *El Capitán de los Andes* (2 vols), Quito, 1960; L. C. Marquez, *Independencia de las colonias Hispano-Americanas: Participación de la Gran Bretaña y de los Estados Unidos, Legión Británica*, Bogotá, 1935, vol. 2, p. 199.
 9 D. Scott, *Mary English: A Friend of Bolívar*, Lewes, Sussex, 1991, p. 35; see A. Hasbrouck, *Foreign Legionaries in the Liberation of South America*, New York, 1928, pp. 370–1, *passim*; C. Marquez, op. cit., *passim*.
10 Carrera Damas, *Culto*, *passim*; id., 'Bolívar', pp. 107–45.
11 Lievano Aguirre, op. cit., p. 7; see O. Albornoz Peralta, *Bolívar: Vison Critica*, Quito, 1990; see also Masur, op. cit., pp. 488–9; D. Sommer, 'Irresistible Romance: The Foundational Fictions of Latin America', in *Nation and Narration*, Homi K. Bhabha (ed.), London, 1990, p. 76.
12 F. Larrazabel (ed.), *Correspondencia general del Libertador Simón Bolívar* (2 vols), New York, 1865–6; J. F. Blanco and R. Azpurúa (eds), *Documentos para la historia de la vida pública del Libertador* (14 vols), Caracas, 1875–8; S. B. O'Leary (ed.), *Memorias del general O'Leary* (32 vols), Caracas, 1879–88; V. Lecuna (ed.), *Cartas del Libertador* (12 vols), Caracas, 1929–59; id., *Proclamas y Discursos del Libertador*, Caracas, 1939; M. Pérez Villa (comp.), *Bolívar y su epoca: Cartas y testimonios de extranjeros notables* (2 vols), Caracas, 1953; V. Lecuna (ed.), *Decretos del Libertador* (3 vols), Caracas, 1961; id., *La entrevista de Guayaquil* (2 vols), Caracas, 1962–3 edn; id., *Obras completas* (3 vols), Havana, 1950; ibid., *Escritos del Libertador*, Caracas, 1964– .
13 J. Lynch on Madariaga, in *The Spanish American Revolutions, 1808–1826*, London, 1973, p. 417.
14 C. L. Mendoza, 'The Cult to the Liberator', in *The Liberator, Simón Bolívar: Man and Image*, D. Bushnell (ed.), New York, 1970, p. 133.
15 Madariaga, op. cit., p. xiv; see Carrera Damas, *Culto*, p. 83, *passim*; see also e.g. Pedro Grasas' introduction to A. Mijares, *The Liberator*, J. Fisher (trans.), Caracas, 1983, p. xix. Not surprisingly this approach has spilled over into many foreign biographies and histories. See e.g. I. Nicholson, *The Liberators: A Study of Independence Movements in Spanish America*, New York, 1969, pp. 20, 32; J. A. Crow, *The Epic of Latin America*, Berkeley, 1992 edn, p. 450; G. Saurat, *Simón Bolívar: Le Libertador*, Paris, 1990; A. Bernieri, *Simón Bolívar, Libertador*, Florence, 1989.
16 See J. Lynch, *The Spanish American Revolutions 1808–1826*, New York, 1986 edn, chs 6–7. On the competing and contradictory attitudes among classes and

races to Spanish rule, see J. Lynch (ed.), *Latin American Revolutions, 1808–1826: Old and New World Origins*, Norman, OK, 1994.

17 A. J. Kuethe, *Military Reform and Society in New Granada*, Gainsville, FL, 1978, pp. 186, 188.
18 See e.g. V. Lecuna (ed.), *Cartas del Libertador*, Cartagena Manifesto, vol. 1, pp. 35ff.; Madariaga, op. cit., p. 158.
19 Quoted in Masur, op. cit., p. 101.
20 Madariaga, op. cit., p. 184; Mijares, op. cit., ch. 15.
21 O'Leary (ed.), *Memorias*, vol. 1, pp. 103–4.
22 Letter of 7 May 1813, quoted in Madariaga, op. cit., pp. 192–3; see also Masur, op. cit., p. 118.
23 O'Leary (ed.), *Memorias*, vol. 1, p. 213.
24 See e.g. McNerney (ed.), *Bolívar*, p. 52.
25 Masur, op. cit., p. 125; Madariaga, op. cit., pp. 199–203.
26 Lecuna (ed.), *Cartas*, vol. 2, p. 113.
27 McNerney (ed.), *Bolívar*, p. 50; see Madariaga, op. cit., p. 207.
28 R. Urdaneta, *Memorias del General Rafael Urdaneta*, Madrid, 1917, p. 13; Larrazabel (ed.), op. cit., vol. 1, p. 141.
29 Madariaga, op. cit., p. 206; Masur, op. cit., pp. 122ff.
30 O'Leary, *Bolívar*, p. 73; Madariaga, op. cit., p. 212.
31 J. F. Heredia, *Memorias sobre las Revoluciones de Venezuela*, Paris, 1895, pp. 126–7.
32 Masur, op. cit., p. 130.
33 McNerney (ed.), *Bolívar*, p. 61; see Masur, op. cit., p. 144. Even the sympathetic biographer Augusto Mijares admits that 'lack of experience' among 'newly formed forces' created 'frightful disorder'. Mijares, op. cit., p. 297.
34 Masur, op. cit., p. 149.
35 J. Lynch, *Caudillos in Spanish America, 1800–1850*, Oxford, 1992, p. 55; Masur, op. cit., pp. 144ff. On Boves and the class struggle, see G. Carrera Damas, *Boves: Aspectos socio-económicos de su acción historica*, Caracas, 1968.
36 Madariaga, op. cit., p. 229.
37 Ibid., pp. 220–5.
38 Masur, op. cit., p. 153.
39 Madariaga, op. cit., p. 228.
40 P. de Lacroix, *Diaro de Bucaramanga*, Madrid, 1924, p. 225.
41 Madariaga, op. cit., p. 245.
42 Ibid., p. 248.
43 Lynch, *Caudillos*, pp. 35, 55.
44 Madariaga, op. cit., p. 259.
45 See S. K. Stoan, *Pablo Morillo and Venezuela, 1815–1820*, Columbus, OH, 1974.
46 Lecuna (ed.), *Proclamas*, pp. 147–9.
47 Letter to General Marion, 27 June 1816, quoted in Madariaga, op. cit., p. 280.
48 Masur, op. cit., pp. 198–201.
49 R. Sevilla, *Memorias de un oficial del Ejército Español*, Madrid, 1916, pp. 22–4.
50 M. L. Woodward, 'The Spanish Army and the Loss of America, 1810–1824', *Hispanic American Historical Review*, 1968, vol. 48, pp. 590ff.; L. Ullrick, 'Morillo's Attempt to Pacify Venezuela', *Hispanic American Historical Review*, 1920, vol. 3, p. 545.
51 On Páez, see *Autobiografia del General José Antonio Páez*, Caracas, 1973, vol. 1.
52 See Masur, op. cit., ch. 17; Mijares, op. cit., pp. 303–6.
53 Lecuna (ed.), *Escritos*, vol. 9, pp. 94–5; O'Leary, *Memorias*, vol. 15, pp. 264–8. On the Piar episode, see Masur, op. cit., p. 311; Mijares, op. cit., pp. 311ff.
54 McNerney (ed.), *Bolívar*, pp. 124–5.

55　Stoan, op. cit., pp. 213ff.; Madariaga, op. cit., pp. 305ff.

56　Quoted in Madariaga, op. cit., p. 307; see McNerney (ed.), *Bolívar*, p. 127. In defence of the Caracas strategy, see Mijares, op. cit., pp. 307–8.

57　Madariaga, op. cit., p. 321.

58　H. A. Bierck (ed.), *Selected Writings of Bolívar*, New York, 1951, vol. 1, p. 165.

59　Madariaga, op. cit., p. 309; see also Lecuna, *Cartas*, vol. 2, pp. 30–1.

60　Bierck (ed.), *Selected Writings*, vol. 1, p. 153.

61　See Nicholson, op. cit., p. 206; see also Mijares, op. cit., p. 315.

62　McNerney (ed.), *Bolívar*, p. 146.

63　Stoan, op. cit., pp. 220, 204; see e.g. Madariaga, op. cit., p. 393.

64　Lecuna, *Cartas*, vol. 2, p. 229. On the trials and tribulations of the foreign volunteers, see Hasbrouck, op. cit., *passim*, and Cuervo Marquez, op. cit., *passim*. A sense of the disillusionment felt by the first volunteers can be found in Gustav Hippisley's *A Narrative of the Expedition to the Rivers Orinoco and Apuré in South America*, London, 1819.

65　Masur, op. cit., p. 239.

66　See e.g. Mijares, op. cit., p. 354.

67　Ibid., p. 243.

68　Madariaga, op. cit., p. 342.

69　McNerney (ed.), *Bolívar*, p. 151; Masur, op. cit., pp. 263–4.

70　McNerney (ed.), op. cit., pp. 157ff.; Masur, op. cit., pp. 267–9.

71　V. Lecuna (ed.), *Cartas de Santander*, Caracas, 1942, vol. 1, p. 57.

72　Madariaga, op. cit., p. 346. On Vargas, see Mijares, op. cit., pp. 361–2.

73　See Bierck (ed.), *Selected Writings*, vol. 1, p. 205.

74　Madariaga, op. cit., p. 346.

75　A. R. Villa, *El teniente general Don Pablo Morillo*, Madrid, 1910, vol. 4, p. 49. On Boyacá, see e.g. J. Friede (ed.), *La Batalla de Boyacá, 7 de agosto de 1819, a través de los Archivos Españoles*, Bogotá, 1969.

76　Bierck (ed.), *Selected Writings*, vol. 1, p. 208.

77　See C. H. Bowman, 'The Activities of Manuel Torres As Purchasing Agent, 1820–1821', *Hispanic American Historical Review*, 1968, vol. 48, pp. 234–46.

78　Bierck (ed.), *Selected Writings*, vol. 1, p. 222.

79　Ibid., pp. 218–19.

80　M. P. Costeloe, *Response to Revolution: Imperial Spain and the Spanish American Revolutions, 1810–1840*, Cambridge, 1986, pp. 83ff.

81　Stoan, op. cit., p. 222; see Mijares, op. cit., pp. 383–4.

82　Madariaga, op. cit., pp. 391–2.

83　McNerney (ed.), *Bolívar*, pp. 185–6.

84　Quoted in Madariaga, op. cit., pp. 419–20.

85　Hasbrouck, op. cit., pp. 233ff.; Madariaga, op. cit., pp. 396–7; M. E. Rosales, *La Batalla de Carabobo*, Caracas, 1911.

86　Quoted in Madariaga, op. cit., p. 399.

87　Ibid., pp. 421, 423, 428.

88　Ibid., pp. 455–6; see Miller, op. cit., p. 105.

89　See ibid., pp. 113ff., 149, 154, 156, 188–9.

90　Madariaga, op. cit., pp. 430–2, 482, 483. For a more detailed (if biased) assessment of Bomboná and Pichincha, see J. R. Ibañez Sanchez, *Campaña del Sur, 1822*, Bogotá, 1972.

91　Quoted in Miller, op. cit., pp. 158–9.

92　Madariaga, op. cit., p. 487.

5 THE VOORTREKKERS, BLOOD RIVER, AND THE ZULU WAR OF 1838–40

1 Dispatch on the battle of Blood River, dated 31 December, quoted in H. F. Schoon (ed.), *The Diary of Erasmus Smit*,W. G. A. Mears (trans.), Cape Town, 1972 edn, p. 155.

2 Account of the battle of Dlokweni, in M. M. Funze, *The Black People and Whence They Came: A Zulu View*, H. C. Lugg (trans.), A. T. Cope (ed.), Pietermaritzburg, 1979, p. 77.

3 K. Smith, *The Changing Past: Trends in South African Historical Writing*, Athens, OH, 1989, pp. 36–7, 58–9, 67–8; F. A. van Jaarsveld, *The Afrikaner's Interpretation of South African History*, Cape Town, 1964, pp. 34ff., 63, 78–9. On Theal, see also C. Saunders, *The Making of the South African Past: Major Historians on Race and Class*, Totowa, NJ, 1988, pp. 9–49; D. Schreuder, 'The Imperial Historian as Colonial Naturalist: George McCall Theal and the Making of South African History', in *Studies in British Imperial History: Essays in Honour of A. P. Thorton*, G. Martel (ed.), London, 1986, pp. 95–158.

4 D. H. Akenson, *God's Peoples: Covenant and Land in South Africa, Israel, and Ulster*, Ithaca, NY, 1992, pp. 67, 69–70, 72–3; L. Thompson, *The Political Mythology of Apartheid*, New Haven, CT, 1985, ch. 5. See also J. A. Templin, *Ideology and Frontier: The Theological Foundation of Afrikaner Nationalism, 1652–1910*, Westport, CT, 1984.

5 D. Harrison, *The White Tribe of Africa: South Africa in Perspective*, London, 1981, ch. 8; C. Blomberg, *Christian Nationalism and the Rise of the Afrikaner Broederbond in South Africa, 1918–1948*, London, 1990, pp. 117–22.

6 Thompson, *Political Mythology*, p. 39. For descriptions and analysis of the Voortrekker Monument, see Harrison, op. cit., pp. 9–15; J. Morris, *Destinations*, New York, 1990, pp. 103–5.

7 V. February, *The Afrikaners of South Africa*, London, 1991, p. 98; Harrison, op. cit., ch. 16; M. Walker, 'History and History Teaching in Apartheid South Africa', in *History From South Africa: Alternative Visions and Practices*, J. Brown *et al.* (eds), Philadelphia, 1991, p. 269; R. E. van der Ross, 'The Place of History and History Teaching in Our Educational System', in *The Meaning of History*, A König and H. Keane (eds), Pretoria, 1980, p. 155; Blomberg, op. cit., p. 27; M. Cornevin, *Apartheid: Power and Historical Falsification*, Paris, 1980, p. 52; B. Villet, *Blood River: The Passionate Saga of South Africa's Afrikaners and of Life in their Embattled Land*, New York, 1982, p. 89.

8 Harrison, op. cit., pp. 10, 18–19; Thompson, *Political Mythology*, p. 144. This was eventually scaled down to six small wagons made of cement along with other attractions. G. Schutte, *What Racists Believe: Race Relations in South Africa and the United States*, Thousand Oaks, CA, 1995, p. 55.

9 van Jaarsveld, 'Historical Mirror', pp. 36–41.

10 Harrison, op. cit., p. 10.

11 J. Morris, op. cit., p. 105; Thompson, *Political Mythology*, p. 220.

12 See Schutte, op. cit., pp. 103, 240, *passim*; G. Mendel, 'Promised Land', in *History From South Africa*, J. Brown *et al.* (eds), Philadelphia, 1991, pp. 245–56; A. Hochschild, *The Mirror at Midnight: A South African Journey*, New York, 1990, pp. 251–4; Akenson, op. cit., p. 295.

13 Quoted in van Jaarsveld, 'Historical Mirror', p. 16.

14 Ibid.

15 J. Naido, *Tracking Down Historical Myths: Eight South African Cases*, Johannesburg, 1989, pp. 82–105; Smith, op. cit., p. 46.

16 Thompson, *Political Mythology*, pp. 213–14; see Smith, op. cit., pp. 74–6; van Jaarsveld, 'Historical Mirror', pp. 16–17; Schutte, op. cit., p. 43.

17 van Jaarsveld, 'Historical Mirror', p. 16; see e.g. J. Meintjes, *The Voortrekkers: The Story of the Great Trek and the Making of South Africa*, London, 1973, p. 134, the first general history of the trek by an Afrikaner, and C. F. J. Muller's *Five Hundred Years: A History of South Africa*, Pretoria, 1981 edn, p. 166, a popular history textbook in South Africa in the 1970s.

18 G. M. Theal, *History of the Boers in South Africa*, London, 1887, p. 117. On the popularity of this and other Theal works, see Smith, op. cit., p. 36; Thompson, *Political Mythology*, pp. 54–8. For a more contemporary but nevertheless highly sympathetic interpretation of Blood River and the Afrikaner experience see G. H. L. Le May, *The Afrikaners: An Historical Interpretation*, Oxford, 1995, p. 49.

19 See J. J. Durand, 'God in History – An Unresolved Problem' and responses, in *The Meaning of History*, A. König and H. Keane (eds), Pretoria, 1980, pp. 171–89.

20 See views of J. B. Liebenberg as recounted in van Jaarsveld, 'Historical Mirror', p. 17; see also Cornevin, op. cit., p. 60. For Zulu pride in White Umfolozi, see Fuze, op. cit., pp. 78–9; J. Y. Gibson, *The Story of the Zulus*, London, 1910, p. 72.

21 On the problems of reclaiming Zulu history, see D. Golan, *Inventing Shaka: Using History in the Construction of Zulu Nationalism*, Boulder, CO, 1994. See also van Jaarsveld, 'Historical Mirror', pp. 13–14.

22 For the traditional view of Dingane and the Retief massacre, see e.g. P. Becker, *Rule of Fear: The Life and Times of Dingane, King of the Zulus*, London, 1964.

23 J. K. Ngubane, *Ushaba: The Hurtle to Blood River*, Washington, DC, 1974, p. 37; see F. N. C. Okoye, 'Dingane: A Reappraisal', *Journal of African History*, 1969, vol. 10, pp. 221–35.

24 Retief to Dingane, 8 November 1857, in J. Bird (ed.), *Annals of Natal*, Pietermaritzburg, 1888, vol. 1, p. 362.

25 Naido, op. cit., ch. 6; Okoye, op. cit., p. 235; C. V. Mutwa, *My People*, Johannesburg, 1969, pp. 189–95. See also Hochschild, op. cit., pp. 67–8; Fuze, op. cit., p. 75; B. Roberts, *The Zulu Kings*, London, 1974, pp. 275–6, 279, 285.

26 Cilliers account in D. C. F. Moodie, *The History of the Battles and Adventures of the British, the Boers and the Zulus in Southern Africa*, London, 1888, vol. 1, pp. 441–2. On the role of the Cilliers account in Covenant mythology, see Thompson, *Political Mythology*, ch. 5.

27 A. du Toit, 'No Chosen People: The Myth of the Calvinist Origins of Afrikaner Nationalism and Racial Ideology', *American Historical Review*, 1983, vol. 88, pp. 920–52; Thompson, *Political Mythology*, pp. 158–61; Akenson, op. cit., pp. 60–1.

28 Bantjes in J. C. Chase (ed.), *The Natal Papers*, Cape Town, 1968 edn, pt II, pp. 62–3; see Thompson, op. cit., pp. 164–5.

29 Ibid., pp. 162–4.

30 See n. 1; Pretorius dispatch, 22 December 1838, in Bird, op. cit., vol. 1, p. 453.

31 Thompson, *Political Mythology*, p. 165; Smith, op. cit., pp. 58–9.

32 Thompson, *Political Mythology*, p. 164.

33 Quoted in Smit diary, Schoon, op. cit., p. 158; see ibid., diary entries for 8 and 10 December 1838, p. 151.

34 Harrison, op. cit., pp. 17–18; see also van Jaarsveld, 'Historical Mirror', p. 19.

35 Pretorius dispatch of 22 December 1858, in Bird, op. cit., vol. 1, p. 453; Cilliers account in Moodie, op. cit., p. 443.

36 For example, 'The weird appearance created by this circle of light, as seen from

a distance, worked on the superstitious fears of the Zulus, who believed that the white invaders had some powerful magic.' J. C. Voigt, *Fifty Years of the History of the Republic in South Africa (1795–1845)*, Cape Town, 1969 reprint, vol. 2, p. 96.

37 Hochschild, op. cit., p. 247.

38 van Jaarsveld, 'Historical Mirror', p. 19.

39 Pretorius dispatch of 22 December 1858, in Bird, op. cit., vol. 1, p. 454.

40 Cilliers account in Moodie, op. cit., p. 444.

41 Bantjes journal in Chase, op. cit., pt II, p. 66; see Pretorius dispatch, 22 December 1858, in Bird, op. cit., vol. 1, p. 454.

42 Cachet quoted in Meintjes, op. cit., p. 139. For the factors involved in the victory, see van Jaarsveld on Liebenberg, 'Historical Mirror', p. 16.

43 Pretorius letter of 3 January 1839 quoted in Smit diary, Schoon, op. cit., p. 156.

44 Pretorius dispatch, 22 December 1838, in Bird, op. cit., vol. 1, pp. 454–5; Bantjes journal, in Chase, op. cit., pt II, p. 66; Cilliers account in Moodie, op. cit., p. 438.

45 See Smit diary, 20 November 1838, Schoon, op. cit., p. 3. Only two Boers were killed. For an account of the battle, see Meintjes, op. cit., pp. 57–9.

46 Calculations are based on individual Boer firepower against the Matabele being approximately three times that at Blood River due to pre-loading by the women. 'As the battle raged the women . . . calmly went on loading, handing the guns upright to their men. The man never had to look for the next rifle [*sic*], but merely put out his hand with the word "*Gee*" ("Give"), found it put into his hand, aimed and fired.' Meintjes, op. cit., p. 58.

47 D. R. Morris, *The Washing of the Spears: A History of the Rise of the Zulu Nation under Shaka and its Fall in the Zulu War of 1879*, New York, 1965, pp. 387, 392, 402, 416–17.

48 A summary account of these events can be found in L. Thompson, 'Co-operation and Conflict: The Zulu Kingdom and Natal', in *The Oxford History of South Africa*, M. Wilson and L. Thompson (eds), Oxford, 1969, vol. 1, pp. 363–73.

49 See J. T. Marcus, 'The World Impact of the West: The Mystique and the Sense of Participation in History', in *Myth and Mythmaking*, H. A. Murray (ed.), New York, 1960, ch. 13.

6 THE ARMIES OF THE HEAVENLY KINGDOM AND THE TAIPING REBELLION IN CHINA, 1850–68

1 Book on the Principles of the Heavenly Nature, Doc. 50 in F. Michael (ed.), *The Taiping Rebellion. History and Documents: Volume II, Documents and Comments*, Seattle, 1971, p. 402.

2 Open Letter to the Gentry of Hunan, quoted in Kung-chan Hsiao, *Rural China: Imperial Control in the Nineteenth Century*, Seattle, 1960, p. 476.

3 Ho Ping-ti, *Studies in the Population of China, 1368–1953*, Cambridge, MA, 1959, p. 247; S. Y. Teng, *The Taiping Rebellion and the Western Powers: A Comprehensive Survey*, Oxford, 1971, p. 411.

4 J. D. Spence, *God's Chinese Son: The Taiping Heavenly Kingdom of Hong Xiuquan*, New York, 1996, pp. 114–15, 126–7.

5 V. Shih, 'Interpretations of the T'ai-p'ings by Non-Communist Writers', *Far Eastern Quarterly*, 1951, vol. 10, pp. 248–57; C. H. Peake, *Nationalism and Education in Modern China*, New York, 1932, p. 187; Teng, *Taiping Rebellion*, pp. 1–2.

6   Mao Tse-tung, 'The Chinese Revolution and the CCP', *Selected Works of Mao Tse-tung*, New York, 1954, vol. 3, pp. 74, 76.
7   D. E. Apter and T. Saich, *Revolutionary Discourse in Mao's Republic*, Cambridge, MA, 1994, pp. 16–17, 104, 121–2.
8   Kwang-Ching Liu, 'World View and the Peasant Rebellion: Reflections on Post-Mao Historiography', *Journal of Asian Studies*, 1981, vol. 60, p. 295.
9   A. Feutwerker and S. Cheng, *Chinese Communist Studies of Modern Chinese History*, Cambridge, MA, 1961, pp. 77ff.; R. H. T. Lin, 'The Taiping Revolution: A Comparative Historical and Sociological Study of a Movement – From the Perspective of Intercivilizational Encounters and Missions', Ph.D. Thesis, New School of Social Research, 1977, p. v.
10   See S. Uhalley, Jr, 'The Controversy over Li Hsiu-ch'eng: An Ill-Timed Centenary', *Journal of Asian Studies*, 1966, vol. 25, pp. 305–17; C. A. Curwen (ed.), *Taiping Rebel: The Deposition of Li Hsiu-ch'eng*, Cambridge, 1977, pp. 46ff.
11   Liu, 'World View and Peasant Rebellion', pp. 296ff.; L. R. Sullivan, 'The Controversy over "Feudal Despotism": Politics and Historiography in China, 1978–82', in *Using the Past to Serve the Present: Historiography and Politics in Contemporary China*, J. Unger (ed.), Armonk, NY, 1993, p. 174.
12   See C. Calhoun, *Neither Gods nor Emperors: Students and the Struggle for Democracy in China*, Berkeley, CA, 1994, p. 163; D. Kellog, *In Search of China*, London, 1989, pp. 43, 45; L. Feigon, *China Rising: The Meaning of Tiananmen*, Chicago, 1990, p. 4, *passim*; G. C. Chu and Y. Ju, *The Great Wall in Ruins: Commemoration and Cultural Change in China*, Albany, NY, 1993, p. 292.
13   Quote from Chou T'un, *The Taiping Army in Yangchow* (1957), cited in Ssu-yu Teng, *Historiography of the Taiping Rebellion*, Cambridge, MA, 1962, p. 86; see Feurwerker and Cheng, op. cit., *passim*; review by M. C. Wright of *Symposium on the T'ai-p'ing Revolutionary Movement* (1950), in *Far Eastern Quarterly*, 1953, vol. 12, p. 324.
14   Quote from Lo Erh-kang, *Commentaries on the Falsehoods in the Historical Record of the Taiping Kingdom* (1955), and Hua Kang, *A History of the Taiping Revolutionary War* (1955), cited in Feurwerker and Cheng, op. cit., pp. 88, 79.
15   See Lo Erh-kang, excerpt from the preface of *The Mobile Warfare of the New Taiping Army* (1955), in E. J. Perry (ed.), *Chinese Perspectives on the Nien Rebellion*, Armonk, NY, 1980, pp. 70–1; Teng, *Historiography*, pp. 68–9, 74; review by Kung-chuan Hsiao of Hua Kang, *A History of the Revolutionary War of the Taiping* (1951), in *Far Eastern Quarterly*, 1953, vol. 12, p. 219; Feurwerker and Cheng, op. cit., *passim*.
16   Jen Yu-wen, *The Taiping Revolutionary Movement*, New Haven, CT, 1973, p. 36. On the works of Jen, see Teng, *Historiography*, pp. 59–62.
17   T. T. Meadows, *The Chinese and Their Rebellions*, Stanford reprint, 1953, pp. 458–61; see Teng, *Taiping Rebellion*, p. 188.
18   J. Gray, *Rebellions and Revolutions: China from the 1800s to the 1980s*, Oxford, 1990, p. 63.
19   Prosper Giquel diary, 15 July 1864, in S. A. Leibo (ed.), *A Journal of the Chinese Civil War, 1864*, Honolulu, 1985, p. 86.
20   Meadows, op. cit., p. 148.
21   Jen, op. cit., p. 46.
22   Quoted in ibid., p. 158. See Doc. 34, E. C. Bridgeman letter; Doc. 12, L. G. Delaplace letter; Doc. 14, Rizzolati letter in: P. Clarke and J. S. Gregory (eds), *Western Reports on the Taiping: A Selection of Documents*, Honolulu, 1982, pp. 148, 30, 24.
23   Meadows, op. cit., pp. 147–8; see Spence, op. cit., p. 152.

24 Michael, *Taiping Rebellion*, vol. 1, pp. 66–7.
25 See e.g. Docs 14, 34, 35 in Clarke and Gregory, op. cit., pp. 30, 148, 152, 162.
26 Jen, op. cit., p. 91. Overall losses here may have approached 10,000. See Spence, op. cit., pp. 158–9.
27 See Teng, *Taiping Rebellion*, p. 331; Michael, *Taiping Rebellion*, vol. 1, pp. 67–8.
28 See Teng, *Taiping Rebellion*, p. 55; Jen, op. cit., pp. 96, 187; Michael, *Taiping Rebellion*, vol. 1, p. 66; J. L. Withers, 'The Heavenly Capital Nanjing under the Taiping, 1853–1864', Ph.D. Thesis, Yale University, 1983, pp. 93–4.
29 Doc. 14, Clarke and Gregory, op. cit., p. 30.
30 Doc. 23, Decree of 14 September 1851 in Michael, *Taiping Rebellion*, vol. 2, p. 105; see ibid., pp. 103, 106, 108–9; Meadows, op. cit., pp. 242–3; Spence, op. cit., pp. 129, 132, 135.
31 Doc. 50, Clarke and Gregory, op. cit., p. 236; see Doc. 93, ibid., p. 417; see Vt Wolseley, *The Story of a Soldier's Life, Volume II*, New York, 1903, p. 94, for a more jaundiced view.
32 Jen, op. cit., p. 106.
33 Hsiao, op. cit., p. 476; see Doc. 47, Clarke and Gregory, op. cit., p. 218.
34 See Jen, op. cit., p. 60; Teng, *Taiping Rebellion*, p. 98; Meadows, op. cit., p. 173.
35 Hsiao, op. cit., p. 476; Doc. 86, Clarke and Gregory, op. cit., p. 395.
36 Quoted in Withers, op. cit., p. 73.
37 J. T. K. Wu, 'The Impact of the Taiping Rebellion upon the Manchu Fiscal System', *Pacific Historical Review*, 1950, vol. 19, p. 272; Michael, *Taiping Rebellion*, vol. 1, pp. 192–3. Taxes in the countryside rose, moreover, as the military situation deteriorated and the need for funds grew desperate. See e.g. K. Bernhardt, 'Rural Society and the Taiping Rebellion: The Jaingnan from 1820 to 1911', Ph.D. Thesis, Stanford University, 1984, p. 156; see also id., *Rents, Taxes, and Peasant Resistance: The Lower Yangzi Region, 1840–1950*, Stanford, CA, 1992, pp. 103–16.
38 Doc. 61, Clarke and Gregory, op. cit., p. 288.
39 Those with bound feet found heavy labour – unheard of for women under the old order – virtually impossible, and even the true believers among the Taipings grew restive about the separation of the sexes at a time when the Taiping princes were taking hundreds of concubines. See Michael, *Taiping Rebellion*, vol. 1, p. 108; Teng, *Taiping Rebellion*, pp. 98, 99; Withers, op. cit., pp. 119, 129, 132–3.
40 See F. Michael, 'Regionalism in Nineteenth-Century China', in S. Spector, *Li Hung-chang and the Huai Army: A Study in Nineteenth Century Chinese Regionalism*, Seattle, 1964, pp. xxxii–xxxv.
41 Doc. 12, Clarke and Gregory, op. cit., p. 24.
42 Quoted in Meadows, op. cit., p. 158.
43 *Tung hua-lu* for 7 September 1852, quoted in J. C. Cheng, *Chinese Sources for the Taiping Rebellion*, Hong Kong, 1963, p. 21; see Docs 14, 21, Clarke and Gregory, op. cit., pp. 30, 59.
44 Michael, *Taiping Rebellion*, vol. 2, p. 131; Lin, 'Taiping Revolution', pp. 42–3; V. C. Y. Shih, *The Taiping Ideology: Its Sources, Interpretations, and Influences*, Seattle, 1967, pp. 259–64.
45 Teng, *Taiping Rebellion*, p. 143; Michael, *Taiping Rebellion*, p. 116; Jen, op. cit., pp. 321–2.
46 Curwen, op. cit., p. 141; see Teng, *Taiping Rebellion*, pp. 331–4; Withers, op. cit., pp. 181–4.
47 Doc. 43, Clarke and Gregory, op. cit., p. 203; see Bernhardt, op. cit., p. 122.
48 See Teng, *Taiping Rebellion*, pp. 178–9.
49 Jen, op. cit., pp. 182–3.

50   Yung Wing, *My Life in China and America*, New York, 1909, p. 121.
51   Doc. 86, Clarke and Gregory, op. cit., p. 395; see G. J. Wolseley, *Narrative of the War in China in 1860*, London, 1862, p. 350; Withers, op. cit., p. 218.
52   Doc. 86, Clarke and Gregory, op. cit., p. 397; see Withers, op. cit., p. 184.
53   Doc. 93, ibid., p. 418; see Wolseley, *Narrative*, p. 351.
54   For an overview of the development of the local militia see Michael, 'Regionalism', pp. xxii–xxxii, xxxv–xliii. For a more detailed analysis, see P. A. Kuhn, *Rebellion and Its Enemies in Late Imperial China: Militarization and Social Structure, 1796–1864*, Cambridge, MA, 1970. For the significance of the So-li ambush, see Michael, *Taiping Rebellion*, p. 67. On the debate surrounding underlying motives of the gentry, see P. A. Cohen, *Discovering History in China: American Historical Writings on the Recent Chinese Past*, New York, 1994, pp. 27–8.
55   Summary biographies of Tseng and other leading figures of the period on both sides can be found in A. W. Hummel (ed.), *Eminent Chinese of the Ch'ing Period (1644–1912)* (2 vols), Washington, DC, 1943–4.
56   On Tseng and the Hunan Army, see J. Porter, *Tseng Kuo-fan's Private Bureaucracy*, Berkeley, CA, 1962; Kuhn, op. cit., pp. 135–52; W. J. Hail, *Tseng Kuo-fan and the Taiping Rebellion*, New York, 1964 edn, pp. 147ff.; Wu, op. cit., p. 274.
57   See Spector, op. cit., pp. 39ff.; Hail, op. cit., chs 8, 10–11.
58   On the problematic Chinese relations with the Western powers in this period, see e.g. F. Wakeman, Jr, *Strangers at the Gate: Social Disorder in South China, 1839–1861*, Berkeley, CA, 1966.
59   On the rather naïve dealings of the Taipings with the Western powers, see Teng, *Taiping Rebellion*, pt 3.
60   See J. K. Fairbank (ed.), *The Chinese World Order: Traditional China's Foreign Relations*, Cambridge, MA, 1968.
61   Meadows, op. cit., pp. 307–8.
62   Curwen, op. cit., pp. 134–5.
63   Wing, op. cit., pp. 109–10; see Teng, *Taiping Rebellion*, pp. 162, 166.
64   Spence, op. cit., pp. 237–8, 311–12.
65   Wolseley, *Narrative*, p. 350; see Meadows, op. cit., pp. 166, 229.
66   Spence, op. cit., pp. 299–300.
67   On the Ever-Victorious Army, see C. Carr, *The Devil Soldier: The Story of Frederick Townsend Ward*, New York, 1992; H. Cahill, *A Yankee Adventurer: The Story of Ward and the Taiping Rebellion*, New York, 1930; A. Wilson, '*The Ever-Victorious Army': A History of the Chinese Campaign under Lt.-Col. C. G. Gordon*, Edinburgh, 1868; see also P. C. Elliott, 'The Role of Frederick Townsend Ward in the Suppression of the Taiping Rebellion', Ph.D. Thesis, St John's University, 1976.
68   See Leibo, op. cit., introduction.
69   Curwen, op. cit., p. 140.
70   Quoted in Cheng, op. cit., p. 110.
71   A. E. Hake, *Events in the Taiping Rebellion, being reprints of the mss compiled by General Gordon*, London, 1891, p. 508.
72   On Western neutrality and the tilt towards Peking, see Teng, *Taiping Rebellion*, chs 10–11. On the Taipings' desperate weapons situation, see ibid., p. 355 and e.g. Doc. 92, Clarke and Gregory, op. cit., p. 413; Wolseley, *Narrative*, pp. 347, 365.
73   L. Oliphant, *Narrative of the Earl of Elgin's Mission to China and Japan in the Years 1857, '58, and '59*, New York, 1860, p. 525.
74   Wolseley, diary entry, 21 March 1861, *Narrative*, p. 371.

75 Compare e.g. Sun-tzu, *The Art of War*, R. D. Sawyer (trans.), New York, 1994, with V. D. Hanson, *The Western Way of War*, New York, 1989.
76 See e.g. Doc. 79, Michael, *Taiping Rebellion*, vol. 2, pp. 373–4; Jen, op. cit., pp. 121–2; Withers, op. cit., pp. 189–90.
77 Curwen, op. cit., p. 65; see also Bernhardt, 'Rural Society', pp. 158–9.
78 Cheng, op. cit., Li Hung-chang memorial, 6 December 1864, p. 125.
79 Ibid., p. 126.
80 Ibid., 31 December 1861 memorial, p. 129.
81 Leibo, op. cit., diary entry for 19 June 1864, p. 72.
82 Ibid., 27 August 1864, p. 101; see ibid., 26 August 1864, p. 101; 15 July 1864, p. 86; 22 June 1864, p. 75; 29 June 1864, p. 80.
83 Curwen, op. cit., pp. 151–3.
84 Teng, *Taiping Rebellion*, p. 409.
85 See Hsiao Kung-chuan review of Hua Kang, *A History of the Revolutionary War of the Taiping Kingdom* (1951), in *Far Eastern Quarterly*, 1953, vol. 12, p. 219. See also Teng, *Historiography*, pp. 73–4; Harrison, op. cit., p. 222.
86 Perry, op. cit., p. 71; see Teng, *Historiography*, pp. 68–9.
87 S. Y. Teng, *The Nien Army and Their Guerrilla Warfare, 1851–1868*, Paris, 1961, p. 9.
88 The term is borrowed from E. J. Hobsbawm, *Primitive Rebels: Studies in Archaic Forms of Social Movement in the 19th and 20th Centuries*, New York, 1965.
89 See Michael, *Taiping Rebellion*, vol. 1, p. 181; S. Y. Teng, *Nien Army, passim*; Siang-tseh Chiang, *The Nien Rebellion*, Seattle, 1954.
90 See Teng, *Taiping Rebellion*, p. 383; see also Yu Sheng-wu and Chang Chen-kun, 'China and India in the Mid-19th Century', in P. C. Joshi (ed.), *Rebellion 1857: A Symposium*, New Delhi, 1957, pp. 346–8.

7 SEPOYS IN THE INDIAN MUTINY, 1857–9

1 'Victory of the Mohammedan Faith' pamphlet in S. A. A. Rizvi and M. L. Bhargava (eds), *Freedom Struggle in Uttar Pradesh*, Delhi, 1958, vol. 2, p. 159.
2 Ibid., spy report, 22 December 1857, p. 260.
3 Paradoxically, this kind of nationalist thought was very much along Western lines. For a critical analysis of 'modern' history in India, see D. Chakrabarty, 'Postcoloniality and the Artifice of History: Who speaks for "Indian" Pasts?', *Representations*, 1992, vol. 37, pp. 1–26.
4 V. D. Savarkar, *The Indian War of Independence of 1857*, London, 1909. On the significance of this work see S. N. Sen, *The Historiography of the Indian Revolt of 1857*, Calcutta, 1992, ch. 7; S. B. Chaudhuri, *English Historical Writings on the Indian Mutiny, 1857–1859*, Calcutta, 1979, pp. 170–1; T. R. Metcalfe, *The Aftermath of Revolt: India 1857–1870*, Princeton, NJ, 1964, p. 57.
5 V. D. Savarkar, *The Indian War of Independence, 1857*, Bombay, 1947. Foreign-language and later Indian editions of this work are listed in the National Union and British Library catalogues.
6 See e.g. A. Mehta, *1857: The Great Rebellion*, Bombay, 1946, p. 8; N. Chatterji, 'Was the Great Revolt of 1857 a Fight for National Freedom?', *Journal of Indian History*, 1955, vol. 33, pp. 341–7.
7 Metcalfe, *Aftermath*, p. 58. A sense of Indian opinion in this period can be gathered from H. Tinker, '1857 and 1957: The Mutiny and Modern India', *International Affairs*, 1957, vol. 34, p. 57. Pressure to conform to the 'orthodox' view in official centenary publications is discussed in R. C. Majumdar, *The*

Sepoy Mutiny and the Revolt of 1857, Calcutta, 1963, preface. The results can be seen in: Publications Division, Ministry of Information, Government of India, *1857: A Pictorial Presentation*, New Delhi, 1957; A. S. Misra, *Nana Saheb Peshwa and the Fight for Freedom*, Lucknow, 1961, publisher's note; H. R. Ghosal, *An Outline History of the Indian People*, Delhi, 1962 edn, preface; S. A. A. Rizvi and M. L. Bhargava (eds), *Freedom Struggle*, *passim*. That the nationalist interpretation lived on subsequently in India can be gathered from the content and often the title of works such as: K. K. Datta, *History of the Freedom Movement in Bihar: Volume One, 1857–1928*, Patna, 1957; S. B. Chaudhuri, *Civil Rebellion in the Indian Mutinies (1857–1859)*, Calcutta, 1957; id., *Theories of the Indian Mutiny (1857–59)*, Calcutta, 1965; id., *English Historical Writings*, op. cit., *passim*; P. C. Joshi (ed.), *Rebellion 1857: A Symposium*, New Delhi, 1957. Hagiographic biographies based on the same assumptions also continued to pour forth. See e.g. D. Pal, *Tatya Tope: The Hero of India's First War of Independence, 1857–1859*, Delhi, 1955; K. K. Datta, *Biography of Kunwar Singh*, Patna, 1957; K. C. Yadev, *Rao Tula Ram – A Hero of 1857*, Hoshiapur, 1965; C. Bhatnagar, 'Rao Tula Ram, Rebel Chief of Rewari', *Journal of Indian History*, 1964, vol. 42, pp. 471–7; R. Devi, 'Raja Arjun Singh – The Hero of the Mutiny in Singhbhum', *Journal of Indian History*, 1972, vol. 50, pp. 555–60; I. Sheorey, *Tatya Tope*, New Delhi, 1973; S. N. Sinha, *Rani Lakshmi Bai of Jhansi*, Allahabad, 1980; M. L. Bhargava, *Architects of Indian Freedom Struggle*, New Delhi, 1981.

8 See e.g. V. S. Naipual, *India: A Million Mutinies Now*, New York, 1991, p. 353. Pakistan, it is worth noting, has developed a parallel heroic tradition. See e.g. I. H. Qureshi, *The Muslim Community of the Indo-Pakistan Subcontinent (610–1947)*, The Hague, 1962, pp. 229–31; S. M. Haq, *The Great Revolution of 1857*, Karachi, 1968; see also B. Umar, *The Indian National Movement*, A. Islam (trans.), Dhaka, 1993, p. 22.

9 See e.g. J. Lebra-Chapman, *The Rani of Jhansi: A Study in Female Heroism in India*, Honolulu, 1986, p. 162; Chaudhuri, *English Historical Writings*, pp. 175–6, 178–90; id., *Theories of the Indian Mutiny*, pp. xi–xiii, 12. Majumdar, no shrinking violet, continued to uphold his unpopular views – first put forth in 1957 – in subsequent works. See R. C. Majumdar (ed.), *The History and Culture of the Indian People: British Paramountcy and Indian Renaissance, Part I*, Bombay, 1963, chs 12–18; id., *History of the Freedom Movement in India, Volume I*, Calcutta, 1962. The debate over the nature of 1857 continues. See Sen, *Historiography*, op. cit., p. 252.

10 Foreword by Surendra Mohan to S. N. Sen (ed.), *Mutiny Telegrams*, Lucknow, 1988; see also the more moderate R. Tapti, *The Politics of a Popular Uprising: Bundelkhand in 1857*, Delhi, 1994, pp. 45, 65, 258.

11 Lebra-Chapman, op. cit., pp. 157–8, chs 10–11; see Datta, *Kunwar Singh*, p. 159; S. S. Chakravarty, *National Identity in Indian Popular Cinema, 1947–1987*, Austin, TX, 1993, p. 158; S. M. Burke and S. Al-Din Quraishi, *The British Raj in India: An Historical Overview*, Karachi, 1995, p. 43. See also J. Nehru, *The Discovery of India*, New York, 1946, p. 289. On the lack of distinction between myth and history in India see R. Panikkar, 'Time and History in the Tradition of India', *Cultures and Time*, Paris, 1976, pp. 63–88.

12 As noted, the patriot case is made most strongly by V. D. Savarkar; but other nationalist writers, even if they disagree with some elements of his case – such as the existence of a plot or the abilities of particular leaders – all adhere to a patriotic viewpoint. Even the generally sceptical S. N. Sen concluded that 'what began as a fight for religion ended as a war of independence'. S. N. Sen, *Eighteen Fifty-seven*, Delhi, 1957, p. 252.

13 See e.g. Misra, op. cit., pp. 215–18, 302.
14 See e.g. Yadev, op. cit., pp. 26–7; Datta, *Kunwar Singh*, p. 144; Savarkar, *Six*, p. 462; Pal, op. cit., pp. 109–18; Rizvi, op. cit., vol. 1, ch. 2.
15 See e.g. Misra, op. cit., p. 302; Savarkar, *Indian War*, pp. 112–13; K. C. Yadev, 'Battle of Narnaul (A Forgotten Battle of the Indian Uprising of 1857)', *Journal of Indian History*, 1965, vol. 43, pp. 657–63.
16 Mehta, op. cit., p. 39; see P. C. Joshi, '1857 in Our History', *Rebellion 1857: A Symposium*, P. C. Joshi (ed.), New Delhi, 1957, pp. 185ff.
17 U. Dutt, *The Great Rebellion*, Calcutta, 1986, p. 34.
18 Savarkar, *Indian War*, p. 114.
19 See Sheorey, op. cit., pp. 2, 77–89; Pal, op. cit., ch. 10; Haq, op. cit., pp. 522–3; Joshi, op. cit., p. 194; Datta, *Kunwar Singh*, pp. 150ff.
20 Majumdar, *Sepoy Mutiny*, p. 473; see E. Stokes, *The Peasant Armed: The Indian Revolt of 1857*, Oxford, 1986, pp. 19–20.
21 See Savarkar, *Indian War*, pp. 92–3, 129–30; Mehta, op. cit., p. 25; Misra, op. cit., p. 211; Bhargarva, op. cit., p. 25; Nehru, op. cit., p. 324; Haq, op. cit., p. 75.
22 Savarkar, *Indian War*, p. 442; see Haq, op. cit., p. 552; K. M. Panikar, *A Survey of Indian History*, London, 1964 edn, p. 224; Mehta, op. cit., pp. 62–3; see also T. Khaldun, 'The Great Rebellion', *Rebellion 1857: A Symposium*, P. C. Joshi (ed.), New Delhi, 1957, pp. 44ff.; Dutt, op. cit., *passim*, and Joshi, '1857 in Our History', pp. 166ff. for a Marxist class-analysis variations on the 'traitor' theme. At the same time some historians have attempted to suggest that regions such as the Punjab usually considered loyal to the *Raj* were in fact rebellious too. See e.g. S. Malik, 'The Panjab and the Indian "Mutiny" ', *Journal of Indian History*, 1972, vol. 50, pp. 343–54.
23 Mehta, op. cit., pp. 60–1; see Ghosal, op. cit., p. 97.
24 Haq, op. cit., pp. 551–3; Khaldun, op. cit., p. 52; Savarkar, *Indian War*, pp. 262, 272; M. P. Srivastava, *The Indian Mutiny 1857*, Allahabad, 1979, pp. 143–4; Chatterji, op. cit., pp. 345–6.
25 See e.g. Rizvi, op. cit., vol. 1, ch. 7; ibid., vol. 5, ch. 4; Khaldun, op. cit., pp. 36–44; Joshi, op. cit., p. 188; Savarkar, op. cit., p. 286; Pal, op. cit., p. 80, *passim*.
26 On nineteenth-century British accounts see Chaudhuri, *English Historical Writings*, pp. 256ff.; id., *Theories*, pp. 15–17. For an example of racial assumptions at work, see V. D. Majendie, *Up Among the Pandies: Or, a Year's Service in India*, Allahabad, 1974 edn, p. 282.
27 Roberts, op. cit., pp. 83, 85; J. Cave-Brown, *The Punjab and Delhi in 1857*, Delhi, 1970 edn, vol. 1, pp. 316, 320; H. Grant, *Incidents in the Sepoy War, 1857–58*, London, 1873, pp. 63–5.
28 Stokes, op. cit., p. 68. Contemporary estimates of rebel strength in Delhi were wildly inflated (40,000 was not an uncommon guess), but the fact remains that the normal force ratio in sieges – besiegers outnumbering the besieged – was reversed.
29 See Rizvi, op. cit., vol. 5, pp. 126–7.
30 Ibid., p. 128; Lord Roberts, *Forty-One Years in India*, New York, 1901, p. 116.
31 Cave-Brown, op. cit., vol. 1, pp. 332–5.
32 Majumdar, *Sepoy Mutiny*, p. 133.
33 Ibid., p. 477. On the mutiny at Kanpur, see Sen, op. cit., ch. 4.
34 Majumdar, *Sepoy Mutiny*, pp. 477–8.
35 On the various relief columns sent towards Lucknow, see M. Edwardes, *Battles of the Indian Mutiny*, London, 1963, pt 2. For a relatively balanced account of

the surrender and subsequent massacre at Kanpur, see Sen, *Eighteen Fifty-seven*, pp. 144–50.

36 J. C. Marshman (comp.), *Memoirs of Major-General Sir Henry Havelock*, London, 1867, pp. 290–2.

37 Ibid., pp. 306–13; Edwardes, op. cit., pp. 78–80.

38 Marshman, op. cit., pp. 339–40, 352, 354–6; Edwardes, op. cit., pp. 83–90. An argument can be made that this campaign was a strategic victory for the rebels, in that Havelock was eventually forced to call off his advance on Lucknow (Stokes, op. cit., pp. 60–1). On the other hand, Havelock was never actually defeated in battle, and rebel battlefield losses were consistently higher – an important point even granting that the rebels had many more men to lose. See Marshman, op. cit., pp. 306–13.

39 Edwardes, op. cit., p. 97.

40 Ibid., pp. 104–15; B. Watson, *The Great Indian Mutiny: Colin Campbell and the Campaign at Lucknow*, New York, 1991, p. 82.

41 Ibid., pp. 79–81.

42 Ibid., pp. 82–91; Edwardes, op. cit., ch. 15.

43 Ibid., pp. 69–71; see e.g. Rizvi, op. cit., vol. 2, pp. 52–73.

44 Edwardes, op. cit., pp. 117–18; see e.g. Sheorey, op. cit., pp. 56–7.

45 On British blunders see Edwardes, op. cit., *passim*. A more favourable assessment of Colin Campbell can be found in Watson, op. cit.

46 See e.g. Misra, op. cit., pp. 302, 309, on the battles of Bithoor and 2nd Kanpur, and Savarakar, op. cit., pp. 238–9, on the rebel attempts to push the British off the Delhi ridge.

47 See e.g. W. H. Russell, *My Indian Mutiny Diary*, M. Edwardes (ed.), London, 1957, p. 150. On the strength of the East India Company's three armies see Stokes, op. cit., p. 19. For a list of units of the Bengal Army which stayed loyal, see H. Chattopadhyaya, *The Sepoy Mutiny 1857: A Social Study and Analysis*, Calcutta, 1957, app. A.

48 F. C. Maude, *Memories of the Mutiny*, London, 1894, p. 25; see Cave-Brown, op. cit., vol. 2, p. 323; Stokes, op. cit., p. 59, n. 19; Marshman, op. cit., p. 290.

49 Ibid., p. 291.

50 Rizvi, op. cit., vol. 2, pp. 249–50; see Russell, op. cit., p. 59; Stokes, op. cit., p. 59.

51 Russell, op. cit., p. 105; see Watson, op. cit., p. 96.

52 See n. 22.

53 Rizvi, op. cit., vol. 1, pp. 451–3; ibid., vol. 4, pp. 589–90; see Majumdar, *Sepoy Mutiny*, p. 263.

54 C. T. Metcalfe (ed.), *Two Native Narratives of the Mutiny at Delhi*, Delhi, 1974 edn, pp. 134, 146, 171, 177, 209; J. Hewitt (ed.), *Eye-Witnesses to the Indian Mutiny*, Reading, 1972, p. 27.

55 Rizvi, op. cit., vol. 1, pp. 453ff. The King himself, though old and weak willed, appears to have suspected quite early on that the rebels, for whom he was both monarch and captive, would lose. See Metcalfe, op. cit., Lal narrative, *passim*.

56 Rizvi, op. cit., vol. 1, p. 443.

57 Watson, op. cit., p. 64.

58 Sen, op. cit., pp. 353–4.

59 Majumdar, *Sepoy Mutiny*, pp. 351, 392, 475.

60 Ibid., pp. 479–80.

61 Ibid., pp. 181–3. This is an episode nationalists tend to gloss over. See T. R. Sareen, 'Gwalior under the Mutineers', *Journal of Indian History*, 1965, vol. 43, pp. 630–1.

62 Joshi, '1857 in Our History', p. 167.

63 Leasor, op. cit., p. 64. For a list of the sepoy units which converged on Delhi, see Rizvi, op. cit., vol. 5, pp. 126–8.
64 Metcalfe, *Two Narratives*, Mandoin Hassan Khan narrative, pp. 58–9, 65–6, Lal narrative, pp. 85, 91, 96, 99, 101–2, 123.
65 Ibid., pp. 104–5.
66 Ibid., pp. 139, 123, 128, 93–4, 95, 100, 108–9. Some Indian Marxists seem to view this as a laudable instance of direct democracy – see Joshi, op. cit., pp. 188–9 – but the results in terms of action were catastrophic.
67 H. H. Greathed, *Letters Written during the Siege of Delhi*, London, 1858, pp. 46–7. See Metcalfe, *Two Narratives*, Mandoin Hassan Khan narrative, pp. 65–6, Lal narrative, p. 94, *passim*.
68 Greathed, op. cit., p. 71.
69 Metcalfe, *Two Narratives*, Mandoin Hassan Khan narrative, p. 68; see W. W. Ireland, *History of the Siege of Delhi*, Edinburgh, 1861, pp. 95, 114, *passim*; Greathed, op. cit., p. 44, *passim*.
70 Ibid., p. 154; see Metcalfe, *Two Narratives*, Lal narrative, pp. 117–18, 121, 123, 171, 177; Grant, op. cit., pp. 87–9, *passim*.
71 See e.g. Vibart, op. cit., p. 139; Ireland, op. cit., p. 92; D. Blomfield (ed.), *The Indian Mutiny Journal of Arthur Moffatt Lang*, London, 1992, p. 136.
72 See e.g. Blomfield, op. cit., p. 60; Sherer in N. A. Chick (comp.), *Annals of the Indian Rebellion, 1857–58*, D. Hutchinson (ed.), London, 1974 edn, pp. 174–5.
73 Metcalfe, *Two Narratives*, Lal narrative, pp. 108, 118, 183, 209; Greathed, op. cit., p. 100.
74 Ibid., p. 108. See Roberts, op. cit., p. 83.
75 Vibart, op. cit., p. 139.
76 Grant, op. cit., p. 114.
77 On the mood in Delhi, see Stokes, op. cit., p. 91; Ireland, op. cit., p. 230; Metcalfe, *Two Narratives*, Lal narrative, September entries. On the final assault, see Stokes, op. cit., pp. 95–8.
78 Savarkar, *Indian War*, pp. 272, 281.
79 Rizvi, op. cit., vol. 4, native diary of events at Kanpur up to 12 June 1857, pp. 504–9.
80 Ibid., statement of Jahingir Khan, p. 502.
81 Ibid., proclamation of Nana Sahib, 6 July 1857, p. 607; see G. B. Mallenson, *History of the Indian Mutiny 1857–1858: Volume III*, London, 1880, p. 515.
82 Rizvi, op. cit., vol. 4, proclamation of Nana Sahib, 7 July 1857, p. 608.
83 Ibid., native diary, p. 506.
84 Ibid., p. 508.
85 See Sen, *Eighteen Fifty-seven*, pp. 139–44.
86 Marshman, op. cit., pp. 306–9.
87 For unbiased discussion of the massacres, see Majumdar, *Sepoy Mutiny*, pp. 201–3, 264; Sen, op. cit., pp. 145–51, 158–60.
88 Quoted in Maude, op. cit., p. 114.
89 Rizvi, op. cit., vol. 2, statement at trial of Jai Lal Singh, p. 112; T. H. Kavanaugh, *How I Won the Victoria Cross*, London, 1860, p. 129.
90 Ibid., p. 128; see Sen, *Eighteen Fifty-seven*, pp. 209–10.
91 Grant, op. cit., p. 371.
92 Kavanaugh, op. cit., pp. 130–4; Rizvi, vol. 2, intelligence reports November–December 1857, pp. 248–59.
93 Ibid., p. 260.
94 Russell, op. cit., p. 71.
95 L. E. R. Rees, *A Personal Narrative of the Siege of Lucknow*, London, 1858, p. 137; see Majendie, op. cit., p. 197.

96   F. Tucker (ed.), *The Chronicle of Private Henry Metcalfe*, London, 1953, p. 38; Rees, op. cit., p. 144.
97   Ibid., pp. 140, 220; Kavanaugh, op. cit., p. 131.
98   W. Forbes-Mitchell, *Reminiscences of the Great Mutiny, 1857–59*, London, 1904, p. 43.
99   Ibid., p. 195.
100 Ibid., p. 42. On the campaign for Lucknow, see Watson, op. cit.
101 See e.g. Ireland, op. cit., p. 95; Majendie, op. cit., p. 193. See also Stokes, op. cit., p. 60.
102 Russell, op. cit., p. 73.
103 Forbes-Mitchell, op. cit., p. 245.
104 Watson, op. cit., p. 113.
105 The term 'primitive rebel' is used here to distinguish premodern guerrilla behaviour from the organized Maoist-style movements of the second half of the twentieth century. See E. Hobsbawm, *Primitive Rebels: Studies in Archaic Forms of Social Movement in the 19th and 20th Centuries*, New York, 1965.
106 See Russell, op. cit., p. 270; Rizvi, op. cit., vol. 2, Aulad Hussain letter, 8 April 1858, p. 375.
107 Ibid., vol. 3, Tatya Tope to Nana Sahib, 10 February 1858, p. 266; see also 'Young Lady' in Chick, op. cit., p. 193.
108 Mallenson, *History of the Indian Mutiny*, III, app. 1, deposition of Tatya Tope, pp. 518–24; see also Rizvi, op. cit., vol. 3, deposition of Rao Sahib, pp. 683ff.
109 The best case against a plot is made in Majumdar, *Sepoy Mutiny*, books 3 and 4.
110 See Palmer, op. cit., pp. 5–6, ch. 2 on events at Meerut. On earlier mutinies, see C. A. Bayly, *The New Cambridge History of India, II.1: Indian Society and the Making of the British Empire*, Cambridge, 1987, pp. 178–80; P. Chinnian, *The Vellore Mutiny 1806*, Madras, 1906.
111 See Stokes, op. cit., pp. 54–5; Metcalfe, op. cit., Lal narrative, pp. 104–5; Tucker, op. cit., p. 28; E. Vibart, *The Sepoy Mutiny as seen by a Subaltern: From Delhi to Lucknow*, London, 1898, pp. 20–1, 25–6, 38, 48; id., narrative of A. R. D. Mackenzie, pp. 224–5, 237–8; Russell, op. cit., pp. 250, 270; Dr Murray's narrative in Chick, op. cit., p. 207.
112 Rizvi, op. cit., vol. 2, Sepoy petition to King of Nepal, 1858.
113 See e.g. Vibart, op. cit., pp. 18, 38; Forbes-Mitchell, op. cit., p. 43; Maude, op. cit., p. 154.
114 Vibart, op. cit., p. 139; see Rees, op. cit., pp. 115, 144, 220, 323; Russell, op. cit., p. 263; C. J. Griffiths, *A Narrative of the Siege of Delhi*, London, 1910, p. 108; Marshman, op. cit., p. 356.
115 Forbes-Mitchell, op. cit., pp. 80–1; Rees, op. cit., p. 322; Majendie, op. cit., pp. 147, 183–4, 214–16; Russell, op. cit., p. 87.
116 J. Lunt (ed.), *From Sepoy to Subedar, being the Life and Adventures of Subedar Sita Ram, a Native Officer of the Bengal Army written and related by himself*, London, 1988 edn, p. 167.
117 On the nationalism issue, see Majumdar, *Sepoy Mutiny*, pp. 406ff.; Sen, *Eighteen Fifty-seven*, ch. 11. On the special conditions in Awadh, see R. Mukherjee, *Awadh in Revolt, 1857–1858: A Study of Popular Resistance*, Delhi, 1984.
118 See Stokes, op. cit., pp. 22–3; Tucker, op. cit., p. 38; Greathed, op. cit., pp. 118–19; Rees, op. cit., p. 344; 'Young Lady' and Inglis in Chick, op. cit., pp. 192, 249.
119 Hewitt, op. cit., p. 27; see Tapti, op. cit., pp. 38, 49–50.
120 Watson, op. cit., p. 120.

121 Ibid., p. 67, *passim*; Stokes, op. cit., pp. 55–6.
122 See Stokes, op. cit., pp. 66, 90–1; Metcalfe, op. cit., pp. 199–200, 204–5, 209, 218–19; Russell, op. cit., p. 270.
123 S. A. Khan, *The Causes of the Indian Revolt*, Benares, 1873, pp. 51–3.
124 See Hewitt, op. cit., p. 28.
125 See Metcalfe, *Two Narratives*, Lal narrative, p. 176; Rizvi, vol. 2, Sepoy petition to King of Nepal, p. 604; ibid., Victory of the Mahomedan Faith, p. 152.
126 Stokes, op. cit., p. 66; Watson, op. cit., pp. 67–6, 96–8, 111–13.

8 THE INTERNATIONAL BRIGADES IN THE SPANISH CIVIL WAR, 1936–9

1 J. Gurney, *Crusade in Spain*, London, 1974, p. 111.
2 L. Lee, *A Moment of War: A Memoir of the Spanish Civil War*, New York, 1991, pp. 80–1.
3 See R. de España, 'Images of the Spanish Civil War in Spanish Feature Films, 1939–1985', *Journal of Film, Radio and Television*, 1986, vol. 6, p. 225.
4 For political commitment and the intellectuals in and after the Spanish Civil War, see P. Monteath, *Writing the Good Fight: Political Commitment in the International Literature of the Spanish Civil War*, Westport, CT, 1994; J. Perez and W. Aycock (eds), *The Spanish Civil War in Literature*, Lubbock, TX, 1990; V. Cunningham (ed.), *Spanish Front: Writers on the Civil War*, Oxford, 1986; K. B. Hoskins, *Today the Struggle: Literature and Politics in England during the Spanish Civil War*, Austin, TX, 1969; and S. Weintraub, *The Last Great Cause: Intellectuals and the Spanish Civil War*, London, 1968.
5 For an overview of historiographical developments, see P. Preston, 'War of Words: The Spanish Civil War and the Historians', in *Revolution and War in Spain, 1931–1939*, P. Preston (ed.), London, 1984, pp. 1–13. See also H. Thomas, *The Spanish Civil War*, New York, 1986 edn, 1977 preface.
6 G. Esenwein and A. Schubert, *Spain at War: The Spanish Civil War in Context, 1931–1939*, London, 1995, pp. 1–3. See e.g. J. Cook, *Apprentices of Freedom*, London, 1972, p. iii. Even some of the best postwar historians in Britain, such as E. P. Thompson, have found it difficult to maintain an attitude of critical dispassion with regard to the civil war. Raymond Carr himself has admitted that 'I find writing on the civil war a painful exercise, since it entails, if one is to tell what seems to one to be the truth, a severe and sometimes savage criticism of the errors of one's side [the Republic]'. R. Carr, *The Spanish Tragedy: The Civil War in Perspective*, London, 1977, p. vii; see also D. E. Puzzo, *The Spanish Civil War*, New York, 1969, p. 3.
7 Esenwein and Schubert, op. cit., p. 154, n. 15, p. 273, n. 17.
8 M. Jackson, *Fallen Sparrows: The International Brigades in the Spanish Civil War*, Philadelphia, 1994, p. 20.
9 G. Cox, *The Defence of Madrid*, London, 1937, pp. 66–7; *The Book of the XV Brigade: Records of British, American, Canadian, and Irish Volunteers in the XV International Brigade in Spain, 1936–1938*, Newcastle, 1975 reprint, p. 20; R. Secourt, *Spain's Ordeal*, New York, 1940, pp. 185–6; L. Fischer, *Men and Politics: An Autobiography*, New York, 1941, p. 393; A. Kantorowicz letter, 8 January 1937, in M. Acier (ed.), *From the Spanish Trenches: Letters from Spain*, London, 1937, p. 80; S. Dewez, *Gloire aux volontaires internationaux*, Madrid, 1937, p. 24; H. L. Matthews, *Two Wars and More to Come*, New York, 1938, p. 209; F. Copeman, *Reason in Revolt*, London, 1948, p. 78; C. G. Bowers, *My Mission to Spain: Watching the Rehearsal for World War II*, New York,

1954, p. 316; R. G. Colodny, *The Struggle for Madrid: The Central Epic of the Spanish Conflict (1936–37)*, New York, 1958, pp. 66–7, 70.

10 See *Brigada Internacional is unser Ehrenname . . . Erlebnisse ehemaliger deutscher Spanienkämpfer Ausgewählt und eingeleitet von Hanns Massen*, Berlin, 1975, vol. 1, pp. 89ff.; W. C. Beeching, *Canadian Volunteers: Spain, 1936–1939*, Regina, 1989, p. 35; R. D. Richardson, *Comintern Army: The International Brigades and the Spanish Civil War*, Lexington, KY, 1982, pp. 81–2; R. A. Rosenstone, *Crusade of the Left: The Lincoln Battalion in the Spanish Civil War*, New York, 1969, pp. 23–4; V. B. Johnson, *Legions of Babel: The International Brigades in the Spanish Civil War*, University Park, PA, 1967, p. 56; V. Brome, *The International Brigades: Spain, 1936–1939*, London, 1965, pp. 80–1; see also Esenwein and Schubert, op. cit., p. 161; T. Buchanan, *The Spanish Civil War and the British Labour Movement*, Cambridge, 1991, p. 77; G. Jackson, *A Concise History of the Spanish Civil War*, London, 1974, pp. 92, 176–7; J. Gibbs, *The Spanish Civil War*, London, 1973, p. 62; R. Goldston, *The Civil War in Spain*, New York, 1966, pp. 74–5, 102–3; J. Cleugh, *Spanish Fury: The Story of a Civil War*, London, 1962, p. 104.

11 See e.g. T. Wintringham, *English Captain*, London, 1939, pp. 294–5; Fischer, op. cit., p. 394; W. Rust, *Britons in Spain: The History of the British Battalion of the XVth International Brigade*, London, 1939, p. 16; W. Alexander, *British Volunteers for Liberty: Spain, 1936–1939*, London, 1982, pp. 63–4.

12 See e.g. P. Broué and E. Témine, *The Revolution and the Civil War in Spain*, T. White (trans.), London, 1972, p. 246; G. Jackson, *The Spanish Republic and the Civil War, 1931–1939*, Princeton, NJ, 1965, p. 328; Goldston, op. cit., pp. 102–3; Gibbs, op. cit., p. 62.

13 Cox, op. cit., p. 76; *Book of the XV Brigade*, pp. 24, 25, 34, 67; Colodny, op. cit., p. 68; Broué and Témine, op. cit., p. 375; Hoskins, op. cit., p. 262; Esenwein and Schubert, op. cit., pp. 156–7; Puzzo, op. cit., p. 46; E. de Guzmán, *Madrid, rojo y negro*, Barcelona, 1938, p. 164; J. Zugazagoitia, *Historia de la Guerra en España*, Buenos Aires, 1940, p. 195; J. Pérez Salas, *Guerra en España 1936–39*, Mexico City, 1947, p. 128; E. Rolfe, *The Lincoln Battalion: The Story of the Americans who Fought in Spain in the International Brigades*, New York, 1939, p. 280; L. Renn, *Der Spanische Krieg*, Berlin, 1955, pp. 71–2; W. Bredel, *Spanienkrieg: Zur Geschichte der 11. Internationalen Brigade*, Berlin, 1977, p. 386; B. Bolloten, *The Spanish Civil War: Revolution and Counterrevolution*, Chapel Hill, NC, 1991, p. 316.

14 Wintringham, op. cit., p. 308; Alexander, op. cit., p. 49; J. Tisa, *Recalling the Good Fight: An Autobiography of the Spanish Civil War*, South Hadley, MA, 1985, pp. 171–2; M. Alpert, *A New International History of the Spanish Civil War*, New York, 1994, p. 150.

15 See e.g. *Book of the XV Brigade*, p. 34; Wintringham, op. cit., pp. 278–93; Acier, op. cit., p. 113; Alexander, op. cit., p. 60; Rust, op. cit., pp. 24–5, 36, 89, 97; Rolfe, op. cit., p. 26; Tisa, op. cit., pp. 25, 29; Cook, op. cit., p. 37; Esenwein and Schubert, op. cit., pp. 156–7; Goldston, op. cit., pp. 74–5, 102–3; see also Gurney, op. cit., p. 84.

16 Alexander, op. cit., pp. 78, 53–4.

17 See R. Taylor letter, 20 April 1937, in Acier, op. cit., p. 151, *passim*; *Book of the XV Brigade*, *passim*; Gurney, op. cit., p. 84; Matthews, op. cit., p. 219; A. Bessie, *Men in Battle: A Story of Americans in Spain*, Berlin, 1960 edn, p. 87; Alexander, op. cit., p. 39; Tisa, op. cit., p. xiv; Brome, op. cit., p. 83; Rosenstone, op. cit., p. 360; G. Regler, *The Great Crusade*, New York, 1940, p. 155; see Jackson, *Fallen Sparrows*, p. 119.

18 *Book of the XV Brigade*, p. 217; Soviet War Veterans' Committee, Academy of

Sciences of the USSR, *International Solidarity with the Spanish Republic,
1936–1939*, Moscow, 1975, p. 95; J. Gates, *The Story of an American
Communist*, New York, 1958, p. 47; M. Merriman and W. Lerude, *American
Commander in Spain: Robert Hale Merriman and the Abraham Lincoln Brigade*,
Reno, NV, 1986, p. 114; V. Sheean, *Not Peace But a Sword*, New York, 1939,
p. 68; Fischer, op. cit., p. 394.

19 Gates, quoted in P. N. Carroll, *The Odyssey of the Abraham Lincoln Brigade:
Americans in the Spanish Civil War*, Stanford, CA, 1994, p. 96; see Alexander,
op. cit., pp. 78–9, 100, 177, 212; Rust, op. cit., p. 18; Rolfe, op. cit., pp. 103–5;
Tisa, op. cit., pp. 25, 56, *passim*; S. Nelson *et al.*, *Steve Nelson: American
Radical*, Pittsburgh, 1981, pp. 224–5, *passim*; Wintringham, op. cit., pp. 113–14;
Johnston, op. cit., p. 76; Richardson, op. cit., p. 120; see also Copeman, op. cit.,
p. 107; G. Regler, *The Owl of Minerva*, N. Denny (trans.), London, 1959, p. 283.
20 H. L. Matthews, *Half of Spain Died: A Reappraisal of the Spanish Civil War*,
New York, 1973, p. 202; Tisa, op. cit., p. 172; Cook, op. cit., pp. 4, 6.
21 Colodny, op. cit., p. 74; see K. S. Watson, *Single to Spain*, New York, 1937,
p. 122; R. Pacciardi, *Il Battaglione Garibaldi*, Lugano, 1938, p. 71.
22 Richardson, op. cit., p. 199, n. 5; Johnston, op. cit., pp. 53–4.
23 A. Kantorowicz letter, 8 January 1937, quoted in Acier, op. cit., p. 80.
24 Colodny, op. cit., pp. 103, 214, n. 49; Regler, *Crusade*, pp. 182–4; *International
Solidarity*, p. 167; Richardson, op. cit., p. 83.
25 Regler, *Crusade*, pp. 267–79.
26 Wintringham, op. cit., p. 195.
27 Carroll, *Odyssey*, pp. 100–2.
28 Colodny, op. cit., p. 229, n. 158; Johnston, op. cit., p. 175, n. 26.
29 Rolfe, op. cit., p. 5; see *Book of the XV Brigade*, pp. 40, 52, 68; Matthews, *Half
of Spain*, p. 6; P. Wyden, *The Passionate War: The Narrative History of the
Spanish Civil War*, New York, 1983, p. 301; Puzzo, op. cit., p. 48; Beeching, op.
cit., p. 51.
30 See *International Solidarity*, pp. 146, 148, 242, 342; Rolfe, op. cit., p. 102;
Copeman, op. cit., p. 99; Rust, op. cit., p. 41; Alexander, op. cit., pp. 95, 97, 103;
Wintringham, op. cit., p. 180; J. Kallerborm letter, 21 April 1937, in Acier, op.
cit., p. 173; Tisa, op. cit., p. 75; see also Rosenstone, op. cit., p. 48.
31 Merriman and Lerude, op. cit., p. 113; for the heavy losses + commitment =
success equation, see also e.g. *Book of the XV Brigade*, p. 46, *passim*;
International Solidarity, p. 166, *passim*.
32 Carroll, *Odyssey*, pp. 143–4; Alexander, op. cit., pp. 123–4, 127; A. H. Landis,
The Abraham Lincoln Brigade, New York, 1967, p. 233.
33 See *Book of the XV Brigade*, p. 130; S. Nelson, *The Volunteers*, New York, 1953,
p. 174; Rosenstone, op. cit., p. 188; Landis, *Abraham Lincoln Brigade*, p. 229;
Rolfe, op. cit., p. 107; *International Solidarity*, p. 120; Beeching, op. cit., p. 55;
see also Puzzo, op. cit., p. 68.
34 L. Muñiz, *La Batalla de Madrid*, Madrid, 1943, p. 43; see M. J. Iribarren,
General Mola, Madrid, 1945, p. 241; A. Kindelán, *Mis Caudernos de Guerra*,
Madrid, 1945, pp. 24–5; see also M. Aznar, *Historia militar de la guerra de
España* (3 vols), Madrid, 1969 edn, p. 460; A. Castells, *Las Brigadas
Internacionales de la guerra de España*, Barcelona, 1974, p. 134; P. Kemp in P.
Toynbee (ed.), *The Distant Drum: Reflections on the Spanish Civil War*,
London, 1976, p. 69; K. Hommel, *Die Internationale Brigaden im Spanischen
Bürgerkrieg, 1936–1939*, Regensburg, 1990, p. 99. Not all nationalists, however,
adopted this line. See e.g. J. M. Martínez Bande, *Brigadas Internacionales*,
Barcelona, 1972, p. 86; R. de la Cierva y de Hoces, *Lyenda y Tragedia de las
Brigadas Internacionales*, Madrid, 1970, p. 62.

35 Quoted in Johnston, op. cit., p. 46.
36 On the war as a crusade, see e.g. Matthews, *Two Wars*, p. 207; A. Osheroff, 'Reflections of a Civil War Veteran', in *The Spanish Civil War in Literature*, J. Pérez and W. Aycock (eds), Lubbock, TX, 1990, p. 10; Monteath, op. cit., p. xii; Rosenstone, op. cit., p. 360; Brome, op. cit., p. 1.
37 D. Corkhill and S. J. Rawnsley (eds), *The Road to Spain: Anti-Fascists at War 1936–1939*, Dunfermline, 1981, p. xvi; see Beeching, op. cit., p. 55.
38 Matthews, *Half of Spain*, p. 215; see Esenwein and Schubert, op. cit., p. 159; Hoskins, op. cit., p. 262.
39 Carroll, *Odyssey*, pp. 235–9, 316–18. Hemingway's portrait was in fact quite accurate. See J. Meyers, '*For Whom the Bell Tolls* as Contemporary History', in *The Spanish Civil War in Literature*, J. Pérez and W. Aycock (eds), Lubbock, TX, 1990, pp. 97–107.
40 See Alexander, op. cit., p. 282.
41 Witness the reaction to Cecil Eby's *Between the Bullet and the Lie* (New York, 1969), a book which, though problematic in many respects, seems to have been attacked mainly because the author's bias was anti- rather than pro-communist. See e.g. Matthews, *Half of Spain*, pp. 200, 202, 215; Carroll, *Odyssey*, p. ix. See also Alexander, op. cit., p. 280.
42 This was in response to Jason Gurney's *Crusade in Spain*, London, 1974. Nelson, *Steve Nelson*, p. 438, n. 5; Alexander, op. cit., p. 278; see also Jackson, *Fallen Sparrows*, p. 20; Carroll, *Odyssey*, p. 335; and the 1960 footnote to Alvah Bessie's *Men in Battle: A Story of Americans in Spain*, Berlin, 1960 edn, p. 324.
43 See Carroll, *Odyssey*, p. 319; Esenwein and Schubert, op. cit., p. 273, n. 17. As one true-believer veteran lamented in the mid-1980s, 'for the young of this generation, and perhaps even for their fathers, the war in Spain, with its million casualties [*sic*], is as remote as the Napoleonic wars or the struggles of the Romans and Carthaginians'. Colodny preface to C. Geiser, *Prisoners of the Good Fight: The Spanish Civil War, 1936–1939*, Westport, CT, 1986, pp. vi–vii. Yet some veterans have themselves become victims of their own imagination. See P. N. Carroll, *Keeping Time: Memory, Nostalgia, and the Art of History*, Athens, GA, 1990, p. 177.
44 See e.g. C. Williams *et al.*, *British Memorials of the Spanish Civil War*, Phoenix Mill, 1996.
45 See e.g. *Book of the XV Brigade*, pp. 24–9; *The Battle of Jarama, 1937: The Story of the British Battalion of the International Brigade's baptism of fire in the Spanish War*, Newcastle, 1987, p. 7; Beeching, op. cit., pp. 7–9; A. H. Landis, *Death in the Olive Groves: American Volunteers in the Spanish Civil War, 1936–1939*, New York, 1989, pp. 225–6.
46 Jackson, *Fallen Sparrows*, pp. 89–90.
47 See Richardson, op. cit., ch. 3, *passim*.
48 See e.g. Fischer, op. cit., p. 389; Wintringham, op. cit., pp. 77, 79, 115, 116–17; J. Brown and J. Peet in Corkhill, op. cit., pp. 50, 108; Gurney, op. cit., pp. 78, 79, 81, 83, 90, 103; B. Bailey in Gerassi, op. cit., p. 111; T. A. R. Hyndman and J. H. Bassett in Toynbee, op. cit., pp. 125–6, 137; Colodny, op. cit., p. 121; F. Graham in *Battle of Jarama*, p. 66.
49 Thomas, op. cit., pp. 980–2; M. Alpert, 'The Republican Army in the Spanish Civil War of 1936–1939', Ph.D. Thesis, Reading University, 1973, pp. 310, 371.
50 Johnston, op. cit., p. 89; Richardson, op. cit., p. 53; Puzzo, op. cit., p. 46; *International Solidarity*, pp. 116–17, 291; Pacciardi, op. cit., p. 59; Hemingway in Regler, *Crusade*, p. vii; L. Falusi in Dokumentationsarchiv des österreichischen Widerstandes, *Für Spaniens Freiheit: Österreicher an der Seite der Spanischen Republik 1936–1939: Eine Dokumentation*, Vienna, 1986, p. 125.

51 Ibid., op. cit., p. 65; P. v. zur Mühlen, *Spanien war ihre Hoffnung: Die deutsche Linke im Spanischen Bürgerkrieg, 1936 bis 1939*, Bonn, 1983, p. 193; T. A. R. Hyndman in Toynbee, op. cit., p. 123; Carroll, *Odyssey*, p. 65; Gurney, op. cit., p. 41; B. Clark, *No Boots for My Feet: Experiences of a Britisher in Spain, 1937–38*, Stoke-on-Trent, 1984, p. 27.

52 See e.g. E. Romilly, *Boadilla*, London, 1971 edn, pp. 28–9; Clark, op. cit., p. 18.

53 See Jackson, *Fallen Sparrows*, pp. 47–54; J. Angus, *With the International Brigade in Spain*, Loughborough, 1983, p. 2; C. Morgan in Cook, op. cit., p. 68; J. Jones in Corkhill, op. cit., p. 143; Lee, op. cit., p. 28; J. R. Jump and J. H. Bassett in Toynbee, op. cit., pp. 113, 132; Bessie, op. cit., p. 174; D. Hyde, *I Believed: The Autobiography of a former British Communist*, London, 1951, p. 59; H. Francis, *Miners Against Fascism: Wales and the Spanish Civil War*, London, 1984, pp. 180–1, 213; S. Spender, *World Within World*, London, 1977 edn, p. 229. For the orthodox response to any hint of politically incorrect motivation, see e.g. Alexander, op. cit., p. 32.

54 This may well have happened once news of the losses at Jarama and Brunete began to deter potential volunteers and the Party grew more desperate for new drafts to replace losses. See Francis, op. cit., pp. 158, 165–6, 167; Hyde, op. cit., p. 60; H. G. Dahms, *Der Spanische Bürgkrieg 1936–1939*, Tübingen, 1962, p. 325, n. 23.

55 N. Gillain, *Le Mercenaire*, Paris, 1938, p. 18.

56 See G. Leeson in Corkhill, op. cit., p. 79; Gurney, op. cit., pp. 53–4.

57 On the tendency to equate the picket line with the firing line, see R. Schoher in *Für Spaniens Freiheit*, p. 164; Colodny, op. cit., p. 79; Richardson, op. cit., p. 56; Alexander, op. cit., p. 38; *International Solidarity*, pp. 41–2; Rosenstone, op. cit., pp. 100–1; Broué and Témine, op. cit., p. 246; Gurney, op. cit., pp. 64–5.

58 See Citrine quote in Buchanan, op. cit., p. 78; Alexander, op. cit., p. 38.

59 L. Renn, *Der Spanische Krieg*, Berlin, 1955, p. 30.

60 Copeman, op. cit., p. 125.

61 J. Monks, *With the Reds in Andalusia*, London, 1985, pp. 26–7; Wintringham, op. cit., p. 85; Romilly, op. cit., p. 57.

62 V. Hoar, *The Mackenzie-Papineau Battalion: Canadian Participation in the Spanish Civil War*, Toronto, 1969, pp. 115, 148; Beeching, op. cit., pp. 58, 70–8; see Rust, op. cit., p. 89; Rolfe, op. cit., pp. 133–4; Alexander, op. cit., pp. 153–4; L. Levenson letter, 30 August 1937, in C. Nelson and J. Henricks (eds), *Madrid 1937: Letters from the Abraham Lincoln Brigade from the Spanish Civil War*, London, 1996, p. 171.

63 See Copeman, op. cit., p. 133; Carroll, *Odyssey*, pp. 95, 99, 141–2; Brome, op. cit., p. 208; see also Tisa, op. cit., p. 25; Beeching, op. cit., p. 58. On the stress given to advancing in formation rather than entrenching, see e.g. Sommerfield, op. cit., pp. 31–2; Gurney, op. cit., p. 76.

64 Rust, op. cit., p. 36; Tisa, op. cit., p. 29; Beeching, op. cit., p. 58.

65 Alexander, op. cit., pp. 53–4; see Gurney, op. cit., p. 76; Copeman, op. cit., p. 80; Wintringham, op. cit., p. 63; see also Richardson, op. cit., p. 56; Jackson, *Fallen Sparrows*, p. 101; L. Falusi in *Für Spaniens Freiheit*, p. 125.

66 M. Levin and G. Murray in Cook, op. cit., pp. 45, 66; Clark, op. cit., p. 22; Gurney, op. cit., p. 87; B. Baily and O. Hunter in Gerassi, op. cit., pp. 106–7, 151; Rosenstone, op. cit., pp. 34, 38; Hoar, op. cit., p. 115. British volunteer Walter Gregory believed that he was relatively well prepared after having fired a total of fifteen rounds on a rifle range. Gregory, op. cit., p. 33.

67 For example, Cook, op. cit., p. 37.

68 Bessie, op. cit., p. 63; see J. Freeman letter, 14 July 1938, in Nelson and Hendricks, op. cit., p. 394; Gregory, op. cit., p. 116.

69 F. Deegan, *There's No Other Way*, Liverpool, 1980, p. 34; see A. Inglis, *Australians in the Spanish Civil War*, Sydney, 1987, p. 141.

70 See B. Doyle in Cook, op. cit., p. 109; W. Paynter, *My Generation*, London, 1972, p. 67; D. Goodman in Corkhill, op. cit., pp. 97–8; Inglis, op. cit., p. 141; H. Smith letter, 16 May 1937, in Nelson and Hendricks, op. cit., p. 143.

71 See e.g. Bessie, op. cit., p. 80; Gurney, op. cit., p. 84; Wintringham, op. cit., p. 101; J. Jones in Corkhill, op. cit., p. 144; R. Taylor in Acier, op. cit., p. 151; Romilly, op. cit., p. 146; C. Geiser letter, 3 June 1937, in Nelson and Hendricks, op. cit., p. 157.

72 Wintringham, op. cit., p. 100; see J. R. Jump in Toynbee, op. cit., pp. 116–17; D. Cook in Acier, op. cit., p. 99; Romilly, op. cit., pp. 48–9.

73 Regler, *Crusade*, pp. 99–102, 217; Wintringham, op. cit., pp. 94, 105–8; Rust, op. cit., pp. 28–31; Alexander, op. cit., p. 54; L. Longo, *Die Internationalen Brigaden in Spanien*, Berlin, 1976, p. 53; H. Rubin letter, 27 July 1937, in Nelson and Hendricks, op. cit., p. 164.

74 Memorandum reproduced in Alexander, op. cit., p. 75.

75 J. H. Basset in Toynbee, op. cit., p. 133; see Lee, op. cit., pp. 40–1; Gurney, op. cit., p. 84; Romilly, op. cit., pp. 165, 169; Regler, *Crusade*, p. 236; Bessie, op. cit., p. 73. On Marty's position, see Romilly, op. cit., p. 53; see also Paynter in Francis, op. cit., p. 285.

76 Jackson, *Fallen Sparrows*, p. 121; see the comment by a Russian officer in Romilly, op. cit., p. 53.

77 Gurney, op. cit., p. 104; Lee, op. cit., pp. 90–1; see J. Tisa in Gerassi, op. cit., p. 136; M. Levin in Cook, op. cit., p. 73.

78 Hoar, p. 116; see Monks, op. cit., p. 23; Mühlen, op. cit., p. 193; Beeching, op. cit., pp. 58–9; Clark, op. cit., p. 27.

79 See e.g. Wintringham, op. cit., pp. 174–5; T. A. R. Hyndman in Toynbee, op. cit., p. 126; Carroll, *Odyssey*, pp. 134–5; Mühlen, op. cit., p. 194. On political appointments, see Monks, p. 21; Hoar, op. cit., pp. 122–3. On movements and the mis-siting of trenches, see Cornford to Heinmann, 8 December 1936, in P. Sloan, *John Cornford: A Memoir*, Dunfermline, 1978 reprint, p. 239; Carroll, *Odyssey*, p. 99. On other blunders of inexperienced officers, see e.g. Gurney, op. cit., pp. 126–7.

80 On Nathan (who had been in the Black and Tans), see Monks, op. cit., pp. 6, 12, 15; Nelson *et al.*, *Steve Nelson*, pp. 224–5; id., *Volunteers*, pp. 145–6, 165; Copeman, op. cit., pp. 83–4; Sid Quinn in Cook, op. cit., p. 44. On Pacciardi (who was not a communist), see Regler, *Owl*, p. 290.

81 See Copeman, op. cit., pp. 137, 138–40; Richardson, op. cit., pp. 104–10.

82 Controversy still swirls, for example, around the promotion of Oliver Law, an African–American, to command of the Lincoln Battalion as part of a conscious effort on the part of the US party to highlight racial equality in Spain (see Frank Alexander in Collum, op. cit., pp. 142–3). Veterans are divided as to whether he was a foolish coward or a genuine hero (see Nelson, *Volunteers*, p. 151; Eby, op. cit., pp. 69–70, 134–5; W. Herrick, *Hermanos!*, London, 1969, pp. 266–9, where Law appears as 'Cromwell Webster'; Carroll, *Odyssey*, pp. 138, 304, 335; Jackson, *Fallen Sparrows*, pp. 103–4; Harry Fisher letter, 29 July 1937, in Nelson and Hendricks, op. cit., p. 187). Questions have also been raised about the abilities of Robert Merriman, a (white) American who served as battalion CO at Jarama and rose to become XV Brigade Chief of Staff. See Carroll, *Odyssey*, p. 335; Merriman and Lerude, op. cit., p. 173, *passim*; Eby, op. cit., pp. 30–4, *passim*.

83 On leading by example and the officer casualty problem, see Deegan, op. cit., p. 44; Merriman and Lerude, op. cit., p. 173; Wintringham, op. cit., p. 289;

Beeching, op. cit., pp. 73, 74. Without direction men might retreat, go to ground, or – if particularly committed to the cause – fight on until surrounded and killed rather than retire. See e.g. Colodny, op. cit., p. 214, n. 49; Regler, *Owl*, p. 287.

84 R. C. Nation, *Black Earth, Red Star: A History of Soviet Security Policy, 1917–1991*, Ithaca, NY, 1992, p. 95; see e.g. D. Glantz, 'Batov', and J. Erickson, 'Malinowsky', in *Stalin's Generals*, H. Shukman (ed.), New York, 1993, pp. 36, 118.

85 Richardson, op. cit., pp. 57–8, 67, 70, 72.

86 See W. G. Krivitsky, *I Was Stalin's Agent*, London, 1940, p. 116.

87 On backgrounds, see n. 85.

88 On events in Russia, see O. Khlevnyuk, 'The Objectives of the Great Terror, 1937–38', in *Soviet History, 1917–1953: Essays in Honor of R. W. Davies*, J. Cooper and M. Perrie (eds), London, 1995, pp. 158–76; R. Conquest, *The Great Terror: A Reassessment*, New York, 1990. On the effect on Soviet officers serving in Spain, see Louis Fischer in *The God That Failed: Six Studies in Communism*, London, 1950, pp. 222–3.

89 It is more likely that Delasalle was simply as incompetent as many other new commanders. See Monks, op. cit., p. 18; Wintringham, op. cit., pp. 82–3; Gillain, op. cit., pp. 29–37; L. Longo, *Le Brigate Internazionali in Spagna*, Rome, 1956, pp. 151–60.

90 Wintringham, op. cit., p. 189; see ibid., pp. 146, 152–3, 156; see also Gurney, op. cit., pp. 104, 109, 119.

91 Wintringham, op. cit., pp. 191–2, 195.

92 Merriman and Lerude, op. cit., p. 106.

93 Carroll, *Odyssey*, p. 100; see Merriman diary, 13 March 1937, in Nelson and Hendricks, op. cit., p. 86.

94 Hoar, op. cit., pp. 144–7; Beeching, op. cit., pp. 70–8; see also Carroll, *Odyssey*, pp. 156–7; Merriman and Lerude, op. cit., pp. 161–2.

95 See Gurney, op. cit., pp. 156–61; Copeman, op. cit., p. 136; Carroll, *Odyssey*, pp. 144–5, 156–7; Beeching, op. cit., pp. 101–2. For a more positive view of such actions, see Alexander, op. cit., p. 130; Rolfe, op. cit., p. 198; Rosenstone, op. cit., pp. 87–8; Nelson, *American Radical*, pp. 224–5, 228.

96 See Regler's depiction in *Crusade, passim*, and in *Owl*, pp. 279–80, 297; I. Ehrenburg, *Eve of War 1933–1941*, T. Shebunina (trans.), London, 1963, p. 155.

97 Thomas, op. cit., p. 953; see P. I. Barta, 'The Writing of History: Authors Meet on the Soviet–Spanish Border', *Spanish Civil War in Literature*, p. 79. For more positive assessments of the humanity of men like Marty and Čopić, see Beeching, op. cit., p. 114; Clark, op. cit., p. 82; Gregory, op. cit., pp. 58–9.

98 See Romilly, op. cit., pp. 110, 112–13; Rosenstone, op. cit., pp. 169–70; Kurzman, op. cit., p. 265; Alexander, op. cit., pp. 113–14; Corkhill, op. cit., p. 39; Johnston, op. cit., p. 62; Jackson, *Fallen Sparrows*, p. 18; Nelson, *Volunteers*, p. 88; Sommerfield, op. cit., p. 36; Regler, *Crusade*, pp. 4, 32, 64–5; *Für Spaniens Freiheit*, p. 128.

99 Gurney, op. cit., pp. 96–7; see Regler, *Crusade*, pp. 39, 58; Gates, op. cit., p. 46.

100 See Rosenstone, op. cit., pp. 316–17; Brome, op. cit., pp. 252–3; Bessie, op. cit., pp. 148, 191–2; *Für Spaniens Freiheit*, pp. 125–6, 128. For the best that could be achieved, see Gregory, op. cit., pp. 94–5.

101 See J. Dollard, *Fear In Battle*, New Haven, CT, 1943, pp. 56–7; Hoar, op. cit., pp. 20–1, 26; J. Gates in J. W. Muste, *Say That We Saw Spain Die: Literary Consequences of the Spanish Civil War*, Seattle, 1966, p. 27, n. 19; Rust, op. cit., p. 58; Alexander, op. cit., p. 81.

102 Tisa, op. cit., p. 56.

103 See e.g. Bessie, op. cit., p. 303; Regler, *Owl*, p. 287; Sheean, op. cit., p. 68; Hoar, op. cit., p. 205.
104 On the realities of fear, see Romilly, op. cit., p. 169.
105 Gurney, op. cit., pp. 107–8; see W. Gregory, *The Shallow Grave: A Memoir of the Spanish Civil War*, London, 1986, pp. 47–8.
106 Copeman, op. cit., pp. 94–5; G. Aitkin in Cook, op. cit., p. 68; Alexander, op. cit., pp. 98–9.
107 M. Brown to W. Greenhalgh in Cook, op. cit., p. 40.
108 Angus, op. cit., p. 7; Carroll, *Odyssey*, pp. 112–15; Gurney, op. cit., pp. 128, 129; Copeman, op. cit., p. 91; Alexander, op. cit., p. 80.
109 Beeching, op. cit., p. 78.
110 Jackson, *Fallen Sparrows*, p. 120.
111 See e.g. Paynter and Morgan in Cook, op. cit., pp. 53, 69; Francis, op. cit., p. 237; Richardson, op. cit., pp. 120–1.
112 Geiser, op. cit., p. 5.
113 Nelson, *Volunteers*, p. 85; see Sommerfield, op. cit., p. 120; B. Conon letter in Francis, op. cit., p. 270; Romilly, op. cit., p. 146; see also Castells, op. cit., p. 89.
114 Monks, op. cit., p. 29.
115 On the narrowing of horizons at the front, see e.g. Sommerfield, op. cit., pt 2; Romilly, op. cit., p. 142; H. Garner letters in Hoar, op. cit., pp. 79–81; see also Jackson, *Fallen Sparrows*, p. 122. On commissars in the role of welfare officers, see Angus, op. cit., pp. 7ff.; Paynter, op. cit., pp. 69–70; Nelson, *Volunteers*, pp. 82–3.
116 Quinn in Cook, op. cit., pp. 87–8. Cockburn frankly saw himself as a propagandist first and a journalist second. See T. Royle, *War Report: The War Correspondent's View of Battle from the Crimea to the Falklands*, London, 1987, ch. 5. Cockburn, however, was far from alone in engaging in propaganda work. See P. Knightly, *The First Casualty: From the Crimea to Vietnam: The War Correspondent as Hero, Propagandist, and Myth Maker*, New York, 1975, ch. 9.
117 See e.g. Tisa, op. cit., p. 69; Lee, op. cit., pp. 93–4. Though see also Clark, op. cit., pp. 39–40; Deegan, op. cit., p. 53.
118 See John H. Basset in Toynbee, op. cit., pp. 134–5; Sheean, op. cit., pp. 250–1; Bessie, op. cit., pp. 87–9; Paul Wendorf letter, 16 June 1938, in Nelson and Hendricks, op. cit., p. 388.
119 Brome, op. cit., pp. 130–1. On the high reputation of the Thaelmann, see Romilly, op. cit., p. 130.
120 J. M. M. Bande, *La ofensiva sobre Segovia y la Batalla de Brunete*, Madrid, 1972, p. 222, n. 268; Richardson, op. cit., p. 203, n. 60; Brome, op. cit., pp. 176–7.
121 Spender, op. cit., p. 222.
122 See *In Spain . . .*, *passim*; Francis, op. cit., p. 274; Hoar, op. cit., p. 127; Carroll, *Odyssey*, pp. 180–1.
123 See Angus, op. cit., p. 7; Francis, op. cit., p. 167; John H. Basset in Toynbee, op. cit., pp. 134–5; O. Hunter in Gerassi, op. cit., p. 151; Richardson, op. cit., pp. 168–70.
124 Paynter in Cook, op. cit., p. 53; Carroll, *Odyssey*, pp. 190–1; Gates, op. cit., p. 55.
125 See e.g. Nelson, *Volunteers*, p. 86; Richardson, op. cit., p. 165.
126 See e.g. Francis, op. cit., pp. 162, 163; Hyde, op. cit., p. 60.
127 See e.g. Carroll, *Odyssey*, pp. 190–1.
128 Brome, op. cit., p. 215; Copeman, op. cit., p. 132; W. Paynter, *There's No Other Way*, London, 1972, p. 70; Carroll, *Odyssey*, p. 48; Carr, op. cit., p. 143.

129 Alexander, op. cit., p. 81; G. Thompson, *Front-Line Diplomat*, London, 1959, p. 119; Richardson, op. cit., p. 170; Mühlen, op. cit., p. 202.

130 *In Spain with the International Brigade: A Personal Narrative*, London, 1938, pp. 17ff.; Paynter, op. cit., p. 71; Alexander, op. cit., pp. 80–1; Francis, op. cit., p. 231; Hoar, op. cit., p. 22; Paynter in Cook, op. cit., p. 55; Carroll, *Odyssey*, pp. 177–8; Spender, op. cit., p. 237.

131 Richardson, op. cit., p. 166; Francis, op. cit., p. 231.

132 Spender, op. cit., pp. 237–8; see Gates in Gerassi, op. cit., p. 86; Rosenstone, op. cit., pp. 145–6.

133 See Jackson, *Fallen Sparrows*, p. 107; Richardson, op. cit., pp. 103, 135; Copeman, op. cit., p. 108; Carroll, *Odyssey*, pp. 181–7.

134 Richardson, op. cit., p. 161; Krivitsky, op. cit., p. 113.

135 Fischer, op. cit., pp. 404–5; see Lee, op. cit., *passim*. On Marty, see Regler, *Owl*, pp. 277–8; Gurney, op. cit., p. 54; Meyers, op. cit., p. 101; Hoar, op. cit., p. 211.

136 Jackson, *Fallen Sparrows*, pp. 107–8.

137 See Francis, op. cit., p. 270; Bessie, op. cit., pp. 184–5; Carroll, *Odyssey*, pp. 190–1; Tisa, op. cit., p. 69; A. Horner, *Incorrigible Rebel*, London, 1960, p. 158.

138 See Jackson, *Fallen Sparrows*, p. 106.

139 Thomas, op. cit., pp. 850–1; Carr, op. cit., p. 225; Jackson, *Fallen Sparrows*, p. 69. See, however, Matthews, *Half of Spain*, p. 215.

140 Gallo in Tisa, op. cit., p. 172; see Dahms, op. cit., p. 252; E. Wolf in *Für Spaniens Freiheit*, p. 256; Inglis, op. cit., p. 166; Mühlen, op. cit., p. 203.

141 Carroll, *Odyssey*, p. 102; Thomas, op. cit., pp. 480, 780, 982; A. Beevor, *The Spanish Civil War*, London, 1982, p. 283; G. Hills, *The Battle for Madrid*, London, 1977, pp. 99, 109, 111; Hommel, op. cit., p. 100.

142 Richardson, op. cit., p. 62.

143 On the national pride issue, see Bessie, op. cit., p. 148; Gurney, op. cit., p. 115. On the 'cannon fodder' issue, see Jackson, *Fallen Sparrows*, p. 105. For more enthusiastic relations between Spaniards and internationals, see e.g. Sommerfield, op. cit., p. 25; Tisa, op. cit., pp. 187–8.

144 On problems in the early loyalist militias, see Regler, *Owl*, p. 273; Thomas, op.cit., pp. 375–6; Alpert, 'Republican Army', ch. 3. On morale and co-ordination problems among the Spanish conscripts, see Alpert, *passim*; see also e.g. Gurney, op. cit., p. 115; Bessie, op. cit., pp. 219, 226, 229; W. Brandt, *Essays, Reflections and Letters, 1933–1947*, R. W. Last (trans.), London, 1971, letter of 15 March 1937. On Francoist strategy, see P. Preston, *Franco: A Biography*, New York, 1994, pp. 202ff.; J. Benet, 'Military Strategy in the Spanish Civil War', in *Rewriting the Good Fight: Critical Essays on the Literature of the Spanish Civil War*, F. S. Brown *et al.* (eds), East Lansing, MI, 1989, pp. 19–22.

145 For example, losses for the British Battalion on their first day at Jarama were in the region of 68 per cent, as compared with around 50 per cent for British units attacking on the first day of the battle of the Somme (1 July 1916). M. Middlebrook, *The First Day of the Somme: 1 July 1916*, London, 1971, ch. 15; Wintringham, op. cit., p. 195. For comparisons with loss rates in the Second World War, see Jackson, *Fallen Sparrows*, p. 104. For the losses of the Italian forces, see J. F. Coverdale, *Italian Intervention in the Spanish Civil War*, Princeton, NJ, 1975, p. 418.

146 See e.g. D. Diamant, *Combattants Juifs de L'Armée Espagnole, 1936–1939*, Paris, 1979, p. 60.

9 THE WAFFEN-SS IN THE SECOND WORLD WAR, 1939–45

1 Quoted in E. L. Blandford, *Hitler's Second Army: The Waffen SS*, Osceola, WI, 1994, p. 31.

2 Quoted in ibid., p. 125.

3 E. Nolte, *Der europäische Burgerkrieg 1917–1945: Nationalsozialismus und Bolschewismus*, Frankfurt, 1987, p. 495.

4 R. Humble, 'The Waffen-SS – A European Crusade?', *Hitler's War Machine*, S. Goodenough (ed.), London, 1975, p. 106. The number of 'buff books' on the Waffen-SS is too large to list in full. Examples of varying quality include: G. Williamson, *The Blood-Soaked Soil: The Battles of the Waffen-SS*, Osceola, WI, 1995; M. Windrow and J. Bun, *The Waffen SS*, Men-at-Arms No. 34, London, 1982; D. Littlejohn, *Foreign Legions of the Third Reich* (4 vols), San Jose, CA, 1985–7; B. L. Davis, *Waffen-SS*, Poole, 1986; R. J. Bender and H. P. Taylor, *Uniforms, Organization and History of the Waffen SS* (2 vols), Mountain View, CA, 1969–71.

5 On the structure of the SS-VT and relations with the Army, see R. Absolon, *Die Wehrmacht im Dritten Reich, Band IV, 5. Februar 1938 bis 31. August 1939*, Boppard am Rhein, 1979, pp. 54–93.

6 K. Hummelkeier quoted in Blandford, op. cit., p. 40. On SS-VT training, see Hausser testimony in International Military Tribunal, *Trials of the German Major War Criminals*, HMSO, 1948, vol. 20, p. 294; P. Neumann, *Other Men's Graves*, C. Fitz Gibbon (trans.), London, 1958, pp. 92–3; F. Steiner, *Die Armee der Geächteten*, Göttingen, 1963, pp. 33–4; H. Höhne, *The Order of the Death's Head: The Story of Hitler's SS*, R. Barry (trans.), London, 1972, pp. 409–12; C. W. Syndor, Jr, *Soldiers of Destruction: The SS Death's Head Division, 1933–1945*, Princeton, NJ, 1977, pp. 47–53. On the development of the elite mystique within the Waffen-SS, see e.g. G. M. Kren and L. H. Rappoport, 'The Waffen SS: A Social Psychological Perspective', *Armed Forces and Society*, 1976, vol. 3, pp. 94ff.

7 L. Lochner (ed.), *The Goebbels Diaries*, London, 1948, p. 12. See also H. R. Trevor-Roper (ed.), *Hitler's Secret Conversations 1941–1944*, New York, 1953, pp. 138–9.

8 Höhne, op. cit., pp. 422ff.; V. O. Lumans, *Himmler's Auxiliaries: The Volkdeutsche Mittelstelle and the German National Minorities of Europe, 1933–1945*, Chapel Hill, NC, 1993, pp. 213ff.

9 A sketch order of battle for the Waffen-SS divisions can be found in J. Keegan, *Waffen SS: The Asphalt Soldiers*, New York, 1970, pp. 156–9. A more detailed summary of Waffen-SS units can be found in K.-G. Klietmann, *Die Waffen-SS – eine Dokumentation*, Osnabrück, 1965.

10 See W. L. Combs, *The Voice of the SS: A History of the SS Journal 'Das Schwarze Korps'*, New York, 1986, pp. 148–9; K. W. Estes, 'A European Anabasis: Western European Volunteers in the German Army and SS, 1940–1945', Ph.D. Thesis, University of Maryland, 1984, pp. 13–14, 65; G. H. Stein, *The Waffen SS: Hitler's Elite Guard at War, 1939–1945*, Ithaca, NY, 1966, p. 145; R. L. Koehl, *The Black Corps: The Structure and Power Struggles of the Nazi SS*, Madison, WI, 1983, pp. 211–12; see also US War Department, *Handbook on German Military Forces*, Baton Rouge, LA, 1990 edn, p. 200.

11 A. Camus, *Resistance, Rebellion, and Death*, J. O'Brien (trans.), New York, 1961, p. 21.

12 See *Trials of the German Major War Criminals*, vol. 20, pp. 281ff.; C. Messenger, *Hitler's Gladiator: The Life and Times of Oberstgruppenführer and Panzergeneral-Oberst der Waffen-SS Sepp Dietrich*, London, 1988, chs 10–11; J. M. Weingartner, *Crossroads of Death: The Story of the Malmédy*

Massacre and Trial, Berkeley, CA, 1979; B. J. S. MacDonald, *The Trial of Kurt Meyer*, Toronto, 1954.

13 G. Reitlinger, *The SS: Alibi of a Nation, 1922–1945*, New York, 1957.

14 K. P. Tauber, *Beyond Eagle and Swastika: German Nationalism since 1945*, Middletown, CT, 1967, vol. 1, pp. 333, 346, vol. 2, p. 1149, n. 161. See also D. Abenheim, *Reforging the Iron Cross: The Search for Tradition in the West German Armed Forces*, Princeton, NJ, 1988, p. 213.

15 D. C. Large, 'Reckoning without the Past: The HIAG of the Waffen-SS and the Politics of Rehabilitation in the Bonn Republic, 1950–1961', *Journal of Modern History*, 1987, vol. 59, p. 102, *passim*. On the publishing links of HIAG, see C. W. Syndor, Jr, 'The History of the *SS Totenkopfdivision* and the Postwar Mythology of the *Waffen SS*', *Central European History*, 1973, vol. 6, p. 340.

16 Ibid.; J. Dornberg, *Schizophrenic Germany*, New York, 1961, pp. 112–13; T. H. Tetens, *The New Germany and the Old Nazis*, New York, 1961, pp. 99–107; Tauber, vol. 1, pp. 344–62; G. Zwerenz, '*Soldaten sind Mörder': Die Deutschen und der Krieg*, Munich, 1988, pp. 252–3. See G. L. Mosse, *Fallen Soldiers: Reshaping the Memory of the World Wars*, New York, 1990, p. 210.

17 On Schönhuber, the Republicans, and the far right, see D. L. Bark and D. R. Gress, *Democracy and Its Discontents, 1963–1988*, Oxford, 1989, p. 477; R. Stöss, *Politics Against Democracy: Right-wing Extremism in West Germany*, L. Batson (trans.), New York, 1992, pp. 11, 139, 200–5, *passim*. It remains to be seen if the Freedom Party in Austria, led by Jorge Haider – who associates with Waffen-SS veterans – will capitalize on its success in the October 1996 elections to promote the Waffen-SS cause. See *New York Times*, 8 February 1996, sect. A, p. 12, col. 3.

18 P. Hausser, *Soldaten wie andere auch; Der Weg der Waffen-SS*, Osnabrück, 1966; F. Steiner, *Die Armee der Geächteten*, Göttingen, 1963.

19 P. Hausser, *Waffen-SS im Einsatz*, Göttingen, 1953, pp. 7, 66, 104; see also O. Kumm and O. Hummel in J. Seinhoff *et al.*, *Voices from the Third Reich: An Oral History*, Washington, DC, 1989, pp. 117, 274.

20 F. Steiner, *Die Freiwilligen: Idee und Opefergang*, Göttingen, 1958, pp. 46, 50, 13ff.

21 E. Vernier, 'Freiwillige für Europa: Waffen-SS und europäischer Nationalismus', *Der Freiwillige*, April–May 1976, vol. 22, pp. 6–9.

22 *Waffen-SS im Bild*, Göttingen, 1957, p. 116. See *Verweht sind die Spuren: Bibliodokumentation SS-Panzerregiment 5 'Wiking'*, Osnabrück, 1979; *Panzer Grenadiere der Panzerdivision 'Wiking' im Bild*, Osnabrück, 1984.

23 O. Weidinger, *Division Das Reich, Der Weg der 2. SS-Panzer-Division 'Das Reich': Die Geschichte der Stammdivision der Waffen-SS* (5 vols), Osnabrück, 1977–82. For a recent example of this genre see *Zwölf Jahre: 1. Kopanie, Leibstandarte SS Adolf Hitler: Ein Buch der Kameradenschaft*, Rossenheim, 1993. A sometimes rather romanticized summary account of Waffen-SS units can be found in Klietmann, op. cit. The number of books put out by Munin Verlag and Plesse Verlag, along with Verlag 'Der Freiwillige', is simply too large to list, but includes volumes on practically every German formation (regiments, divisions, and even corps) and many on foreign units as well. A few glossy works of similar provenance have been translated or adapted into English. See H. Walther, *The 12th SS Armoured Division: A Documentation in Words and Pictures*, E. Force (trans.), West Chester, PA, 1989; id., *The 1st SS Panzer Division Leibstandarte: A Pictorial History*, Atglen, PA, 1994; id., *The Waffen-SS: A Pictorial History*, Atglen, PA, 1994.

24 See e.g. C. de la Mazière, *The Captive Dreamer*, F. Stuart (trans.), New York, 1974; Neumann, op. cit.

25 For example, in English, L. Degrelle, *Epic: The Story of the Waffen SS*,

Torance, CA, 1983; id., *Campaign in Russia: The Waffen SS on the Eastern Front*, Torance, CA, 1985. See also M. Conway, *Collaboration in Belgium: Léon Degrelle and the Rexist Movement, 1940–1944*, New Haven, CT, 1993, pp. 280–1. Other foreign volunteer accounts include 'Saint-Loup', *Les S.S. de la Toison d'or: Flamands et Wallons au combat, 1941–1945*, Paris, 1975; M. Augier, *Götterdamerung*, Leoni an Sturnberger See, 1957; id., *Legion der Aufrechten: Frankreichs Freiwillige an der Ostfront*, Leoni an Sturnberger See, 1977.

26 On the 'year zero' tendency and its effects on the most important memory of all, see e.g. C. Koonz, 'Between Memory and Oblivion: Concentration Camps in German Memory', *Commemorations: The Politics of National Identity*, J. R. Gills (ed.), Princeton, NJ, 1994, pp. 262–3, *passim*. It is noteworthy how comparatively easy it was for lower-ranking SS figures to assume alternative identities after 'zero hour'. See e.g. A. Allen, 'Open Secret', *Lingua Franca*, March/April 1996, pp. 28–41.

27 R. Landwehr, *Narva 1944: The Waffen-SS and the Battle for Europe*, Silver Spring, MD, 1981, p. 11.

28 Id., *Lions of Flanders: Flemish Volunteers of the Waffen-SS, 1941–1945*, Silver Spring, MD, 1983, foreword.

29 Id., *Charlemagne's Legionnaires: French Volunteers of the Waffen-SS, 1943–1945*, Silver Spring, MD, 1989, pp. 17, 19.

30 Id., *Fighting for Freedom: The Ukrainian Volunteer Division of the Waffen SS*, Silver Spring, MD, 1985, p. 13. Other books by Landwehr include: *Frontfighters: The Norwegian Volunteer Legion of the Waffen-SS, 1941–1943*, Madison, WI, 1986; *Italian Volunteers of the Waffen-SS*, Bennington, VT, 1987; *Romanian Volunteers of the Waffen SS, 1944–1945*, Brookings, OR, 1991; *Britisches Freikorps: British Volunteers of the Waffen-SS, 1943–1945*, Brookings, OR, 1992. Rather less overtly fascistic works of a similar nature by other authors include: G. L. Simpson, *Tiger Ace: The Life of Panzer Commander Michael Wittmann*, Atglen, PA, 1994; M. C. Yerger, *Knights of Steel: The Structure, Development and Personalities of the 2. SS-Panzer Division 'Das Reich'* (2 vols), Lancaster, PA, 1994.

31 As successful efforts to obtain them through inter-library loan revealed. On the Institute for Historical Review, see D. Lipstadt, *Denying the Holocaust: The Growing Assault on Truth and Memory*, New York, 1994.

32 Jean Mabire has written a dozen divisional histories – too many to list here – on the Waffen-SS, concentrating on the foreign volunteers (especially the French) and the fighting in Normandy. See e.g. *La Division Charlemagne: les combats des SS français en Poméranie*, Paris, 1974; *Les S.S. Français: La Brigade Frankreich*, Paris, 1973.

33 Blandford, op. cit., p. 179, *passim*; G. Williamson, *Loyalty is My Honour: Personal Accounts from the Waffen-SS*, London, 1995.

34 Keegan, op. cit., pp. 13–14. See also his introduction to A. Wykes, *Hitler's Bodyguard: SS Leibstandarte*, New York, 1974, p. 6.

35 R. A. Beaumont, *Military Elites*, Indianapolis, 1974, p. 156.

36 J. Lucas, *Das Reich: The Fighting Role of the 2nd SS Division*, London, 1991, pp. 12, 13, 22, 221; id., *War on the Eastern Front, 1941–1945: The German Soldier in Russia*, New York, 1982, pp. 37–9.

37 B. Quarrie, *Waffen-SS Soldier, 1940–1945*, London, 1993, pp. 28, 17–27; id., *Hitler's Teutonic Knights: SS Panzers in Action*, Wellingborough, 1986, p. 7; id., *Hitler's Samurai: The Waffen-SS in Action*, New York, 1983, p. 7; see also R. Butler, *The Black Angels: A History of the Waffen-SS*, New York, 1979.

38 A. Hillgruber, *Zweierlei Untergang: Die Zerschlagung des Deutschen Reiches und das Ende des europäischen Judentums*, Berlin, 1986, pp. 33–4, 47.

39 On the *Historikerstreit*, see R. J. Evans, *In Hitler's Shadow: West German Historians and the Attempt to Escape from the Nazi Past*, New York, 1989; C. S. Maier, *The Unmasterable Past: History, Holocaust, and German National Identity*, Cambridge, MA, 1988; G. Thomas (ed.), *The Unresolved Past: A Debate in German History*, New York, 1990; P. Baldwin (ed.), *Reworking the Past: Hitler, the Holocaust, and the Historians' Debate*, Boston, 1990; A. D. Low, *The Third Reich and the Holocaust in German Historiography: Toward the Historikerstreit of the mid-1980s*, Boulder, CO, 1994.

40 A. Hillgruber, *Die Zerstörung Europas: Beiträge zur Weltkriesepoche 1914 bis 1945*, Berlin, 1988, p. 57.

41 On the Bitburg affair, see Bark and Gress, op. cit., pp. 425–7; G. Hartman (ed.), *Bitburg in Moral and Historical Perspective*, Bloomington, IN, 1986.

42 F. Schönhuber, *Ich war dabei*, Munich, 1981, p. 348.

43 Ibid., pp. 438–9.

44 See e.g. R. Woollcombe, *Lion Rampant*, London, 1970 edn, pp. 73, 108, 109.

45 On humane actions in the West, see e.g. B. Pitt in Keegan, op. cit., pp. 6–7; C. Whiting, *A Bridge at Arnhem*, London, 1974, p. 138. On war crimes by Allied personnel, see e.g. Senate of Canada, *Proceedings of the Standing Senate Subcommittee on Veterans Affairs*, Ottawa, 1993, vol. 9A, pp. 107–10, vol. 10, pp. 40–1; A. M. de Zayas, *The Wehrmacht War Crimes Bureau, 1939–1945*, Lincoln, NE, 1989.

46 O. Bartov, *Hitler's Army: Soldiers, Nazis, and War in the Third Reich*, New York, 1991; id., *The Eastern Front, 1941–1945: The Barbarization of Warfare*, New York, 1986.

47 See C. Jolly (ed.), *The Vengeance of Private Pooley*, London, 1956; L. Aitkin, *Massacre on the Road to Dunkirk: Wormhout 1940*, London, 1977.

48 J. M. Bauserman, *The Malmédy Massacre*, Shippensburg, PA, 1995; M. Hastings, *Das Reich: The March of the 2nd SS Panzer Division through France*, New York, 1982; R. Mackness, *Massacre at Oradour*, New York, 1989; see n. 12.

49 Höhne, op. cit., pp. 428–9.

50 See e.g. *Trials of the German Major War Criminals*, vol. 20, pp. 304–10; Neumann, op. cit., p. 140.

51 See E. Jackel, *Hitler's World View: A Blueprint for Power*, Cambridge, MA, 1981.

52 On Wehrmacht foreign units from the East, see J. Hoffman, *Die Ostlegionen 1941–1943*, Freiburg, 1976. On those from the West, see Estes, op. cit. See also J. L. Ready, *The Forgotten Axis: Germany's Partners and Foreign Volunteers in World War II*, Jefferson, NC, 1987. Such units appear to excite significantly less popular interest than their more glamorous SS counterparts. For an example of a 'buff' book on the subject, see C. C. Jurado, *Foreign Volunteers of the Wehrmacht 1941–45*, Osprey Men-at-Arms Series, London, 1983.

53 Office of the United States Chief Consul for the Prosecution of Axis Criminality, *Nazi Conspiracy and Aggression*, Washington, DC, 1946–8, vol. 2, Doc. 1919-PS; see Stein, op. cit., pp. 146–8.

54 W. Rings, *Life with the Enemy: Collaboration and Resistance in Hitler's Europe, 1939–1945*, J. M. Brown (trans.), New York, 1982, pp. 86–105; R. O. Paxton, *Parades and Politics at Vichy: The French Officer Corps under Marshal Pétain*, Princeton, NJ, 1966, pp. 273–6. Degrelle's postwar accounts cannot conceal the fact that even if he was trying to preserve a united Belgium by linking the Walloon Legion with the Waffen-SS in 1943 and not making a fuss like other collaborationists, his efforts would have come to naught in the event of a German victory. See Höhne, op. cit., p. 440; Conway, op. cit., pp. 170–2.

55 Gilbert, op. cit., pp. 147–8. For the ideological problems encountered in raising

Russian units, see R. Gehlen, *The Service: The Memoirs of Reinhard Gehlen*, D. Irving (trans.), New York, 1972, ch. 3.

56 Stein, op. cit., p. 154.
57 Estes, op. cit., pp. 23–5, 33, 39, 62, 63; Stein, op. cit. pp. 158, 159, 160; Koehl, op. cit., p. 206. See also H. W. Woltersdorf, *Gods of War: A Memoir of a German Soldier*, N. Benvenga (trans.), Novato, CA, 1990, pp. 26–7.
58 Estes, op. cit., pp. 110–11; Stein, op. cit., pp. 161–2. On army efforts at sensitivity training, see D. S. Detwiler (ed.), *World War II German Military Studies*, New York, 1979, vol. 19: D. von Heygendorff, 'Commanding Foreign Peoples', MS C-043.
59 Steiner, *Armee der Geächteten*, p. 121.
60 D. Littlejohn, *The Patriotic Traitors: A History of Collaboration in German-Occupied Europe, 1940–45*, London, 1972, p. 70.
61 Stein, op. cit., p. 140.
62 This was the percentage for the Netherlands. The percentage dipped elsewhere as low as 0.041 per cent. Estes, op. cit., p. 196. In July 1941 Quisling had expected to raise a force of 30,000. Only 1,000 Norwegians departed for training in Germany. Hoidal, op. cit., p. 606. For reactions to the recruiting drive, see Conway, op. cit., pp. 96–7; Estes, op. cit., pp. 143–5.
63 Buss and Mollo, op. cit., p. 51.
64 Stein, op. cit., pp. 154–5.
65 Ibid., p. 141.
66 Estes, op. cit., pp. 143, 156ff. See e.g. de la Mazière, op. cit.
67 For example, the IRA fighter Frank Ryan, a senior figure in the British Battalion, who was captured in Spain and went on to engage in recruiting activities for an Irish brigade unit in wartime Germany. See A. Weale, *Renegades: Hitler's Englishmen*, London, 1995, p. 133; M. Jackson, *Fallen Sparrows: The International Brigades in the Spanish Civil War*, Philadelphia, 1994, p. 124.
68 Estes, op. cit., pp. 189–91. See also C. Rofe, *Against the Wind*, London, 1956, p.80.
69 This was in reference to the Flemish volunteers. Buss and Mollo, op. cit., p. 31. Even partisan statistical sources admit that idealism was not the only motive for signing on. See Estes, op. cit., pp. 32–3, 193–4.
70 Stein, op. cit., pp. 182ff.
71 Ibid., p. 193.
72 See S. Steenberg, *Vlasov*, A. Farbstein (trans.), New York, 1970, ch. 6.
73 Estes, op. cit., pp. 63, 48, 43, 55–6.
74 Ibid., p. 29; see Stein, op. cit., pp. 158–9.
75 J. Olafsen in Blandford, op. cit., p. 113.
76 Estes, op. cit., p. 41.
77 Ibid., p. 28.
78 Ibid., pp. 173, 39–40.
79 Buss and Mollo, op. cit., p. 11. Knowledge that the Soviets routinely killed foreign volunteers may also have been an incentive to fight hard. See e.g. G. Sajer, *The Forgotten Soldier*, L. Emmet (trans.), New York, 1971, p. 102.
80 Estes, op. cit., p. 26. These figures are contrary to veteran claims that the division 'was an international volunteer force, formed exclusively of foreigners who volunteered'. Hummel in J. Steinhoff, *Voices From the Third Reich*, New York, 1989, p. 274. See also Kumm in ibid., p. 117.
81 Estes, op. cit., p. 120.
82 Ibid., p. 200; Steiner, *Freiwilligen*, p. 373. There is, to be sure, a good deal of uncertainty and confusion concerning the number of foreigners in the Waffen-SS. See Robert A. Gelwick, 'Personnel Policies and Procedures of the Waffen-SS', Ph.D. Thesis, University of Nebraska, 1971, p. 536.

83 Hummel in Steinhoff *et al.*, op. cit., p. 274; Steiner, *Armee der Geächteten*, p. 127.

84 See e.g. Beaumont, op. cit., p. 23; Lucas, *Das Reich*, p. 12; Quarrie, *Lightning Death*, p. 8; Keegan, op. cit., p. 143.

85 Höhne, op. cit., pp. 438–9; see Woltersdorf, op. cit., pp. 26–7.

86 Combs, op. cit., p. 143.

87 Lumans, op. cit., pp. 213–14, 224, 235, *passim*; G. Rempel, 'Gottlob Berger and Waffen-SS Recruitment, 1939–1945', *Militargeschichtliche Mitteilungen*, 1980, vol. 27, p. 112.

88 See e.g. J. Munk in Williamson, *Loyalty is My Honour*, p. 109.

89 Stein, op. cit., p. 192.

90 Höhne, op. cit., p. 423.

91 P. Zahnfeld in Blandford, op. cit., pp. 34–5; see K. Kempe in ibid., pp. 37; T. Loch in Steinhoff *et al.*, op. cit., p. 260; Williamson, *Loyalty is My Honour*, pp. 21–3; B. Wegner, *Hitlers Politische Soldaten: Die Waffen-SS 1933–1945*, Paderborn, 1982, p. 239.

92 H. F. Ziegler, *Nazi Germany's New Aristocracy: The SS Leadership, 1925–1939*, Princeton, NJ, 1989, p. 56.

93 Neumann, op. cit., p. 237; see Woltersdorf, op. cit., pp. 27, 103; Koehl, op. cit., p. 208; R. Brill testimony, *Trials of the German Major War Criminals*, vol. 20, p. 284; Loch in Steinhoff, op. cit., p. 100; see also Hastings, *Das Reich*, pp. 13–14. On SS recruitment policies, see Remple, 'Gottlob Berger', pp. 107–22.

94 Höhne, op. cit., pp. 436–7, 401–2; see also I. Kershaw, *The 'Hitler Myth': Image and Reality in the Third Reich*, Oxford, 1987, pp. 181–2.

95 See Hastings, *Das Reich*, p. 13.

96 H. W. Koch, *The Hitler Youth: Origins and Development 1922–45*, London, 1975, p. 245; G. Rempel, *Hitler's Children: The Hitler Youth and the SS*, Chapel Hill, NC, 1989, pp. 200–2, 213–19; A. Jodl testimony, *Trials of the German Major War Criminals*, vol. 16, p. 380; H. Beyer, *A Dog's Life*, R. Miller (trans.), Lanham, MD, 1993, pp. 34–5; W. Gorlitz (ed.), *The Memoirs of Field-Marshal Keitel*, D. Irving (trans.), London, 1965, p. 169.

97 Stein, op. cit., pp. 171, 204; R. Helm in Blandford, op. cit., p. 136; Gorlitz, op. cit., p. 172; Remple, 'Gottlob Berger', p. 116.

98 Göring evidence, *Trials of the German Major War Criminals*, vol. 9, p. 185.

99 C. Wilmot, *The Struggle for Europe*, London, 1952, p. 343; C. W. H. Luther, *Blood and Honor: The History of the 12th SS Panzer Division 'Hitler Youth', 1943–1945*, San Jose, CA, 1987, pp. 62ff.; W. Fecht in Williamson, *Loyalty is My Honour*, pp. 88–9; Hastings, *Das Reich*, p. 14; Keegan, op. cit., p. 137.

100 See e.g. T. N. Dupuy *et al.*, *Hitler's Last Gamble: The Battle of the Bulge, December 1944–January 1945*, New York, 1994, p. 47; R. J. Kershaw, *'It Never Snows in September': The German View of Market-Garden and the Battle for Arnhem, September 1944*, New York, 1994, p. 47.

101 See Hastings, *Das Reich*, pp. 13–14, 216; Beyer, op. cit., p. 70.

102 Ibid., pp. 84, 93; E. Kinscher in Williamson, *Loyalty*, p. 47; J. Lucas, *Experiences of War: The Third Reich*, London, 1990, pp. 161, 162; 'The 300 prisoners outnumbered the rifle brigade assault companies', W. Moore, *Panzer Bait: With the Third Royal Tank Regiment, 1939–1945*, London, 1991, pp. 156–7; J. J. How, *Hill 112: Cornerstone of the Normandy Campaign*, London, 1984, p. 205; see also H. C. Butcher, *My Three Years With Eisenhower: The Personal Diary of Captain Harry C. Butcher, USNR*, New York, 1946, entry for 22 July 1944; Woollcombe, op. cit., p. 56. This was, it should be remembered, in the face of the most intense supporting air and artillery fire that any

German soldier had yet faced in the war. See M. Thom in Williamson, *Loyalty*, p. 94; Luther, op. cit., p. 151; Hausser in Wilmot, op. cit., pp. 345–6; M. Hastings, *Overlord: D-Day and the Battle for Normandy, 1944*, London, 1993 edn, *passim*.

103 Kershaw, '*It Never Snows in September*', p. 168; see Whiting, op. cit., p. 113.

104 J. Munk in Williamson, *Loyalty*, p. 124; see also F.-K. Wacker in ibid., p. 46.

105 See A. Stahlberg, *Bounden Duty: The Memoirs of a German Officer 1932–45*, P. Crampton (trans.), London, 1990, pp. 268, 330; Gorlitz, op. cit., p. 225; Neumann, op. cit., p. 260; J. Munk in Williamson, *Loyalty*, p. 124; see also H. Krüger, *A Crack in the Wall: Growing Up Under Hitler*, R. Hein (trans.), New York, 1986, p. 156; M. Bates, *A Wilderness of Days*, Victoria, BC, 1978, p. 97.

106 Kershaw, '*It Never Snows in September*', p. 53; see S. Knappe, *Soldat: Reflections of a German Soldier, 1936–1945*, T. Brusaw (trans.), New York, 1992, p. 39.

107 On the career of Eicke, see Syndor, *Soldiers of Destruction, passim*. On Dietrich, see Messenger, *Hitler's Gladiator, passim*.

108 Wegner, op. cit., p. 140.

109 See Steiner, *Armee der Geächteten*, p. 117.

110 Neumann, op. cit., p. 157. On Dietrich's relations with his men, see Bayer, op. cit., p. 68; Messenger, op. cit., p. 111 *passim*.

111 Williamson, *Loyalty*, p. 46; see statements in ibid., pp. 43–4, 47–8; de la Mazière, op. cit., p. 32; Neumann, op. cit, pp. 92–3.

112 *Hitler's Secret Conversations 1941–1944*, New York, 1953, p. 139; see also F. W. von Mellenthin, *German Generals of World War II as I Saw Them*, Norman, OK, 1977, p. 227.

113 H. Köhne in Williamson, *Loyalty*, p. 47.

114 F.-K. Wacker in Williamson, *Loyalty*, p. 46.

115 On the problems with the 'primary group' in the *Ostheer*, see Bartov, *Hitler's Army, passim*. On the effects of the turnover in the Waffen-SS, see e.g. K. Hummelkeier in Blandford, op. cit., pp. 121–2; Neumann, op. cit., p. 237.

116 On army transfers to the SS, see Ziegler, op. cit., pp. 132–3. On the stringency of officer promotion qualifications, see J. S. Corum, *The Roots of Blitzkrieg: Hans von Seeckt and German Military Reform*, Lawrence, KS, 1992, p. 78, ch. 4, *passim*.

117 M. van Creveld, *Fighting Power: German and U.S. Army Performance, 1939–1945*, Westport, CT, 1982, pp. 123, 129; S. J. Lewis, *Forgotten Legions: German Army Infantry Policy 1918–1941*, New York, 1985, p. 62; M. Cooper, *The German Army 1933–1945*, Lanham, MD, 1990 edn, pp. 130–1; S. G. Fritz, *Frontsoldaten: The German Soldier in World War II*, Lexington, KY, 1995, p. 159; J. E. Förster, 'The Dynamics of *Volksgemeinschaft*: The Effectiveness of the German Military Establishment in the Second World War', in *Military Effectiveness Volume III: The Second World War*, A. R. Millet and W. Murray (eds), Boston, 1988, p. 208.

118 Steiner, *Armee der Geächteten*, p. 118; see Wegner, op. cit., pp. 236–7.

119 1936 *Truppenführung*, point 8, in van Creveld, op. cit., pp. 128–9; D. Fraser, *Knight's Cross: A Life of Field Marshal Erwin Rommel*, London, 1994 edn, p. 118; see Fritz, op. cit., p. 158; Lewis, op. cit., p. 62. Even in the Reichswehr it is worth noting that officer candidates always underwent a period of standard recruit training to familiarize them with the life of the men they would command. Corum, op. cit., p. 80.

120 P. H. Weidenreich, 'Why He Fights', *Infantry Journal*, 1945, vol. 56, no. 2, pp. 43–4. Though see also M. G. Steinert, *Hitler's War and the Germans: Public*

Mood and Attitude during the Second World War, T. E. J. de Witt (trans.), Athens, OH, 1977, p. 227.

121 See e.g. J. Munk and W. Völkner in Williamson, *Loyalty*, pp. 35–6, 39–40. Conversely, 'bull' or 'chickenshit' was less common in the German Army than is often supposed. See Fritz, op. cit., p. 25.

122 Ibid., pp. 23, 16ff.; van Creveld, op. cit., pp. 36, 72–3; de la Mazière, op. cit., pp. 67–8; see also Lewis, op. cit., p. 93. It was in the Reichswehr that the principle that an officer or NCO should think aggressively and be able to function at the next level of command was established. Corum, op. cit., pp. 71–3, *passim*.

123 E. Brörup in Williamson, *Loyalty*, p. 33; see Sajer, op. cit., pp. 1–12, 155–68.

124 Quoted in van Creveld, op. cit., pp. 128–9. On von Seeckt, see Corum, op. cit., p. 40.

125 Detwiler, op. cit., vol. 20, D-178, Generalmajor der Waffen-SS Werner Doerffler-Schuband, 'Officer Procurement in the Waffen-SS', pp. 2, 11.

126 For example, Stahlberg, op. cit., pp. 187–8; see also R. A. Doughty, *The Breaking Point: Sedan and the Fall of France*, Hamden, CT, 1990, *passim*.

127 Stein, op. cit., pp. 92, 130–2.

128 Neumann, op. cit., p. 237.

129 Woltersdorf, op. cit., p. 103.

130 G. Astor, *A Blood-Dimmed Tide: The Battle of the Bulge by the Men Who Fought It*, New York, 1992, p. 246.

131 Stein, op. cit., pp. 209–10; Cooper, op. cit., pp. 450; see Mellenthin, op. cit., p. 321; G. Rommel in Williamson, *Loyalty*, p. 40.

132 C. Chant, *Kursk*, London, 1975, pp. 10–11, 38.

133 Dupuy, *Hitler's Last Gamble*, pp. 410, 412. The quantitative difference was apparent as early as 1940. See A. Seaton, *The German Army 1933–45*, London, 1982, pp. 158–9, 241–2.

134 W. S. Dunn, Jr, *Hitler's Nemesis: The Red Army, 1930–1945*, Westport, CT, 1994, pp. 83–4, 144–5; Dupuy, op. cit., p. 412; D. M. Glanz and J. House, *When Titans Clashed: How the Red Army Stopped Hitler*, Lawrence, KS, 1995, p. 180.

135 Fritz Laganke quoted in Hastings, *Overlord*, p. 214. For the comparative strengths of German and Allied armour, see ibid., pp. 220ff.

136 T. Dupuy, *A Genius for War: The German Army and General Staff, 1807–1945*, New York, 1979, pp. 234–5; van Creveld, op. cit., pp. 7–8; see Dupuy, *Hitler's Last Gamble*, p. 498; Hastings, *Normandy*, p. 219.

137 G. Williamson, *The Iron Cross: A History, 1813–1957*, Poole, 1984, p. 93. HIAG, needless to say, makes much of Waffen-SS winners. See E.-G. Krätschmer, *Die Ritterkreuzträger der Waffen-SS*, Göttingen, 1955. At least some of the crosses awarded to SS men, furthermore, were undeserved (though this may also have been true for the Wehrmacht in the latter years of the war). See Stahlberg, op. cit., p. 368.

138 For the problems of Allied forces in Normandy, see e.g. C. d'Este, *Decision in Normandy: The Unwritten Story of Montgomery and the Normandy Campaign*, London, 1983, ch. 17; Wilmot, op. cit., p. 428; Hastings, *Normandy*, pp. 220ff.; J. A. English, *The Canadian Army and the Normandy Campaign: A Study of Failure in High Command*, New York, 1991.

139 See e.g. Steiner, *Armee der Geächteten*, p. 166. Some former SS men were willing to concede that the Waffen-SS did indeed suffer disproportionate losses. See Wünster in Steinhoff *et al.*, op. cit., pp. 260–1.

140 Calculations on the basis of figures provided in Williamson, *Loyalty*, p. 25; Hausser, *Waffen-SS im Einsatz*, pp. 15–16; M. K. Sorge, *The Other Price of Hitler's War: German Military and Civilian Losses Resulting from World War II*, New York, 1986, p. 42; I. C. B. Dear and M. R. D. Foot (eds), *The Oxford Companion to World War II*, Oxford, 1995, pp. 468, 469. Suggestions that the

higher death toll was due to fewer rear-area troops in the Waffen-SS cannot be sustained. See Reitlinger, op. cit., p. 195.

141 See e.g. Sajer, op. cit., p. 111. On the cult of death in the Waffen-SS and in Nazi ideology see J. W. Baird, *To Die for Germany: Heroes in the Nazi Pantheon*, Bloomington, IN, 1990, pp. 209, 212–13, 216–20, 233; G. N. Kren and L. H. Rappoport, 'The Waffen SS: A Social and Psychological Perspective', *Armed Forces and Society*, 1976, vol. 3, November, p. 95.

142 See Höhne, op. cit., p. 416; Messenger, op. cit., pp. 74–5, 80–1. Moreover, such aggressiveness was no guarantee of success even in 1940. See K. Gebert (ed.), *Generalfeldmarscall Feder von Bock: The War Diary, 1939–1945*, Atglen, PA, 1996, 10 May 1940, p. 137.

143 On losses in training and at the front, see e.g. Syndor, op. cit., pp. 99–100, 119, 147, 167, 197, 222; Messenger, op. cit., p. 75; Luther, op. cit., p. 64; Weingartner, op. cit., pp. 67, 76–7, 94, 103; Weidinger, op. cit. vol. 2, pp. 523–4. In obeying Hitler's order not to withdraw an inch in the winter of 1941–2 in Russia, for instance, the Waffen-SS units won the Führer's admiration but suffered huge losses – ultimately to no avail since the German line was in places pushed back to the positions that the generals had wanted to retire to in the first place. See T-28, Hans von Greffenberg, 'Battle of Moscow, 1941–42', in Detwiler, op. cit., vol. 16, p. 122; Cooper, op. cit., pp. 449, 342–3.

144 Neumann, op. cit., p. 120; see also Messenger, op. cit., p. 131.

145 K. Meyer, *Grenadiere*, Munich, 1957, p. 64.

146 R. Wünster in Steinhoff *et al.*, op. cit., p. 260.

147 Quoted in Blandford, op. cit., p. 163.

148 Luther, op. cit., pp. 121, 168; Hastings, *Overlord*, pp. 147–8; O. Haller, 'The Defeat of the 12th SS, 7–10 June 1944', *Canadian Military History*, 1994, vol. 3, pp. 9–25.

149 Kershaw, '*It Never Snows in September*', pp. 129–31; M. Middlebrook, *Arnhem 1944*, Boulder, CO, 1994, pp. 292–5. Graebner and most of his men were killed.

150 B. Horrocks, *A Full Life*, London, 1960, p. 221; see Höhne, op. cit., p. 425.

151 L. Rühl in Steinhoff *et al.*, op. cit., p. 434; *The Memoirs of Field-Marshal Kesselring*, London, 1953, p. 290; see M. G. Steinert, *Capitulation 1945: The Story of the Doenitz Regime*, R. Barry (trans.), London, 1969, p. 180.

152 N. von Below, *Als Hitlers Adjutant, 1937–1945*, Mainz, 1980, p. 236.

153 S. Westphal, *The German Army in the West*, London, 1951, p. 54; see E. von Manstein, *Lost Victories*, A. G. Powell (trans.), Chicago, 1958, p. 188; Syndor, *Soldiers of Destruction*, pp. 99–100; Stahlberg, op. cit., p. 288.

154 The reference was to Dietrich. F. Taylor (ed.), *The Goebbels Diaries, 1939–41*, London, 1982, p. 158.

155 Wegner, op. cit., p. 227.

156 See Syndor, *Soldiers of Destruction*, ch. 1.

157 *Hitler's Secret Conversations, 1941–1944*, New York, 1953, p. 138; see Stahlberg, op. cit., p. 291. For comments on Dietrich's plain-speaking loyalty, see von Below, op. cit., p. 30; Lochner, pp. 12, 219, 231; A. Speer, *Inside the Third Reich*, R. and C. Winston (trans.), London, 1970, pp. 364, 418; H. Guderian, *Panzer Leader*, C. Fitzgibbon (trans.), New York, 1952, p. 272. Messenger, op. cit., *passim*; Weingartner, op. cit., pp. 69–70. Dietrich may, however, have known about the plot to kill Hitler in July 1944. See H. von Luck, *Panzer Commander*, New York, 1989, p. 202; Messenger, op. cit., p. 124.

158 Gilbert, op. cit., pp. 113–14. On Hausser, see R. Brett-Smith, *Hitler's Generals*, London, 1976, pp. 151–3.

159 Syndor, *Soldiers of Destruction*, pp. 92, 267.

160 Manstein, op. cit., p. 188.

161 Messenger, op. cit., p. 106. For an earlier example of disobedience, see Guderian, op. cit., p. 117.
162 Stahlberg, op. cit., p. 289; see Messenger, op. cit., pp. 118, 131.
163 Ibid., p. 125.
164 O. N. Bradley, *A Soldier's Story*, New York, 1951, p. 491; Messenger, op. cit., pp. 117, 161–2, 109; see Mellenthin, op. cit., pp. 235, 237; Westphal, op. cit., pp. 183–4; W. Warlimont, *Inside Hitler's Headquarters*, R. H. Barry (trans.), New York, 1964, p. 312; Brett-Smith, op. cit., p. 155. Apart from von Rundstedt, army critics included Hasso von Manteuffel, Alfred Jodl, Walter Warlimont, Siegfried Westphal, Geyr von Schweppenburg, and Joachim von Mellenthin. See also F. Kurowski, 'Dietrich and Manteuffel', *Hitler's Generals*, C. Barnett (ed.), London, 1989, p. 411.
165 Höhne, op. cit., p. 430; Stahlberg, op. cit., p. 289; Weingartner, op. cit., p. 69.
166 Höhne, op. cit., p. 441.
167 Moore, op. cit., p. 152; see Brett-Smith, op. cit., p. 162.
168 Glantz and House, op. cit., p. 147.
169 Woltersdorf, op. cit., p. 104.
170 See Knappe, op. cit., p. 24; Lucas, *War on the Eastern Front*, p. 40; Kesselring, op. cit., pp. 287–8; Luck, op. cit., p. 35; Gorlitz, op. cit., p. 169; Westphal, op. cit., p. 54.
171 O. Lauer in Steinhoff *et al.*, op. cit., p. 272; H. Metelmann, *Through Hell for Hitler*, Wellingborough, 1990, pp. 171–3; see D. Edgar, *The Stalag Men*, London, 1982, p. 189. On battlegroup problems, see Lucas, *Experience of War*, pp. 161, 162. These instances of Waffen-SS killing Wehrmacht personnel do not include official action against supposed deserters, for which see e.g. Neumann, op. cit., pp. 244–5; Rühl and Leo Welt in Steinhoff *et al.*, op. cit., pp. 433–5, 437; A. Heck, *A Child of Hitler: Germany in the Days Where God Wore a Swastika*, Frederick, CO, 1985, p. 171. On the Wehrmacht success with battle-groups and SS dislike of them, see Quarrie, *Waffen-SS Soldier*, p. 29; van Creveld, op. cit., p. 44; Hastings, *Overlord*, pp. 201–3. Co-operating with elite Wehrmacht units like the 'Gross Deutschland' Division was easier. See Sajer, op. cit., p. 296. It is hard to disagree with those German commanders who believed that the build-up of the Waffen-SS involved unnecessary duplication. See Kesselring, op. cit., pp. 287–8; Manstein, op. cit., p. 188; Gorlitz, op. cit., p. 169; Stahlberg, op. cit., p. 254.

10 THE VIET CONG IN THE SECOND INDOCHINA WAR, 1960–75

1 R. Stetler (ed.), *The Military Art of People's War: Selected Writing of General Vo Nguyen Giap*, New York, 1970, pp. 175–6.
2 S. J. Tourison, *Talking With Victor Charlie: An Interrogator's Story*, New York, 1991, p. 164.
3 On Vietnamese communist strategy, see P. J. McGarvey, *Visions of Victory: Selected Communist Military Writings, 1964–1968*, Stanford, CA, 1969; Vo Nguyen Giap, '*Big Victory, Great Task': North Viet-Nam's Minister of Defense Assesses the Course of the War*, New York, 1968. For a brief examination of Maoist strategy and links with Vietnam, see J. Shy and T. Collier, 'Revolutionary War', in *Makers of Modern Strategy*, P. Paret (ed.), Princeton, NJ, 1986, pp. 815–62.
4 See R. J. Asprey, *War in the Shadows: The Guerrilla in History*, New York, 1994, ch. 57. On the penchant on the New Left for peasant insurrection, see e.g. J. Murphy, *Harvest of Fear*, Boulder, CO, 1994 edn, pp. 235–6.

5 Asprey, op. cit., ch. 92. On the contrast between the Western image and the reality of the guerrillas in Afghanistan, see e.g. P. Moorcroft, *What the Hell am I Doing Here? Travels with an Occasional War Correspondent*, London, 1995, pp. 82ff.

6 This may be the result of efforts to confirm northern dominance in Vietnam. See Troung Nhu Tang, *A Vietcong Memoir*, with D. Chanoff and Doan Van Toai, New York, 1985, pp. 264–5; R. Shaplin, *Bitter Victory*, New York, 1986, p. 144; Ngo Vinh Long, 'Post-Paris Agreement Struggles and the Fall of Saigon', in *The Vietnam War: Vietnamese and American Perspectives*, J. S. Werner and Luu Doan Huynh (eds), New York, 1992, p. 205; H. Kamm, *Dragon Ascending: Vietnam and the Vietnamese*, New York, 1996, pp. 174, 236. For the party line on the war, see D. Chanoff and D. V. Toai, *Portrait of the Enemy*, New York, 1986, p. xvii.

7 On the success of the PLA in the Chinese Civil War, see S. I. Levine, *Anvil of Victory: The Communist Revolution in Manchuria, 1945–1948*, New York, 1987; E. R. Hooton, *The Greatest Tumult: The Chinese Civil War, 1936–49*, London, 1991. On the problems in Korea, see A. L. George, *The Chinese Communist Army in Action: The Korean War and its Aftermath*, New York, 1967; Shu Guang Zhang, *Mao's Military Romanticism: China and the Korean War, 1950–1953*, Lawrence, KS, 1996. It should be noted that even in the Chinese Civil War communist successes were heavily dependent on nationalist weaknesses – not all of which were induced by the Party. See Hsi-Sheng Ch'i, *Nationalist China at War: Military Defeats and Political Collapse, 1937–45*, Ann Arbor, MI, 1982.

8 See D. Kinnard, *The War Managers: American Generals Reflect on Vietnam*, New York, 1991 edn, p. 67. On the NVA, see D. Pike, *PAVN: People's Army of Vietnam*, Novato, CA, 1986.

9 T. Page and J. Pimlott (eds), *Nam: The Vietnam Experience 1965–75*, New York, 1995, p. 107; see D. Pike, 'Conduct of the Vietnam War: Strategic Factors, 1965–1968', in *The Second Indochina War: Proceedings of a Symposium Held at Airlie, Virginia, 7–9 November 1984*, J. Schlight (ed.), Washington, DC, 1986, p. 103; see also e.g. G. E. Smith, *P.O.W. Two Years with the Viet Cong*, Berkeley, CA, 1971, p. 12.

10 Troung Nhu Tang, op. cit., pp. 173–4.

11 'Why I Joined the VC', in *Nam*, p. 270.

12 L. Borton, *After Sorrow: An American Among the Vietnamese*, New York, 1995, p. 116.

13 J. Leslie, *The Mark: A War Correspondent's Memoir of Vietnam and Cambodia*, New York, 1955, p. 148; see M. Hess, *Then the Americans Came: Voices from Vietnam*, New York, 1993, p. 149; T. Mangold and J. Pennycate, *The Tunnels of Cu Chi*, London, 1985, *passim*.

14 See Tourison, op. cit., pp. 32, 174, 255–6; A. F. Krepinevich, Jr, *The Army and Vietnam*, Baltimore, MD, 1986, pp. 207, 210.

15 F. Fitzgerald, *Fire in the Lake: The Vietnamese and the Americans in Vietnam*, Boston, 1972, p. 142, *passim*.

16 M. Clodfelter, *Mad Minutes and Vietnam Months*, Jefferson, NC, 1988, p. 163.

17 J. R. MacDonough, *Platoon Leader*, Novato, CA, 1985, p. 51; see M. Herr, *Dispatches*, New York, 1977 edn, p. 12.

18 Don F. Brown in T. Wallace, *Bloods: An Oral History of the Vietnam War by Black Veterans*, New York, 1984, p. 169; see J. M. G. Bown, *Rice Paddy Grunt: Unfading Memories of the Vietnam Generation*, Lake Bluff, IL, 1986, p. 42; R. Herrod, *Blue's Bastards: A True Story of Valor Under Fire*, Washington, DC, 1989, p. 122; T. Wolff, *In Pharaoh's Army: Memories of the Lost War*, New

York, 1994, pp. 4, 7; E. M. Bergerud, *The Dynamics of Defeat: The Vietnam War in Hau Nghia Province*, Boulder, CO, 1990, p. 132.

19 C. L. Powell, *My American Journey*, with J. E. Persico, New York, 1995, p. 88; see B. Fair, *Headhunters: Stories from the 1st Squadron, 9th Cavalry in Vietnam, 1965–1971*, Novato, CA, 1987, p. 44; H. R. Simpson, *Tiger in the Barbed Wire: An American in Vietnam, 1952–1991*, Washington, DC, 1992, p. 198.

20 J. Sack, *Lieutenant Calley: His Own Story*, New York, 1971, p. 57; see M. D. Mahler, *Ringed in Steel: Armored Cavalry, Vietnam 1967–68*, Novato, CA, 1986, pp. 167–8; C. Gadd, *Line Doggie: Foot Soldier in Vietnam*, Novato, CA, 1987, p. 14.

21 P. Caputo, *A Rumour of War*, New York, 1994 edn, pp. 101, 124, 148, 203.

22 L. B. Lewis, *The Tainted War: Culture and Identity in Vietnam War Narratives*, Westport, CT, 1985, p. 95.

23 R. L. Stevens, *Mission on the Ho Chi Minh Trail: Nature, Myth, and War in Vietnam*, Norman, OK, 1995, p. 8.

24 A. N. Garland (ed.), *Infantry in Vietnam*, Nashville, TN, 1982 edn (first published 1967), p. 13.

25 M. Russ, *Happy Hunting Ground*, New York, 1968, p. 37; see Robert L. Daniels in Terry, op. cit., p. 237.

26 Robert L. Mountain in Terry, op. cit., p. 182.

27 D. Kitchin, *War in Aquarius: Memoir of an American Infantryman in Action Along the Cambodian Border During the Vietnam War*, Jefferson, NC, 1994, p. 4.

28 B. Fall, *Viet-Nam Witness, 1953–66*, London, 1966, p. 296.

29 M. Baker, *Nam: The Vietnam War in the Words of the Men and Women Who Fought There*, New York, 1981, pp. 72–3; see J. L. Esten, *Comanche Six: Company Commander, Vietnam*, Novato, CA, 1991, p. 38; F. Downs, *The Killing Zone: My Life in the Vietnam War*, New York, 1978, p. 45; C. Coe, *Young Man in Vietnam*, New York, 1968, p. 46; Herrod, op. cit., pp. 109–10; Page and Pimlott, op. cit., pp. 109, 147; Lewis, op. cit., p. 96.

30 N. Schwarzkopf, *It Doesn't Take a Hero*, with P. Petre, New York, 1992, p. 166; E. Hammel, *Ambush Valley*, Novato, CA, 1990, p. 108; see Carlton Sherwood and David Sherman in M. L. Lanning and D. Cragg, *Inside the VC and the NVA*, New York, 1992, pp. 219, 223; D. Kirk, *Tell It to the Dead: Stories of a War*, Armonk, NY, 1996 edn, p. 98.

31 P. Arnett, *Live from the Battlefield: From Vietnam to Baghdad, 35 Years in the World's War Zones*, New York, 1994, p. 164.

32 Lanning and Cragg, op. cit., p. 204; see K. Knoebl, *Victor Charlie: The Face of War in Viet-Nam*, New York, 1967, p. 12.

33 Sack, op. cit., p.79; see Clodfleter, op. cit., p. 163; M. Bilton and K. Sim, *Four Hours in My Lai*, New York, 1992; D. Lang, *Casualties of War*, New York, 1969, p. 19; P. Goldman and T. Fuller, *Charlie Company: What Vietnam Did to Us*, New York, 1983, p. 125; Terry, op. cit., pp. 56, 98, 261; Baker, op. cit., pp. 170–1; Schwarzkopf, op. cit., p. 164; Anson, op. cit., pp. 49–50, 51, 56; D. Duncan, *The New Legions*, New York, 1967, pp. 169, 229; T. O'Brien, *If I Die in a Combat Zone (Box Me Up and Send Me Home)*, New York, 1973, p. 188.

34 Herr, op. cit., p. 47; see R. Mason, *Chickenhawk*, New York, 1983, pp. 181, 208–10; W. G. Bainbridge in Lanning and Cragg, op. cit., p. 229; H. Behret in H. Maurer, *Strange Ground: Americans in Vietnam, 1945–1975, An Oral History*, New York, 1989, p. 181.

35 On avoiding contact, see Schwarzkopf, op. cit., pp. 163, 167; Santolini, op. cit., pp. 24, 127; O'Brien, op. cit., p. 99. On the VC 'owning' the night, see A. B. Herbert, *Soldier*, with J. T. Wooten, New York, 1973, pp. 211, 233; Brown,

op. cit., p. 328; R. L. Daniels in Terry, op. cit., p. 237; Herr, op. cit., p. 12; Santolini, op. cit., p. 24.

36 J. Murphy, *Harvest of Fear: A History of Australia's Vietnam War*, Boulder, CO, 1994 edn, p. 166; see G. Walker in *Memories of Vietnam*, K. Maddock (ed.), Sydney, 1991, p. 196; J. Ross, 'Australia's Soldiers in Vietnam: product and performance', *Australia's Vietnam: Australia in the Second Indo-China War*, P. King (ed.), Sydney, 1983, p. 83. On attitudes to the South Vietnamese, see e.g. Goldman and Fuller, op. cit., pp. 126–7; Bergerud, op. cit., pp. 226–8; H. P. Hall, Jr, 'The Enlisted Man's War: A Study of the Vietnam War Novels', Ph.D. Thesis, University of Texas at Austin, 1984, p. 95.

37 D. Luce and J. Summer, *Viet Nam: The Unheard Voices*, Ithaca, NY, 1969, p. 192; J. R. Ebert, *A Life in a Year: The American Infantryman in Vietnam, 1965–1972*, Novato, CA, 1993, p. 211; see Bergerud, op. cit., p. 228.

38 Archie Biggers in Terry, op. cit., p. 113.

39 Joseph B. Anderson in Terry, op. cit., p. 232; see I. Fergusson in G. McKay, *Vietnam Fragments: An Oral History of Australians at War*, St Leonards, NSW, 1992, p. 93; Graham Walker in *Memories of Vietnam*, op. cit., p. 167.

40 D. H. Hackworth and J. Sherman, *About Face*, New York, 1989, p. 694; see K. Maddock, op. cit., p. 152.

41 W. Pearson, *Vietnam Studies: The War in the Northern Provinces, 1966–1968*, Washington, DC, 1975, p. 45.

42 Lanning and Cragg, op. cit., pp. 201, 202; see W. K. Jones in ibid., p. 213.

43 Kinnard, op. cit., p. 67.

44 R. S. McNamara, *In Retrospect: The Tragedy and Lessons of Vietnam*, with B. VanDeMark, New York, 1995, p. 242; Lanning and Cragg, op. cit., p. 211.

45 Knoebl, op. cit., pp. 5–6; see D. C. Hallin, *The 'Uncensored' War: The Media and Vietnam*, New York, 1986, p. 147. On the rarity of face-to-face contact, see D. Rather, *The Camera Never Blinks: Adventures of a TV Journalist*, New York, 1977, p. 194; R. S. Anson, *War News: A Young Reporter in Indochina*, New York, 1989, p. 86; Arnett, op. cit., p. 248. Left-wing correspondents overtly in sympathy with the NLF cause also promoted the image of the heroic underdog. See e.g. W. G. Burchett, *Vietnam: Inside Story of the Guerrilla War*, New York, 1965.

46 Leslie, op. cit., p. 75; see also H. Behret in Maurer, op. cit., p. 181.

47 See C. D. Wyatt, *Paper Soldiers: The American Press and the Vietnam War*, New York, 1983, p. 182; Hallin, op. cit., pp. 166–7.

48 P. Braestrup, *Big Story: How the American Press and Television Reported and Interpreted the Crisis of Tet 1968 in Vietnam and Washington*, New Haven, CT, 1983 abridged edn, pp. 132, 157, 159–60, 162–3, 166; see also D. Burnham in Maurer, op. cit., p. 308.

49 Herr, op. cit., p. 71; see Arnett, op. cit., pp. 245, 250.

50 See Fitzgerald, op. cit., pp. 138–9. On links made with the War of Independence, see J. Shy, *A People Numerous and Armed: Reflections on The Military Struggle for American Independence*, New York, 1976, pp. 168, 193, 196, 244, 254; Duncan, op. cit., pp. 339–40; Lanning and Cragg, op. cit., pp. 37–8; and the film documentary *In the Year of the Pig* (1968).

51 W. Van Zanten, *Don't Bunch Up: One Marine's Story*, Hamden, CT, 1993, p. 188.

52 M. L. Lanning, *Vietnam at the Movies*, New York, 1994, p. ix. On the problems of celluloid history, see A. Kaes, 'History and Film: Public Memory in the Age of Electronic Dissemination', *History and Memory*, 1990, vol. 2, pp. 111–29.

53 For example, see *Casualties of War* (1989) and – for the NVA – *Hamburger Hill* (1987); see also *The Deer Hunter* (1978). Among the few films which do seek to view the war from the Vietnamese perspective are *The Iron Triangle* (1988) and

Heaven and Earth (1992). On the myths perpetuated in Vietnam films, see J. W. Davidson and M. H. Lyttle, *After the Fact: The Art of Historical Detection*, New York, 1992 edn, pp. 358–84; B. Taylor, 'The Vietnam War Movie', in *The Legacy: The Vietnam War in the American Imagination*, M. D. Shafer (ed.), Boston, 1990, ch. 9; T. Prasch, '*Platoon* and the Mythology of Realism', in *Search and Clear: Critical Responses to Selected Literature and Films of the Vietnam War*, W. J. Searle (ed.), Bowling Green, OH, 1988, pp. 195–215; D. Culbert, 'Television's Vietnam and Historical Revisionism in the United States', *Historical Journal of Film, Radio and Television*, 1988, vol. 8, pp. 253–67; J. Hellman, *American Myth and the Legacy of Vietnam*, New York, 1986; A. Auster and L. Quart, *How the War is Remembered: Hollywood & Vietnam*, New York, 1988, pp. 63–4.

54 See C. A. Thayer, *War by Other Means: National Liberation and Revolution in Viet-Nam, 1954–1960*, Sydney, 1988; W. R. Andrews, *The Village War: Vietnamese Communist Revolutionary Activities in Dinh Tuong Province, 1960–1964*, Columbia, MS, 1973; G. K. Tanham, *Communist Revolutionary Warfare: From the Vietminh to the Viet Cong*, New York, 1967; D. Pike, *Viet Cong: The Organization and Techniques of the National Liberation Front of South Vietnam*, Cambridge, MA, 1966.

55 See Bergerud, op. cit.; J. W. Trullinger, Jr, *Village at War: An Account of Revolution in Vietnam*, New York, 1980; J. Race, *War Comes to Long An: Revolutionary Conflict in a Vietnamese Province*, Berkeley, CA, 1972; S. T. Hosmer, *Viet Cong Repression and its Implications for the Future*, Lexington, MA, 1970; see also N. Leites, *The Viet Cong Style of Politics*, RM-5487-1-ISA/ARPA, Santa Monica, CA, 1969; K. Kellen, *Conversations with Enemy Soldiers in Late 1968/Early 1969: A Study of Motivation and Morale*, RM-6131-1-ISA/ARPA, Santa Monica, CA, 1970.

56 Lanning and Cragg, op. cit., p. 229.

57 S. L. Stanton, *The Rise and Fall of an American Army: U.S. Ground Forces in Vietnam, 1965–1973*, Novato, CA, 1985, pp. 89–90; Krepinevich, op. cit., p. 201; Shaplin, op. cit., pp. 174, 175–6, 194; Lanning and Cragg, op. cit., pp. 177–8.

58 See e.g. Stanton, op. cit., pp. 193–4; R. Harris in Maddock, op. cit., pp. 62–3; C. Gannon in ibid., pp. 82–3; R. McKormack in McKay, op. cit., p. 159; M. Anderson *et al.*, *Insurgent Organization and Operations: A Case Study of the Viet Cong in the Delta, 1964–1966*, RM-5239-1-ISA/ARPA, Santa Monica, CA, 1967, pp. 55–7.

59 Appy, op. cit., pp. 204–5; Tanham, op. cit., pp. 181–2; Burchett, op. cit., p. 21; Anderson *et al.*, op. cit., pp. 54–5; L. Goure and C. A. H. Thompson, *Some Impressions of Viet Cong Vulnerabilities: An Interim Report*, RM-4699-1-ISA/ARPA, Santa Monica, CA, 1965, pp. 10, 46.

60 Krepinevich, op. cit., p. 200; Tanham, op. cit., p. 183; Troung Nhu Tang, op. cit., p. 170; Webb, op. cit., p. 40; L. Goure *et al.*, *Some Findings of the Viet Cong Motivation and Morale Study: June–December 1965*, RM-4911-2-ISA/ARPA, Santa Monica, CA, 1966, pp. 4–5; see Trinh Duc and Houng Vab Ba in Chanoff and Toai, op. cit., pp. 109–10, 154.

61 Krepinevich, op. cit., p. 197; Thayer, op. cit., p. 27.

62 J. Shulimson, *Marines in Vietnam: An Expanding War, 1966*, Washington, DC, 1982, pp. 281–2; Herbert, op. cit., pp. 140–1; Thayer, op. cit., p. 94.

63 For the Westmoreland vs. CBS case, see D. Koet, *A Matter of Honor*, New York, 1984; B. Benjamin, *Fair Play: CBS, General Westmoreland, and How a Television Documentary Went Wrong*, New York, 1988; C. Clifford, *Counsel to the President*, New York, 1991, p. 468; McNamara, op. cit., pp. 239–42.

64 For a rather partisan view of the CIA vs. MACV dispute on VC numbers, see

S. Adams, *War of Numbers: An Intelligence Memoir*, South Royalston, VT, 1994, p. 84, *passim*.

65 Spector, op. cit., p. 40.

66 S. Zaffiri, *Westmoreland: A Biography of General William C. Westmoreland*, New York, 1994, pp. 7–8.

67 See W. C. Westmoreland, *A Soldier Reports*, New York, 1976, pp. 177ff.; *The Pentagon Papers*, Boston, 1971–2, vol. 4, pp. 277ff.

68 Thayer, op. cit., p. 95; see *Pentagon Papers*, vol. 4, p. 458.

69 Krepinevich, op. cit., p. 188.

70 Thayer, op. cit., p. 95. For a thorough critique of the attrition strategy, see Krepinevich, op. cit., *passim*.

71 L. P. Holliday and R. M. Garfield, *Viet Cong Logistics*, RM-5432-1-ISA/ARPA, Santa Monica, CA, 1968, pp. 89–90; Lanning and Cragg, op. cit., p. 146.

72 Tourison, op. cit., p. 239.

73 Page and Pimlott, op. cit., p. 273.

74 Holliday and Garfield, op. cit., p. 74; Spector, *After Tet*, pp. 48–9; Appy, op. cit., pp. 205–13.

75 Bergerud, op. cit., p. 90; Stanton, op. cit., pp. 47–8.

76 Appy, op. cit., pp. 198–200.

77 Kellen, *Conversations*, pp. 8–9, 17.

78 See Kinnard, op. cit., pp. 45–6.

79 On the failures of the GVN in pacification, see e.g. *Pentagon Papers*, vol. 4, pp. 374, 376, 398–9.

80 Krepinevich, op. cit., pp. 172–7, 180, 188, 190; Shulimson, op. cit., pp. 13–14.

81 Ibid., p. 14; see Lt-Col. W. Corson in A. Hemmingway, *Our War Was Different: Marine Combined Action Platoons in Vietnam*, Annapolis, MA, 1994, p. 89.

82 See L. Sorley, *Thunderbolt: General Creighton Abrams and the Army of His Times*, New York, 1992, pp. 232ff.; R. H. Spector, 'The Vietnam War and the Army's Self-Image', in *The Second Indochina War*, J. Schlight (ed.), Washington, DC, 1986, pp. 179–81.

83 Stanton, op. cit., p. 27; T. Thayer, op. cit., p. 114; see Hackworth, op. cit., ch. 22; Herbert, op. cit., pp. 240–2, 134–6, 154–6.

84 Spector, *After Tet*, pp. 207–10; Appy, op. cit., pp. 239–40.

85 *Pentagon Papers*, vol. 4, p. 371.

86 Appy, op. cit., p. 239.

87 Krepinevich, op. cit., pp. 199–200, 254–5; see Herr, op. cit., pp. 61–2; Powell, op. cit., pp. 146–7; J. Schnell, *The Real War*, New York, 1987.

88 See N. Sheehan, *A Bright Shining Lie: John Paul Vann and America in Vietnam*, New York, 1988; Thi Tuyet Mai Nguyen, *The Rubber Tree: Memoir of a Vietnamese Woman*, M. Senderowitz (ed.), Jefferson, NC, 1994, p. 206; Kinnard, op. cit., p. 46; McNamara, op. cit., p. 243; Bergerud, op. cit., pp. 28–9; Fitzgerald, op. cit., pp. 9–10.

89 Hackworth, op. cit., p. 594; Stanton, op. cit., pp. 23–4.

90 See J. J. Zasloff, *Political Motivation of the Viet Cong: The Vietminh Regroupees*, RM-4703/2-ISA/ARPA, Santa Monica, CA, 1968 edn.

91 J. C. Donnell *et al.*, *Viet Cong Motivation and Morale in 1964: A Preliminary Report*, RM-4507/3-ISA, Santa Monica, CA, 1965, pp. viii–ix, 20ff.; Leites, op. cit., pp. 153–4; Sheehan, *Bright Shining Lie*, pp. 381–2; *Pentagon Papers*, vol. 4, p. 295.

92 See W. C. Duiker, 'Waging Revolutionary War: The Evolution of Hanoi's Strategy in the South, 1959–1965', in *The Vietnam War: Vietnamese and American Perspectives*, J. S. Werner and Doan Huynh Luu (eds), Armonk, NY,

1992, pp. 124–36; D. Pike, 'The Vietnam War: Strategic Factors', in *The Second Indochina War: Proceedings of a Symposium Held at Airlie, Virginia, 7–9 November 1984*, Washington, DC, 1986, pp. 106–7; J. T. Wirtz, *The Tet Offensive: Intelligence Failure in War*, Ithaca, NY, 1991, pp. 24–30.

93 Ibid., pp. 30–5; Knoebl, op. cit., pp. 57–8; Goure and Thomson, *Impressions of Viet Cong Vulnerabilities*, pp. 24–5, 29, 30, 31; Davison and Zasloff, *Profile of Viet Cong Cadres*, p. 38.

94 D. W. P. Elliott and C. A. H. Thomson, *A Look at the VC Cadres: Dinh Tuoung Province, 1965–1966*, RM-5114-1-ISA/ARPA, Santa Monica, CA, 1967, pp. 59–62, 66, 68.

95 Wirtz, op. cit., pp. 42–4; L. Goure *et al.*, *Some Findings of the Viet Cong Motivation and Morale Study: June–December 1965*, RM-4911-2-ISA/ARPA, Santa Monica, CA, 1966, p. 3; Goure and Leon, *Impressions of Viet Cong Vulnerabilities*, pp. 66–7. On the tunnel mythology, see e.g. Tourison, op. cit., p. 253; E. W. Williamson in Lanning and Cragg, op. cit., p. 205.

96 *Pentagon Papers*, vol. 4, p. 370; Elliott and Thomson, *A Look at the VC Cadres*, pp. 66, 71; M. Gurtov, *The War in the Delta: Views from Three Viet Cong Battalions*, RM-5353-1-ISA/ARPA, Santa Monica, CA, 1967, pp. 24–5. On the psychological stresses on women created by the absence of casualty news, see Li Thi Dau in Chanoff and Toai, op. cit., p. 112.

97 *Pentagon Papers*, vol. 4, p. 371; Goure *et al.*, *Findings of the Viet Cong Motivation and Morale Study*, p. 19; Gurtov, *War in the Delta*, pp. 9–12, 37ff.; Leites, op. cit., pp. 51ff., 140–2, 157–9; see L. L. Hayslip with J. Wurts, *When Heaven and Earth Changed Places: A Vietnamese Woman's Journey from War to Peace*, New York, 1989, pp. 70, *passim*.

98 F. Denton, *Volunteers for the Viet Cong*, RM-5647-ISA/ARPA, Santa Monica, CA, 1968, p. 7.

99 Leites, op. cit., pp. 92, 73, 182, 76–7.

100 See Long in Lanning and Cragg, op. cit., p. 226; Parrish, op. cit., p. 71; R. Briand, *No Tears to Flow: Woman at War*, Melbourne, 1969, p. 60; D. Donovan, *Once a Warrior King: Memories of an Infantry Officer in Vietnam*, London, 1987 edn, p. 184; Kitchin, op. cit., p. 81.

101 R. H. Spector, ' "How do You Know if You're Winning?" Perception and Reality in America's Military Performance in Vietnam, 1965–1970', in *The Vietnam War: Vietnamese and American Perspectives*, J. S. Werner and Doan Huynh Luu (eds), Armonk, NY, 1992, p. 156; McDonough, op. cit., p. 100; Hackworth, op. cit., p. 692; Herbert, op. cit., pp. 233, 312; Smith *et al.* in Lanning and Cragg, op. cit., pp. 211, 216, 223; see Chris Gannon in Maddock, op. cit., pp. 70, 78.

102 Hop Brown in Hemmingway, op. cit., p. 25.

103 Lanning and Cragg, op. cit., pp. 205–6; see Parrish, op. cit., pp. 95, 191–9; Minutes of the *Kiem Thao* Session on the Counter-Sweep Operation on 3 May 1967, in D. W. P. Elliott and M. Elliott (comps), *Documents of an Elite Viet Cong Delta Unit: The Demolition Platoon of the 514th Battalion – Part Three: Military Organization and Activities*, RM-5850-ISA/ARPA, Santa Monica, CA, 1969, pp. 48–9.

104 Page and Pimlott, op. cit., pp. 273–4.

105 Davison and Zasloff, *Profile of Viet Cong Cadres*, p. 47; Goure *et al.*, *Findings of the Viet Cong Motivation and Morale Study: June–December 1965*, p. 24; Goure and Thompson, *Impressions of Viet Cong Vulnerabilities*, p. 40.

106 Tran Van Nham in Hess, op. cit., p. 107.

107 Thayer, op. cit., pp. 195–8. It was easy to verify the authenticity of rallier figures, in marked contrast to body counts. See Adams, op. cit.

108 Adams, op. cit., p. 63; see Goure *et al.*, *Findings of the Viet Cong Motivation and Morale Study: June–December 1965*, p. 19; Goure and Thompson, *Impressions of Viet Cong Vulnerabilities*, p. 42; S. Sheehan, *Ten Vietnamese*, New York, 1967, pp. 159–60.

109 Tourison, op. cit., pp. 174, 222; see Elliott and Thomson, *Look at VC Cadres*, pp. 63–4; Zasloff, *Political Motivation of the Viet Cong*, p. xiv; Davison and Zasloff, *Profile of Viet Cong Cadres*, pp. 35ff.

110 *Pentagon Papers*, vol. 4, p. 387.

111 Hayslip, op. cit., p. 46.

112 See Bergerud, op. cit., p. 159.

113 Thayer, op. cit., p. 196; see Tourison, op. cit., p. 80.

114 Wirtz, op. cit., p. 45.

115 See e.g. Race, op. cit., p. 217.

116 On the planning of Tet, see Wirtz, op. cit., pp. 58ff.; R. E. Ford, *Tet 1968: Understanding the Surprise*, London, 1995, pp. 66ff.

117 Tran Van Tra, op. cit., p. 35; see id., 'Tet: The 1968 General Offensive and General Uprising', in *The Vietnam War: Vietnamese and American Perspectives*, J. S. Werner and Doan Huynh Luu (eds), Armonk, NY, 1992, pp. 52–3; Wirtz, op. cit., p. 230; Bergerud, op. cit., pp. 201–2.

118 Westmoreland, op. cit., p. 332; Adams, op. cit., p. 151; see Macdonald, op. cit., p. 266. As one VC village organizer remembered, losses were 'very, very high and the spirit of the soldiers dropped to a low point'. Trinh Duc in Chanoff and Toai, op. cit., p. 107.

119 Houng Van Ba in Chanoff and Toai, op. cit., p. 157.

120 Wirtz, op. cit., pp. 242–3; Stanton, op. cit., pp. 273–5.

121 Thayer, op. cit., p. 198; see Bergerud, op. cit., pp. 243, 246, 249.

122 See S. Popkin, 'Commentary: The Village War', *Viet Nam as History*, Peter Braestrup (ed.), Washington, DC, 1984, p. 102; Troung Nhu Tang, op. cit., pp. 153–4; J. Jones, *Viet Journal*, New York, 1973, pp. 91–3.

123 P. Macdonald, *Giap: The Victor in Vietnam*, New York, 1993, p. 268.

124 See W. E. Komer, *Bureaucracy at War: U.S. Performance in the Vietnam Conflict*, Boulder, CO, 1986, pp. 115ff.; R. A. Hunt, 'The Challenge of Counterinsurgency', in *The Second Indochina War: Proceedings of a Symposium Held at Airlie, Virginia, 7–9 November 1984*, J. Schlight (ed.), Washington, DC, 1986, pp. 121–41; E. P. Metzner, *More than a Soldier's War: Pacification in Vietnam*, College Station, TX, 1995, pp. 83ff.

125 See Troung Nhu Tang, op. cit. p. 201; Maurer, op. cit., p. 341; T. Thayer, op. cit., pp. 208ff.; Bergerud, op. cit., pp. 255ff.; D. Valentine, *The Phoenix Program*, New York, 1990; see Trullinger, op. cit., pp. 143–4; Race, op. cit., pp. 269–70; Tran Dinh Tho, *Pacification*, Washington, DC, 1980.

126 Trinh Duc in Chanoff and Toai, op. cit., p. 109.

127 T. Thayer, op. cit., p. 202; Bergerud, op. cit., p. 288; Troung Nhu Tang, op. cit., pp. 182–3.

128 On the 1972 and 1975 offensives see: Van Tien Dung, *Our Great Spring Victory*, J. Spragens, Jr (trans.), New York, 1977; Ngo Vinh Long, 'Post-Paris Agreement Struggles and the Fall of Saigon', in *The Vietnam War: Vietnamese and American Perspectives*, J. S. Werner and Doan Huynh Luu (eds), Armonk, NY, 1992, pp. 203–15; S. T. Hosmer *et al.*, *The Fall of South Vietnam: Statements by Vietnamese Military and Civilian Leaders*, New York, 1980. For arguments for and against the idea that greater American involvement would have prevented this collapse, see A. J. Joes, *Modern Guerrilla Insurgency*, Westport, CT, 1992, pp. 138ff.; H. G. Summers, Jr, *On Strategy: A Critical Analysis of the Vietnam War*, Novato, CA, 1982; Krepinevich, op. cit.,

pp. 261–3; L. J. Matthews and D. E. Brown (eds), *Assessing the Vietnam War: A Collection from the Journal of the U.S. Army College*, Washington, DC, 1987; G. R. Vickers, 'U.S. Military Strategy and the Vietnam War', in *The Vietnam War: Vietnamese and American Perspectives*, J. S. Werner and Doan Huynh Luu (eds), Armonk, NY, 1992, pp. 113–29.

129 See Bergerud, op. cit., p. 327; Race, op. cit., pp. 272–3, 141ff.; Trullinger, op. cit., chs 7, 11. On the respite 'Vietnamization' gave the VC, see Houng Van Ba in Chanoff and Toai, op. cit., p. 157.

130 Kitchin, op. cit., p. 52.

131 James H. Webb in Lanning and Cragg, op. cit., p. 215.

132 Elvy B. Roberts in ibid., p. 210.

133 Giap in Stetler, op. cit., p. 164.

CONCLUSION

1 See G. L. Mosse, *Fallen Soldiers: Reshaping the Memory of the World Wars*, New York, 1990. Even the Second World War on the Allied side, 'the good war', has been subject to critical analysis in recent years. See e.g. P. Fussell, *Wartime: Understanding and Behavior in the Second World War*, New York, 1989.

2 J. R. Adelman, *Revolution, Armies, and War: A Political History*, Boulder, CO, 1985, p. 26.

3 G. M. Theal, *History of the Boers in South Africa*, London, 1887, p. 117.

4 J. Gray, *Rebellions and Revolutions: China from the 1880s to the 1980s*, Oxford, 1990, p. 63.

5 Which is why apologists for the Waffen-SS tend to link it with the revolutionary forces of the Romantic Era. See e.g. F. Steiner, *Die Freiwilligen: Idee und Opefergang*, Göttingen, 1958.

6 This is, to be sure, an inevitable result of a comparative approach, and stems from a tendency among all historians to try and impose order on the natural chaos of events. See S. C. Ausband, *Myth and Meaning, Myth and Order*, Macon, GA, 1983, ch. 7.

7 See e.g. T. T. Meadows, *The Chinese and Their Rebellions*, Stanford reprint, 1953, pp. 548–61.

8 See ch. 2, n. 38; ch. 8, n. 18; ch. 10, n. 50.

9 See M. van Creveld, *The Transformation of War*, New York, 1991.

Index

1st Air Cavalry Division 163
I SS Panzer Corps 156
IV SS Panzer Corps 156
9th Infantry Division (US) 163, 165, 166, 169
XI International Brigade 117–19, 122–3, 128, 132
11th Light Infantry Brigade (US) 161
XII International Brigade 117, 118, 119, 123, 126
XIII International Brigade 126, 128, 130–1
XIV International Brigade 119, 126
XV International Brigade 118, 119, 123, 126, 127, 128
23rd Infantry Division (US) 162
25th Infantry Division (US) 161, 162
101st Airborne Division 160, 163
173rd Airborne Brigade 161, 162, 163, 166, 167

Abraham Lincoln Battalion (IB) 119, 120, 123, 127, 128
Abrams, Creighton 168
Adams, John 19
Adelman, Johnathan 1, 8, 36
Afghanistan 159
Afrikaner Resistance Movement (AWB) 69, 70
Aisne 40
Alabcete 117, 131
Alambagh (battle of) 102
Alexander the Great 182 n. 65
Allahabad 101
America 22
Americal Division (US) 161
American Revolution 19–32, 34, 176
André Marty Battalion (IB) 119, 124
Anhwai Province 83, 87, 89

Anking 92
Apocalypse Now 164, 176
Araure (battle of) 57
Ariege 40
armées revolutionnaires 40
Army of Africa (Spanish) 129
Army of Italy (French) 46
Army of the Moselle (French) 34, 46
Army of the North (French) 35, 42, 43, 44, 45
Army of the North and Ardennes (French) 35, 47
Army of the Republic of Vietnam (ARVN) 160, 161, 162, 169, 170
Army of the Rhine (French) 44
Arnett, Peter 162
Arnhem (battle of) 154
Arnold, Benedict 28
Assyrians 1
Astley, Lord 14, 15
Attleboro (Operation) 166
Aurillac 40
Austrian army 41, 42, 48, 50, 193 n. 108
Auverge 50
Awadh (Begam of) 96, 109
Awadh (Kingdom of) 96, 110, 113
Ayacucho (battle of) 66–7

Bad Tölz 143, 152
Badli-ke-Serai (battle of) 100
Bahadur Shah 104, 106, 107, 112, 206 n. 55
Baillie, Robert 12
Bakht Khan 104
Baldock, T. S. 7
Bantjes, J. B. 73, 75
Bareilly 104–5, 111
Barnes Review 139
Barquisimeto (battle of) 57

Barrieiro, José 63
Basle, treaty of 48
Baxter, Richard 6
Belchite (battle of) 116
Bengal Army 98ff., 175
Berger, Gottlob 135–6, 144, 147
Bertaud, Jean-Paul 36
Bessie, Alvah 123
Bianco, Vincenzo 131
Bihn Dinh Province 161
Biron, Duc de 41
Bitburg affair 141
Blandford, Edmund L. 140
Blomberg, Werner von 151
Blood River (battle of) 69–77
Bolívar, Simon 51–67
Bolton, Charles K. 20
Bombay Army 103
Bomboná (battle of) 66
Boorstin, Daniel J. 21
Boston 23, 24, 30
Bouchotte, Jean-Baptiste 33, 34
Boves, José 57
Boyacá (battle of) 63
Brissot, Jacques-Pierre 34
British Battalion (IB) 119, 127, 129
British Legion 61–2, 63, 64, 65, 66
Brittany 50
Brunete (battle of) 119, 123–4, 129, 130
Brunswick, Duke of 41, 42
Bundestag 137
Bundeswehr 136
Bunker Hill [Breed's Hill] (battle of) 23
Burgoyne, John 21, 28, 30, 31

Caesar, Julius 52
Calabozo (battle of) 60
Calley, William 162
Cambodia 167, 173
Campbell, Colin 101, 102, 110, 206 n. 45
Campofiormo (treaty of) 46
Camus, Albert 136
Caputo, Philip 161
Carabobo (battle of) 65
Caracas 56, 60, 61
Carlton, Charles 16
Carlton, Guy 28
Carlyle, Thomas 7, 8
Carnot, Lazare 44, 45
Carr, Raymond 209 n. 6
Carúpano 58
Castro, Fidel 159
casualties 17, 58, 60, 63, 66, 75–80, 78,

87, 93, 108, 118, 119, 127, 129, 130,
132, 133, 153–4, 161, 170, 173
Casualties of War 164
Caudillos 52, 58, 62
cavaliers 8, 16
Cedar Falls (Operation) 166
Cedeños, General 60
Central Intelligence Angency (CIA)
166, 172
Central Office for South Vietnam
(COSVN) 169, 173
Cerro de los Angeles (battle of) 118
Chaing Chung-yuan 88
Chapiev Battalion (IB) 128
chaplains 8, 13
Charente 40
Charlemagne (SS Div.) 146
Charles I 5, 8–10, 12–15, 17
Charles, Archduke 48
Châteauneuf 40
Chekiang 87, 91
Cheriton (battle of) 13
Chiang Kai-shek 80
Chieu Hoi 171–3
Chinese Communist Party (CCP) 80, 81
Ch'ing armies 85–6
Ch'ing dynasty 78, 81
Chinhat (battle of) 97, 102, 109
Chin-t'ien 79, 82, 83
Chorley, Katherine 1, 22, 36
Chou dynasty 86
Chou T'ien-chüeh 82, 86
Chou Wen-chia 93
Cilliers, Sarel 72, 73, 74
Civil Operations and
Revolutionary/Rural Development
Support (CORDS) 173
Clarendon, Earl of 7
Clausewitz, Carl von 2, 51
Clinton, Henry 28
Cockburn, Claud 130
Combined Action Platoons 168, 171
Comintern 121, 125–6, 131
Commager, Henry Steele 21
Committee of Public Safety 34, 35, 36,
43, 44, 45
Concord (battle of) 23, 185 n. 29
conscription 11, 25, 38, 50, 54, 56, 132,
133, 170
Continental Army 19–32, 118, 164, 174
Continental Congress 19, 23, 24, 25, 26,
29, 31
Čopić, Vladimir 127

Cornwallis, Lord 26, 28, 31
Cory, G. E. 70
Courtrai 41
Cowpens (battle of) 24
Crimean War 103
Cromwell 8
Cromwell, Oliver 5–13, 16–18, 20, 31,
    70, 118, 177
Cuban Revolution (1959) 159
Cúcata 55
Cultural Revolution, 80
Custine, A.-P. 43, 44

de Clerq, Staff 143
de Lacroix, Peru 58
Delbrel, P. 35
Dell, William 6
Derrida, Jacques 3
desertion 13, 19, 23, 28–9, 37, 39–40, 45,
    49, 57, 59–60, 62–6, 73, 87, 92–3,
    128–9, 131–2, 152
Diderot, Denis 34
Diggers 10
Dillon, Théobold 41
Discipline 12, 13, 14, 23, 26, 28, 29–30,
    39, 40, 43, 45, 49, 54–8, 60–2, 73,
    82–7, 94, 106–10, 113–14, 124–5, 147
Doc, Tran Van 173
drunkenness 12–13, 58, 124
Dumouriez, Charles 42, 43
Dutch Wars 14

Easter Offensive 172
Eastern Association 6, 12, 17
Ebro (battle of the) 133
Ecuador 65–6
Eden, Anthony 130
Edgar André Battalion (IB) 118
Edgehill (battle of) 8
Edkins, Joseph 84
Eicke, Theodore 147, 149, 154–6
Elgin, Lord 92
Elie, Jacob 42
Ellis, John 1, 185 n. 26
El Semen (battle of) 60
English Civil War 5–18, 31
Enrico, Robert 36
Essex, Earl of 9, 10, 17
Ever-Triumphant Army 91, 93
Ever-Victorious Army 90–1

Fairfax, Thomas 5–7, 9, 13, 16, 17, 31,
    181 n. 28

Fall, Bernard 161–2
Fatehpur (battle of) 101
Fegelein, Hermann 149
Finistère 40
Firth, C. H. 7
Flandern (SS regiment) 144
Foreign legionnaries (South America)
    61–2
For Whom the Bell Tolls 120, 121
Foucault, Michel 1
Franco, Francisco 116, 119, 120
Franco-Prussian War 50
Franklin, Benjamin 32
Frederick the Great 45
Freikorps 135
Freikorps Denmark 144, 145
Der Freiwillige 138
Freiwilligen-Legion Niederlande 143
Freiwilligen-Legion Norwegen 144
French and Indian War *see* Seven Years
    War
French Revolution 3, 32, 33–50, 67
French Revolutionary armies 3,
    33–50, 118
French Royal Army 31, 33, 37, 39
Fromentin, General 44
Fu-chou 87
Fuentes del Ebro (battle of) 127, 129
Fukiyama, Francis 115

Gage, Thomas 26, 27, 28
Gainsborough (battle of) 6
Galicz, Janos 126–7
Gard 40
Gardiner, S. R. 7
Garibaldi Battalion (IB) 118, 128
Gates, Horatio 27, 28, 30, 31
Gates, John 118
Gentles, Ian ix
George Washington Battalion (IB) 119
Giap, Vo Nguyen 158, 173
Gille, Herbert 156
Giquel, Prosper 93
Goebbels, Josef 135
Goethe, Johann Wolfgang von 34–5
Goetz von Berlichingen (SS Division) 134
Goguet, Jacques 45
Goldstein, Ben 125
González, Juan Vicente 52
Gordon, Charles 91
Goring, Lord 17
Government of Viet Nam (GVN) 164–5,
    168, 173–4

Graebner, Viktor 154
Gran Colombia 67
Gray, Jack 81
Great Terror 126
Greene, Nathanael 25, 29
Grégoiré, Abbé 50
Griffith, D. W. 22
Guayaquil 65–6
Guderian, Heinz 138
Guevara, Ernesto 'Che' 159
guerilla war 24, 94, 98, 110–11, 158
Guibert, Comte de 47
Gurkhas 98
Gurney, Jason 128
Gwalior 105

Hackworth, David 163
Haiti expedition 58–9
Halbwachs, Maurice 1
Hancock, John 24
Handschar (SS Division) 145
Hannibal 62
Hanoi 159
Hanovarian army 42
Harlem Heights (battle of) 31
Harsh, Joseph C. 163–4
Harvey, F. W. 87
Hausser, Paul 136, 137–8, 155, 156
Havelock, Henry 101, 103, 104, 108, 206
   n. 38
Hemingway, Ernest 120
Herbert, Anthony 163
Hessians 19, 22, 27
Higginbotham, Don 22
Hill, Christopher 7, 8, 17
Hillgruber, Andreas 141
Hilsgemeinschaft auf Gegenseitigkeit der
   ehemaligen Angehorigen der Waffen-
   SS (HAIG) 137–8, 139
Himmler, Heinrich 135, 142, 143, 144,
   147, 152
Hippersley, G. 62
Historikerstreit 141
Hitler, Adolf 120, 135, 141 142–3,
   150, 155
Hitlerjugend (SS Division) 147, 148,
   149, 154
Hitler Youth (HJ) 143, 148
Hoche, Louis-Lazare 43
Ho Chi Minh Trail 167
Hoepner, Erich 154
Hondschoote (battle of) 42
Hong Kong Register 87

Horrocks, Brian 154
Houchard, Jean Nicolas 44
Houng Van Ba 173
Howe, Richard 28
Howe, William 28, 30
Huai Army 89, 91, 93, 94
Hua Kang 81, 84
Hunan Army 88–9
Hunan Province 83, 87, 88, 93
Hung Hsiu-ch'üan 78–9, 80, 84, 87, 93
Hung Jen-kan 90
Huntington 5
Hupeh Province 83, 87

Indian Mutiny 95, 96–115, 176
Institute for Historical Review 139
International Brigades 116–33, 134, 157,
   175, 176
Ireton, Henry 10, 15, 16
Irish Legion 62
Ironsides 6, 8, 11, 12
Isandhlwana (battle of) 76
Israeli Defence Forces 140
Italieni (battle of) 71, 74

Jaarsveld, F. A. van 70
Jacobins 35, 39, 40, 44, 45
Jarama (battle of) 116, 119, 123,
   127, 132
Jemappes (battle of) 41–2
Jen Yu-wen 81
Jodl, Alfred 227 n. 164
Joseph II 48
Jourdan Jean-Baptiste 43, 44
Journal of Historical Review 139
Junction City (Operation) 166
Junger, Ernst 150
Junín (battle of) 66

Kahle, Hans 118
Kama (SS Division) 145
Kanpur 100–2, 104, 108–9, 113, 114
Kao Yung-k'uan 93
Kay, John William 96
Keegan, John 140
Kerrigan, Peter 131
Kesselring, Albert 154
Khan Bahadur Khan 98, 104–5, 111
Kharkov 156
Khe Sanh 172
Khmer Rouge 2
Kiangsi Province 83, 87
King's Mountain (battle of) 24

Kleber [Manfred Stern], General 126
Kleist, Ewald von 150, 156
Korean War 159, 163
Krulak, Walt 168
Kuei-lin 83
Kumm, Otto 137
Kunshan 91
Kunwar Singh 98, 104
Kuomintang (KMT) 80, 81
Kwangsi Province 78, 82, 83, 85, 93

Lacroix, Sebastian 35
Lafayette, Marquis de 27, 43
La Guaita 57
Lai Wen-kuang 94
Lal, Mushi Ali Jeeluan 106–7
Land and Freedom 121
Landwehr, Richard 139
Langport (battle of) 5, 17
Laos 167
Larrázabal, Felipe 52
Las Rozas 118
Law, Oliver 214 n. 82
Lawrence, Henry 101–2
Lecourbe, Claude Jacques 44
Lee, Charles 24, 27, 28
Lefebvre, Georges 36
Legion Bibliophile Books 139
Legion Falndern 145
*Légion des voluntaires français contre le
   bolshevisme* (LVF) 145
Legion Wallonien 146
Legislative Assembly (France) 34, 37, 38
Leibenberg, J. B. 71
Leibstandarte Adolf Hitler 134, 154,
   155, 156
Leslie, Jacques 163
Levée en masse 34–5, 37, 175
Levellers 10
Lexington (battle of) 20, 185 n. 29
Li Hsiu-ch'eng 80, 91
Li Hung-chang 88–9, 90, 91, 93
Lindley, Augustus 87
Llaneros 52, 57, 59, 60, 63, 65
Lo Erh-kang 81, 94, 95
Long Kahn Province 173
Lopera (battle of) 126
Los Angeles Times 163
Lucas, James 140
Lucknow 100–2, 109–11, 113, 114
Lynn, John ix, 36
London Trained Bands 10
Louis XVI 37, 39

Louis Philippe 42
Lowenthal, David 1
Luckner, Nicholas 41
Luke, Samuel 5, 13
Lynn, John ix

Mabire, Jean 139–40
MacCartney, Wilfred 124
Mackenzie-Papineau Battalion (IB) 123,
   127, 129
Madras Army 103
Madrid 117–20, 123, 126, 128, 131, 132
Majumadar, R. C. 97, 204 n. 9
Malleson, George Bruce 96
Malmédy 142
Manchester, Earl of 9, 10, 12, 17
Manning, Brian 7
Manstein, Erich von 154–5
Mao Tse-tung 4, 13, 80, 81, 158, 159,
   208 n. 105
Maria Theresa 48
Mariño, Santiago 59
Marston Moor (battle of) 6
Marseillaise, La 36
Marty, André 120, 124, 131, 132
Masur, Gerhard 56
Matabele 72, 76
Mathiez, Albert 35–6
Matthews, Herbert 120
McGee, Frank 164
McLay, R. S. 87
McNamera, Robert S. 163, 169
Meadows, Thomas 81, 83
Meerut 98, 106, 112, 113
Mehta, Asoka 98, 99
Mellenthin, Jachim von 227 n. 164
Merriman, Robert 127, 215 n. 82
Metcalfe, Henry 110
Meyer, Kurt 136, 138, 154
Michelet, Jules 35
Military Assistance Command Vietnam
   (MACV) 163, 166, 168
Militia (Spanish) 117, 133
Militia (US) 23, 24, 164
Millius, John 22
Miranda, Francisco 54
Mompox 54
Monagas, General 60
Monmouth (battle of) 31
Montague, F. C. 7
Montesquieu, Charles Louis de
   Secondat 34
Monteverde, Domingo 54, 55, 57

Montgomery, Richard 27
Mooyman, Gerdus 136, 146
Morale 2, 11–12, 14, 15–17, 20–2, 25,
  33–5, 38, 84–5, 90–1, 97–8, 104, 109,
  111, 113, 114, 118, 124, 128–30, 139,
  145–6, 149, 152, 159, 170–3, 178–9 n.
  10, 182 n. 65
Morgan, Edmund S. 21
Morillo, Pablo 58, 59, 60, 62, 63, 64
Morris, James R. 22
Mpande 77
Mujahidin 159
Munin Verlag 137
Mussert, Anton 143
Mussolini, Benito 120
mutiny 29–30, 37, 62, 96–115, 129,
  130–1, 145, 182 n. 77
My Lai 162
Mzilikazi 72

Nana Sahib 104, 108–9, 111–2
Nanking 79–84, 89, 92–4
Napoleon 43, 46, 48, 52, 56, 58, 62,
  193 n. 103
Naseby (battle of) 5, 8, 14–7, 166,
  175, 176
Natal, Republic of 77
Nathan, George 125
National Assembly (France) 38
National Convention (France) 34, 38,
  39, 43, 44, 49
National Guard (France) 37
National Liberation Front (NLF) 158,
  164–5, 169, 170, 174
National Party (South Africa) 68–9
Ndlela 74
Neerwinden (battle of) 42
Nelson, Steve 130
Nepal 109, 113
Nevins, Allan 21
New England 23–4
New Grenada 53–65
New Jersey Line 29
New Model Army 5–18, 31, 67, 118,
  140, 176, 177
Newport Pagnell 13
New York 24–5, 30, 31
Niebelungen (SS Division) 149
Niederlande (SS unit) 145–6
Nien Rebellion 94
Nine Nations Battalion 128
Ningpo 87, 91
NKVD 126, 132

Nolte, Ernst 134, 141
Norde (SS unit) 152
Nordland (SS unit) 146
Nordwest (SS unit) 146
North Atlantic Treaty Organization
  (NATO) 136–7, 141–2
North, Lord 19, 27
North Vietnamese Army (NVA) 159,
  166, 168, 170–4
Northern Army 17
Northern Expedition 86–7
Northern Horse 16
Norwegen Legion 146
Nujufghur (battle of) 100, 107–8

Oath of the Covenant 68, 70, 72–3
Ocaña 54
Oise 40
Okey, John 15–16
O'Leary, Daniel F. 53, 54, 55, 56, 60,
  61, 65
Oliphant, Laurence 92
Opium War (1839–42) 85
Oradur-sur-Glane 142
Ortiz 60
Ostendorff, Werner 134

Pacciardi, Randolfo 125
Pàez, José 59, 60, 62
Panzer Group West 156
Paris 38, 41, 43, 50
Pas-de-Calais 40
Pay 11, 12, 29, 54, 55, 60, 85, 87,
  106, 108
Pecklam, Howard H. 21
Peking 88, 89, 91
Pelzer, A. N. 70
Pennsylvania Line 29
People's Liberation Army (China) 4,
  81, 159
Père Duchesne 35, 40
Peru 51, 65–6
Peter the Great 47
Peters, Hugh 6, 13
Phillips, William 27
Phoenix Programme 173
Phu Yen Provoince 172
Piar, Manuel 59
Pichincha (battle of) 66
Pieper, Joachim 142, 152
Plesse Verlag 137
plundering 13, 28, 45, 55, 57, 64, 84, 85,
  87, 107, 108–9

Poland 42
Pollitt, Harry 124
Potgieter, Andries 71, 74
Powell, Colin 161
Preller, G. S. 68
Pretorius, Andries 68, 71, 72, 74, 76
Princeton (battle of) 31
prisoners of war (POWs) 12, 25, 27, 29, 167, 171–2
professionalism 17–8, 19, 24, 25, 36, 31, 46, 113–14; *see* training
Prussian Army 41, 42, 47, 48, 50
La Puerta (battle of) 58
Punjab 103
Putney Debates 17

Quarrie, Bruce 140–1
Quito 66

Ranke Leopold von 3, 53
recruiting 10–11, 25, 27, 29, 38–9, 54, 57–9, 61, 63–5, 83–4, 86–7, 118, 121–2, 137–8, 144–5, 147–9, 150–1, 169, 170
Red Army 4, 125, 152–3
Red Dawn 22
Das Reich (SS Division) 134, 135, 138, 142, 147, 149, 152–3, 156
Reich Labour Service (RAD) 143, 148
Reichswehr 149–50, 155, 224 n. 119
Reichsführer-SS (SS Division) 150
Republikaner Party 137
Research and Development Corporation (RAND) 167, 172
Restoration 7
Retief, Piet 70, 71–2, 75
revolution (definition) 179 n. 13
Reynier, Jean Louis 44
Rhani of Jhansi 97, 104–5
Roberts, Ely R. 174
Robespierre, Maximilien 34, 43, 45, 46
Rohilkhand 104–5
Rommel, Erwin 156
Rooke, James 63
Rorke's Drift (battle of) 76–7
Rose, Hugh 105
Rostov 155
Rothenberg, Gunther E. 37
Rousseau, Jean-Jacques 34, 45
Royal Navy 31
Royster, Charles ix
Rundstedt, Gerd von 156
Rupert, Prince 14, 15, 16, 17

Russian Army of Liberation 145
Russian Civil War 4, 126
Russian Imperial Army 47

Saint-Céré 40
Saint-Cyr, Gouvoin 45
Saint-Just, Louis 35, 43, 44, 45
San Martín, José de 62, 63
sans-culottes 35, 36, 40, 46, 50
Santandar, Francisco 63, 64, 65
Saratoga (campaign and battle) 24, 30
Sata y Bussy, José de 51
Savakar, V. D. 96–7, 98, 99
Saxe, Maurice de 47
Scharnhorst, Gerhard von 48
Schönhuber, Franz 137
Schuyler, Philip 28
Das Schwarze Korps 147
Schwarzkopf, Norman 162
Schweppenburg, Geyr von 156, 227 n. 164
Seaforth Highlanders 29
Seeckt, Hans von 151
Self-Denying Ordinance 9, 10, 17
Sen, S. N. 97, 204 n. 12
Seven Years War 20, 24, 27
Shaka 71
Shanghai 90
Siegrunen 139
Sikhs 98, 176
Sikonyela 71, 72
Simon, Max 150
Sixth of February Battalion (IB) 119
Sixth Panzer Army 149, 155, 156
Skanderberg (SS Division) 145
Skippon, Philip 9, 10, 14, 15, 16
Smith, Lacey Baldwin 8
Soboul, Albert 36
So-li (battle of) 83, 88
Sombrero (battle of) 60
Soochow 91, 93
South Vietnam, army, *see* Army of the Republic of Vietnam (ARVN)
South Vietnam, government *see* Government of Viet Nam (GVN)
Soviet Union 4
Spanish Army 48, 55, 58, 59, 60–1, 64, 117, 127
Spanish Civil War 52, 116–33, 134
Sprigge, Joshua 6
Spring Offensive (Vietnam) 175
SS-Verfügungstruppe (SS-VT) 135, 148, 152

Steiner, Felix 135, 137, 138, 143, 150
strategy 26, 30, 62–3, 65, 83, 88–9,
   167–8, 169–70, 174
Sucre, Antonio José de 66
Sullivan, John 28
Sun Yat-sen 80
Suti Chaura Ghat 109
Suvorov, A. V. 47

tactics 15–6, 26, 47, 60–1, 74–5, 83,
   90–1, 107, 110, 111, 122–3, 153–4,
   158–62, 168, 182 n. 65
Tagaunes (battle of) 56
Taiping armies 78–95, 175, 176
Taitsang 91
Tang, Troung Nhu 160
Tarn 40
Tatya Tope 98, 102, 104, 105, 111
Teng Kuang-ming 93
Terror, the 35, 44, 49
Tet Offensive 163–4, 172–3
Thael, George M. 68, 70
Thaelmann Battalion (IB) 118, 122, 130
Thom, H. B. 69
Thomas, Hugh 120
Thompson, E. P. 209 n. 6
Tisa, John 128, 129
La Torre, Miguel de 65
Totenkopf (SS Division) 142, 147,
   149, 155
Tournai 41
Tra, Tran Van 172
training 26, 33, 40, 43, 66, 113–4, 120,
   122, 123, 135, 143, 149, 151–2, 153,
   161, 171
Trevelyen, George M. 7
Tseng Ku-fan 78, 88, 91, 94
Tuchman, Barbara 22
Tung Jung-hai 93
Turnham Green (battle of) 10
Tuy Hoa 161

US Army 21, 22, 51, 168–74
US Marine Corps 161, 162, 164,
   166, 168
Upton, Emory 21
Urdaneta, Rafael 62, 64
Uys, Piet 71, 74

Valencia 131
Valmy (battle of) 33, 34, 35, 36, 37, 41
Vane, Henry 5
Vann, John 11

Vargas (battle of) 63
Vendée 40, 49
Venezuela 51–65
Viet Cong 158–74, 176
Vieusseux, Jean-Louis 32
Volksdeutsche 136, 146, 147
Voltaire 34
Volunteer for Liberty 128
Voortrekker Monument 69
Voortrekkers 3, 68–77

Waffen-SS 3, 134–57, 175, 176
Waller, William 10
Walterdorf, Hans 156
Wang An-chün 93
Wang Hua-pan 93
War of 1812 31
Ward, Frederick Townsend 90
Warlimont, Walter 227 n. 164
Washington, George 19–20, 22–31, 39
Watson, Bruce 114
Wattignies (battle of) 42
Wehrmacht 136
Welle, Hans-Jurgen 134
Westland (SS unit) 144
Westmoreland, William 160, 163, 166
Westphal, Siegfried 155
Wheeler, Hugh 101, 108, 109
White Unfolozi (battle of) 71, 77
Wiking (SS Division) 135, 138, 143,
   146–52, 156
Williams, G. 109
Williamson, Ellis E. 162, 171
Williamson, Gordon 140
Wilson, I. 62
Wintringham, Tom 127
Wisch, Theodore 156
Wolesley, Garnet 92

Yang Hsiu-ch'ing 78, 83
York, Duke of 42
Yorktown (battle of) 20, 31
Young, Peter 18
Yung-an 79
Yung Wing 90

Zakla, Máté 126, 127
Zeisser, Wilhelm 126
Zulu War (1838–40) 68–77
Zulu War (1879) 76–7

Made in the USA
Middletown, DE
10 March 2020

86107471R00144